Middle School 2-2

중간고사 완벽대비

적중 100

영어 기출 문제집

중2

지학 | 민찬규

Best Collection

구성과 특징

교과서의 주요 학습 내용을 중심으로 학습 영역별 특성에 맞춰 단계별로 다양한 학습 기회를 제공하여 단원별 학습능력 평가는 물론 중간 및 기말고사 시험 등에 완벽하게 대비할 수 있도록 내용을 구성

Words & Expressions

Step1 Key Words 단원별 핵심 단어 설명 및 풀이
Key Expression 단원별 핵심 숙어 및 관용어 설명
Word Power 반대 또는 비슷한 뜻 단어 배우기
English Dictionary 영어로 배우는 영어 단어

Step2 실력평가 단원별 수시평가 대비 주관식, 객관식 문제풀이

Step3 서술형 대비 학업성취도 및 수행능력평가 대비 서술형 문제풀이

Conversation

Step1 핵심 의사소통 의사소통에 필요한 주요 표현 방법 요약
핵심 Check 기본적인 표현 방법 및 활용능력 확인

Step2 대화문 익히기 상황에 따른 대화문 활용 및 연습

Step3 기본평가 시험대비 기초 학습 능력 평가

Step4 실력평가 단원별 수시평가 대비 주관식, 객관식 문제풀이

Step5 서술형 대비 학업성취도 및 수행능력평가 대비 서술형 문제풀이

Grammar

Step1 주요 문법 단원별 주요 문법 사항과 예문을 알기 쉽게 설명

핵심 Check 기본 문법사항에 대한 이해 여부 확인

Step2 기본평가 시험대비 기초 학습 능력 평가

Step3 실력평가 단원별 수시평가 대비 주관식, 객관식 문제풀이

Step4 서술형 대비 학업성취도 및 수행능력평가 대비 서술형 문제풀이

Reading

Step1 구문 분석 단원별로 제시된 문장에 대한 구문별 분석과 내용 설명
확인문제 문장에 대한 기본적인 이해와 인지능력 확인

Step2 확인학습A 빈칸 채우기를 통한 문장 완성 능력 확인

Step3 확인학습B 제시된 우리말을 영어로 완성하여 작문 능력 키우기

Step4 실력평가 단원별 수시평가 대비 주관식, 객관식 문제풀이

Step5 서술형 대비 학업성취도 및 수행능력평가 대비 서술형 문제풀이
교과서 구석구석 교과서에 나오는 기타 문장까지 완벽 학습

Composition

|영역별 핵심문제|

단어 및 어휘, 대화문, 문법, 독해 등 각 영역별 기출문제의 출제 유형을 분석하여 실전에 대비하고 연습할 수 있도록 문제를 배열

|서술형 실전 및 창의사고력 문제|

학교 시험에서 점차 늘어나는 서술형 시험에 집중 대비하고 고득점을 취득하는데 만전을 기하기 위한 학습 코너

|단원별 예상문제|

기출문제를 분석한 후 새로운 시험 출제 경향을 더하여 새롭게 출제될 수 있는 문제를 포함하여 시험에 완벽하게 대비할 수 있도록 준비

|단원별 모의고사|

영역별, 단계별 학습을 모두 마친 후 실전 연습을 위한 모의고사

INSIGHT on the textbook

교과서 파헤치기

- **단어Test1~2** 영어 단어 우리말 쓰기와 우리말을 영어 단어로 쓰기
- **대화문Test1~2** 대화문 빈칸 완성 및 전체 대화문 쓰기
- **본문Test1~5** 빈칸 완성, 우리말 쓰기, 문장 배열연습, 영어 작문하기 복습 등 단계별 반복 학습을 통해 교과서 지문에 대한 완벽한 습득
- **구석구석지문Test1~2** 지문 빈칸 완성 및 전문 영어로 쓰기

이책의 차례 Contents

Lesson 5

I Don't Have a Clue

의사소통 기능

- 설명 요청하기
  Can you explain how to use the buttons?

- 열거하기
  First, fold the paper in half. Second, turn it over.
  Then, draw a face.

언어 형식

- 수동태
  The cheese **was eaten by** a mouse.

- 조동사의 수동태
  Bright stars **can be seen** at night.

Words & Expressions

Key Words

- **accident** [ǽksidənt] 명 사고
- **bat** [bæt] 명 배트, 방망이
- **bean** [biːn] 명 콩
- **block** [blɑk] 명 구역, 블록
- **bottom** [bátəm] 명 맨 아래 (부분)
- **button** [bʌ́tən] 명 단추
- **candle** [kǽndl] 명 양초
- **clue** [kluː] 명 단서, 실마리
- **congratulation** [kəngrætʃuléiʃən] 명 축하
- **cross** [krɔːs] 동 건너다
- **delete** [dilíːt] 동 삭제하다
- **detective** [ditéktiv] 명 탐정, 형사
- **disappear** [dìsəpíər] 동 사라지다
- **dragon** [drǽgən] 명 용
- **enter** [éntər] 동 입장하다, 들어가다
- **escape** [iskéip] 동 탈출하다
- **explain** [ikspléin] 동 설명하다
- **finally** [fáinəli] 부 마침내
- **fold** [fould] 동 접다
- **half** [hæf] 명 반, 절반
- **hide** [haid] 동 숨기다, 숨다

- **inside** [ìnsáid] 전 ~의 안에, ~의 내부에
- **lie** [lai] 동 거짓말하다
- **luckily** [lʌ́kili] 부 다행히
- **none** [nʌn] 대 하나도 ~ 않다
- **outside** [áutsàid] 전 ~ 밖에 부 밖으로, 밖에
- **prize** [praiz] 명 상
- **riddle** [rídl] 명 수수께끼
- **safely** [séifli] 부 안전하게
- **scene** [siːn] 명 장면
- **solve** [sɑlv] 동 해결하다
- **somewhere** [sʌ́mhwɛ̀ər] 부 어딘가에
- **space** [speis] 명 공간, 우주
- **stamp** [stæmp] 명 우표
- **straight** [streit] 부 똑바로, 일직선으로
- **strange** [streindʒ] 형 이상한
- **suspect** [səspékt] 명 용의자
- **thief** [θiːf] 명 도둑
- **throw** [θrou] 동 던지다
- **triangle** [tráiæ̀ŋgl] 명 삼각형
- **twice** [twais] 부 두 번, 두 배
- **win** [win] 동 얻다, 이기다

Key Expressions

- **at the time of**: ~이 일어나던 때에
- **catch a thief**: 도둑을 잡다
- **fill A with B**: A를 B로 채우다
- **for free**: 공짜로

- **help yourself**: 마음껏 드세요
- **make it to** ~: ~에 이르는 데 성공하다
- **turn over**: ~을 뒤집다
- **write down**: ~을 적다

Word Power

※ 서로 반대되는 뜻을 가진 단어

☐ **appear** 나타나다 ↔ **disappear** 사라지다

☐ **top** 맨 위 ↔ **bottom** 맨 아래쪽

☐ **throw** 던지다 ↔ **catch** 잡다

☐ **win** 이기다 ↔ **lose** 지다

☐ **dark** 어두운 ↔ **bright** 밝은

☐ **inside** ~의 안에 ↔ **outside** ~의 밖에

☐ **safe** 안전한 ↔ **dangerous** 위험한

☐ **special** 특별한 ↔ **general** 일반적인

☐ **straight** 똑바른, 일직선의 ↔ **curved** 굽은

☐ **fold** 접다 ↔ **unfold** 펴다

English Dictionary

☐ **accident** 사고
→ an event in which a car, train, plane, etc. is damaged and often someone is hurt
자동차, 기차, 비행기 등이 손상되고 때로는 누군가가 다치는 사건

☐ **bat** 방망이, 배트
→ a long wooden stick with a special shape that is used in some sports and games
몇몇 스포츠와 게임에서 사용되는 특별한 모양을 가진 긴 나무 막대

☐ **bean** 콩
→ a seed or a pod that comes from a climbing plant and is cooked as food
덩굴나무에서 나오며 음식으로 요리되는 씨앗 또는 꼬투리

☐ **bottom** 맨 아래 (부분)
→ the flat surface on the lowest side of an object
물체의 가장 낮은 부분의 평평한 표면

☐ **clue** 단서, 실마리
→ an object or piece of information that helps someone solve a crime or mystery
누군가가 범죄나 미스터리를 풀도록 도와주는 물체나 정보

☐ **cross** 건너다
→ to go from one side of something such as a road, river, room, etc. to the other
길, 강, 방 등과 같은 무언가의 한 쪽에서 다른 쪽으로 가다

☐ **delete** 삭제하다
→ to remove something that has been written down or stored in a computer
적어 놓았거나 컴퓨터에 저장해 놓은 무언가를 제거하다

☐ **detective** 탐정
→ someone who is paid to discover information about someone or something
누군가 또는 무언가에 대한 정보를 발견하도록 돈을 받는 사람

☐ **enter** 입장하다
→ to go or come into a place
한 장소로 들어가거나 들어오다

☐ **escape** 탈출하다
→ to leave a place when someone is trying to catch you or stop you, or when there is a dangerous situation
누군가가 당신을 잡으려 하거나 당신을 멈출 때, 또는 위험한 상황이 있을 때 한 장소를 떠나다

☐ **half** 반, 절반
→ exactly or about 50% of an amount, time, distance, number, etc.
양, 시간, 거리, 수 등의 정확히 또는 거의 50%

☐ **riddle** 수수께끼
→ a question that is deliberately very confusing and has a humorous or clever answer
의도적으로 매우 혼란스럽게 하는 그리고 재미있거나 재기 넘치는 대답을 갖는 질문

☐ **suspect** 용의자
→ someone who is thought to be guilty of a crime
어떤 범죄의 죄가 있다고 생각되는 사람

☐ **thief** 도둑
→ someone who steals things from another person or place
다른 사람이나 장소로부터 물건들을 훔치는 사람

서답형

01 다음 짝지어진 단어의 관계가 같도록 빈칸에 알맞은 말을 쓰시오.

> agree: disagree = appear : _____

02 다음 영영풀이가 가리키는 것을 고르시오.

> to remove something that has been written down or stored in a computer

① enter ② delete ③ shift
④ throw ⑤ cross

 03 다음 중 밑줄 친 부분의 뜻풀이가 바르지 않은 것은?

① Clues can be found somewhere inside the room. 어딘가에
② Luckily, he wasn't badly hurt. 다행히
③ The thief escaped from the police station. 탈출했다
④ Where did you hide your gold? 찾다
⑤ The players are dragons and seahorses. 해마

서답형

04 다음 우리말에 맞게 빈칸에 알맞은 말을 쓰시오.

(1) 나는 셜록 홈즈가 위대한 탐정들 중 한 명이었다고 생각한다.
  ➡ I think Sherlock Holmes was one of the greatest _____.
(2) 수건을 반으로 접으세요.
  ➡ _____ the towel in _____.
(3) 그는 1분 만에 수학 퍼즐을 해결했다.
  ➡ He _____ the math puzzle in just one minute.

서답형

05 다음 문장의 빈칸에 들어갈 말을 〈보기〉에서 골라 쓰시오.

> ┤ 보기 ├
> made it to / turn over / help yourself / for free

(1) The soccer team _____ the finals.
(2) I got this T-shirt _____.
(3) You should _____ the sweet potato before it burns.
(4) _____ to anything you like on the table.

06 다음 주어진 문장의 밑줄 친 suspects와 같은 의미로 쓰인 것은?

> The detective met some suspects and asked questions.

① The spoiled food is suspected of causing food poisoning.
② Who is the suspect in the crime?
③ I suspected that he stole my wallet.
④ The police suspect that he is a spy.
⑤ We suspected him to be a liar.

07 다음 문장에 공통으로 들어갈 말을 고르시오.

> • There is enough space for three people to _____ down.
> • I don't want to _____ to my parents anymore.
> • I promise not to _____ again.

① explain ② solve ③ throw
④ win ⑤ lie

01 다음 짝지어진 단어의 관계가 같도록 빈칸에 알맞은 말을 쓰시오.

> top : bottom = inside : _____

02 다음 우리말에 맞게 빈칸에 알맞은 말을 쓰시오.

(1) 너는 이것을 일주일에 두 번 볼 수 있다.

➡ You can see this _____ in a week.

(2) 그녀는 사고가 일어나던 때에 아침을 만들고 있었다.

➡ She was making breakfast _____ _____ of the accident.

(3) 당신은 우리 가게에서 일곱 가지 상품을 무엇이든 무료로 고를 수 있다.

➡ You can choose any seven items from our store _____.

03 다음 우리말을 주어진 어구를 배열하여 영작하시오.

(1) 그 이야기를 제게 설명해 주실 수 있나요?

(you / me / to / the story / can / explain)

➡ _____

(2) 너는 하루에 두 번 약을 먹어야 한다.

(twice / a day / the pills / should / you / take)

➡ _____

(3) 나는 빵을 삼각형으로 잘랐다.

(triangles / the bread / into / I / cut)

➡ _____

04 다음 우리말에 맞게 빈칸에 알맞은 말을 쓰시오.

(1) 그녀는 어제 차 사고를 당했다.

➡ She got in a car _____ yesterday.

(2) Mary가 게임하는 중에 다쳤니?

➡ Did Mary get _____ during the game?

(3) 경찰이 오후에 용의자를 심문할 것이다.

➡ The police will _____ the suspect in the afternoon.

(4) 네 컴퓨터에 공간을 만들기 위해 모든 사진을 지워야 한다.

➡ You should _____ all of the pictures on your computer to make more space.

05 다음 우리말을 주어진 단어를 이용하여 영작하시오.

(1) 경찰은 도둑을 잡을 수 있을 것이라고 확신했다. (catch, sure)

➡ _____

(2) 페이지를 넘겨 그림을 보세요. (turn, look)

➡ _____

(3) 이 병을 물로 채워 주시겠어요? (would, fill, with)

➡ _____

06 다음 대화의 빈칸을 완성하시오.

> A: Try to solve this riddle.
> B: Sure.
> A: This has three to four legs but it can't walk. Can you explain why?
> B: Yes! It's because it's a _____.

Conversation

1 설명 요청하기

Can you explain how to use the buttons? (버튼 사용법을 설명해 줄 수 있니?)

■ 'Can you explain ~?'은 '너는 ~을 설명해 줄 수 있니?'라는 뜻으로, 상대방에게 설명을 요청할 때 쓰는 표현이다. 'Can you explain' 다음에 'how to ~' 표현을 사용하여 어떤 절차나 방법을 물어볼 수 있다.

설명 요청하기

- I don't get it. Can you explain why? (이해가 안돼요. 이유를 설명해 줄 수 있나요?)
- Can you show me how to use this machine? (어떻게 이 기계를 사용할 수 있는지 보여줄 수 있나요?)
- Can you tell me how to draw this character? (이 캐릭터를 어떻게 그릴 수 있는지 말해 줄래요?)
- Let me know how to make the cookies. (쿠키 만드는 법을 알려 주세요.)

핵심 Check

1. 다음 우리말과 일치하도록 빈칸에 알맞은 말을 쓰시오.

   (1) A: Can you _____ a little bit more? (좀 더 설명을 해 주시겠습니까?)

   B: No problem. (그럼요.)

   (2) A: _____ how to use the copier. (복사기 사용법 좀 알려 주세요.)

   B: Sure. Look at this. (물론이지. 여기를 봐.)

   (3) A: _____? (어제 무슨 일이 일어났었는지 말해줄 수 있니?)

   B: Well, I got hurt in a car accident. (차 사고로 다쳤어.)

② 열거하기

First, fold the paper in half. Second, turn it over. Then, draw a face.
(먼저, 종이를 반으로 접어. 두 번째로, 뒤집어. 그리고 나서, 얼굴을 그려.)

■ 서수를 사용하여 어떤 절차의 순서를 열거할 수 있다. 이때, 'Second, Third' 대신에 'Next, Then'을 쓸 수 있다.

열거하기

- First, draw a circle. Second, put a star inside. Then, put a triangle on top of the circle.
(첫째로, 원을 그리세요. 둘째, 안에 별을 놓으세요. 그리고 나서, 원의 맨 위에 삼각형을 놓으세요.)

- First, he looked around the school. Then, he met some suspects and asked questions.
Finally, he found the thief. (첫째로, 그는 학교를 둘러봤어. 그리고 나서, 몇몇의 용의자를 만나서 질문을 했지. 마침내, 그는 도둑을 찾았어.)

핵심 Check

2. 다음 우리말과 일치하도록 빈칸에 알맞은 말을 쓰시오.

(1) A: Can you explain how to make a taco? (타코 만드는 법을 설명해 주실 수 있어요?)

B: _____, fill your tortilla with vegetables and meat. _____, add some sauce on the top. (먼저, 토르티야를 채소와 고기로 채워. 그 다음, 위에 약간의 소스를 추가하렴.)

(2) A: _____, the farmer buys a fox, a duck, and a bag of beans. _____, the farmer needs to cross a river. (먼저 농부는 여우, 오리, 콩 자루를 하나씩 사. 그리고 나서, 농부는 강을 건너야 해.)

B: What's the problem? (뭐가 문제인데?)

(3) A: _____, fold a paper in half to make a triangle. _____, fold the top of the triangle to the bottom line. _____, fold both ends of the bottom line to the top to make ears. _____, turn it over and draw a face. (먼저, 종이를 반으로 접어서 세모를 만들어. 두 번째로, 세모의 꼭대기를 맨 아랫선 쪽으로 접어. 세 번째로, 맨 아랫선 양쪽 끝을 위로 접어서 귀를 만들어. 그리고 나서, 그것을 뒤집어서 얼굴을 그려.)

B: That sounds easy. (쉽구나.)

Listen and Speak 2-B

> **Jane:** Minsu, do you know the TV show about the student ❶detective?
>
> **Minsu:** Yes. I love ❷that show, but I didn't see ❷it this week. What was ❷it about?
>
> **Jane:** Well, all of the bikes at school disappeared.
>
> **Minsu:** So, what did ❸he do?
>
> **Jane:** ❹First, he looked around the school. ❹Then, he met some suspects and ❺asked questions. ❹Finally, he found the thief. The thief was....
>
> **Minsu:** No, don't tell me! I'll watch it later.

Jane: 민수야, 학생 탐정이 나오는 TV쇼를 아니?
Minsu: 응, 나는 그 쇼를 아주 좋아하지만 이번 주에는 못 봤어. 무슨 내용이었어?
Jane: 음, 학교의 모든 자전거들이 사라졌어.
Minsu: 그래서 그가 무엇을 했어?
Jane: 첫째로, 그는 학교를 둘러봤어. 그러고 나서, 몇몇의 용의자를 만나서 질문을 했지. 마침내, 그는 도둑을 찾았어. 도둑은...
Minsu: 안 돼, 말하지 마! 내가 나중에 볼 거야.

❶ detective: 탐정
❷ that show와 it 모두 the TV show about the student detective를 가리킨다.
❸ he는 the student detective를 가리킨다.
❹ 학생 탐정이 한 일을 열거하고 있다.
❺ met과 병렬구조이다.

Check(√) True or False

(1) Minsu loves the TV show about the student detective. T ☐ F ☐

(2) Jane knows who the thief was. T ☐ F ☐

 Real Life Communication

> **Emily:** Junsu, do you want to solve a riddle?
>
> **Junsu:** Sure, what is ❶it?
>
> **Emily:** There is a farmer. First, the farmer buys a fox, a duck, and a bag of beans. Then, the farmer needs to cross a river.
>
> **Junsu:** What's the problem?
>
> **Emily:** The boat can only hold the farmer and one more thing.
>
> **Junsu:** ❷Are you saying that the farmer can take only one thing ❸at a time?
>
> **Emily:** Yes. Also, the fox will eat the duck or the duck will eat the beans if the farmer isn't there. Can you explain how to move everything across the river safely?
>
> **Junsu:** Hmm ....

Emily: 준수야, 수수께끼 하나 풀어볼래?
Junsu: 물론이지, 뭔데?
Emily: 한 농부가 있어. 먼저 농부는 여우, 오리, 콩 자루를 하나씩 사. 그러고 나서, 농부는 강을 건너야 해.
Junsu: 뭐가 문제인데?
Emily: 보트는 단지 농부와 한 가지만 더 옮길 수 있어.
Junsu: 농부가 한 번에 오직 한 가지만 옮길 수 있다는 말이니?
Emily: 응. 또한 만약 농부가 없다면 여우가 오리를 먹거나, 오리가 콩을 먹을 거야. 전부를 강 건너로 안전하게 옮길 방법을 설명할 수 있겠니?
Junsu: 음....

❶ it은 riddle(수수께끼)을 가리킨다.
❷ 자신의 이해를 한 번 더 점검하고 있다.
❸ at a time: 한 번에

Check(√) True or False

(3) The farmer should cross a river with only one thing. T ☐ F ☐

(4) Without the farmer, the fox will eat the beans. T ☐ F ☐

Listen and Speak 1-A

Jimin: Do you want to play the new game **❶**that I bought?

Brian: Sure, what is it, Jimin?

Jimin: It's **❷**like a soccer game but the players are dragons and **❸**seahorses. You need to use these buttons to play.

Brian: That sounds fun. **❹**Can you explain how to use the buttons?

Jimin: Sure.

❶ that은 목적격 관계대명사로 which로 바꾸어 쓸 수 있다.
❷ like는 전치사로 '~와 같은'을 뜻한다.
❸ seahorse: 해마
❹ 버튼 사용법에 대한 설명을 요청하는 표현이다. how to+동사원형: ~하는 방법

Listen and Speak 2 -A

Tom: Yujin, **❶**look at my paper fox.

Yujin: That's cute. How did you make **❷**it?

Tom: First, **❸**fold a paper **❹**in half to make a triangle. Second, fold the top of the triangle to the bottom line. Third, fold both ends of the bottom line to the top to make ears. Then, **❺**turn it over and draw a face.

Yujin: That sounds easy.

❶ look at: ~을 보다
❷ it은 Tom's paper fox를 가리킨다.
❸ 동사로 시작하는 명령문이다.
❹ in half: 반으로
❺ turn over: 뒤집다

Listen and Speak 1-B

Jack: Kelly, here's a riddle. You can see this twice in a week, once in a year, but never in a day. What is this?

Kelly: **❶**I have no idea.

Jack: It's the letter "E."

Kelly: **❷**I don't get it. Can you explain why?

Jack: Well, there are two "E"s in the word "week," one "E" in the word "year" but no "E"s in the word "day."

Kelly: Aha! **❸**Now I get it.

❶ I have no idea. = I don't know.
❷ I don't get it. = I don't understand.
❸ I get it. = I understand. = I see.

Let's Check

Minjun: Wow! Something smells really good, Mom. What is it?

Mom: We're going to have tacos for dinner. **❶**Help yourself.

Minjun: Can you explain how to make a taco?

Mom: First, **❷**fill your tortilla with vegetables and meat. Then, add some sauce on the top.

Minjun: **❸**Sounds delicious!

Mom: Would you like some cheese?

Minjun: No, thanks.

❶ Help yourself.: 마음껏 드세요.
❷ fill A with B: A를 B로 채우다
❸ Sounds delicious.: 맛있을 거 같아요.

● 다음 우리말과 일치하도록 빈칸에 알맞은 말을 쓰시오.

Listen & Speak 1 - A

Jimin: Do you want to play the new game _____ I _____?

Brian: Sure, what is it, Jimin?

Jimin: It's _____ a soccer game but the players are _____ and _____. You _____ _____ _____ these buttons _____ _____.

Brian: That _____ fun. _____ _____ _____ _____ _____ _____ the buttons?

Jimin: Sure.

Jimin: 내가 산 새로운 게임을 하고 싶니?
Brian: 물론이야. 그게 뭐니, 지민아?
Jimin: 축구 시합 같은 것인데 선수들이 용과 해마야. 게임을 하려면 이 버튼들을 사용해야 해.
Brian: 재밌을 거 같아. 버튼 사용법을 설명해 줄 수 있니?
Jimin: 물론이지.

Listen & Speak 1 - B

Jack: Kelly, here's a _____. You can see this _____ in a week, _____ in a year, but _____ _____ _____ _____. What is this?

Kelly: _____ _____ _____ _____.

Jack: It's the letter "E."

Kelly: I don't _____. _____ _____ _____ _____ _____?

Jack: Well, there are two "E"s in the word "week," one "E" in the word "year" but no "E"s in the word "day."

Kelly: Aha! Now I _____ _____.

Jack: Kelly, 수수께끼가 있어. 넌 이것을 1주에 두 번, 1년에 한 번 볼 수 있어, 하지만 1일에는 전혀 볼 수가 없어. 이게 뭐게?
Kelly: 전혀 모르겠어.
Jack: 알파벳 'E'야.
Kelly: 이해가 안 가. 이유를 설명해 줄 수 있니?
Jack: 음, 단어 week에는 'E'가 2개 있고, 단어 year에는 'E'가 1개 있고, 단어 day에는 'E'가 없잖아.
Kelly: 아! 이제 이해했다.

Listen & Speak 2 - A

Tom: Yujin, _____ _____ my paper fox.

Yujin: That's cute. _____ _____ _____ _____ _____ _____ _____?

Tom: _____, fold a paper _____ _____ to make a triangle. _____, fold the top of the triangle to the _____ _____. _____, fold _____ _____ of the bottom line to the top to make ears. _____, _____ it _____ and draw a face.

Yujin: That sounds _____.

Tom: 유진아, 내 종이 여우를 봐.
Yujin: 귀엽다. 어떻게 만들었니?
Tom: 먼저, 종이를 반으로 접어서 세모를 만들어. 두 번째로, 세모의 꼭대기를 맨 아랫선 쪽으로 접어. 세 번째로, 맨 아랫선 양쪽 끝을 위로 접어서 귀를 만들어. 그리고 나서, 그것을 뒤집어서 얼굴을 그려.
Yujin: 쉽구나.

Listen & Talk 2 - B

Jane: Minsu, do you know the TV show about the student _____?

Minsu: Yes. I love that show, but I _____ _____ it _____ _____. What was it _____?

Jane: Well, _____ _____ the bikes at school _____.

Minsu: So, what _____ he _____?

Jane: _____, he _____ _____ the school. _____, he met some _____ and asked questions. _____, he found the _____. The thief was ....

Minsu: No, _____ _____ me! I'll _____ it _____.

Real Life Communication

Emily: Junsu, do you want to _____ a riddle?

Junsu: Sure, what is it?

Emily: There is a farmer. _____, the farmer buys a fox, a duck, and _____ _____ _____ _____. Then, the farmer _____ _____ _____ _____ _____.

Junsu: What's the problem?

Emily: The boat can only _____ the farmer and _____ _____ thing.

Junsu: Are you saying that the farmer can _____ only one thing _____ _____ _____?

Emily: Yes. Also, the fox will eat the duck or the duck will eat the beans if the farmer isn't there. _____ _____ _____ _____ _____ _____ _____ _____ the river safely?

Junsu: Hmm ....

Let's Check

Minjun: Wow! Something _____ really _____, Mom. What is it?

Mom: We're _____ _____ have tacos _____ _____. _____ _____.

Minjun: _____ _____ _____ _____ _____ _____ _____ a taco?

Mom: _____, _____ your tortilla _____ vegetables and meat. _____, add some sauce _____ _____ _____.

Minjun: Sounds _____!

Mom: _____ you _____ some cheese?

Minjun: No, _____.

01 다음 대화가 자연스럽게 이어지도록 주어진 문장을 알맞게 배열하시오.

> (A) Sure, what is it, Jimin?
> (B) That sounds fun.
> (C) It's like a soccer game but the players are dragons and seahorses. You need to use these buttons to play.
> (D) Do you want to play the new game that I bought?

➡ _____

[02~04] 다음 대화를 읽고 물음에 답하시오.

Tom: Yujin, look at my paper fox.

Yujin: That's cute. How did you make it?

Tom: First, fold a paper in half to make a triangle. (A)둘째, fold the top of the triangle to the bottom line. (B)셋째, fold both ends of the bottom line to the top to make ears. Then, turn it over and draw a face.

Yujin: That sounds easy.

02 위 대화에서 다음의 영영풀이가 가리키는 말을 찾아 쓰시오.

> a shape that is made up of three lines and three angles

➡ _____

03 위 대화에서 (A)와 (B)의 우리말을 영어로 쓰시오.

➡ (A) _____, (B) _____

04 위 대화의 내용과 일치하지 않는 것은?

① Yujin은 Tom에게 종이 여우 만드는 법에 대해 물어보았다.
② 종이 여우를 만들기 위해 먼저 종이를 반으로 접어서 세모를 만들어야 한다.
③ 두 번째로, 맨 아랫선을 사용하여 세모로 접어야 한다.
④ 세 번째로, 맨 아랫선 양쪽 끝을 위로 접어 귀를 만든다.
⑤ 네 번째로, 귀를 만든 면을 뒤집어 얼굴을 그린다.

[01~02] 다음 대화를 읽고 물음에 답하시오.

Jimin: Do you want to play the new game that I bought?

Brian: Sure, what is it, Jimin?

Jimin: It's like a soccer game but the players are dragons and seahorses. You need to use these buttons to play.

Brian: That sounds fun. (A)Can you explain how to use the buttons?

Jimin: Sure.

01 위 대화의 밑줄 친 (A)와 의도가 다른 것은? (2개)

① Would you show me how to use the buttons?

② Do you understand how to use the buttons?

③ Can you tell me how to use the buttons?

④ Let me know how to use the buttons, please.

⑤ Why don't you explain how to use the buttons?

02 위 대화의 내용과 일치하지 않는 것은?

① Jimin bought the new game.

② Brian wants to play soccer with Jimin on the playground.

③ The game is similar to a soccer game.

④ The dragons and seahorses are the players in the new game.

⑤ The buttons are used to play the game.

[03~04] 다음 대화를 읽고 물음에 답하시오.

Jack: Kelly, here's a riddle. You can see this twice in a week, once in a year, but never in a day. What is this?

Kelly: I have no idea.

Jack: It's the letter "(A)_____."

Kelly: (B)I don't get it. Can you explain why?

Jack: Well, there are two "(A)_____"s in the word "week," one "(A)_____" in the word "year" but no "(A)_____"s in the word "day."

Kelly: Aha! Now I get it.

서답형

03 위 대화의 빈칸 (A)에 공통으로 들어갈 수수께끼의 답을 쓰시오.

➡ _____

04 위 대화의 밑줄 친 (B)와 바꾸어 쓸 수 있는 말은?

① Not at all.

② I don't understand.

③ It doesn't matter.

④ I can't believe this.

⑤ It's not fair.

[05~07] 다음 대화를 읽고 물음에 답하시오.

Tom: Yujin, look at my paper fox.

Yujin: That's cute. How did you make (A)it?

Tom: First, fold a paper in half to make a triangle. Second, fold the top of the triangle to the bottom line. Third, fold both ends of the bottom line to the top to make ears. Then, turn it over and draw a face.

Yujin: That sounds easy.

서답형

05 위 대화에서 밑줄 친 (A)it이 가리키는 것을 찾아 쓰시오.

➡ _____

06 To make the paper fox, what should Yujin do after making a triangle by folding a paper in half?

➡ _____

07 What should Yujin make just before drawing a face?

➡ _____

[08~09] 다음 대화를 읽고 물음에 답하시오.

> Jane: Minsu, do you know the TV show about the student detective?
> Minsu: (A) Yes. I love that show, but I didn't see it this week. What was it about?
> Jane: (B) Well, all of the bikes at school disappeared.
> Minsu: (C) So, what did he do?
> Jane: (D) Then, he met some suspects and asked questions. Finally, he found the thief. The thief was ....
> Minsu: (E) No, don't tell me! I'll watch it later.

08 위 대화의 (A)~(E) 중 주어진 문장이 들어가기에 가장 적절한 곳은?

> First, he looked around the school.

① (A) ② (B) ③ (C) ④ (D) ⑤ (E)

09 위 대화를 읽고 대답할 수 없는 것은?

① What show does Minsu like?
② What happened at school?
③ Who was the thief who had stolen all the bikes at school?
④ What did the student detective do to catch the thief?
⑤ Why didn't Minsu want to know who the thief was?

[10~13] 다음 대화를 읽고 물음에 답하시오.

> Minjun: Wow! Something smells really good, Mom. What is it?
> Mom: We're going to have tacos for dinner. (A)Help yourself.
> Minjun: (B)타코 만드는 법을 설명해 주실 수 있어요?
> Mom: First, fill your tortilla (a)____ vegetables and meat. Then, add some sauce on the top.
> Minjun: Sounds (b)_____!
> Mom: (C)Would you like some cheese?
> Minjun: No, thanks.

10 위 대화의 밑줄 친 (A)의 의미를 우리말로 간략히 쓰시오.

➡ _____

11 위 대화의 밑줄 친 (B)의 우리말을 〈보기〉에 주어진 단어를 배열하여 완성하시오.

┌─ 보기 ─┐
> make / how / a taco / can / to / you / explain

➡ _____

12 위 대화의 밑줄 친 (C)와 바꾸어 쓸 수 있는 것은?

① Do you want some cheese?
② Do you like cheese?
③ Have you tried some cheese?
④ Do you know some cheese?
⑤ Do you mind if I have some cheese?

13 위 대화의 빈칸 (a)에는 알맞은 전치사를, (b)에는 대화의 흐름에 어울리는 d로 시작되는 단어를 쓰시오.

➡ (a)_____, (b) _____

[01~04] 다음 대화를 읽고 물음에 답하시오.

Emily: Junsu, do you want to solve a riddle?

Junsu: Sure, what is it?

Emily: There is a farmer. First, the farmer buys a fox, a duck, and a bag of beans. Then, the farmer needs to cross a river.

Junsu: What's the problem?

Emily: The boat can only hold the farmer and one more thing.

Junsu: Are you saying that the farmer can take only one thing at a time?

Emily: Yes. Also, the fox will eat the duck or the duck will eat the beans if the farmer isn't there. Can you explain (A)옮길 방법 everything across the river safely?

Junsu: Hmm ....

01 What did the farmer buy before crossing the river?

➡ _____

02 How many things could the farmer load on the boat at a time?

➡ _____

03 What will happen to the fox and the duck if the farmer isn't there?

➡ _____

04 밑줄 친 우리말 (A)를 move를 이용하여 3 단어의 영어로 쓰시오.

➡ _____

05 다음 대화가 자연스럽게 이어지도록 순서대로 배열하시오.

(A) Can you explain how to make a taco?

(B) We're going to have tacos for dinner. Help yourself.

(C) First, fill your tortilla with vegetables and meat. Then, add some sauce on the top.

(D) Wow! Something smells really good, Mom. What is it?

➡ _____

06 다음 대화를 읽고 대화의 내용과 일치하도록 빈칸 (A)~(C)를 명령문 형태로 완성하시오.

Tom: Yujin, look at my paper fox.

Yujin: That's cute. How did you make it?

Tom: First, fold a paper in half to make a triangle. Second, fold the top of the triangle to the bottom line. Third, fold both ends of the bottom line to the top to make ears. Then, turn it over and draw a face.

Yujin: That sounds easy.

⬇

How to make a paper fox
Fold a paper in half to make a triangle.
(A) _____
(B) _____ _____
(C) _____

Grammar

① 수동태

> The author **wrote** many books. 그 작가는 많은 책을 썼다. 〈능동태〉
> Many books **were written by** the author. 많은 책이 그 작가에 의해 쓰여졌다. 〈수동태〉

- 수동태는 'be+p.p.+by'의 형태로, 행동의 주체보다는 행동의 대상에 초점을 맞춘다. 'by+행위자'는 동작의 주체가 일반인이거나 막연한 사람일 때, 그리고 동작의 주체가 명확하지 않을 때 생략한다.
  - Jerry **was taken** to the hospital **by** Tom. Jerry는 Tom에 의해 병원으로 데려가졌다.
  - Nelson **is loved by** many people. Nelson은 많은 사람들에게 사랑받는다.
  - All the flowers **were planted** yesterday. 어제 모든 꽃들이 심어졌다.

- 4형식 문장의 수동태는 두 가지 형태를 갖는다. 직접목적어를 주어로 한 수동태에서는 간접목적어에 특정한 전치사를 쓴다. 전치사 to를 쓰는 동사는 'give, tell, teach, show, bring' 등이고, 전치사 for를 쓰는 동사는 'buy, make, cook, get' 등이며, 전치사 of를 쓰는 동사는 'ask'가 있다.
  - A picture **was given to** me. 사진 한 장이 내게 주어졌다.
  - A chicken soup **was cooked for** Jimmy. Jimmy를 위해 닭고기 수프가 요리되었다.

- 5형식 문장의 목적격 보어가 원형부정사인 경우, 수동태 문장에서는 to부정사로 바뀐다. 그 외에는 모든 목적격 보어를 그대로 쓸 수 있다.
  - Mom **allowed** me **to hang** out with my friends. 엄마는 내가 친구들과 놀도록 허락하셨다.
    (= I **was allowed to hang** out with my friends by Mom.)
  - He **made** me **do** the job. 그는 내가 그 일을 하게 했다.
    (= I **was made to do** the job by him.)

- by 이외의 전치사를 사용하는 수동태에 유의한다.
  - Jane **is interested in** playing tennis. Jane은 테니스를 치는 것에 흥미가 있다.
  - Cheese **is made from** milk. 치즈는 우유로 만들어진다.
  - Katherine **was surprised at** the news. Katherine은 그 소식을 듣고 놀랐다.

핵심 Check

1. 다음 우리말과 같도록 빈칸에 알맞은 말을 쓰시오.
   (1) 우리는 그 벽을 칠했다.
   ➡ The wall _____ _____ _____ us.
   (2) 나는 그에게서 영어를 배웠다.
   ➡ I _____ _____ English by him.

② 조동사의 수동태

- We **can delay** the plan. 우리는 그 계획을 연기할 수 있다. 〈능동태〉
- The plan **can be delayed**. 그 계획은 연기될 수 있다. 〈수동태〉

■ 조동사의 수동태는 '조동사+be+p.p.+by ~'의 형태로, 수동태 구문 앞에 조동사를 넣어 사용한다.

- A pizza **will be delivered**. 피자가 배달될 것이다.
- Many messages **must be deleted**. 많은 메시지들이 지워져야 한다.
- Any puzzle **can be solved** by Jason. 어떠한 퍼즐이든 Jason에 의해 해결될 수 있어.

■ 조동사 수동의 부정문은 조동사 뒤에 not을 붙여 '주어+조동사+not+be+p.p.(+by 행위자)'를 쓴다. 의문문은 '조동사+주어+be+p.p.(+by 행위자)?' 형태로 쓴다.

- The information **will not be provided**. 그 정보는 제공되지 않을 것입니다.
- It **cannot be completed** in an ordinary way. 그것은 평범한 방법으로 완성될 수 없다.
- **Will** the bike **be bought** by Jerry? Jerry가 그 자전거를 살까?
- **Can** the book **be borrowed** by any student? 어떤 학생이건 그 책을 빌릴 수 있나요?
- **Should** the car **be parked** by me? 내가 그 차를 주차해야만 하나요?

핵심 Check

2. 다음 우리말을 능동태와 수동태로 쓰시오.

(1) 나는 그 방을 청소할 거야.

➡ I _____.

➡ The room _____.

(2) 우리는 우리의 숙제를 해야만 한다.

➡ We _____.

➡ Our homework _____.

(3) 그가 그녀를 도와 줄 거야.

➡ He _____.

➡ She _____.

Grammar 시험대비 기본평가

01 다음 문장에서 어법상 <u>어색한</u> 부분을 바르게 고치시오.

(1) My sweater made in England.

_____ ➡ _____

(2) The building will complete next month.

_____ ➡ _____

(3) Careless driving is caused many accidents.

_____ ➡ _____

(4) The window can't open by me.

_____ ➡ _____

02 주어진 동사를 어법에 맞게 빈칸에 쓰시오.

(1) The car _____ last weekend. (steal)

(2) The letter should _____ by this Friday. (send)

(3) Hundreds of people _____ the place every day. (visit)

(4) The Olympic Games _____ every four years. (hold)

(5) Karl _____ as a great teacher now. (look up to)

(6) The children will _____ with toys. (play)

(7) Badminton can _____ by two or four people. (play)

03 주어진 단어를 바르게 배열하여 다음 우리말을 영어로 쓰시오. 필요하다면 단어를 변형하거나 추가하시오.

(1) 그 교실은 매일 청소된다. (clean / every day / the classroom)

➡ _____

(2) 이 건물은 언제 지어졌니? (when / build / this building / was)

➡ _____

(3) 우리는 그에게서 표를 받지 못했다. (tickets / give / were / we / not / him / by)

➡ _____

(4) 이것은 오늘 밤이 되기 전에 되어져야만 해. (tonight / this / do / must / before)

➡ _____

(5) 그 문은 10분 후에 닫힐 겁니다. (10 minutes / the door / close / will / in)

➡ _____

01 다음 괄호 안의 동사의 알맞은 형태를 고르시오.

> Two people (injure) in the accident yesterday.

① injure
② injured
③ is injured
④ was injured
⑤ were injured

02 다음 빈칸에 들어갈 말로 가장 적절한 것은?

> Meat _____ in a refrigerator, or it will spoil.

① was kept
② keeps
③ kept
④ must be kept
⑤ must keep

03 주어진 문장과 같은 의미의 문장은?

> You should return these books by next Wednesday.

① You return these books by next Wednesday.
② These books should return by next Wednesday.
③ These books should be returned by you by next Wednesday.
④ Next Wednesday is returned by you these books.
⑤ These books are going to be returned by you by next Wednesday.

서답형

04 다음 두 문장이 같은 의미가 되도록 빈칸에 알맞은 말을 쓰시오.

> The noise did not wake me up.
> = I _____ by the noise.

05 다음 중 우리말을 영어로 바르게 옮기지 <u>않은</u> 것은?

① 그 사진은 내 남동생이 찍은 거야.
　→ The picture was taken by my brother.
② 그 나무를 너의 부모님이 심으셨니?
　→ Was the tree planted by your parents?
③ 나는 아침마다 오렌지 주스를 마셔.
　→ I drink orange juice every morning.
④ 우리는 그 노래를 불렀다.
　→ The song sang by us.
⑤ 그가 상자를 옮길 거야.
　→ The box will be moved by him.

06 다음 빈칸에 들어갈 말이 바르게 짝지어진 것은?

> My car _____ last month, but the next day it _____ by the police.

① is lost – is found
② lost – found
③ was lost – was found
④ was lost – was founded
⑤ was lost – will be found

07 다음 중 밑줄 친 부분을 생략할 수 <u>없는</u> 것은?

① The moon can be seen <u>by us</u> at night.
② Lots of bikes are ridden <u>by people</u> in China.
③ My pencil case was stolen <u>by someone</u>.
④ BTS is loved <u>by people</u> all over the world.
⑤ The vase was broken <u>by Thomson</u>.

서답형

08 주어진 문장을 수동태로 쓰시오.

> She will cook the fish.

➡ _____

09 다음 빈칸에 들어갈 말로 가장 적절한 것은?

> The hospital was _____ down for a day.

① shutting ② shutted ③ shut
④ shuted ⑤ shutten

서답형

10 주어진 어구를 바르게 배열하여 다음 우리말을 영어로 쓰시오. 필요하다면 단어를 변형하시오.

> 그 편지가 올바른 주소로 보내질까?
> (the right address / the letter / send / will / to / be)

➡ _____

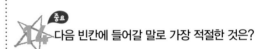

11 다음 중 빈칸에 들어갈 단어 play의 형태가 <u>다른</u> 하나는?

① The game is _____ on a court.
② Boys are _____ on the playground.
③ The role is _____ by a British actor.
④ The audio is _____ from the beginning.
⑤ A violin is _____ with a bow.

서답형

12 주어진 단어를 활용하여 다음 우리말을 영어로 쓰시오.

> 너희들은 그 선생님에게 벌 받을 거야.
> (punish)

➡ _____

13 다음 우리말을 영어로 바르게 옮긴 것은?

> Julia의 친구들은 그녀에 대해 좋게 말한다.

① Julia's friends speak well with her.
② Julia is spoken well with her friends.
③ Julia's friends are spoken well of by her.
④ Julia is spoken well of by her friends.
⑤ Julia is talked about by her friends.

14 다음 빈칸에 들어갈 말로 가장 적절한 것은?

> It was cold, so the heater was turned _____ Jason.

① on at ② at by ③ on by
④ off by ⑤ into by

15 다음 중 어법상 바르지 <u>않은</u> 것은?

① The woman typed all the reports.
② My father was born in Canada.
③ A book must be written by him by tomorrow.
④ The glass was filled with chocolate milk.
⑤ James is interested by taking pictures.

16 다음 중 수동태로의 전환이 바르지 <u>않은</u> 것은?

① Someone ate my sandwich.
 → My sandwich was eaten by someone.
② Mom made me a candy bar.
 → A candy bar was made for me by Mom.
③ Ms. Han runs a restaurant.
 → A restaurant is ran by Ms. Han.
④ A stranger spoke to me.
 → I was spoken to by a stranger.
⑤ Melisa prepared an interview.
 → An interview was prepared by Melisa.

서답형

17 다음 대화의 빈칸에 알맞은 말을 쓰시오.

> A: Who takes care of your children while you are here?
> B: My children _____ my mother.

18 다음 빈칸에 공통으로 들어갈 말로 가장 적절한 것은?

> • The restaurant is crowded _____ many people.
> • Are you satisfied _____ your birthday present?

① at　　　　② by　　　　③ from
④ about　　　⑤ with

서답형

19 주어진 문장을 수동태로 바르게 전환하시오.

> They sell stamps in a post office.

➡ _____

서답형

20 다음 우리말을 수동태를 활용하여 영어로 쓸 때 다섯 번째로 오는 단어는?

> 많은 사람들이 이 공연을 볼 거야.

➡ _____

서답형

21 다음 문장을 능동태는 수동태로, 수동태는 능동태로 전환하시오.

(1) I saw him dancing.
➡ _____

(2) Jack will buy the cake.
➡ _____

(3) Did you drink the juice?
➡ _____

22 다음 중 어법상 바르지 <u>않은</u> 것은?

① The car was repaired by a man.
② A terrible accident was happened last night.
③ The illness was cured by a doctor.
④ A boy was hit by a truck.
⑤ The package was delivered by a young girl.

23 다음 중 빈칸에 들어갈 말로 가장 적절한 것은?

> Do your brothers help you?
> = _____ your brothers?

① Do you help　　　② Are you helping
③ Were you helped　④ Are you helped
⑤ Are you helped by

24 다음 빈칸에 공통으로 들어갈 말로 가장 적절한 것은?

> • Were the pants bought _____ you?
> • Was the chocolate made _____ his mother?

① for　　　　② to　　　　③ about
④ of　　　　⑤ in

서답형

25 주어진 문장과 같은 의미가 되도록 빈칸에 알맞은 말을 쓰시오.

> I will take care of your cats.
> = Your cats _____.

서답형

26 주어진 단어를 활용하여 다음 우리말을 다섯 단어의 영어 문장으로 쓰시오.

> 이 다리는 수리되어야만 해. (repair)

➡ _____

01 다음 문장을 수동태로 쓰시오.

> We will not give up the project.

➡ _____

02 다음 문장에서 어법상 틀린 것을 바르게 고쳐 올바른 문장으로 다시 쓰시오.

> My parents will be used the treadmill.

➡ _____

03 다음 대화의 빈칸에 알맞은 말을 쓰시오.

> A: How many solutions will they offer?
> B: As far as I know, three solutions _____ _____ _____ by them.

04 같은 의미의 문장이 되도록 빈칸에 알맞은 말을 쓰시오.

> David put on the pants.
> = The pants _____.

05 괄호 안에 주어진 단어를 어법에 맞게 고쳐 쓰시오.

> A: You are going to throw a party for Jenny, right?
> B: Yes. A cake will (make) by me, some balloons will (buy) by James, some friends will (invite).

➡ _____

06 주어진 동사를 어법과 내용에 맞게 빈칸에 쓰시오.

> arrest / cut / serve / laugh at / eat

(1) Julia _____ by her classmates. She was really embarrassed.
(2) Don't worry. I'm sure that the suspect will _____ by the police.
(3) My dog _____ all the pizza on the table last night.
(4) The news that tuition fees will _____ in half makes me happy.
(5) The cook _____ customers himself. So they feel satisfied.

07 다음 대화의 빈칸에 알맞은 말을 쓰시오.

> A: Who will write a script for our play?
> B: A script _____ by Colin. He is good at writing.

08 주어진 단어를 활용하여 다음 우리말을 영어로 쓰시오.

> 이 집은 언제 지어졌니? (build)

➡ _____

09 같은 의미의 문장이 되도록 빈칸에 알맞은 말을 쓰시오.

> Someone should tell James the news
> = James _____.

10 다음 각 문장을 능동태는 수동태로, 수동태는 능동태로 전환하시오.

(1) The company may offer Chris a job.

➡ _____

➡ _____

(2) You must send this letter before June 1.

➡ _____

(3) The electric light bulb was invented by Thomas Edison in 1879.

➡ _____

(4) I will divide the class into two sections.

➡ _____

(5) Rice is grown in many countries by people.

➡ _____

11 두 문장이 같은 의미가 되도록 빈칸에 알맞은 말을 쓰시오.

> We must wear seat belts during takeoff and landing.
> = Seat belts _____ during takeoff and landing.

12 주어진 단어를 활용하여 대화를 완성하시오.

> A: Andy, your chores (should, finish) by the time I get home.
> B: Don't worry, Dad. I'll do everything you told me to do.

➡ _____

13 주어진 단어를 어법에 맞게 빈칸에 쓰시오.

> Jim is wearing a gold band on his fourth finger. He (marry).

➡ _____

14 주어진 단어를 어법에 맞게 빈칸에 쓰시오.

> introduce / originate / grow

> Bananas _____ in Asia but now _____ _____ by people all around the world. They _____ to the Americas in 1516.

15 주어진 어휘를 활용하여 문장을 완성하시오.

> When we are in the middle school, we _____ (require / to wear uniforms).

➡ _____

16 같은 의미의 문장이 되도록 빈칸에 알맞은 말을 쓰시오.

> Timmy dropped a plate after dinner last night.
> = A plate _____.

17 다음 문장을 수동태로 전환하시오.

(1) You must not bring food into the lab.

➡ _____

(2) You should turn off cell phones.

➡ _____

(3) We cannot explain UFO sightings.

➡ _____

The Great Escape

Welcome to the Escape Tower. You will enter the first room in our
<small>~에 들어가다(타동사)</small>

tower. You need to solve some riddles to escape. Clues can be found
<small>~해야 한다(= have to. should)   ~하기 위해서(to부정사의 부사적 용법)   조동사의 수동태는 '조동사+be+p.p.' 형태임</small>

somewhere inside the room. So, are you ready to think like Sherlock
<small>~처럼 생각하다</small>

Holmes?

Room #1

Mr. Doodle was hit by a car on Sunday afternoon. Luckily, he wasn't
<small>~에 의해 …되다   문장 수식 부사: 운 좋게도</small>

badly hurt, but he didn't see the driver. Three suspects were questioned
<small>(= A police officer questioned three suspects.)</small>

by a police officer. Ms. A said she was reading a book at the time of

the accident. Mr. B said he was walking his dog. Ms. C said she was
<small>said (that): 명사절 접속사 that 생략</small>

making breakfast. Who hit Mr. Doodle? Can you explain why? Do you

have the answer? Write it down. Then you can move to the next room.
<small>down이 부사이고 목적어가 인칭대명사이므로 it이 동사와 부사 사이에 위치함</small>

Clue The accident happened in the afternoon.
<small>자동사(수동태 불가능)</small>

Congratulations! You made it to the second room. However, the

second room is much harder to escape than the first one. Good luck!
<small>비교급 강조 부사 '훨씬' (= still. far. even. a lot)   =room</small>

escape: 탈출하다
riddle: 수수께끼
clue: 단서
somewhere: 어딘가에
be ready to: ~할 준비가 되어 있다
hurt: 다친
suspect: 용의자
question: 심문하다
at the time of: ~이 일어나던 때에
accident: 사고
write down: 적다
make it to: ~에 이르는 데 성공하다

 확인문제

● 다음 문장이 본문의 내용과 일치하면 T, 일치하지 않으면 F를 쓰시오.

1 You should solve some riddles to escape from the tower. ☐

2 Clues will be given to you by the tower manager. ☐

3 The car accident happened on Saturday afternoon. ☐

4 If you write down the answer to the first riddle, you can escape from the tower. ☐

Room #2

Jay gets an email from his favorite clothing store. The title reads "You won our Lucky Day event!" Jay is surprised. He quickly opens it.

JayJr@kmail.com

You won our 'Lucky Day' event!

Congratulations!

You have won a special prize. During our Lucky Day event, you can choose any seven items from our store for free! Come to our store on November 31. We can't wait to see you.

Truly yours,

Kay Brown

However, Jay thinks that the event isn't real and deletes the email. Can you explain why?

Clue There are usually 30 or 31 days in a month.

Do you have the answer? Write it down and then you are free to go!

📎 **확인문제**

● 다음 문장이 본문의 내용과 일치하면 T, 일치하지 <u>않으면</u> F를 쓰시오.

1 Jay gets many emails from his favorite clothing store. ☐

2 Jay is surprised at the title of the email. ☐

3 Seven items can be chosen by Jay on November 30. ☐

4 Jay wants to meet Kay Brown. ☐

5 Jay thinks the event is not true. ☐

6 Jay deletes the email before reading it. ☐

● 우리말을 참고하여 빈칸에 알맞은 말을 쓰시오.

The Great Escape

1 Welcome _____ the Escape Tower.

2 You will _____ _____ _____ _____ in our tower.

3 You need _____ _____ _____ _____ to escape.

4 Clues can _____ _____ somewhere _____ the room.

5 So, _____ you ready _____ _____ like Sherlock Holmes?

Room # 1

6 Mr. Doodle _____ _____ _____ a car _____ Sunday afternoon.

7 _____, he wasn't _____ _____, but he didn't _____ the driver.

8 Three suspects _____ _____ _____ a police officer.

9 Ms. A said she was _____ _____ _____ at the time of _____ _____.

10 Mr. B said he _____ _____ his dog.

11 Ms. C said she _____ _____ _____.

12 _____ _____ Mr. Doodle? Can you _____ why?

13 Do you have the answer? _____ _____ _____.

14 Then you can _____ _____ the next room.

15 **Clue** The accident _____ _____ the afternoon.

16 Congratulations! You _____ _____ _____ the second room.

대탈출

1 '탈출탑'에 오신 것을 환영합니다.

2 당신은 저희 탑의 첫 번째 방에 들어갈 것입니다.

3 당신은 탈출하기 위하여 몇 개의 수수께끼를 풀어야 합니다.

4 단서들은 방 어딘가에서 발견될 수 있습니다.

5 그러면 당신은 셜록 홈스처럼 생각할 준비가 되었나요?

방 # 1

6 Doodle씨는 일요일 오후에 차에 치였습니다.

7 다행히 그는 심하게 다치지 않았으나 그는 운전자를 보지 못했습니다.

8 세 명의 용의자들이 경찰에게 심문을 받았습니다.

9 A씨는 사고가 일어난 시간에 책을 읽고 있었다고 말했습니다.

10 B씨는 그의 개를 산책시키고 있었다고 말했습니다.

11 C씨는 아침을 만들고 있었다고 말했습니다.

12 누가 Doodle씨를 치었을까요? 왜 그런지 설명할 수 있나요?

13 답을 가지고 있나요? 적어 보세요.

14 그런 다음, 당신은 다음 방으로 갈 수 있습니다.

15 단서: 사건은 오후에 일어났습니다.

16 축하합니다! 당신은 두 번째 방에 오는 데 성공하셨습니다.

17 However, the second room is _____ _____ _____ _____ the first one. Good luck!

Room #2

18 Jay _____ an email _____ his favorite clothing store.

19 The title _____ "You _____ our Lucky Day event!"

20 Jay is _____. He quickly opens it.

21 JayJr@kmail.com

You _____ our 'Lucky Day' event!

22 _____! You_____ _____ a special prize.

23 _____ our Lucky Day event, you can _____ any seven items _____ our store _____ _____!

24 Come _____ our store _____ November 31.

25 We can't _____ _____ _____ you.

26 _____ _____, Kay Brown

27 _____, Jay thinks that the event _____ _____ and _____ the email.

28 _____ you explain _____?

29 **Clue** _____ _____ _____ 30 or 31 _____ in a month.

30 Do you _____ _____ _____?

31 Write _____ down and then you _____ _____ _____ _____!

17 그러나 두 번째 방은 첫 번째 방보다 탈출하기 훨씬 더 어렵습니다. 행운을 빕니다!

방 # 2

18 Jay는 그가 가장 좋아하는 옷 가게로부터 이메일을 받습니다.

19 제목은 "당신은 '행운의 날' 행사에 당첨되었습니다!"라고 적혀 있습니다.

20 Jay는 놀랍니다. 그는 재빨리 그것을 엽니다.

21 JayJr@kmail.com
당신은 우리의 '행운의 날' 행사에 당첨되었습니다!

22 축하합니다! 당신은 특별한 상품을 받게 되었습니다.

23 '행운의 날' 행사 동안, 당신은 우리 가게에서 일곱 가지 상품을 아무거나 무료로 선택할 수 있습니다!

24 11월 31일에 우리 가게로 오세요.

25 우리는 몹시 당신을 보기를 기대합니다.

26 안녕히 계십시오, Kay Brown

27 그러나 Jay는 그 행사가 사실이 아니라고 생각하고 이메일을 삭제합니다.

28 왜 그런지 설명할 수 있나요?

29 단서: 한 달은 주로 30일 또는 31일이 있습니다.

30 답을 가지고 계신가요?

31 그것을 적으면, 당신은 자유롭게 가실 수 있습니다!

● 우리말을 참고하여 본문을 영작하시오.

The Great Escape

1 '탈출 탑'에 오신 것을 환영합니다.

➡ _____

2 당신은 저희 탑의 첫 번째 방에 들어갈 것입니다.

➡ _____

3 당신은 탈출하기 위하여 몇 개의 수수께끼를 풀어야 합니다.

➡ _____

4 단서들은 방 어딘가에서 발견될 수 있습니다.

➡ _____

5 그러면 당신은 셜록 홈스처럼 생각할 준비가 되었나요?

➡ _____

Room #1

6 Doodle씨는 일요일 오후에 차에 치였습니다.

➡ _____

7 다행히 그는 심하게 다치지 않았으나 그는 운전자를 보지 못했습니다.

➡ _____

8 세 명의 용의자들이 경찰에게 심문을 받았습니다.

➡ _____

9 A씨는 사고가 일어난 시간에 책을 읽고 있었다고 말했습니다.

➡ _____

10 B씨는 그의 개를 산책시키고 있었다고 말했습니다.

➡ _____

11 C씨는 아침을 만들고 있었다고 말했습니다.

➡ _____

12 누가 Doodle씨를 치었을까요? 왜 그런지 설명할 수 있나요?

➡ _____

13 답을 가지고 있나요? 적어 보세요.

➡ _____

14 그런 다음, 당신은 다음 방으로 갈 수 있습니다.

➡ _____

15 단서: 사건은 오후에 일어났습니다.

➡ _____

16 축하합니다! 당신은 두 번째 방에 오는 데 성공하셨습니다.

➡ _____

17 그러나 두 번째 방은 첫 번째 방보다 탈출하기 훨씬 더 어렵습니다. 행운을 빕니다!

➡ _____

Room #2

18 Jay는 그가 가장 좋아하는 옷 가게로부터 이메일을 받습니다.

➡ _____

19 제목은 "당신은 '행운의 날' 행사에 당첨되었습니다!"라고 적혀 있습니다.

➡ _____

20 Jay는 놀랍니다. 그는 재빨리 그것을 엽니다.

➡ _____

21 JayJr@kmail.com
당신은 우리의 '행운의 날' 행사에 당첨되었습니다!

➡ JayJr@kmail.com _____

22 축하합니다! 당신은 특별한 상품을 받게 되었습니다.

➡ _____

23 '행운의 날' 행사 동안, 당신은 우리 가게에서 일곱 가지 상품을 아무거나 공짜로 선택할 수 있습니다!

➡ _____

24 11월 31일에 우리 가게로 오세요.

➡ _____

25 우리는 몹시 당신을 보기를 기대합니다.

➡ _____

26 안녕히 계십시오, Kay Brown

➡ _____

27 그러나 Jay는 그 행사가 사실이 아니라고 생각하고 이메일을 삭제합니다.

➡ _____

28 왜 그런지 설명할 수 있나요?

➡ _____

29 단서: 한 달은 주로 30일 또는 31일이 있습니다.

➡ _____

30 답을 가지고 계신가요?

➡ _____

31 그것을 적으면, 당신은 자유롭게 가실 수 있습니다!

➡ _____

[01~03] 다음 글을 읽고 물음에 답하시오.

Welcome to the Escape Tower. You will enter the first room in our tower. You need (A)to solve some riddles to escape. Clues can be found somewhere inside the room. So, are you ready to think like Sherlock Holmes?

서답형
01 다음과 같이 풀이되는 단어를 위 글에서 찾아 쓰시오.

something that helps a person find something, understand something, or solve a mystery or puzzle

➡ _____

중요
02 다음 중 위 글의 내용과 일치하지 <u>않는</u> 것은?

① There are some riddles to solve.
② In order to escape, you need to solve some riddles.
③ It is necessary to find clues inside the room.
④ Clues are hidden inside the room.
⑤ Sherlock Holmes used to think many things in the tower.

03 다음 중 밑줄 친 (A)와 쓰임이 같은 것은?

① Is there anything to eat?
② She hopes to meet you someday.
③ Bradley woke up early not to be late.
④ Kathy is happy to see him.
⑤ He must be generous to buy you shoes.

[04~08] 다음 글을 읽고 물음에 답하시오.

Room #1
Mr. Doodle (A)_____ by a car on Sunday afternoon. ①Unfortunately, he wasn't badly hurt, but he didn't see the driver. Three suspects were questioned by ②a police officer. Ms. A said she was reading a book at the time of the accident. Mr. B said he was walking his dog. Ms. C said she was making breakfast. ③Who hit Mr. Doodle? Can you explain why? Do you have the answer? Write it down. Then you can ④move to the next room.
Clue: The accident happened ⑤in the afternoon.
Congratulations! You made it to the second room. However, the second room is much harder to escape than the first one. Good luck!

04 다음 중 빈칸 (A)에 들어갈 말로 가장 적절한 것은?

① is hit   ② hit   ③ hits
④ was hit   ⑤ can be hit

중요
05 다음 중 위 글을 읽고 답할 수 <u>없는</u> 것은?

① When was Mr. Doodle hit by a car?
② Why didn't Mr. Doodle see the driver?
③ What was Ms. A doing on Sunday afternoon?
④ What was Mr. B doing at the time of the accident?
⑤ How many people were questioned by a police officer?

서답형

06 ①~⑤ 중 글의 흐름상 어색한 것은?

①   ②   ③   ④   ⑤

서답형

07 How many suspects are there? Answer in English with a full sentence.

➡ _____

서답형

08 다음 물음에 완전한 문장의 영어로 답하시오.

> Q: After you escape from the first room, where do you have to go?

➡ _____

[09~14] 다음 글을 읽고 물음에 답하시오.

Room #2

Jay gets an email from his favorite clothing store. The title reads "You won our Lucky Day event!" Jay (A)_____(surprise). He quickly opens (B)it.

JayJr@kmail.com

You won our 'Lucky Day' event!

Congratulations!

You have won a special prize. During our Lucky Day event, you can choose any seven items from our store for free! Come to our store (C)_____ November 31. We can't wait to see you.

Truly yours,
Kay Brown

However, Jay thinks (D)that the event isn't real and deletes the email. Can you explain why?

Clue: There are usually 30 or 31 days in a month.

서답형

09 빈칸 (A)에 괄호 안에 주어진 동사를 어법에 맞게 쓰시오.

➡ _____

서답형

10 밑줄 친 (B)가 가리키는 것을 위 글에서 찾아 쓰시오.

➡ _____

11 다음 중 빈칸 (C)에 들어갈 말로 가장 적절한 것은?

① in   ② at   ③ on   ④ by   ⑤ to

12 다음 중 밑줄 친 (D)와 쓰임이 다른 하나는?

① Did you just say that she loves me?
② The fact that you stole it doesn't change.
③ Jason knew that they couldn't arrive in time.
④ Where is the box that came yesterday?
⑤ It is impossible that they come together.

서답형

13 According to the email, what can Jay do during their Lucky Day event? Answer in English with eleven words.

➡ _____

중요

14 다음 중 위 글의 내용과 일치하지 않는 것은?

① Jay's favorite clothing store sent an email to Jay.
② The email that the clothing store sent had no title.
③ The person who sent Jay an email is Kay Brown.
④ Jay didn't believe what the email said.
⑤ The email was deleted by Jay.

[15~22] 다음 글을 읽고 물음에 답하시오.

Welcome to the Escape Tower. You will enter the first room in our tower. You need to solve some riddles to escape. ⓐClues can be found somewhere inside the room. So, are you ready to think like Sherlock Holmes?

Room #1

Mr. Doodle was hit by a car on Sunday afternoon. Luckily, he wasn't badly hurt, but he didn't see the driver. Three suspects were questioned by a police officer. Ms. A said she was reading a book ⓑ____ the time of the accident. Mr. B said he was walking his dog. Ms. C said she (A)[was making / was made] breakfast. Who hit Mr. Doodle? Can you explain why? Do you have the answer? Write (B)[it / them] down. Then you can move to the next room.

Clue: The accident (C)[happened / was happened] in the afternoon.

서답형
15 밑줄 친 ⓐ와 같은 의미의 문장이 되도록 빈칸에 알맞은 말을 쓰시오.

You _____.

16 다음 중 빈칸 ⓑ에 들어갈 말로 가장 적절한 것은?

① on ② at ③ to ④ in ⑤ by

중요
17 (A)~(C)에서 어법상 옳은 것끼리 바르게 짝지어진 것은?

① was making – it – happened
② was making – them – happened
③ was making – it – was happened
④ was made – them – happened
⑤ was made – them – was happened

서답형
18 위 글의 내용에 맞게 빈칸에 알맞은 말을 쓰시오.

Q: Did Mr. Doodle see the driver?
A: No. The driver _____ Mr. Doodle.

서답형
19 What was Ms. A doing when Mr. Doodle was hit by a car? Answer in English with a full sentence.

➡ _____

_____

20 다음 중 위 글의 내용과 일치하지 않는 것은?

① Solving some riddles lets you get away from the room.
② A car hit Mr. Doodle on Sunday.
③ Mr. Doodle was hardly hurt.
④ According to Ms. C, she was making breakfast when Mr. Doodle was hit by a car.
⑤ Mr. B has a dog.

서답형
21 위 글의 내용에 맞게 빈칸에 알맞은 말을 쓰시오.

If the right answer _____, you can move to the next room.

서답형
22 다음과 같이 풀이되는 단어를 위 글에서 찾아 쓰시오.

a sudden event that is not planned and that causes damage or injury

➡ _____

[23~30] 다음 글을 읽고 물음에 답하시오.

Congratulations! You made it to the second room. (A)_____, the second room is much harder to escape than the first one. Good luck!

Room #2

Jay gets an email (B)_____ his favorite clothing store. The title reads "You won our Lucky Day event!" Jay is surprised. He quickly opens it.

JayJr@kmail.com

You won our 'Lucky Day' event!

Congratulations!

You have won a special prize. During our Lucky Day event, you can choose any seven items from our store (C)for free! Come to our store on November 31. We can't wait to see you.

Truly yours,

Kay Brown

However, Jay thinks that the event isn't real and deletes the email. Can you explain why?

Clue: There are usually 30 or 31 days in a month.

Do you have the answer? Write it down and then (D)당신은 자유롭게 가실 수 있습니다!

23 다음 중 빈칸 (A)에 들어갈 말로 가장 적절한 것은?

① Therefore
② For example
③ However
④ On the other hand
⑤ As a result

24 다음 중 빈칸 (B)에 들어갈 말로 가장 적절한 것은?

① to
② about
③ in
④ from
⑤ by

25 밑줄 친 (C)의 의미로 가장 적절한 것은?

① freely
② for yourself
③ at no cost
④ with paying money
⑤ for anything

26 서답형 주어진 단어를 활용하여 밑줄 친 우리말 (D)를 영어로 쓰시오.

> free

➡ _____

27 서답형 글의 내용에 맞게 다음 물음에 대한 대답을 완성하시오.

> Q: By whom is the email deleted?
> A: It _____.

28 중요 다음 중 위 글을 읽고 답할 수 없는 것은?

① From whom did Jay get an email?
② What is the title of the email?
③ How many items can Jay choose from the store on the event day?
④ What does Jay think about the email?
⑤ When did Jay get the email?

29 서답형 글의 내용에 맞게 빈칸에 알맞은 말을 쓰시오.

> Q: Why doesn't Jay believe the email?
> A: It's because the event is _____ but there are only _____ in November.

30 서답형 글의 내용에 맞게 빈칸에 알맞은 말을 세 단어로 쓰시오.

> The second room is not as _____ as the first room.

[01~03] 다음 글을 읽고 물음에 답하시오.

Welcome to the Escape Tower. (A)You will enter into the first room in our tower. You need to solve some riddles to escape. You can find clues somewhere inside the room. So, are you ready to think like Sherlock Holmes?

01 What do you need to do to escape from the tower? Answer in English with a full sentence.

➡ _____

02 밑줄 친 (A)에서 틀린 곳을 고쳐 다시 쓰시오.

➡ _____

03 글의 내용에 맞게 빈칸에 알맞은 말을 쓰시오.

In order to _____ from the room, you should think _____.

[04~08] 다음 글을 읽고 물음에 답하시오.

Room #1
(A)Mr. Doodle was hit by a car on Sunday afternoon. Luckily, he wasn't badly hurt, but (B) he didn't see the driver. Three suspects were questioned by a police officer. Ms. A said she was reading a book at the time of the accident. Mr. B said he was walking his dog. Ms. C said she was making breakfast. Who hit Mr. Doodle? Can you explain why? Do you have the answer? Write it down. Then you can move to the next room.

Clue: The accident happened in the afternoon.

Congratulations! You made it to the second room. However, (C)두 번째 방은 첫 번째 방보다 탈출하기가 훨씬 더 어렵습니다. Good luck!

04 밑줄 친 (A)를 능동태로 전환하시오.

➡ _____

05 다음은 밑줄 친 문장 (B)와 같은 의미의 문장이다. 빈칸에 알맞은 말을 쓰시오.

The driver _____.

06 What was the second suspect doing when Mr. Doodle was hit by a car?

➡ _____

07 According to the passage, what happened to Mr. Doodle on Sunday afternoon? Answer in English.

➡ _____

08 주어진 어구를 바르게 배열하여 밑줄 친 우리말 (C)를 영어로 쓰시오.

(the first one / the second room / than / is / harder / escape / much / to)

➡ _____
_____

[09~13] 다음 글을 읽고 물음에 답하시오.

Room #2

Jay gets an email from his favorite clothing store. The title reads "You won our Lucky Day event!" Jay is surprised. (A)He quickly opens it.

JayJr@kmail.com

You won our 'Lucky Day' event!

Congratulations!

You have won a special prize. During our Lucky Day event, you can choose any seven items from our store for free! Come to our store on November 31. We can't wait to see you.

Truly yours,
Kay Brown

However, Jay thinks that the event isn't real and deletes the email. Can you explain why?

Clue: (B)한 달은 주로 30일 또는 31일이 있습니다.

Do you have the answer? Write it down and then you are free to go!

09 다음 빈칸에 알맞은 말을 써서 밑줄 친 (A)와 같은 의미의 문장을 만드시오.

It _____ .

10 주어진 단어를 활용하여 밑줄 친 우리말 (B)를 영어로 쓰시오.

there

➡ _____

11 According to the email, what did Jay win?

➡ _____

12 What does Jay do after reading the email? Answer in English with a full sentence.

➡ _____

13 글의 내용에 맞게 빈칸에 알맞은 말을 쓰시오.

Q: What surprises Jay?
A: He _____ the title of the email.

[14~17] 다음 글을 읽고 물음에 답하시오.

It was last Sunday. Dohun was at home. Suddenly, (A)he heard a sound in the next room. When he went into the room, the window was broken. When he looked outside, Sujin was holding a baseball bat and Ted was throwing a ball to his dog. (B)Who broke the window? How can it be explained?

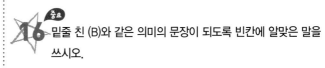

14 밑줄 친 (A)를 수동태로 전환하시오.

➡ _____

15 When was the window broken? Answer in English with five words.

➡ _____

16 밑줄 친 (B)와 같은 의미의 문장이 되도록 빈칸에 알맞은 말을 쓰시오.

By whom _____ ?

17 What was Sujin holding? Answer in English with a full sentence.

➡ _____

Listen and Speak 1-C

A: Try to solve this riddle.
　　try to: ~하려고 노력하다 try ~ing: 시험 삼아 ~해 보다

B: Sure.

A: Four people are under one umbrella, but nobody gets wet.
　　　　　　　　　　　　　　　　nobody는 부정대명사로 3인칭 단수 취급하여 동사에 -s가 붙는다.

　 Can you explain why?
　　　　　　　　　　=why nobody gets wet

B: Yes! It's because it's a sunny day!
　　　　　　　A가 말한 내용　비인칭 주어

구문해설 • riddle: 수수께끼 • wet: 젖은 • explain: 설명하다

A: 이 수수께끼를 풀어봐.
B: 그래.
A: 4명의 사람들이 하나의 우산 아래 있는데 아무도 젖지 않아. 이유를 설명할 수 있겠니?
B: 응! 왜냐하면 맑은 날이기 때문이야.

Let's Write

It was last Sunday. Dohun was at home. Suddenly, he heard a
비인칭 주어

sound in the next room. When he went into the room, the
　　sound를 수식하는 형용사구

window was broken.
　　　　행위자가 불분명 할 때 'by+행위자' 생략

When he looked outside, Sujin was holding a baseball bat and
　　　　　　　　　　　　　　　　　　과거진행형

Ted was throwing a ball to his dog. Who broke the window?
　　　　　　　　　　　　　　　~에게

How can it be explained?
　　주체가 행위의 대상이 되므로 수동태를 씀

구문해설 • suddenly: 갑자기 • break: ~을 깨뜨리다 (-broke-broken) • hold: ~을 쥐다, 잡다
　　　　　　 • throw: ~을 던지다 • explain: ~을 설명하다

지난 일요일이었다. 도훈이는 집에 있었다. 갑자기, 그는 옆방에서 나는 어떤 소리를 들었다. 그가 그 방으로 갔을 때, 창문이 깨져 있었다. 도훈이가 밖을 보았을 때, 수진이는 야구 방망이를 들고 있었고 Ted는 그의 개에게 공을 던지고 있었다. 누가 창문을 깼을까? 그것은 어떻게 설명될 수 있을까?

Culture & Life

This is the famous riddle of the Sphinx. Oedipus needs to solve it to go into
　　　　　　　　　　　　　　　　　　　　　　　need to V: V할 필요가 있다　부사적 용법(목적)

Thebes. This is the question that the Sphinx asks him.
　　　　　　　　　　　　　　목적격 관계대명사

Which creature walks on four legs in the morning, two legs in the afternoon,
의문형용사로 creature 수식

and three legs in the evening?

구문해설 • famous: 유명한 • solve: 해결하다 • question: 질문 • creature: 생명체

이것은 스핑크스의 유명한 수수께끼이다. 오이디푸스는 Thebes에 들어가기 위해 그것을 풀어야 한다. 이것은 스핑크스가 그에게 묻는 질문이다.

어느 생명체가 아침에는 네 다리로 걷고, 오후에는 두 다리로 걷고, 저녁에는 세 다리로 걷는가?

영역별 핵심문제

01 다음 영영풀이가 가리키는 것을 고르시오.

> someone who steals things from another person or place

① detective   ② liar
③ thief   ④ police
⑤ prosecutor

02 다음 중 밑줄 친 부분의 뜻풀이가 바르지 <u>않은</u> 것은?

① She was reading a book at the time of the <u>accident</u>. 사고
② Sujin was holding a baseball <u>bat</u>. 방망이
③ The duck will eat the <u>beans</u>. 콩
④ Do not <u>cross</u> the river by yourself without your parents. 건너다
⑤ Did you watch this week's TV show about the student <u>detective</u>? 회장

03 다음 우리말과 일치하도록 주어진 단어를 사용하여 영작하시오.

(1) 첫 번째, 원을 그리세요. (draw)

➡ _____

(2) 두 번째, 원 안에 별을 놓으세요. (put, inside)

➡ _____

(3) 그리고 나서 원의 맨 위에 삼각형을 놓으세요. (then)

➡ _____

04 다음 문장의 빈칸에 들어갈 말을 〈보기〉에서 골라 쓰시오. 필요하면 어형 변화를 하시오.

> ─┤ 보기 ├─
> delete / clue / suspect / escape

(1) The thief _____ from the police station last week.
(2) The _____ lied to the police officer.
(3) The detective looked for _____ at the scene.
(4) Don't open emails with strange titles. _____ them at once.

05 다음 우리말에 맞게 빈칸에 알맞은 말을 쓰시오.

(1) 나는 이 도시를 떠날 준비가 되어 있다.
➡ I'm _____ leave this city.
(2) 나는 축제가 일어나던 때에 아팠다.
➡ I was ill _____ the festival.
(3) 여기에 당신의 주소를 적으세요.
➡ _____ your address here.

06 다음 주어진 문장의 밑줄 친 cross와 같은 의미로 쓰인 것은?

> My parents needed to <u>cross</u> a river.

① I want to <u>cross</u> the road as soon as possible.
② I drew a <u>cross</u> on the map to mark my office.
③ I want to have a <u>cross</u> as a small tattoo on my hand.
④ You can mark it by a <u>cross</u>.
⑤ My mother always keeps her <u>cross</u> necklace.

[07~08] 다음 대화를 읽고 물음에 답하시오.

Jimin: Do you want to play the new game ⓐ<u>what</u> I bought?

Brian: Sure, what is it, Jimin?

Jimin: It's ⓑ<u>like</u> a soccer game but the players are dragons and seahorses. You need to use these buttons ⓒ<u>to play</u>.

Brian: That sounds ⓓ<u>fun</u>. Can you explain how ⓔ<u>to use</u> the buttons?

Jimin: Sure.

07 위 대화의 밑줄 친 ⓐ~ⓔ 중 어법상 어색한 것을 찾아 바르게 고치시오.

➡ _____

08 위 대화를 읽고 대답할 수 <u>없는</u> 것은?

① What are Jimin and Brian going to do?

② What type of game are Jimin and Brian going to play?

③ What role do dragons and seahorses play in the game?

④ Why does Brian need to know how to use the buttons?

⑤ Why did Jimin buy the game similar to a soccer game?

[09~10] 다음 대화를 읽고 물음에 답하시오.

Jack: Kelly, here's a riddle. You can see this twice in a week, once in a year, but never in a day. What is this?

Kelly: (A) I have no idea.

Jack: (B) It's the letter "E."

Kelly: (C) Can you explain why?

Jack: (D) Well, there are two "E"s in the word "week," one "E" in the word "year" but no "E"s in the word "day."

Kelly: (E) Aha! Now I get it.

09 위 대화에서 다음 영영풀이가 나타내는 말을 찾아 쓰시오.

> a difficult question that is asked as a game and that has a surprising or funny answer

➡ _____

10 위 대화의 (A)~(E) 중 주어진 문장이 들어가기에 적절한 곳은?

> I don't get it.

① (A)   ② (B)   ③ (C)   ④ (D)   ⑤ (E)

[11~12] 다음 대화를 읽고 물음에 답하시오.

Tom: Yujin, ⓐ<u>look at</u> my paper fox.

Yujin: That's cute. How did you make it?

Tom: First, fold a paper ⓑ<u>in half</u> to make a triangle. Second, fold the top of the triangle to the bottom line. (A)Third, fold both ends of the bottom line to the top ⓒ<u>to make</u> ears. Then, ⓓ<u>turn it over</u> and ⓔ<u>drawing</u> a face.

Yujin: That sounds easy.

11 위 대화의 ⓐ~ⓔ 중 어법상 어색한 것을 찾아 바르게 고치시오.

➡ _____

12 위 대화의 (A)와 바꾸어 쓸 수 있는 것은?

① Next   ② Besides   ③ After

④ Before   ⑤ Close

[13~14] 다음 대화를 읽고 물음에 답하시오.

Minjun: Wow! Something smells really good, Mom. What is it?

Mom: We're going to have tacos for dinner. Help yourself. (A)

Minjun: Can you explain how to make a taco? (B)

Mom: First, fill your tortilla with vegetables and meat. (C)

Minjun: Sounds delicious! (D)

Mom: Would you like some cheese? (E)

Minjun: No, thanks.

13 위 대화의 (A)~(E) 중 주어진 문장이 들어가기에 적절한 곳은?

Then, add some sauce on the top.

① (A)　② (B)　③ (C)　④ (D)　⑤ (E)

14 위 대화의 내용과 일치하지 <u>않는</u> 것은?

① 민준이는 좋은 냄새를 맡았다.
② 엄마와 민준이는 저녁식사로 타코를 먹을 것이다.
③ 타코를 만들 때 토르티야와 채소와 고기가 필요하다.
④ 타코 위에 약간의 소스를 추가하여 만든다.
⑤ 민준이는 치즈를 더 원한다.

Grammar

15 다음 중 빈칸에 들어갈 말이 <u>다른</u> 하나는?

① The mountain is covered _____ snow.
② Helen is not satisfied _____ the result.
③ My eyes were filled _____ tears.
④ Terry was surprised _____ his letter.
⑤ He was pleased _____ many gifts.

16 다음 중 어법상 바르지 <u>않은</u> 것은?

① Windows are made of glass.
② The store will be closed at 9 o'clock.
③ Something sad happened last night.
④ A postcard was given to me by Jane.
⑤ Hundreds of people were died in the tornado.

17 다음 빈칸에 들어갈 말로 가장 적절한 것은?

People made fun of him
= He _____ people.

① was made fun　② is made fun
③ was made fun of　④ made fun of
⑤ was made fun of by

18 주어진 단어를 활용하여 다음 우리말을 영어로 쓰시오.

언제 그 음식이 배달될까? (deliver)

➡ _____

19 다음 중 문장의 전환이 바르지 <u>않은</u> 것은?

① The students use the computer.
→ The computer is used by the students.
② Does Vicky help you?
→ Are you helped by Vicky?
③ They asked me a question.
→ A question was asked to me by them.
④ Stars can be seen at night.
→ We can see stars at night.
⑤ Is this umbrella carried by you?
→ Do you carry this umbrella?

20 다음 빈칸에 들어갈 말이 바르게 짝지어진 것은?

• Vietnam _____ in Southeast Asia.
• I think life will _____ on other planets.

① located – existed
② locates – exist
③ located – be existed
④ is located – exist
⑤ is located – be existed

21 다음 밑줄 친 ①~⑤ 중 어법상 틀린 것은?

> According to our teacher, ①all of our compositions ②should write ③in ink. He won't accept ④papers ⑤written in pencil.

22 다음 문장을 수동태로 전환하시오.

> Studying English interests us.

➡ _____

23 다음 문장과 같은 의미의 문장을 모두 고르시오.

> Mr. Kim teaches students Korean.

① Students are taught to Korean by Mr. Kim.
② Students are taught Korean by Mr. Kim.
③ Korean teaches students to Mr. Kim.
④ Korean is taught to students by Mr. Kim.
⑤ Korean is taught students by Mr. Kim.

24 다음 중 어법상 옳은 문장의 개수는?

> ⓐ The pencil will sharpen by Tom.
> ⓑ Did the flowers picked up?
> ⓒ Your dog was taken from a hospital.
> ⓓ Can the concert be canceled?
> ⓔ The piano played by James these days.

① 1개 ② 2개 ③ 3개 ④ 4개 ⑤ 5개

25 다음 중 빈칸에 들어갈 말로 가장 적절한 것은?

> Shakespeare wrote *Romeo and Juliet*.
> = *Romeo and Juliet* _____ Shakespeare.

① is written ② was written
③ is written by ④ was written by
⑤ were written by

26 다음 각 문장을 능동태는 수동태로, 수동태는 능동태로 전환하시오.

(1) We must pick up trash.

➡ _____

(2) Kelly is looked down on by Peter.

➡ _____

Reading

[27~30] 다음 글을 읽고 물음에 답하시오.

> Welcome to the Escape Tower. You will enter the first room in our tower. You need to solve some riddles (A)to escape. Clues can be found somewhere inside the room. So, are you ready to think like Sherlock Holmes?
> Room #1
> Mr. Doodle was hit by a car on Sunday afternoon. ① But he didn't see the driver. ② Three suspects were questioned by a police officer. ③ Ms. A said she was reading a book at the time of the accident. Mr. B said he was walking his dog. ④ Ms. C said she was making breakfast. Who hit Mr. Doodle? ⑤ Can you explain why? Do you have the answer? Write it down. Then you can move to the next room.
> Clue: The accident happened in the afternoon.

27 다음 중 주어진 문장이 들어가기에 가장 적절한 곳은?

> Luckily, he wasn't badly hurt.

①   ②   ③   ④   ⑤

28 다음 중 밑줄 친 (A)와 쓰임이 같은 것은?

① Jason told them not to do it again.
② I just did it to help your mother.
③ Helen needs something to wear.
④ It was easy to handle the situation.
⑤ Tamia was happy to hear the news.

29 According to the clue, when did the accident happen?

➡ _____

30 다음 탐정 수첩에서 위 글의 내용과 일치하지 <u>않는</u> 것을 <u>두</u> <u>개</u> 찾아 바르게 고쳐 쓰시오.

> First Riddle
> • Mr. Doodle was hit by a bike.
> • The accident happened on Sunday afternoon.
> • Ms. A was reading a book and Mr. B was walking his dog. Ms. C was making dinner.

➡ _____

➡ _____

[31~34] 다음 글을 읽고 물음에 답하시오.

Congratulations! You made it to the second room. However, the second room is much harder to escape than the first one. Good luck!
Room #2
Jay gets an email from his favorite clothing store. The (A)_____ reads "(B)You won our Lucky Day event!" Jay is surprised. He quickly opens it.
JayJr@kmail.com
You won our 'Lucky Day' event!
Congratulations!
You have won a special prize. During our Lucky Day event, you can choose any seven items from our store for free! Come to our store on November 31. We can't wait to see you.
Truly yours,
Kay Brown
However, Jay thinks that the event isn't real and deletes the email. Can you explain why?
Clue: There are usually 30 or 31 days in a month.
Do you have the answer? Write it down and then you are free to go!

31 다음과 같이 풀이되는 말을 빈칸 (A)에 쓰시오.

> the name given to something such as a book, song, or movie to identify or describe it

➡ _____

32 밑줄 친 (B)를 수동태로 전환하시오.

➡ _____

33 다음 중 위 글을 읽고 답할 수 <u>있는</u> 것은?

① How hard it was to escape from the first room?
② Where is Jay's favorite clothing store?
③ When did Jay get the email?
④ When did Kay Brown send the email to Jay?
⑤ What do you have to do if you have the answer?

34 다음 중 위 글의 내용과 일치하지 <u>않는</u> 것은?

① The first room is much easier to escape than the second room.
② Jay has his favorite clothing store.
③ Jay deletes the email because he doesn't like the special prize.
④ Jay opens the email with surprise.
⑤ You are free to go if you solve the riddle.

[01~02] 다음 대화를 읽고 물음에 답하시오.

Emily: Junsu, do you want to solve a riddle?

Junsu: Sure, what is it?

Emily: There is a farmer. First, the farmer buys a fox, a duck, and a bag of beans. Then, the farmer needs to cross a river.

Junsu: What's the problem?

Emily: The boat can only hold the farmer and one more thing.

Junsu: (A)Are you saying that the farmer can take only one thing at a time?

Emily: Yes. Also, the fox will eat the duck or the duck will eat the beans if the farmer isn't there. Can you explain how to move everything across the river safely?

Junsu: Hmm ....

출제율 90%

01 위 대화의 밑줄 친 (A)와 바꾸어 쓸 수 있는 것은?

① Do you mean that the farmer can take only one thing at a time?

② Why do you say that the farmer can take only one thing at a time?

③ Why do you think the farmer must take only one thing at a time?

④ Do you know that the farmer can take only one thing at a time?

⑤ Have you heard about that the farmer can take only one thing at a time?

출제율 100%

02 위 대화의 내용과 일치하지 않는 것은?

① Emily는 준수에게 수수께끼를 내주었다.

② 농부는 여우한 마리, 오리 한 마리, 콩 한 자루를 샀다.

③ 농부는 강을 건너야 한다.

④ 배는 한 번에 농부와 두 가지 더 옮길 수 있다.

⑤ 농부가 없다면 오리가 콩을 먹거나 여우가 오리를 먹을 수 있다.

[03~04] 다음 대화를 읽고 물음에 답하시오.

Jane: Minsu, do you know the TV show about the student detective?

Minsu: Yes. I love that show, but I didn't see it this week. What was it about?

Jane: Well, all of the bikes at school disappeared.

Minsu: So, what did he do?

Jane: First, he looked around the school. Then, he met some (A)_____s and asked questions. (B)Finally, he found the thief. The thief was ....

Minsu: No, don't tell me! I'll watch it later.

출제율 90%

03 위 대화의 빈칸 (A)에 다음의 영영풀이가 가리키는 말을 고르시오.

> a person who is believed to be possibly guilty of committing a crime

① lawyer　　　　② suspect

③ victim　　　　④ merchant

⑤ prosecutor

출제율 95%

04 위 대화의 밑줄 친 (B)와 바꾸어 쓸 수 있는 것을 모두 고르시오.

① Though　　　　② Eventually

③ Nevertheless　　④ At last

⑤ Initially

[05~06] 다음 대화를 읽고 물음에 답하시오.

Jack: Kelly, here's a riddle. You can see this twice in a week, once in a year, but never in a day. What is this?

Kelly: I have no idea.

Jack: It's the letter "E."

Kelly: I don't get it. (A)이유를 설명해 줄 수 있니?

Jack: Well, there are two "E"s in the word "week," one "E" in the word "year" but no "E"s in the word "day."

Kelly: Aha! Now I get it.

출제율 90%

05 위 대화에서 밑줄 친 (A)의 우리말을 4단어로 영작하시오.

➡ _____

출제율 85%

06 위 대화의 내용과 일치하는 것을 고르시오.

① Kelly solved the riddle with the help of Jack.

② Kelly asked Jack to give him a hint for the answer.

③ Kelly didn't understand the answer at first.

④ The riddle Jack gave to Kelly is about the diary.

⑤ Jack was confused when he got to know the answer to the riddle.

[07~08] 다음 대화를 읽고 물음에 답하시오.

Minjun: Wow! Something smells really good, Mom. What is it?

Mom: We're going to have tacos for dinner. (A) 맘껏 먹으렴.

Minjun: Can you explain how to make a taco?

Mom: First, fill your tortilla with vegetables and meat. Then, add some sauce on the top.

Minjun: Sounds delicious!

Mom: Would you like some cheese?

Minjun: No, thanks.

출제율 95%

07 위 대화의 밑줄 친 (A)의 우리말을 두 단어로 영작하시오.

➡ _____

출제율 90%

08 위 대화의 내용과 일치하도록 민준이의 일기를 완성하시오.

Sun, Sep 8th, 2019

I had (A)_____ for dinner with Mom. It was so delicious. I wondered how to make tacos. Mom told me that (B)_____ first, and then (C)_____.

Next time, I'll try to make them by myself.

출제율 100%

09 다음 대화가 자연스럽게 이어지도록 순서대로 배열하시오.

(A) That sounds easy.

(B) Look at my paper fox.

(C) That's cute. How did you make it?

(D) First, fold a paper in half to make a triangle. Second, fold the top of the triangle to the bottom line. Third, fold both ends of the bottom line to the top to make ears. Then, turn it over and draw a face.

➡ _____

출제율 90%

10 다음 대화에서 수수께끼의 답이 'E'가 되는 이유를 우리말로 설명하시오.

Jack: Kelly, here's a riddle. You can see this twice in a week, once in a year, but never in a day. What is this?

Kelly: I have no idea.

Jack: It's the letter "E."

Kelly: I don't get it. Can you explain why?

Jack: Well, there are two "E"s in the word "week," one "E" in the word "year" but no "E"s in the word "day."

Kelly: Aha! Now I get it.

➡ _____

11 다음 중 밑줄 친 부분을 생략할 수 있는 것은? 출제율 90%

① Was the vase broken <u>by Katherine</u>?
② The door was locked <u>by my parents</u>.
③ The gold mine was discovered <u>by someone</u> in 1890.
④ The water was boiled <u>by your sister</u>.
⑤ A doll was made <u>by my friend</u>.

12 다음 중 문장의 전환이 바르지 <u>않은</u> 것은? 출제율 100%

① Julia will help the poor.
   = The poor will be helped by Julia.
② I must do my homework.
   = My homework must be done by me.
③ Bob drew many paintings.
   = Many paintings were drawn by Bob.
④ The result disappointed me.
   = I was disappointed by the result.
⑤ Brad gave me some chocolate.
   = Some chocolate was given to me by Brad.

13 주어진 단어를 활용하여 다음 우리말을 영어로 쓰시오. 출제율 90%

식탁이 차려지고 양초들에 불이 켜졌다.
(the table / set / light)

➡ _____

14 빈칸에 들어갈 말이 바르게 짝지어진 것은? 출제율 95%

• The building _____ by the earthquake last year.
• The plane _____ behind a cloud.

① was damaged – was disappeared
② is damaged – was disappeared
③ damaged – disappeared
④ is damaged – is disappeared
⑤ was damaged – disappeared

15 다음 우리말과 같은 의미의 문장을 <u>모두</u> 고르시오. 출제율 90%

그 소녀는 공에 맞았다.

① The ball hit the girl.
② The ball was hit by the girl.
③ The girl was hit the ball.
④ The girl hit the ball.
⑤ The girl was hit by the ball.

16 다음 빈칸에 알맞은 말을 쓰시오. 출제율 85%

Someone will deliver the package to your apartment.
= The package _____ to your apartment.

17 다음 각 문장을 수동태로 전환하시오. 출제율 95%

(1) Someone told the kids to leave.
   ➡ _____
(2) Thomas heard me singing in my room.
   ➡ _____

[18~22] 다음 글을 읽고, 물음에 답하시오.

Welcome to the Escape Tower. You will enter the first room in our tower. You need to solve some riddles to escape. Clues can be found somewhere inside the room. So, are you ready to think like Sherlock Holmes?
Room #1
Mr. Doodle was hit by a car on Sunday afternoon.
(A) Who hit Mr. Doodle? Can you explain why? Do you have the answer? Write it down. Then you can move to the next room.

(B) Ms. A said she was reading a book at the time of the accident. Mr. B said he was walking his dog. Ms. C said she was making breakfast.

(C) ⓐLuckily, he wasn't badly hurt, but he didn't see the driver. Three suspects were questioned by a police officer.

Clue: The accident happened in the afternoon.
Congratulations! ⓑ당신은 두 번째 방에 오는 데 성공하셨습니다. However, the second room is much harder to escape than the first one. Good luck!

출제율 100%

18 자연스러운 글이 되도록 (A)~(C)를 바르게 나열한 것은?

① (A)-(C)-(B)　　② (B)-(A)-(C)
③ (B)-(C)-(A)　　④ (C)-(A)-(B)
⑤ (C)-(B)-(A)

출제율 90%

19 다음 중 밑줄 친 ⓐLuckily를 대신하여 쓰일 수 있는 것은?

① Especially　　② Recently
③ Fortunately　　④ Suddenly
⑤ Particularly

출제율 85%

20 주어진 어구를 바르게 배열하여 밑줄 친 우리말 ⓑ를 영어로 쓰시오.

(the second / you / to / made / room / it)

➡ _____

출제율 90%

21 위 글의 내용에 맞게 빈칸에 알맞은 말을 각각 두 단어로 쓰시오.

A: Do you know that there were _____ in Mr. Doodle's accident?
B: Yes. Actually a police officer _____.

출제율 95%

22 다음 중 위 글의 내용과 일치하지 <u>않는</u> 것은?

① Clues for riddles can be found inside the room.
② Mr. Doodle didn't know who hit him.
③ Ms. A was reading a book on Sunday afternoon.
④ Mr. B was with his dog when Mr. Doodle was hit by a car.
⑤ The second room is as difficult to escape as the first room.

[23~25] 다음 글을 읽고 물음에 답하시오.

It was last Sunday. Dohun was at home. Suddenly, he (A)[heard / was heard] a sound in the next room. When he went into the room, the window (B)[broke / was broken]. When he looked outside, Sujin was holding a baseball bat and Ted was throwing a ball to his dog. Who (C)[broke / was broken] the window? How can it be explained?

출제율 100%

23 (A)~(C)에서 어법상 옳은 것끼리 바르게 짝지은 것은?

① was heard – broke – broke
② was heard – broke – was broken
③ heard – broke – broke
④ heard – was broken – was broken
⑤ heard – was broken – broke

출제율 90%

24 What was Ted doing when Dohun looked outside? Answer in English with a full sentence.

➡ _____

출제율 95%

25 다음 중 글의 내용과 일치하지 <u>않는</u> 것은?

① 도훈은 지난 일요일에 집에 있었다.
② 누군가가 창문을 깼다.
③ 도훈이가 있던 방의 창문이 깨졌다.
④ 도훈은 창문이 깨진 것을 보고 밖을 보았다.
⑤ 도훈은 창문이 깨지는 소리를 들었다.

[01~03] 다음 대화를 읽고 물음에 답하시오.

Jimin: Do you want to play the new game that I bought?

Brian: Sure, what is it, Jimin?

Jimin: It's like a soccer game but the players are dragons and seahorses. You need to use these buttons to play.

Brian: That sounds fun. (A)버튼 사용법을 설명해 줄 수 있니?

Jimin: Sure.

01 위 대화의 밑줄 친 (A)의 우리말을 주어진 〈보기〉의 단어를 모두 배열하여 영어로 쓰시오.

┌─ 보기 ─
the buttons / how / use / the / can / to / you / explain
└─

➡ _____

02 What are Jimin and Brian going to do together?

➡ _____

03 How can Jimin and Brian play the game?

➡ _____

[04~05] 다음 대화를 읽고 물음에 답하시오.

Jane: Minsu, do you know the TV show about the student detective?

Minsu: Yes. I love that show, but I didn't see it this week. What was it about?

Jane: Well, all of the bikes at school disappeared.

Minsu: So, what did he do?

Jane: First, he looked around the school. Then, he met some suspects and asked questions. Finally, he found the thief. The thief was ....

Minsu: No, don't tell me! I'll watch it later.

04 What was the TV show that Minsu had missed about?

➡ It(=The TV show) was about the case that

_____

05 What did the student detective do to find the thief?

➡ _____

_____

06 다음 문장을 수동태로 전환하시오.

(1) Someone already made the coffee.

➡ _____

(2) Did you return the book?

➡ _____

(3) I will invite my friends.

➡ _____

07 다음 빈칸에 알맞은 말을 쓰시오.

Wild animals attacked the villagers.
= The villagers _____
   wild animals.

08 다음 대화의 빈칸에 알맞은 말을 쓰시오.

A: Who will make the decision?
B: The decision _____
   our CEO.

09 주어진 어구를 활용하여 다음 우리말을 영어로 쓰시오.

> 실종 소녀가 어제 경찰에 의해 발견되었다.
> (the missing girl, the police)

➡ _____

10 주어진 단어를 어법에 맞게 활용하여 빈칸에 알맞은 말을 쓰시오.

> A: Is the train going to be late?
> B: No. It _____(expect) to be on time.

[11~13] 다음 글을 읽고 물음에 답하시오.

　Welcome to the Escape Tower. You will enter the first room in our tower. You need to solve some riddles to escape. Clues can be found somewhere inside the room. So, are you ready to think like Sherlock Holmes?
Room #1
　Mr. Doodle was hit by a car on Sunday afternoon. (A)Lucky, he wasn't badly hurt, but he didn't see the driver. (B)A police officer questioned three suspects. Ms. A said she was reading a book at the time of the accident. Mr. B said he was walking his dog. Ms. C said she was making breakfast. Who hit Mr. Doodle? Can you explain why? Do you have the answer? Write it down. Then you can move to the next room.
Clue: The accident happened in the afternoon.

11 밑줄 친 (A)를 알맞은 형으로 고치시오.

➡ _____

12 밑줄 친 (B)와 같은 의미의 문장을 완성하시오.

> Three suspects _____.

13 Where can you find clues? Answer in English. (7 words)

➡ _____

[14~16] 다음 글을 읽고 물음에 답하시오.

　It was last Sunday. Dohun was at home. Suddenly, he heard a sound in the next room. When he went into the room, (A)the window was broken. When he looked outside, Sujin was holding a baseball bat and Ted was throwing a ball to his dog. Who broke the window? (B)How can it be explained?

14 빈칸에 알맞은 말을 써서 밑줄 친 (A)와 같은 의미의 문장을 완성하시오.

> someone _____

15 Where was Dohun last Sunday? Answer in English with a full sentence.

➡ _____

16 주어진 문장의 빈칸에 알맞은 말을 써 넣어 밑줄 친 (B)와 같은 의미의 문장을 완성하시오.

> How can you _____ who broke the window?

01 다음 대화의 내용과 일치하도록 빈칸을 완성하시오.

> Jane: Minsu, do you know the TV show about the student detective?
> Minsu: Yes. I love that show, but I didn't see it this week. What was it about?
> Jane: Well, all of the bikes at school disappeared.
> Minsu: So, what did he do?
> Jane: First, he looked around the school. Then, he met some suspects and asked questions. Finally, he found the thief. The thief was ....
> Minsu: No, don't tell me! I'll watch it later.

> I was fascinated by the TV show about the student detective. I was happy when I heard that Minsu also loved that show. This week, the episode was so exciting. The show was about the crime that (A)_____. I also had the experience of losing my bike, so it was more interesting. When I talked about it to Minsu, he said that he (B)_____ this episode. I told him what (C)_____ had done to find the thief. I know who (D)_____ was, but Minsu didn't want to know it. He said he would watch it later.

02 다음은 Mr. Doodle 사고의 용의자 심문 내용이다. 빈칸에 알맞은 말을 쓰시오.

> A police officer: Ms. A, you said you were reading a book at the time of the accident. Where (A)_____ by you?
> Ms. A: I read the book at a cafe.
> A police officer: Okay. Then Mr. B, nobody saw you walk your dog. It means you (B)_____ to walk your dog by anyone. How can you prove it?
> Mr. B: I went to a pet shop to buy my dog a gum. Ask the clerk who worked on Sunday.
> A police officer: I'll check that out. Ms. C, you said you were making something. What (C)_____ you?
> Ms. C: Breakfast was made by me.

03 주어진 동사와 수동태를 활용하여 다양한 문장을 쓰시오.

> send see show eat borrow

(1) _____

(2) _____

(3) _____

(4) _____

(5) _____

단원별 모의고사

01 다음 짝지어진 단어의 관계가 같도록 빈칸에 알맞은 말을 쓰시오.

> win : lose = s_____ : dangerous

02 다음 영영풀이가 가리키는 것을 고르시오.

> an object or piece of information that helps someone solve a crime or mystery

① clue　　　　② accident

③ fact　　　　④ prize

⑤ scene

03 다음 문장의 빈칸에 들어갈 말을 〈보기〉에서 골라 쓰시오.

> ┤ 보기 ├
> case / candle / triangle / hide

(1) The thief couldn't _____ under the table because there wasn't enough space.

(2) The _____ was solved by the police.

(3) The _____ will be put inside the box.

(4) Fold the opposite corners together to form a _____.

04 다음 문장에 공통으로 들어갈 말을 고르시오.

> • The police officer found the clues in the _____ of the crime.
> • The movie opens with a _____ in the Museum of Modern Art.
> • I was fascinated by a beautiful _____.

① prize　　　　② scene

③ bean　　　　④ space

⑤ stamp

[05~07] 다음 대화를 읽고 물음에 답하시오.

Jane: Minsu, do you know the TV show about the student detective?

Minsu: Yes. I love that show, but I didn't see it this week. What was it about?

Jane: Well, all of the bikes at school (A)[appeared / disappeared].

Minsu: So, what did he do?

Jane: First, he looked around the school. Then, he met some (B)[suspects / suspends] and asked questions. Finally, he found the (C)[thief / chief]. The thief was ....

Minsu: No, don't tell me! I'll watch it later.

05 위 대화에서 다음의 영영풀이가 가리키는 말을 찾아 쓰시오.

> a police officer who investigates crimes and catches criminals

➡ _____

06 위 대화의 흐름상 (A)~(C)에 들어갈 말로 적절한 것끼리 바르게 짝지어진 것은?

	(A)	(B)	(C)
①	appeared	suspects	thief
②	appeared	suspends	chief
③	disappeared	suspects	chief
④	disappeared	suspends	thief
⑤	disappeared	suspects	thief

07 위 대화의 내용과 일치하지 않는 것은?

① Minsu missed the TV show about the student detective this week.

② Jane told Minsu about the episode of the TV show.

③ The TV show dealt with the crime of stealing bikes.

④ The student detective investigated the school and some suspects.

⑤ Minsu asked Jane to let him know who the thief was.

[08~10] 다음 대화를 읽고 물음에 답하시오.

> Emily: Junsu, do you want to solve a riddle?
>
> Junsu: Sure, what is it?
>
> Emily: There is a farmer. First, the farmer buys a fox, a duck, and a bag of beans. Then, the farmer needs to cross a river.
>
> Junsu: What's the problem?
>
> Emily: The boat can only hold the farmer and one more thing.
>
> Junsu: Are you saying that the farmer can take only one thing at a time?
>
> Emily: Yes. Also, the fox will eat the duck or the duck will eat the beans if the farmer isn't there. (A)<u>전부를 강 건너로 안전하게 옮길 방법을 설명할 수 있겠니?</u>
>
> Junsu: Hmm ....

08 위 대화의 밑줄 친 우리말 (A)를 〈보기〉에 주어진 단어를 모두 배열하여 완성하시오.

┌─── 보기 ───┐

explain / to / the / across / river / can / how / move / you / safely / everything

└──────────┘

➡ _____

_____

09 위 대화를 읽고 대답할 수 <u>없는</u> 질문은?

① What is the riddle Emily gave to Junsu?

② What did the farmer buy?

③ Why should the farmer cross the river?

④ Why shouldn't the farmer leave the fox and the duck together?

⑤ How many things could the boat hold at a time?

10 위 대화에서 제시된 수수께끼의 해결책을 완성하시오.

> Junsu: First, the farmer crosses the river with the duck. Second, he comes back and takes (A)_____. Third, he leaves the fox and comes back with (B)_____. Then, he leaves the duck and takes (C)_____. Next, the farmer should leave the beans with the fox. Then, he comes back and crosses the river with (D)_____.

11 다음 대화가 자연스럽게 이어지도록 순서대로 배열하시오.

> (A) It's the letter "E."
>
> (B) I have no idea.
>
> (C) I don't get it. Can you explain why?
>
> (D) Well, there are two "E"s in the word "week," one "E" in the word "year" but no "E"s in the word "day."
>
> (E) Kelly, here's a riddle. You can see this twice in a week, once in a year, but never in a day. What is this?

➡ _____

12 다음 짝지어진 대화가 <u>어색한</u> 것은?

① A: Did I draw it correctly?

　 B: No, you didn't.

② A: Where did you hide your gold?

　 B: It is in the building on your right.

③ A: Can you explain how to buy a train ticket?

　 B: First, choose the station. Then, put in the money.

④ A: Would you like some cheese?

　 B: No, thanks.

⑤ A: How did you make it?

　 B: That sounds interesting.

13 다음 빈칸에 들어갈 말로 가장 적절한 것은?

> I will not forget their stories.
> = Their stories _____.

① are not be able to be forgotten
② is not forgotten by me
③ won't be forgot to me
④ don't have to be forgotten by me
⑤ won't be forgotten by me

14 다음 중 어법상 바르지 <u>않은</u> 것은?

① What happened to you last night?
② This key is belonged to your brother.
③ The party will be held in Jin's garden.
④ A job at a local bank was offered to me.
⑤ This symptom can't be explained.

15 다음 문장을 수동태로 전환하시오.

> Hundreds of fans surrounded the rock star outside the theater.

➡ _____
_____

16 다음 빈칸에 들어갈 말로 가장 적절한 것은?

> The noise annoys me.
> = I _____ the noise.

① am annoyed to
② am annoyed of
③ am annoyed in
④ am annoyed with
⑤ am annoyed from

17 주어진 단어를 어법에 맞게 활용하여 문장을 완성하시오.

> Hudson's house burned down. The fire _____. (cause / lightning)

➡ _____

[18~23] 다음 글을 읽고 물음에 답하시오.

Room #2
  Jay gets an email ①from his favorite clothing store. The title reads "You won our Lucky Day event!" Jay is ②surprised. He quickly opens it.

JayJr@kmail.com
You won our 'Lucky Day' event!
Congratulations!
You have won a special prize. ③During our Lucky Day event, (A)you can choose any seven items from our store for free! Come to our store on November 31. We can't wait to see you.

Truly yours,
Kay Brown

  However, Jay thinks that the event isn't real and ④delete the email. Can you explain why?
Clue There are usually 30 or 31 days ⑤in a month.

  Do you have the answer? Write it down and then you are free to go!

18 밑줄 친 문장 (A)를 우리말로 옮기시오.

➡ _____
_____

19 ①~⑤ 중 어법상 바르지 <u>않은</u> 것은?

①   ②   ③   ④   ⑤

20 다음 중 위 글의 내용과 일치하는 것은?

① Jay deletes the email because he isn't interested in shopping.
② The email was sent to Jay from Jay's favorite shoe store.
③ The email has no title at all.
④ Jay opens the email as soon as he sees it.
⑤ Jay is looking forward to going shopping at the store.

21 다음은 위 사건의 탐정 수첩이다. 글의 내용과 일치하지 <u>않</u> <u>는</u> 것을 두 군데 찾아 바르게 고치시오.

Second Riddle
• Jay will get a special prize.
• The event is on November 30.
• Jay kept his email because it was not true.

➡ _____

➡ _____

22 다음 물음에 완전한 문장의 영어로 답하시오.

Q: How many items are free during the Lucky Day event?

➡ _____

23 다음 중 위 글을 읽고 답할 수 <u>없는</u> 것은?

① Where does Jay get email from?
② Why is Jay surprised?
③ How many people get the email besides Jay?
④ When is the 'Lucky Day' event?
⑤ What do we have to do if we know the answer?

[24~25] 다음 글을 읽고 물음에 답하시오.

It was last Sunday. Dohun was at home. Suddenly, he heard a sound in the next room. When he went into the room, the window was broken. When he looked outside, Sujin was holding a baseball bat and Ted was throwing a ball to his dog. Who broke the window? (A)
_____

24 다음 중 위 글에서 찾아볼 수 <u>없는</u> 것은?

① Dohun who was resting at home on Sunday
② a noise from the next room
③ a ball which was thrown to Dohun's home
④ a girl who was holding a baseball bat
⑤ Dohun looking outside to see who broke the window

25 주어진 단어를 바르게 배열하여 빈칸 (A)에 들어갈 말을 완성하시오. 필요하다면 어형을 변형하시오.

(be / how / explain / it / can)

➡ _____

Lesson **6**

We're Here to Dance

🎤 의사소통 기능

- 의견 표현하기
  In my opinion, he really enjoys dancing.
- 확실성 정도 표현하기
  I'm sure you'll feel great.

🎤 언어 형식

- so ~ that ...
  The dance is **so** popular **that** everybody learns it.
- 원급 비교
  The dancers looked **as** beautiful **as** flowers.

Words & Expressions

Key Words

- □ **bee** [biː] 몡 벌
- □ **behind** [biháind] 전 ~ 뒤에
- □ **between** [bitwíːn] 전 ~ 사이에
- □ **brave** [breiv] 혱 용감한
- □ **bright** [brait] 혱 (색상이) 밝은
- □ **character** [kǽriktər] 몡 등장인물
- □ **cheer** [tʃíər] 됭 응원하다
- □ **comfortable** [kʌ́mfərtəbl] 혱 편안한
- □ **communicate** [kəmjúːnəkèit] 됭 의사소통하다
- □ **couple** [kʌ́pl] 몡 두 사람, 남녀
- □ **costume** [kɑ́stjuːm] 몡 의상, 복장
- □ **doll** [dɑl] 몡 인형
- □ **drop** [drɑp] 됭 떨어뜨리다
- □ **enemy** [énəmi] 몡 적
- □ **express** [iksprés] 됭 표현하다
- □ **fan** [fæn] 몡 부채
- □ **female** [fíːmeil] 혱 암컷의, 여성의
- □ **field** [fiːld] 몡 들판, 경기장
- □ **fight** [fait] 몡 싸움, 다툼
- □ **gracefully** [gréisfəli] 뿐 우아하게
- □ **hide** [haid] 됭 숨다
- □ **hold** [hould] 됭 열다, 개최하다
- □ **interestingly** [íntərəstiŋli] 뿐 흥미 있게도
- □ **male** [meil] 혱 수컷의, 남성의
- □ **movement** [múːvmənt] 몡 움직임, 동작
- □ **nowadays** [náuədèiz] 뿐 오늘날에는
- □ **opinion** [əpínjən] 몡 의견
- □ **originally** [ərídʒənəli] 뿐 원래, 본래
- □ **perform** [pərfɔ́ːrm] 됭 공연하다
- □ **popular** [pɑ́pjulər] 혱 인기 있는
- □ **powerful** [páuərfəl] 혱 강한, 힘 있는
- □ **rugby** [rʌ́gbi] 몡 럭비
- □ **scared** [skɛərd] 혱 겁먹은, 무서워하는
- □ **scary** [skɛ́əri] 혱 무서운
- □ **strength** [strenkθ] 몡 힘
- □ **sure** [ʃuər] 혱 확실한
- □ **through** [θruː] 전 ~을 통해
- □ **totally** [tóutəli] 뿐 완전히
- □ **traditional** [trədíʃənl] 혱 전통적인
- □ **uniform** [júːnəfɔ̀ːrm] 몡 제복, 유니폼
- □ **wild** [waild] 혱 야생의
- □ **windy** [wíndi] 혱 바람이 많이 부는

Key Expressions

- □ **be allowed to** ~이 허용되다
- □ **be good at** ~을 잘하다
- □ **catch a cold** 감기에 걸리다
- □ **give up on** ~을 포기하다
- □ **good and evil** 선과 악
- □ **have fun** 즐거운 시간을 보내다
- □ **in my opinion** 내 의견으로는
- □ **keep up the good work** 계속 열심히 하다
- □ **look like** ~처럼 보이다
- □ **make a sound** 소리를 내다
- □ **on time** 정시에
- □ **sound like** ~처럼 들리다, ~일 것 같다
- □ **take a look** 살펴보다
- □ **try one's best** 최선을 다하다

Word Power

※ 서로 반대되는 뜻을 가진 어휘

□ **bright** 밝은 ↔ **dark** 어두운

□ **comfortable** 편안한 ↔ **uncomfortable** 불편한

□ **good** 선 ↔ **evil** 악

□ **sure** 확실한 ↔ **unsure** 불확실한

□ **enemy** 적 ↔ **friend** 친구

□ **brave** 용감한 ↔ **cowardly** 비겁한

□ **male** 수컷의, 남성의 ↔ **female** 암컷의, 여성의

□ **popular** 인기 있는 ↔ **unpopular** 인기 없는

□ **behind** 뒤에 ↔ **ahead** 앞에

□ **powerful** 강한, 힘 있는 ↔ **weak** 약한

English Dictionary

□ **behind** 뒤에
→ at or towards the back of a thing or person
물건이나 사람의 뒤쪽 또는 뒷부분을 향해

□ **brave** 용감한
→ dealing with danger, pain, or difficult situations with courage and confidence
용기와 자신감을 갖고 위험, 고통 또는 어려운 상황을 다루는

□ **cheer** 응원하다
→ to shout as a way of showing happiness, praise, approval, or support of someone or something
누군가 또는 무언가에 대한 행복, 칭찬, 승인 또는 지지를 보여주는 방식으로 소리치다

□ **comfortable** 편안한
→ making you feel physically relaxed, without any pain or without being too hot, cold, etc.
어떠한 고통이나 너무 뜨겁거나 차가움 없이 신체적으로 편안하게 느끼도록 만드는

□ **drop** 떨어뜨리다
→ to stop holding or carrying something so that it falls
무언가가 떨어지도록 그것을 쥐거나 나르는 것을 멈추다

□ **express** 표현하다
→ to tell or show what you are feeling or thinking by using words, looks, or actions
말, 표정 또는 행동을 사용하여 당신이 느끼고 있거나 생각하고 있는 것을 말하거나 보여주다

□ **fan** 부채
→ a flat object that you wave with your hand which makes the air cooler
당신이 손을 움직여 공기를 더 시원하게 만드는 평평한 물체

□ **field** 들판
→ an area of land in the country, especially one where crops are grown or animals feed on grass
특히 곡식이 자라거나 동물들이 풀을 먹는 시골에 있는 땅의 한 지역

□ **movement** 움직임
→ an act of moving
움직이는 행동

□ **originally** 원래, 본래
→ in the beginning, before other things happened or before things changed
맨 처음에, 다른 일들이 발생하기 전이나 상황이 변하기 전에

□ **popular** 인기 있는
→ liked by a lot of people
많은 사람들이 좋아하는

□ **strength** 힘
→ the physical power and energy that makes someone strong
누군가를 강하게 만들어 주는 신체적인 힘과 에너지

□ **uniform** 제복
→ a particular type of clothing worn by all the members of a group or organization such as the police, the army, etc.
경찰, 군인 등과 같이 집단 또는 조직의 모든 구성원들이 입는 옷의 특별한 종류

□ **wild** 야생의
→ living in a natural state, not changed or controlled by people
자연 상태에 사는, 사람들에 의해 바뀌거나 통제되지 않은

서답형

01 다음 짝지어진 단어의 관계가 같도록 빈칸에 알맞은 말을 쓰시오.

man : woman = male : _____

02 다음 영영풀이가 가리키는 것을 고르시오.

dealing with danger, pain, or difficult situations with courage and confidence

① brave
② comfortable
③ scared
④ sure
⑤ traditional

중요
03 다음 중 밑줄 친 부분의 뜻풀이가 바르지 <u>않은</u> 것은?

① <u>Nowadays</u>, many people want to be Youtubers. 오늘날에는
② When did you <u>drop</u> your glasses? 떨어뜨리다
③ I'm interested in Chinese <u>traditional</u> dancing. 전통적인
④ I couldn't sleep well after watching a <u>scary</u> movie. 무서운
⑤ Before the speech, I wrote my <u>opinions</u> about the issue. 사실

서답형
04 다음 우리말에 맞게 빈칸에 알맞은 말을 쓰시오.

(1) 너는 그녀 뒤에 많은 팔들이 보이니?
➡ Do you see many arms _____ her?
(2) 힘이 넘치는 춤꾼들의 힘을 느껴라!
➡ Feel the _____ of the powerful dancers!
(3) 무용수의 우아한 움직임을 보아라.
➡ Look at the _____ movements of a dancer.
(4) 우리는 종종 우리의 손님들을 위해 전통적인 한국 음식들을 요리한다.
➡ We often cook _____ Korean meals for our guests.

05 다음 주어진 문장의 밑줄 친 character와 같은 의미로 쓰인 것은?

I love this cartoon because of its unique <u>characters</u>.

① This book describes the writer's <u>character</u>.
② Generosity is part of American <u>character</u>.
③ She is going to play a main <u>character</u> in the play.
④ The most important thing is the <u>character</u>.
⑤ Tom revealed his real <u>character</u> when he was upset.

중요
06 다음 문장에 공통으로 들어갈 말을 고르시오.

• I have read many stories about ____ and evil.
• Harry is ____ at playing soccer.

① good
② best
③ better
④ bad
⑤ worse

01 다음 짝지어진 단어의 관계가 같도록 빈칸에 알맞은 말을 쓰시오.

> bright : dark = _____ : friend

02 다음 문장의 빈칸에 들어갈 말을 〈보기〉에서 골라 쓰시오.

> ┌─ 보기 ├─
> enemy / expressed / originally / strength / perform

(1) He _____ an interest in meeting her yesterday.

(2) The singers will _____ at Carnegie Hall.

(3) The school _____ belonged to Mr. Bower.

(4) The boxer had no _____ left to punch.

(5) Who is our _____ during the war?

03 다음 주어진 말을 이용하여 우리말에 맞게 빈칸에 알맞은 말을 쓰시오.

(1) 끝날 때 당신은 함께 춤추는 것이 허용된다. (allow)

➡ You _____ dance together at the end.

(2) 몇몇 물고기들은 소리들을 낼 수 있다. (make)

➡ Some fish can _____.

(3) 만약 네가 최선을 다하면 불가능한 것은 없다. (best)

➡ Nothing is impossible if you _____.

04 다음 우리말과 일치하도록 주어진 단어를 모두 배열하여 영작하시오.

(1) 내 의견으로는 무용수들이 인형만큼 귀여워 보인다.

(dancers / my / look / in / opinion / as / as / dolls / cute)

➡ _____

(2) 소년의 신발이 매우 편안해서 그는 그것들을 하루 종일 신을 수 있었다.

(comfortable / are / the boy's / he / can / them / all day / that / wear / shoes / so)

➡ _____
_____

(3) 너는 연기자들 뒤에 많은 사람들이 보이니?

(see / the / many / do / people / behind / actors / you)

➡ _____

05 다음 우리말을 주어진 단어를 이용하여 영작하시오.

(1) 그 춤은 아주 인기 있어서 모두가 이것을 배운다. (so, everybody)

➡ _____
_____

(2) 본래 헝가리에서 공연되었던 이 멋진 공연을 놓치지 마라. (miss, which, great, performed, originally)

➡ _____
_____

(3) 나는 나의 감정을 표현하기 위해 몸을 움직인다. (feelings, move)

➡ _____

Conversation

① 의견 표현하기

In my opinion, he really enjoys dancing.
(내 의견으로는, 그는 정말로 춤을 즐겨.)

■ 'In my opinion, …'은 '내 의견으로는, …'라는 뜻으로 자신의 의견을 표현하는 말이다. 유사한 표현으로는 'I think that …', 'I believe (that) …', 'I would say that …', 'To my mind', 'In my view', 'In my eyes' 등이 있다.

의견 표현하기

- I think that we should have homework because it helps with learning.
  (나는 숙제가 학습에 도움이 되므로 숙제가 있어야 한다고 생각해.)

- I believe that we should not have homework because it takes away our free time.
  (나는 숙제가 우리의 자유 시간을 뺏기 때문에 숙제가 없어야 한다고 믿어.)

- I would say that we should work hard to achieve our goals.
  (나는 우리가 우리 목표를 성취하기 위해 열심히 노력해야 한다고 말하고 싶다.)

- To my mind, wearing a school uniform every day is boring.
  (내 생각에, 교복을 매일 입는 것은 지루해.)

- In my view, it's easy to learn and it's also beautiful. (내가 봤을 땐, 그것은 배우기 쉽고 또한 아름다워.)

- In my eyes, my English teacher is an intelligent person.
  (내가 보기에는, 나의 영어 선생님은 똑똑한 사람이야.)

핵심 Check

1. 다음 주어진 우리말과 일치하도록 빈칸에 알맞은 말을 쓰시오.

(1) A: ＿＿＿＿ ＿＿＿＿ ＿＿＿＿ ＿＿＿＿ ＿＿＿＿ Jenny? (Jenny에 대해 어떻게 생각해?)

　　B: Jenny? ＿＿＿＿ ＿＿＿＿ ＿＿＿＿, she's a nice person.

　　(Jenny? 내 의견으로는, 그녀는 좋은 사람이야.)

(2) A: What do you think about ＿＿＿＿ ＿＿＿＿ ＿＿＿＿ ＿＿＿＿?

　　(너는 교복을 입는 것에 대해 어떻게 생각하니?)

　　B: ＿＿＿＿ ＿＿＿＿ ＿＿＿＿ we ＿＿＿＿ ＿＿＿＿ ＿＿＿＿ ＿＿＿＿ ＿＿＿＿

　　＿＿＿＿ because it's more uncomfortable.

　　(나는 교복이 더 불편하기 때문에 교복을 입지 말아야 한다고 생각해.)

② 확실성 정도 표현하기

I'm sure you'll feel great. (나는 네가 기분이 좋을 것이라고 확신한다.)

■ 'I'm sure ~'는 '나는 ~을 확신한다'라는 뜻으로 자신의 추측이나 생각의 확신을 표현한다. 'I'm certain ~'으로 바꿔 쓸 수 있다.

확신 말하기

- I'm sure (that) ~: 나는 ~을 확신한다
- I'm certain (that) ~: 나는 ~을 확신한다
- I have no doubt that ~: 나는 ~에 대해 의심치 않는다

A: Jane has a great voice. (Jane은 좋은 목소리를 갖고 있어.)

B: I'm certain she will be a great singer. (나는 그녀가 좋은 가수가 될 거라고 확신해.)

A: Jack studies all day. (Jack은 하루 종일 공부해.)

B: I have no doubt that he will get a good grade on the test. (나는 그가 시험에서 좋은 성적을 받을 것이라고 의심치 않아.)

핵심 Check

2. 다음 우리말과 일치하도록 빈칸에 알맞은 말을 쓰시오.

(1) **A:** I'm going to a _____ _____ in our town next weekend. Do you want to join me? (나는 다음 주말에 우리 마을에서 열리는 문화 행사에 갈 거야. 나와 같이 갈래?)

B: Sounds _____ . (재미있겠다.)

A: We can enjoy dances from many countries. _____ _____ we'll have a lot of fun. (우리는 많은 국가에서 온 춤들을 즐길 수 있어. 우리는 매우 즐거울 거라고 확신해.)

(2) **A:** I think Sejun's photo is very funny. (나는 세준이의 사진이 매우 재미있다고 생각해.)

B: _____ _____ he'll win the school photo contest.
(나는 그가 학교 사진 대회에서 우승할 것이라고 확신해.)

Listen and Speak 1-B

Emily: Hojun, did you know that some male birds dance?

Hojun: ❶No. Why do ❷they dance?

Emily: They dance to show their love to female birds.

Hojun: ❸That's interesting. Do you know any other animals that can dance?

Emily: Yes, some bees dance to show where to find food.

Hojun: That's cool! ❹In my opinion, dancing is a great way to communicate.

Emily: ❺I totally agree with you.

Emily: 호준아, 너는 일부 수컷 새들이 춤을 춘다는 것을 알고 있었니?

Hojun: 아니. 왜 춤을 추지?

Emily: 그들은 암컷 새들에게 그들의 사랑을 보여주기 위해 춤을 춰.

Hojun: 그거 흥미로운 걸. 춤을 출 수 있는 또 다른 동물들을 알고 있니?

Emily: 응, 일부 벌들은 먹이를 찾을 수 있는 곳을 보여주기 위해 춤을 춰.

Hojun: 멋지다! 내 의견으로는, 춤을 추는 것은 의사소통을 위한 굉장한 방법인 것 같아.

Emily: 전적으로 너에게 동의해.

---

❶ 'No, I didn't.'의 줄임말이다. ❷ they는 some male birds를 가리킨다.
❸ That's interesting. = Sounds interesting. = How interesting that is!
❹ In my opinion = In my view = In my eyes = To my mind = I would say that ~ 등의 표현을 사용하여 의견을 나타낼 수 있다.
❺ 동의하는 표현으로 'I'm with you on that.', 'I think so, too.' 또는 'I can't agree with you more.' 등으로 바꾸어 표현할 수 있다.

Check(√) True or False

(1) Some male birds dance to show their love to female birds.　　　　　T ☐ F ☐

(2) Some bees dance to get some honey.　　　　　T ☐ F ☐

Listen and Speak 2-B

Tom: What are you reading, Kelly?

Kelly: I'm reading a story about Michaela DePrince.

Tom: Michaela DePrince? Can you tell me more about ❶her?

Kelly: Sure. Michaela lost her parents when she was three. After that, she ❷had a lot of difficulties. But she never ❸gave up on her dream of becoming a dancer.

Tom: Wow, she worked very hard to be a good dancer. Kelly, you also have a dream to be a dancer, right?

Kelly: Yes. I will ❹try my best to be a great dancer like her.

Tom: ❺Keep up the good work. I'm sure you can make it.

Tom: 무엇을 읽고 있니, Kelly?

Kelly: Michaela DePrince에 대한 이야기를 읽고 있어.

Tom: Michaela DePrince? 그녀에 대해 좀 더 얘기해 줄 수 있니?

Kelly: 그래. Michaela는 그녀가 세 살일 때 부모를 잃었어. 그 후 그녀는 많은 역경을 겪었지. 그러나 그녀는 무용수가 되겠다는 꿈을 절대 포기하지 않았어.

Tom: 와, 그녀는 훌륭한 무용수가 되기 위해 굉장히 열심히 노력했구나. Kelly, 너도 무용수가 되려는 꿈이 있지, 그렇지?

Kelly: 응. 그녀처럼 멋진 무용수가 되기 위해 최선을 다할 거야.

Tom: 계속 노력해 봐. 난 네가 해낼 거라고 확신해.

---

❶ her는 Michaela DePrince를 가리킨다. ❷ have a lot of difficulties: 많은 역경을 겪다
❸ give up on: ~을 포기하다　　　　❹ try one's best: 최선을 다하다
❺ keep up the good work: 계속 열심히 하다

Check(√) True or False

(3) Kelly wants to become a dancer in the future.　　　　　T ☐ F ☐

(4) Michaela DePrince gave up on her dream because of her difficulties.　　　　　T ☐ F ☐

Listen and Speak 1 – A-1

Jane: Minsu, ❶what do you think about that painting?

Minsu: Umm ... The people ❷look like they're ❸having fun.

Jane: I agree. In my opinion, the dancing boy really enjoys ❹dancing.

❶ 상대방에게 의견을 묻는 표현으로 'what's your opinion about that painting?'으로 물을 수 있다.
❷ look like: ~처럼 보이다 ❸ have fun: 즐거운 시간을 보내다
❹ enjoy는 동명사를 목적어로 취한다.

Listen and Speak 1 – A-2

Brian: Jimin, what do you think about this painting?

Jimin: In my opinion, it's interesting. I smiled when I first saw it.

Brian: ❶Me, too. The dancers in the painting ❷ look happy.

❶ 'Me, too.'는 'So did I.'로 바꾸어 쓸 수 있다.
❷ look+형용사: ~처럼 보이다

Listen and Speak 2 – A-1

Minji: I use my ❶voice to make music. Listen to my music. My voice is soft and cool. ❷I'm sure you will like ❸it.

Jimin: I move my body to express my feelings. Look at my movements. ❹Why don't you jump like me? I'm sure you'll feel great.

Sujin: I use my hands to ❺make sounds. Come and listen to my music. I'm sure you'll want to dance when you listen to it.

❶ voice: 목소리
❷ 확신을 나타내는 표현으로 'I'm certain ~'으로 바꾸어 쓸 수 있다.
❸ it은 my voice를 가리킨다.
❹ 'Why don't you ~?'는 제안하는 표현으로 'How about ~?', 'What about ~?', 'Let's ~.' 등으로 바꾸어 쓸 수 있다.
❺ make sounds: 소리를 내다

Real Life Communication

Junsu: You know what? The school dance contest will ❶be held soon.

Emily: That's right. I heard Jimin's class is going to perform a taekwondo dance and Tim's class is going to do a K-pop dance.

Brian: We should also decide ❷what to do.

Mina: How about a Buchaechum? In my opinion, it is easy to learn, and it's also beautiful.

Emily: That sounds like a good idea. But who will teach us?

Brian: Mina is good at traditional dances. Can you help us, Mina?

Mina: Of course, I will. I'm sure we'll have a lot of fun.

Junsu: Great. Let's ❸give it a try.

❶ be held: 개최되다, 열리다
❷ what to do: 무엇을 할지 = what we should do
❸ give it a try: 시도하다

Let's Check

Jenny: Look at the dancing girls, Dongjun. ❶ Aren't they amazing?

Dongjun: Girls? I can only see one dancer.

Jenny: Look more closely. Do you see many arms behind her?

Dongjun: Wow. I didn't know that there were other dancers behind her.

Jenny: That's right. I'm sure there are ❷more than 10 dancers.

❶ 부정의문문(=Are they not amazing?)
❷ more than: ~ 이상

● 다음 우리말과 일치하도록 빈칸에 알맞은 말을 쓰시오. (주어진 철자가 있으면 그 철자로 시작할 것)

Listen & Speak 1 A-1

Jane: Minsu, what do you think about that _____?

Minsu: Umm … The people look _____ they're _____ _____.

Jane: I agree. _____ _____ _____, the dancing boy really _____ _____.

Listen & Speak 1 A-2

Brian: Jimin, _____ do you think _____ _____ _____?

Jimin: In my opinion, it's _____. I _____ when I first saw it.

Brian: Me, too. The dancers in the painting _____ _____.

Listen & Speak 1 B

Emily: Hojun, did you know that _____ _____ _____ _____?

Hojun: No. _____ do they dance?

Emily: They dance to show their _____ to _____.

Hojun: That's interesting. Do you know _____ _____ _____ that can dance?

Emily: Yes, some _____ dance to show _____ _____ _____.

Hojun: That's cool! In my opinion, dancing is a great way to _____.

Emily: I totally _____ _____ _____.

Listen & Speak 2 A-1

Minji: I use _____ _____ to make music. Listen to my music. My voice is _____ and _____. I'm _____ you will like it.

Jimin: I move _____ _____ to express my feelings. Look at my _____. _____ _____ you jump like me? I'm _____ you'll feel great.

Sujin: I use my hands to _____ _____. Come and listen to my music. I'm sure you'll want to _____ when you listen to it.

해석

Jane: 민수야, 저 그림에 대해 어떻게 생각해?
Minsu: 음… 사람들이 재미있게 노는 것처럼 보여.
Jane: 나도 동의해. 내 의견으로는, 춤추는 소년이 춤추는 것을 정말로 즐기는 것 같아.

Brian: 지민아, 이 그림에 대해 어떻게 생각해?
Jimin: 내 의견으로는 흥미로워. 처음 이것을 봤을 때 난 미소 지었어.
Brian: 나도 그래. 그림 속 춤추는 사람들은 행복해 보여.

Emily: 호준아, 너는 일부 수컷 새들이 춤을 춘다는 것을 알고 있었니?
Hojun: 아니. 왜 춤을 추지?
Emily: 그들은 암컷 새들에게 그들의 사랑을 보여주기 위해 춤을 춰.
Hojun: 그거 흥미로운 걸. 춤을 출 수 있는 또 다른 동물들을 알고 있니?
Emily: 응, 일부 벌들은 먹이를 찾을 수 있는 곳을 보여주기 위해 춤을 춰.
Hojun: 멋지다! 내 의견으로는, 춤을 추는 것은 의사소통을 위한 굉장한 방법인 것 같아.
Emily: 전적으로 너에게 동의해.

Minji: 나는 음악을 만들기 위해 내 목소리를 사용합니다. 내 음악을 들어 보세요. 내 목소리는 부드럽고 멋지죠. 나는 당신이 그것을 좋아할 거라고 확신해요.
Jimin: 나는 내 감정을 표현하기 위해 내 몸을 움직입니다. 내 동작을 보세요. 나처럼 뛰어올라 보는 게 어때요? 나는 당신이 멋진 기분이 들 거라고 확신해요.
Sujin: 나는 소리를 만들기 위해 내 손을 사용합니다. 와서 내 음악을 들어 보세요. 나는 당신이 이것을 들을 때 춤을 추고 싶을 거라고 확신해요.

Listen & Speak 2 B

Tom: _____ are you _____, Kelly?

Kelly: I'm reading a _____ _____ Michaela DePrince.

Tom: Michaela DePrince? Can you _____ me _____ about her?

Kelly: Sure. Michaela _____ her parents _____ she was three. _____ _____, she had a lot of difficulties. But she never _____ _____ _____ her dream of becoming a dancer.

Tom: Wow, she worked very hard _____ _____ a good dancer. Kelly, you also have a dream _____ _____ a dancer, _____?

Kelly: Yes. I will _____ _____ _____ to be a great dancer like her.

Tom: _____ _____ the good work. I'm sure you can _____ _____.

Real Life Communication

Junsu: You know _____? The school dance contest will be _____ soon.

Emily: That's right. I heard Jimin's class is going to _____ a taekwondo dance and Tim's class is going to do a K-pop dance.

Brian: We should also _____ _____ _____ _____.

Mina: _____ _____ a Buchaechum? In my _____, it is easy to learn, and it's also _____.

Emily: That _____ _____ a good idea. But who will teach us?

Brian: Mina _____ _____ _____ traditional dances. Can you help us, Mina?

Mina: Of course, I will. _____ _____ we'll have a lot of fun.

Junsu: Great. Let's _____ _____ _____ _____.

Let's Check

Jenny: Look at the _____ _____, Dongjun. Aren't they _____?

Dongjun: Girls? I can only see one dancer.

Jenny: _____ _____ closely. Do you see many arms _____ her?

Dongjun: Wow. I didn't know that there were _____ _____ _____ _____.

Jenny: That's _____. _____ _____ there are _____ than 10 dancers.

해석

Tom: 무엇을 읽고 있니, Kelly?

Kelly: Michaela DePrince에 대한 이야기를 읽고 있어.

Tom: Michaela DePrince? 그녀에 대해 좀 더 얘기해 줄 수 있니?

Kelly: 그래. Michaela는 세 살 때 부모를 잃었어. 그 후 그녀는 많은 역경을 겪었지. 그러나 그녀는 무용수가 되겠다는 꿈을 절대 포기하지 않았어.

Tom: 와, 그녀는 훌륭한 무용수가 되기 위해 굉장히 열심히 노력했구나. Kelly, 너도 무용수가 되려는 꿈이 있지, 그렇지?

Kelly: 응. 그녀처럼 멋진 무용수가 되기 위해 최선을 다할 거야.

Tom: 계속 노력해 봐. 난 네가 해낼 거라고 확신해.

Junsu: 있잖아. 학교 춤 경연 대회가 곧 열릴 거야.

Emily: 맞아. 지민이네 반은 태권도 춤을 공연하고, Tim네 반은 K-pop 춤을 출 거라고 들었어.

Brian: 우리도 무엇을 할지 결정해야 해.

Mina: 부채춤은 어때? 내 의견으로는, 그것은 배우기 쉽고 또한 아름다워.

Emily: 좋은 생각인 것 같아. 하지만 누가 우리를 가르치지?

Brian: 미나가 전통 춤을 잘 춰. 우리를 도울 수 있니, 미나야?

Mina: 물론, 그럴 거야. 우리는 매우 즐거울 거라고 확신해.

Junsu: 아주 좋아. 시도해 보자.

Jenny: 춤추는 여자들을 봐, 동준아. 대단하지 않니?

Donjun: 여자들? 난 단지 한 명의 무용수만 보이는 걸.

Jenny: 좀 더 가까이 봐. 그녀 뒤에 많은 팔들이 보이니?

Donjun: 와. 그녀 뒤에 다른 무용수들이 있는지 몰랐어.

Jenny: 맞아. 나는 10명 이상의 무용수들이 있다고 확신해.

[01~02] 다음 대화를 읽고 물음에 답하시오.

Jane: Minsu, what do you think about that painting?

Minsu: Umm ... The people look like they're having fun.

Jane: I agree. (A)_____, the dancing boy really enjoys (B)_____ (dance).

01 위 대화의 빈칸 (A)에 들어갈 말로 나머지와 의미가 <u>다른</u> 것은?

① To my mind

② In my opinion

③ In my view

④ In my eyes

⑤ To sum up

02 위 대화의 빈칸 (B)에 주어진 단어를 알맞은 형태로 쓰시오.

➡ _____

[03~04] 다음 대화를 읽고 물음에 답하시오.

Brian: Jimin, what do you think about this painting?

Jimin: In my opinion, it's (A)[interested / interesting]. I (B)[smiled / smiling] when I first saw it.

Brian: Me, too. The dancers in the painting look (C)[happy / happily].

03 위 대화의 (A)~(C)에 들어갈 말이 바르게 짝지어진 것은?

	(A)	(B)	(C)
①	interested	smiled	happy
②	interested	smiling	happily
③	interesting	smiled	happily
④	interesting	smiling	happily
⑤	interesting	smiled	happy

04 What does Brian think about the dancers in the painting?

➡ _____

[01~03] 다음 대화를 읽고 물음에 답하시오.

Emily: Hojun, did you know that some male birds dance?

Hojun: No. Why do they dance?

Emily: They dance to show their love to female birds.

Hojun: (A)_____ Do you know any other animals that can dance?

Emily: Yes, some bees dance to show where to find food.

Hojun: That's cool! In my opinion, dancing is a great way to communicate.

Emily: I totally agree with you.

01 위 대화의 빈칸 (A)에 들어갈 말로 나머지와 의미가 다른 것은?

① I'm interested in birds.
② What an interesting point!
③ Sounds interesting.
④ How interesting it is!
⑤ That's interesting.

서답형
02 위 대화에서 다음 영영풀이가 나타내는 말을 찾아 쓰시오.

> to give information about something to someone by speaking, writing, moving your hands, etc.

➡ _____

 위 대화의 내용과 일치하지 않는 것은?

① 일부 수컷 새들이 춤을 춘다.
② 수컷 새들은 암컷 새들에게 그들의 사랑을 보여주기 위해 춤을 춘다.
③ 일부 벌들도 춤을 춘다.
④ 벌들은 먹이를 찾을 수 있는 곳을 보여주기 위해 춤을 춘다.
⑤ 호준은 동물들의 춤은 의사소통과는 관계가 없다고 생각한다.

[04~06] 다음 대화를 읽고 물음에 답하시오.

Minji: I use my voice to make music. Listen to my music. My voice is soft and cool. (A)I'm sure you will like it.

Jimin: I move my body to express my feelings. Look at my movements. (B) Why don't you jump like me? I'm sure you'll feel great.

Sujin: I use my hands to make sounds. Come and listen to my music. I'm sure you'll want to dance when you listen to it.

04 위 대화의 밑줄 친 (A)와 바꾸어 쓸 수 있는 것을 모두 고르시오.

① I'm certain you will like it.
② I want to know whether you like it.
③ I wonder if you like it or not.
④ I'm doubtful whether you like it.
⑤ I have no doubt that you will like it.

05 위 대화의 밑줄 친 (B)와 바꾸어 쓸 수 있는 것을 고르시오.

① I wonder how you jump like me.
② Let's jump like me.
③ Why did you jump like me?
④ How about jumping like me?
⑤ Do you know how to jump like me?

 위 대화의 내용과 일치하지 않는 것은?

① 민지는 음악을 만들기 위해 목소리를 사용한다.
② 민지의 목소리는 부드럽고 멋지다.
③ 지민은 자신의 감정을 표현하기 위해 몸을 움직인다.
④ 지민은 자신처럼 뛰어 올라보면 멋진 기분이 들 거라고 확신한다.
⑤ 수진은 춤을 추기 위해 그녀의 손을 사용한다.

[07~09] 다음 대화를 읽고 물음에 답하시오.

Tom: What are you reading, Kelly?

Kelly: I'm reading a story about Michaela DePrince.

Tom: Michaela DePrince? Can you tell me more about her?

Kelly: Sure. Michaela (A)[lost / losing] her parents when she was three. After that, she had a lot of difficulties. But she never gave up on her dream of becoming a dancer.

Tom: Wow, she worked very hard to be a good dancer. Kelly, you also have a dream to be a dancer, right?

Kelly: Yes. I will try my (B)[better / best] to be a great dancer like her.

Tom: (a)계속 노력해 봐. I'm sure you can (C)[make / have] it.

07 위 대화의 (A)~(C)에 들어갈 말로 바르게 짝지어진 것은?

	(A)	(B)	(C)
①	lost	better	make
②	lost	best	have
③	lost	best	make
④	losing	best	have
⑤	losing	better	make

서답형

08 위 대화의 밑줄 친 (a)의 우리말을 <보기>에 주어진 단어를 모두 배열하여 영작하시오.

┌─ 보기 ─┐

the / work / keep / good / up

➡ _____

09 위 대화를 읽고 대답할 수 없는 것은?

① What is Kelly reading?

② When did Michaela's parents pass away?

③ What difficulties did Michaela have after becoming a dancer?

④ What did Michaela want to be?

⑤ What is Kelly going to do to be a great dancer?

[10~12] 다음 대화를 읽고 물음에 답하시오.

Tom: What are you reading, Kelly?

Kelly: I'm reading a story about Michaela DePrince.

Tom: Michaela DePrince? Can you tell me more about her?

Kelly: Sure. Michaela lost her parents when she was three. After that, she had a lot of difficulties. But she never gave up on her dream of becoming a dancer.

Tom: Wow, she worked very hard to be a good dancer. Kelly, you also have a dream to be a dancer, right?

Kelly: Yes. I will try my best to be a great dancer like her.

Tom: Keep up the good work. I'm sure you can make it.

10 What happened to Michaela when she was three?

➡ _____

11 What didn't Michaela give up on despite lots of difficulties?

➡ _____

12 What is Kelly going to do to realize her dream?

➡ _____

01 다음 대화의 내용과 일치하도록 호준이의 일기를 완성하시오.

> Emily: Hojun, did you know that some male birds dance?
>
> Hojun: No. Why do they dance?
>
> Emily: They dance to show their love to female birds.
>
> Hojun: That's interesting. Do you know any other animals that can dance?
>
> Emily: Yes, some bees dance to show where to find food.
>
> Hojun: That's cool! In my opinion, dancing is a great way to communicate.
>
> Emily: I totally agree with you.

⬇

> Mon, Oct 7th, 2019
> Today, I learned about animals' dancing from Emily. She told me that some male birds dance because they want to (A)_____. Moreover, I heard that some bees also dance to (B)_____. It was so interesting. I thought that dancing is a great way to (C)_____ among the animals.

02 다음 대화의 내용과 일치하도록 주어진 표의 빈칸 (A)와 (B)를 완성하시오

> Junsu: You know what? The school dance contest will be held soon.
>
> Emily: That's right. I heard Jimin's class is going to perform a taekwondo dance and Tim's class is going to do a K-pop dance.
>
> Brian: We should also decide what to do.
>
> Mina: How about a Buchaechum? In my opinion, it is easy to learn, and it's also beautiful.

> Emily: That sounds like a good idea. But who will teach us?
>
> Brian: Mina is good at traditional dances. Can you help us, Mina?
>
> Mina: Of course, I will. I'm sure we'll have a lot of fun.
>
> Junsu: Great. Let's give it a try.

<What to Perform at the School Dance Contest>

	Type of dance	The reason
Jimin's class	a taekwondo dance	Taekwondo is a popular sport in the world.
Tim's class	a K-pop dance	It is exciting and popular in the world.
Brian's class	(A) _____	(B) _____

03 다음 대화가 자연스럽게 이어지도록 순서대로 배열하시오.

> Tom: What are you reading, Kelly?
>
> Kelly: I'm reading a story about Michaela DePrince.
>
> (A) Yes. I will try my best to be a great dancer like her.
>
> (B) Michaela DePrince? Can you tell me more about her?
>
> (C) Keep up the good work. I'm sure you can make it.
>
> (D) Wow, she worked very hard to be a good dancer. Kelly, you also have a dream to be a dancer, right?
>
> (E) Sure. Michaela lost her parents when she was three. After that, she had a lot of difficulties. But she never gave up on her dream of becoming a dancer.

➡ _____

Grammar

1 so ~ that ...

> • She was **so** hungry **that** she ordered many dishes.
> 그녀는 너무 배가 고파서 많은 요리를 주문했다.
> • He is **so** happy **that** he wants to talk about it. 그는 너무 행복해서 그것에 관해 말하기를 원한다.

■ 'so ~ that ...'은 '너무 ~해서 …하다'는 뜻으로 that 이하에 결과가 나온다. 이때 that은 주어와 동사가 있는 절을 이끄는 것에 유의한다.

　• She is **so** tired **that** she wants to go home. 그녀는 너무 피곤해서 집에 가고 싶다.

　• There were **so** many children **that** it was noisy. 너무 많은 아이들이 있어서 시끄러웠다.

■ 'so+형용사/부사+that+주어+can't+동사원형'은 '너무 ~해서 …할 수 없다'는 의미로, 형용사나 부사가 that절의 원인이 되고, that절은 그 결과를 이끈다. 'too+형용사/부사+to부정사'로 바꾸어 쓸 수 있다.

　• They are **so** nervous **that** they can't focus. 그들은 너무 초조해서 집중할 수 없다.
　 = They are **too** nervous **to focus**.

　• The boy was **so** short **that** he couldn't ride the bike. 그 소년은 키가 너무 작아서 자전거를 탈 수 없었다.
　 = The boy was **too** short **to ride** the bike.

■ 반면에, '충분히 ~해서 …할 수 있다'는 의미를 나타낼 때에는 '형용사/부사+enough+to부정사'를 쓰고, 이는 'so+형용사/부사+that+주어+can+동사원형'과 같다.

　• He is **so** generous **that** he can forgive you. 그는 아주 관대해서 너를 용서할 수 있다.
　 = He is generous **enough to forgive** you.

　• The candle is **so** bright **that** it can light the room. 그 초는 아주 밝아서 방을 밝힐 수 있다.
　 = The candle is bright **enough to light** the room.

핵심 Check

1. 다음 우리말과 일치하도록 빈칸에 알맞은 말을 쓰시오.
　(1) Clara는 아주 친절해서 모두가 그녀를 좋아한다.
　　➡ Clara is _____ _____ _____ everyone likes her.
　(2) 그 셔츠는 아주 커서 입을 수 없어.
　　➡ The shirt is _____ _____ _____ I can't wear it.
　(3) 그녀는 아주 부자여서 그 차를 살 수 있어.
　　➡ She is _____ _____ _____ she can buy the car.

② 원급 비교

- Sally is **as** diligent **as** Kate. Sally는 Kate만큼 부지런해.
- They did the work **as** much **as** we did. 그들은 우리가 한 만큼 많이 그 일을 했어.

■ 'as ~ as' 원급 비교는 두 개의 대상이 정도가 같을 때 사용할 수 있는 표현이다. 'as+형용사/부사의 원급+as'로 '~만큼 …한[하게]'라고 해석한다. 앞에 쓰인 as는 '그러한, 똑같은 정도로'라는 의미의 부사이며, 뒤에 쓰이고 있는 as는 '~와 같이'라는 의미로 접속사이다.

  - We enjoyed the party **as** much **as** you did. 우리도 너만큼 파티를 즐겼어.
  - That book is **as** cheap **as** this book. 저 책은 이 책만큼 값이 싸.

■ 원급 비교의 부정인 'not as[so]+원급+as ~'는 '~만큼 …하지 않은[않게]'라는 의미로, 비교하는 두 대상의 정도가 같지 않을 때 쓸 수 있다.

  - You are **not as** honest **as** I am. 너는 나만큼 정직하지 않아.
  - This desk is **not as** big **as** my old one. 이 책상은 나의 예전 것만큼 크진 않아.

■ 동등 비교를 이용하여 비교의 배수 표현이 가능하다. '배수사(twice, three times 등)+as+형용사/부사+as'의 형태이며 '~의 몇 배 만큼 …한[하게]'이라는 의미로 쓰인다.

  - This box is **two times as** heavy **as** that box. 이 상자는 저 상자보다 두 배 무겁다.
  - Your rope is **three times as** long **as** my rope. 너의 밧줄은 내 것보다 세 배 길다.

■ 원급을 이용한 관용 표현
  'as+원급+as possible'은 '가능한 한 ~한[하게]'라고 해석되고 이는 'as+원급+as+주어+can[could]'와 같다. 그 외에도 'as quiet as a mouse(쥐 죽은 듯이 조용히)', 'as blind as a bat(시력이 매우 안 좋은)', 'as wise as an owl(매우 현명한)', 'as free as a bird(매우 자유로운)' 등이 있다.

  - Come here **as soon as possible**. 가능한 빨리 이곳으로 오렴.

■ 원급을 이용한 최상급 표현
  'no other+단수 명사+동사+as[so] ~ as …'는 '어떠한 다른 명사도 …만큼 ~하지 않다'는 의미로 최상급을 나타낼 수 있다..

  - **No other** hero in Avengers is **as brave as** Iron Man. Avengers의 다른 어떤 영웅도 아이언맨만큼 용감하지 않다.
    = Iron Man is **the bravest** hero in Avengers.

핵심 Check

2. 다음 우리말과 일치하도록 빈칸에 알맞은 말을 쓰시오.
  (1) 작년만큼 덥지 않아요.
    ➡ It is _____ _____ _____ _____ it was last year.
  (2) 너는 Tom만큼 잘생겼어.
    ➡ You are _____ _____ _____ Tom.

01 다음 문장에서 어법상 <u>어색한</u> 부분을 바르게 고쳐 쓰시오.

(1) Kate was very tired that she went to bed early.

_____ ➡ _____

(2) Robert is as taller as Chuck.

_____ ➡ _____

(3) She was so upset to think clearly.

_____ ➡ _____

(4) This balloon is two time as big as that balloon.

_____ ➡ _____

02 괄호 안의 단어를 이용하여 알맞은 말을 빈칸에 쓰시오.

(1) The meat is _____ _____ _____ it is hard to chew. (tough)

(2) The paper is _____ _____ _____ be written. (thin)

(3) We were _____ _____ _____ we kept dancing. (happy)

(4) She is _____ _____ _____ lend me some money. (generous)

(5) He talks _____ _____ _____ be with. (much)

03 주어진 어구를 바르게 배열하여 다음 우리말을 영어로 쓰시오.

(1) 이 앨범에서 이 노래가 가장 아름다워. (this song / as / as / no / song / other / this album / beautiful / in / is)

➡ _____

(2) 너의 쿠키는 그의 쿠키만큼 맛있지 않아. (his / not / as / as / cookies / your / delicious / are)

➡ _____

(3) 이 산은 남산보다 세 배 높다. (Namsan / this mountain / three / as / as / is / times / high)

➡ _____

(4) 가능한 한 자주 전화하렴. (possible / as / as / me / call / often)

➡ _____

01 다음 빈칸에 들어갈 말로 가장 적절한 것은?

> Brian speaks _____ fast that I can't understand him.

① such ② very ③ so
④ too ⑤ enough

 02 다음 우리말을 영어로 바르게 옮긴 것은?

> 이것은 저것보다 두 배만큼 좋아.

① This is as good as that.
② This is as better as that.
③ This is better than that.
④ This is twice as good as that.
⑤ This is two time as good as that.

03 다음 중 문장의 의미가 서로 같지 않은 것은?

① Maya is so tall that she is good at playing basketball.
　→ Maya is good at playing basketball because she is very tall.
② No other river in Korea is as long as this river.
　→ This river is the longest river in Korea.
③ Kelly was so annoyed that she turned off her cellphone.
　→ Because Kelly turned off her cellphone, she was annoyed.
④ You are too young to work.
　→ You are so young that you can't work.
⑤ He is fast enough to win the race.
　→ He is so fast that he can win the race.

서답형
04 주어진 단어를 이용하여 다음 우리말을 영어로 쓰시오.

> 그녀는 너무 바빠서 지금 우리와 함께 이야기할 수 없어요. (that / busy)

➡ _____

05 다음 빈칸에 들어갈 말로 가장 적절한 것은?

> We were going to meet here at 1 o'clock. You came here at 2 o'clock. Julia came here at 2 o'clock. Julia _____ you.

① came here as early as
② came here two times as late as
③ didn't come as late as
④ came here as late as
⑤ came earlier than

 06 다음 빈칸에 들어갈 말로 가장 적절한 것은?

> He felt so miserable that he couldn't say a word.
> = He felt _____ say a word.

① very miserable to
② miserable enough to
③ so miserable that
④ too miserable to
⑤ too miserable that

서답형
07 다음 우리말을 영어로 쓰시오.

> 네 방은 내 방만큼 깨끗해.

➡ _____

08 다음 두 문장을 하나의 문장으로 바르게 표현한 것은?

> She felt very thirsty. So she drank a bottle of water.

① Although she felt very thirsty, she drank a bottle of water.

② She felt so thirsty that she couldn't drink a bottle of water.

③ She felt very thirsty because she drank a bottle of water.

④ She felt very thirsty although she drank a bottle of water.

⑤ She felt so thirsty that she drank a bottle of water.

09 다음 빈칸에 들어갈 말이 바르게 짝지어진 것은?

> • Olivia felt _____ cold that she couldn't fall asleep.
> • Tom is brave _____ to fight for us.
> • The lamp is not as _____ as my lamp.

① too – too – bright

② too – enough – brighter

③ so – enough – bright

④ so – too – bright

⑤ so – too – brighter

서답형

10 주어진 단어를 사용하여 다음 우리말을 지시에 맞게 영어로 쓰시오.

> 나는 너무 바빠서 숙제를 할 수 없었어. (do)

(1) to부정사를 사용하여

➡ _____

(2) that절을 사용하여

➡ _____

11 다음 중 어법상 틀린 문장은?

① The sun shines as bright as it did yesterday.

② No other planet in space is as beautiful as Earth.

③ The movie was exciting enough to watching two times.

④ She likes to walk so much that she walks every day.

⑤ The weather was so nice that we went to the zoo.

12 다음 주어진 문장과 같은 의미의 문장을 모두 고르시오.

> I can't play with you because I am very busy.

① Although I am very busy, I can play with you.

② I am too busy to play with you.

③ Because I can't play with you, I am very busy.

④ I am so busy that I can't play with you.

⑤ I am busy enough to play with you.

13 다음 빈칸에 들어갈 말로 적절하지 않은 것은?

> Melisa is _____ Betty.

① as lovely as   ② as pretty as

③ as friendly as   ④ not as taller as

⑤ not as smart as

서답형

14 주어진 문장과 같은 의미의 문장을 쓰시오.

> I was too young to see the movie.

➡ _____

서답형

15 아홉 개의 단어를 사용하여 다음 우리말을 영어로 쓸 때 세 번째와 일곱 번째로 오는 단어를 바르게 묶은 것은?

> 목걸이들이 너무 비싸서 우리는 그것들을 살 수 없 었어.

① were – that ② so – we
③ expensive – buy ④ so – couldn't
⑤ were – couldn't

16 다음 중 우리말을 영어로 바르게 옮기지 <u>않은</u> 것은?

① 그는 Jason만큼 크게 말하지 않는다.
 → He doesn't talk as loudly as Jason.
② 나는 너무 열심히 일해서 피곤했다.
 → I worked so hard that I was tired.
③ 너의 다리는 내 다리만큼 길어.
 → Your legs are as long as my legs.
④ 내 친구들 중 Paul이 가장 친절해.
 → No other friend of mine is as kind as Paul.
⑤ 그녀는 책상을 옮기기에 충분히 힘이 세.
 → She is too strong to move the desk.

중요

17 다음 빈칸에 들어갈 말이 바르게 짝지은 것은?

> Julie was so happy that she could invite everyone to her party.
> = Julie was _____ invite everyone to her party.

① too happy to ② happy enough to
③ happy because ④ very happy to
⑤ enough happy to

서답형

18 주어진 단어를 활용하여 다음 우리말을 영어로 쓰시오. (8 words)

> 그들은 우리만큼 가난하지 않아. (poor)

➡ _____

19 다음 대화의 빈칸에 들어갈 말로 적절한 것을 <u>모두</u> 고르시오.

> A: Did you have your dinner?
> B: No, I _____ my dinner.

① was tired enough to have
② was too tired to have
③ was so tired that I could have
④ was tired that I had
⑤ was so tired that I couldn't have

중요

20 다음 우리말을 영어로 옮길 때 빈칸에 들어갈 말로 가장 적절한 것은?

> 사탕은 아이스크림만큼 달콤한 맛이 난다.
> Candies _____ ice cream.

① taste as sweetly as
② taste sweeter than
③ taste as sweet as
④ taste as bitter as
⑤ taste not as sweet as

서답형

21 주어진 단어를 바르게 배열하여 다음 우리말을 영어로 쓰시 오. 필요하다면 어형을 바꾸시오.

> 그녀는 너무 화가 나서 일찍 집으로 갔다.
> (early / she / she / upset / went / was / that / home / so)

➡ _____

서답형

22 다음 빈칸에 알맞은 말을 쓰시오.

(1) James is 170cm tall. Parker is 178cm tall. So James is _____ Parker.
(2) Flowers are expensive these days. A rose is ten thousand won. A lily is also ten thousand won. A rose is _____ a lily.

01 다음 문장과 같은 의미의 문장을 쓰시오.

(1) She is so bright that she can solve all the puzzles.

➡ _____

(2) He runs fast enough to win the race.

➡ _____

(3) It was so hot that I couldn't go out.

➡ _____

(4) They were so poor that they couldn't buy books as much as they wanted.

➡ _____

_____

(5) They studied so hard that they could pass the test.

➡ _____

02 주어진 단어를 사용하여 다음 우리말을 영어로 쓰시오.

너는 네 여동생만큼 똑똑하니?
(clever)

➡ _____

03 다음 우리말을 영어로 옮길 때, 빈칸에 알맞은 말을 쓰시오.

그 책은 너무 어려워서 나는 그것을 읽기를 포기했어.
➡ The book was _____ _____
_____ I gave up reading it.

04 다음 세 학생에 관한 표를 읽고 문장을 완성하시오. 주어진 단어를 활용하시오.

	Kevin	Daisy	Peter
age	17	17	19
height	185	160	178
weight	71	50	71

(heavy / much / short / old)

(1) Kevin is _____ Daisy. But he is _____ Peter.
(2) No other student of them is _____ Daisy.
(3) Peter is _____ Kevin. But He weighs _____ Kevin.
(4) Daisy is _____ Kevin and Peter.

05 주어진 단어를 활용하여 다음 대화의 우리말을 영어로 쓰시오.

A: How was the food?
B: 음식이 너무 뜨거워서 나는 혀를 데였어요.
(burn one's tongue)

➡ _____

06 다음 문장을 읽고 두 사람의 기상 시간을 비교하는 문장을 쓰시오.

Emily gets up at seven o'clock in the morning. Judy gets up at seven o'clock in the morning. Both students get up early in the morning.

➡ _____

07 다음 두 문장을 조건에 맞게 하나의 문장으로 표현하시오.

> I woke up late. So I couldn't attend the meeting.

(1) to부정사를 사용하여

➡ _____

(2) that절을 사용하여

➡ _____

08 다음 그림을 참고하여 개와 고양이를 비교하는 문장을 쓰시오.

4kg   4kg

➡ _____

09 주어진 단어를 활용하여 다음 우리말을 영어로 쓰시오.

> 그녀는 운전을 너무 잘해서 항상 나를 데리러 와요.
> (that / pick up)

➡ _____

10 다음 우리말에 맞게 주어진 단어를 활용하여 빈칸에 알맞은 말을 쓰시오.

> Helen은 자유로운 시간이 결코 없어. 그녀는 매우 바빠.
> ➡ Helen never has any free time. She is
> _____. (bee)

11 다음 글을 읽고 주어진 단어를 활용하여 비교하는 문장을 완성하시오.

> The library is three kilometers away from here. The book store is also three kilometers away from here.

➡ The library is _____ the book store from here. (far)

12 주어진 단어를 이용하여 다음 우리말에 맞게 빈칸을 완성하시오.

> 어제 너는 너무 무례해서 나는 너에게 실망했어.
> (rude / that / disappoint)

➡ Yesterday, _____

_____ .

13 주어진 단어를 활용하여 다음 대화의 빈칸에 알맞은 말을 쓰시오.

> A: _____ ?
> (much / eat / pizza / Tom)
> B: Yes. He ate two pieces of pizza and I ate also two pieces of pizza.

14 다음 문장과 같은 의미의 문장을 쓰시오.

> I know June well enough to ask for help.

➡ _____

15 주어진 단어를 활용하여 다음 우리말을 영어로 쓰시오.

> 그 책은 이 책보다 세 배 두꺼워.
> (thick / as)

➡ _____

Reading

Dance with a Story

Why do people dance? They dance to express feelings, give happiness
to others, or enjoy themselves. Let's take a look at different kinds of
dance around the world.

India: Kathakali

Kathakali tells a story. The dancers tell stories through their body
movements. These stories are usually about a fight between good and
evil. Dancers who are playing good characters paint their faces green.
Those who are playing evil characters wear black make-up.
Interestingly, in *Kathakali*, only men are allowed to dance. The body
movements are so powerful that the dancers need to train for many
years.

express: 표현하다
take a look: 살펴보다
movement: 움직임, 동작
fight 싸움
good and evil: 선과 악
character: 등장인물
make-up 화장, 분장
be allowed to: ~이 허용되다
train 훈련하다

 확인문제

● 다음 문장이 본문의 내용과 일치하면 T, 일치하지 않으면 F를 쓰시오.

1 People dance with one specific reason. ☐

2 By dancing, people enjoy themselves. ☐

3 There are various types of dance around the world. ☐

4 There is no story in the dance *Kathakali*. ☐

5 Dancers who are playing evil characters wear green make-up. ☐

6 Women aren't allowed to dance in *Kathakali*. ☐

New Zealand: *Haka*

When people visit New Zealand, they may meet a group of *haka*
_{시간의 부사절을 이끄는 접속사(~할 때)}   _{추측의 조동사}
dancers. The dancers perform this traditional dance with scary faces.
_{Haka를 의미}
This dance was originally performed by the Maori before a fight.
_{=The Maori originally performed this dance before a fight.}
They wanted to show their strength to the enemy. The dancers looked
_{to부정사를 목적어로 취하는 동사}
as scary as wild animals before fighting. Nowadays, in New Zealand,
_{as+형용사나 부사의 원급+as: ~만큼 …한 (동등비교)}   _{= These days}
rugby players usually perform a *haka* before a game to show their
_{빈도부사(일반동사 앞, be동사나 조동사 뒤에 위치)}   _{to부정사의 부사적 용법 중 목적}
strength to the other team.

Korea: *Buchaechum*

Buchaechum is a traditional Korean fan dance. The dancers wear
colorful *hanbok*. They dance with large fans that are painted in bright
_{주격 관계대명사}
colors. The dancers move the fans gracefully to show different kinds
_{to부정사의 부사적 용법 중 목적}
of beauty. Their movements look as beautiful as flowers or flying
_{as+형용사나 부사의 원급+as: ~만큼 …한 (동등비교)}
birds. In Korea, *Buchaechum* is so popular that people can see it in
_{so+형용사/부사+that …: 너무 ~해서 …하다 (원인과 결과를 나타냄)}
many traditional festivals.

perform: 공연하다, 연주하다
originally: 원래
strength: 힘
enemy: 적
wild: 야생의
colorful: 화려한, 다채로운
fan: 부채
bright: (색상이) 밝은
popular: 인기 있는

 확인문제

- 다음 문장이 본문의 내용과 일치하면 T, 일치하지 않으면 F를 쓰시오.

1 The dancers perform a *haka* to show friendliness. ☐
2 By performing a *haka*, the Maori wanted to show they were scared. ☐
3 To show their strength, rugby players perform a *haka*. ☐
4 The fans used in *Buchaechum* are very simple. ☐
5 The *Buchaechum* dancers move their fans very fast. ☐
6 People are not interested in *Buchaechum* these days. ☐

● 우리말을 참고하여 빈칸에 알맞은 말을 쓰시오.

Dance with a Story

1 _____ do people _____?

2 They dance _____ _____ feelings, give happiness _____ others, or _____ _____.

3 Let's take a look at _____ _____ _____ _____ around the world

India: *Kathakali*

4 *Kathakali* _____ a story.

5 The dancers tell _____ _____ their _____ _____.

6 These stories are usually about _____ _____ _____ _____ _____ _____.

7 Dancers _____ _____ _____ good characters paint their faces _____.

8 Those _____ _____ _____ evil characters _____ _____ make-up.

9 _____, in *Kathakali*, only men _____ _____ _____ dance.

10 The body movements are _____ _____ _____ the dancers need to train _____ many years.

New Zealand: *Haka*

11 When people visit New Zealand, they may _____ a group of _____ _____.

12 The dancers _____ this _____ dance with _____ _____.

이야기가 있는 춤

1 사람들은 왜 춤을 추는 걸까요?

2 사람들은 감정을 표현하고, 다른 사람들에게 행복감을 주거나 스스로 즐기기 위해 춤을 춥니다.

3 세계의 여러 가지 춤을 살펴봅시다.

인도: *Kathakali*

4 *Kathakali*에는 이야기가 있습니다.

5 춤꾼들은 몸동작을 통해 이야기합니다.

6 이러한 이야기들은 대개 선과 악의 싸움에 관한 것입니다.

7 선한 역할을 맡은 춤꾼들은 자신의 얼굴을 초록색으로 칠합니다.

8 악한 역할을 맡은 춤꾼들은 검은색 화장을 합니다.

9 재미있는 것은 *Kathakali* 춤에서 남자들만 춤추는 것이 허락된다는 사실입니다.

10 몸동작이 매우 힘이 넘쳐서 춤꾼들은 수년 동안 연습을 해야 합니다.

뉴질랜드: *Haka*

11 사람들이 뉴질랜드를 방문할 때, 그들은 *haka* 춤꾼들의 무리를 만날지도 모릅니다.

12 그 춤꾼들은 무서운 얼굴로 이 전통 춤을 춥니다.

13 This dance was _____ _____ _____ the Maori before a fight.

14 They wanted _____ _____ _____ _____ to the enemy.

15 The dancers looked _____ _____ _____ wild animals _____ fighting.

16 _____, in New Zealand, rugby players _____ _____ a *haka* before a game _____ _____ their strength to _____ _____ team.

Korea: *Buchaechum*

17 *Buchaechum* is a _____ Korean _____ dance.

18 The dancers _____ _____ _____ .

19 They dance with large fans _____ _____ _____ in bright colors.

20 The dancers _____ the fans _____ to show _____ _____ _____ _____ .

21 Their movements _____ _____ _____ _____ flowers or flying birds.

22 In Korea, *Buchaechum* is _____ _____ _____ people _____ _____ _____ in many traditional festivals.

13 이 춤은 원래 마오리족에 의해 싸움 전에 행해졌습니다.

14 그들은 적에게 그들의 힘을 보여 주고 싶었습니다.

15 춤꾼들은 싸움하기 전의 야생 동물들만큼 무섭게 보였습니다.

16 요즈음, 뉴질랜드에서는 럭비 선수들이 다른 팀에게 그들의 힘을 보여 주기 위해 게임 전에 주로 *haka*를 보여 줍니다.

한국: 부채춤

17 부채춤은 한국 전통 부채춤입니다.

18 춤꾼들은 다채로운 한복을 입습니다.

19 그들은 밝은 색으로 칠해진 커다란 부채를 가지고 춤을 춥니다.

20 그 춤꾼들은 다양한 종류의 미를 보여 주기 위해 부채를 우아하게 움직입니다.

21 그들의 움직임은 꽃 또는 날아다니는 새들처럼 우아하게 보입니다.

22 한국에서, 부채춤은 너무 인기가 있어서 사람들은 많은 전통 축제에서 그것을 볼 수 있습니다.

● 우리말을 참고하여 본문을 영작하시오.

Dance with a Story

1 사람들은 왜 춤을 추는 걸까요?

➡ _____

2 사람들은 감정을 표현하고, 다른 사람들에게 행복감을 주거나 스스로 즐기기 위해 춤을 춥니다.

➡ _____

3 세계의 여러 가지 춤을 살펴봅시다.

➡ _____

India: *Kathakali*

4 *Kathakali*에는 이야기가 있습니다.

➡ _____

5 춤꾼들은 몸동작을 통해 이야기합니다.

➡ _____

6 이러한 이야기들은 대개 선과 악의 싸움에 관한 것입니다.

➡ _____

7 선한 역할을 맡은 춤꾼들은 자신의 얼굴을 초록색으로 칠합니다.

➡ _____

8 악한 역할을 맡은 춤꾼들은 검은색 화장을 합니다.

➡ _____

9 재미있는 것은 *Kathakali* 춤에서 남자들만 춤추는 것이 허락된다는 사실입니다.

➡ _____

10 몸동작이 매우 힘이 넘쳐서 춤꾼들은 수년 동안 연습을 해야 합니다.

➡ _____

New Zealand: *Haka*

11 사람들이 뉴질랜드를 방문할 때, 그들은 *haka* 춤꾼들의 무리를 만날지도 모릅니다.

➡ _____

12 그 춤꾼들은 무서운 얼굴로 이 전통 춤을 춥니다.

➡ _____

13 이 춤은 원래 마오리족에 의해 싸움 전에 행해졌습니다.

➡ _____

14 그들은 적에게 그들의 힘을 보여 주고 싶었습니다.

➡ _____

15 그 춤꾼들은 싸움하기 전의 야생 동물들만큼 무섭게 보였습니다.

➡ _____

16 요즈음, 뉴질랜드에서는 럭비 선수들이 다른 팀에게 그들의 힘을 보여 주기 위해 게임 전에 주로 *haka*를 보여 줍니다.

➡ _____

_____

Korea: *Buchaechum*

17 부채춤은 한국 전통 부채춤입니다.

➡ _____

18 춤꾼들은 다채로운 한복을 입습니다.

➡ _____

19 그들은 밝은 색으로 칠해진 커다란 부채를 가지고 춤을 춥니다.

➡ _____

20 그 춤꾼들은 다양한 종류의 미를 보여 주기 위해 부채를 우아하게 움직입니다.

➡ _____

21 그들의 움직임은 꽃 또는 날아다니는 새들처럼 우아하게 보입니다.

➡ _____

22 한국에서, 부채춤은 너무 인기가 있어서 사람들은 많은 전통 축제에서 그것을 볼 수 있습니다.

➡ _____

[01~02] 다음 글을 읽고 물음에 답하시오.

(A)_____ They dance to express feelings, give happiness to others, or enjoy themselves. Let's take a look (B)____ different kinds of dance around the world.

중요

01 빈칸 (A)에 들어갈 말로 가장 적절한 것은?

① Why do people dance?
② Why do people express feelings?
③ When do people dance?
④ How do people dance?
⑤ How many kinds of dance are there?

02 다음 중 빈칸 (B)에 들어갈 말과 같은 말이 들어가는 것은?

① Minsu was taking care _____ his dog.
② I became interested _____ watching movies.
③ I don't agree _____ you.
④ Jason is good _____ playing the guitar and the piano.
⑤ The glass is full _____ orange juice.

[03~06] 다음 글을 읽고 물음에 답하시오.

India: *Kathakali*

Kathakali tells a story. The dancers tell stories through their body movements. These stories are usually about a fight between good and evil. Dancers (A)_____ are playing good characters paint their faces green. Those who are playing evil characters wear black make-up. Interestingly, in *Kathakali*, only men are allowed to dance. The body movements are so powerful that the dancers need to train for many years.

03 빈칸 (A)에 적절한 말을 모두 고르시오.

① who   ② which   ③ that
④ what   ⑤ whose

서답형

04 다음과 같이 풀이되는 말을 위 글에서 찾아 쓰시오.

the act of moving your body or a part of your body

➡ _____

중요

05 다음 중 위 글을 읽고 답할 수 있는 것은?

① When the dance started?
② Why are only men allowed to dance?
③ Through what do the dancers tell stories?
④ What do women do while men are dancing?
⑤ How long does the dance last?

서답형

06 According to the passage, what do dancers wear to express that they are playing evil characters? Answer in English with a full sentence.

➡ _____

_____

[07~09] 다음 글을 읽고 물음에 답하시오.

New Zealand: *Haka*

When people visit New Zealand, they may meet a group of *haka* dancers. The dancers perform this traditional dance with (A)_____. This dance was originally performed by the Maori before a fight. They wanted to show their strength to the enemy. The dancers looked as scary as wild animals before fighting. Nowadays, in New Zealand, rugby players usually perform a *haka* before a game to show their strength to the other team.

07 빈칸 (A)에 들어갈 말로 가장 적절한 것은?

① funny looks   ② beautiful clothes
③ wild animals   ④ friends and family
⑤ scary faces

08 다음 중 위 글을 읽고 답할 수 있는 것은?

① How many people are needed to perform a *haka*?
② What kind of clothes do dancers need to wear to perform a *haka*?
③ What is the reason why the Maori performed a *haka*?
④ Where is the most popular tourist attraction in New Zealand?
⑤ How many times was a *haka* performed by the Maori?

서답형
09 위 글의 내용에 맞게 빈칸에 알맞은 말을 쓰시오.

> In a way to _____ _____ _____, rugby players perform a *haka* before a game.

[10~12] 다음 글을 읽고 물음에 답하시오.

Korea: *Buchaechum*

  Buchaechum is a traditional Korean fan dance. The dancers wear colorful *hanbok*. They dance with large fans that are painted in bright colors. The dancers move the fans

gracefully to show different kinds of beauty. Their movements look as beautiful as flowers or (A)flying birds. In Korea, *Buchaechum* is so popular that people can see it in many traditional festivals.

10 다음 중 밑줄 친 (A)와 쓰임이 같은 것은?

① David and I enjoyed having conversation with each other.
② My dad was busy with finding the meaning of the word.
③ Your job is keeping this place as clean as possible.
④ Where is my sleeping bag?
⑤ We saw the bus passing by without stopping.

서답형
11 Where can people see *Buchaechum* in Korea? Answer in English with a full sentence.

➡ _____

_____

12 다음 중 위 글의 내용을 제대로 이해한 사람은?

① 민하: 나는 부채춤의 한복 색깔이 매우 단조로운 것에 놀랐어.
② 준영: 이젠 부채춤을 더 이상 볼 수 없다는 것이 참 안타까운 일이야.
③ 세호: 부채가 움직이는 모습이 꽃과 같다니 얼마나 아름다울까.
④ 은종: 부채춤의 격렬한 움직임에서 힘을 느낄 수 있겠어.
⑤ 대민: 한국에서 부채춤이 인기가 없어져서 사라지게 된 것이야.

[13~17] 다음 글을 읽고 물음에 답하시오.

Why do people dance? They dance to express feelings, give happiness to others, or enjoy ⓐ themselves. Let's take a look at different kinds of dance around the world.

India: *Kathakali*

Kathakali tells a story. The dancers tell stories through their body movements. These stories are usually about a fight between good and evil. Dancers who are playing good characters paint their faces green. Those who are playing (A)_____ characters wear black make-up. Interestingly, in *Kathakali*, only men are allowed to dance. The body movements are so powerful that the dancers need to train for many years.

13 다음 중 빈칸 (A)에 들어갈 말로 가장 적절한 것은?

① funny   ② brave   ③ boring
④ evil   ⑤ mysterious

14 다음 중 밑줄 친 ⓐ와 쓰임이 다른 것은?

① Look at yourself! You look terrible.
② Please help yourself to the salad.
③ Did you make this cake yourself?
④ He cut himself on a knife yesterday.
⑤ Have you hurt yourself?

15 다음 중 위 글의 내용으로 보아 알 수 있는 것은?

① the origin of the dance
② the number of dancers
③ people who are allowed to dance
④ the popularity of the dance
⑤ when people dance *Kathakali*

16 다음은 *Kathakali* 춤꾼 중 한 명의 말이다. 글의 내용에 맞게 빈칸에 알맞은 말을 쓰시오.

In order to play a _____ _____, I paint my face green.

서답형

17 Write the reason why the dancers need to train for many years to dance *Kathakali*. Answer in English and use the phrase 'it's because.'

➡ _____

_____

[18~21] 다음 글을 읽고 물음에 답하시오.

New Zealand: *Haka*

When people visit New Zealand, they may meet a group of *haka* dancers.
[A] Nowadays, in New Zealand, rugby players usually perform a *haka* before a game to show their strength to the other team.
[B] They wanted to show their strength to the enemy. The dancers looked as scary as wild animals before fighting.
[C] The dancers perform this traditional dance with scary faces. This dance was originally performed ⓐ_____ the Maori before a fight.

서답형

18 빈칸 ⓐ에 알맞은 말을 쓰시오.

➡ _____

19 자연스러운 글이 되도록 [A]~[C]를 바르게 배열한 것은?

① [A] – [C] – [B]   ② [B] – [A] – [C]
③ [B] – [C] – [A]   ④ [C] – [A] – [B]
⑤ [C] – [B] – [A]

20 글의 내용에 맞게 빈칸에 알맞은 말을 쓰시오.

> A: Alex, do you know what a *haka* is?
> B: Yes, I do. It's _____
>
> _____ .

21 다음 중 위 글의 내용과 일치하지 <u>않는</u> 것은?

① We may meet a group of people who perform a *haka* in New Zealand.

② The Maori used to perform a *haka* before a fight.

③ The dancers who perform a *haka* look scary.

④ People who perform a *haka* can't be seen nowadays.

⑤ Rugby players perform a *haka* in order to show the other team how strong they are.

[22~24] 다음 글을 읽고 물음에 답하시오.

Korea: *Buchaechum*

　Buchaechum is a traditional Korean fan dance. The dancers wear colorful *hanbok*. They dance with large fans that are painted in bright colors. The dancers move the fans gracefully (A)<u>to show</u> different kinds of beauty. Their movements look as beautiful as flowers or flying birds. In Korea, *Buchaechum* is so popular that people can see (B)<u>it</u> in many traditional festivals.

22 다음 중 밑줄 친 (A)와 쓰임이 같은 것은?

① It was nice <u>to see</u> you again.

② What I want is <u>to take</u> a rest.

③ They decided <u>to make</u> a plan.

④ I went to bed early <u>to wake</u> up early.

⑤ Is there anything <u>to sit</u> on?

23 밑줄 친 (B)가 가리키는 것을 우리말로 쓰시오.

➡ _____

24 다음 중 위 글의 내용과 일치하는 것은?

① People who dance *Buchaechum* wear normal clothes.

② *Hanbok* is painted in bright colors in *Buchaechum*.

③ Fans are used to catch a flying bird.

④ *Buchaechum* is popular enough to be seen in many traditional festivals.

⑤ Many flowers are used to decorate the stage of the show.

[25~26] 다음 글을 읽고 물음에 답하시오.

Come and Enjoy the Step Dance

　A step dance is a traditional dance in Ireland. The dancers wear colorful costumes. In my opinion, the dancers look as (A)_____ as dolls. The dancers move their feet so fast that they look like they're flying!

25 단어 cute을 어법에 맞게 (A)에 쓰시오.

➡ _____

26 다음 중 위 글을 읽고 답할 수 <u>없는</u> 것은?

① What is a step dance?

② What do the dancers of a step dance wear?

③ What do the dancers look like when they dance?

④ How do the dancers look in their costumes?

⑤ Why do the people in Ireland perform a step dance?

[01~05] 다음 글을 읽고 물음에 답하시오.

Why do people dance? They dance to express feelings, give happiness to others, or enjoy themselves. Let's take a look at different kinds of dance around the world.

India: *Kathakali*

Kathakali tells a story. The dancers tell stories through their body movements. These stories are usually about a fight between good and evil. Dancers who are playing good characters paint their faces green. Those who are playing evil characters wear black make-up. Interestingly, in *Kathakali*, only men are allowed to dance. (A)Because the body movements are very powerful, the dancers need to train for many years.

01 Write the reason why people dance. Answer in English with a full sentence.

➡ _____

_____

02 When we see people dance *Kathakali* with wearing green make-up, what can we think? Answer in English with the words below.

(think / play)

➡ _____

03 위 글의 내용에 맞게 빈칸에 알맞은 말을 쓰시오.

People _____ for many reasons. For example, in *Kathakali* from _____, dancers dance to express a _____ between _____ _____ _____.

04 How do the *Kathakali* dancers tell stories? Answer in English with a full sentence.

➡ _____

05 주어진 단어를 이용하여 밑줄 친 (A)와 같은 의미의 문장을 쓰시오.

(so / that)

➡ _____

_____

[06~08] 다음 글을 읽고 물음에 답하시오.

New Zealand: *Haka*

When people visit New Zealand, they may meet a group of *haka* dancers. The dancers perform this traditional dance with scary faces. This dance was originally performed by the Maori before a fight. They wanted to show their strength to the enemy. The dancers looked as scary as wild animals before fighting. Nowadays, in New Zealand, rugby players usually perform a *haka* before a game to show their strength to the other team.

06 주어진 단어를 이용하여 다음 물음에 답하시오.

Q: How do dancers perform a *haka*? (with)

➡ _____

07 글의 내용에 맞게 빈칸에 알맞은 말을 쓰시오.

> *Haka* is a traditional dance in New Zealand. The Maori performed the dance to show their strength _____ _____ _____. And now it is performed by rugby players in New Zealand to show _____ _____ _____ _____ _____ _____ .

08 다음 중 위 글의 내용과 일치하지 <u>않는</u> 것을 한 군데 찾아 바르게 고쳐 쓰시오.

> If you want to see people perform a *haka*, go to New Zealand. This traditional dance looks scary. It is usually performed by a single person.

➡ _____ ➡

[09~11] 다음 글을 읽고 물음에 답하시오.

Korea: *Buchaechum*

> *Buchaechum* is a traditional Korean fan dance. The dancers wear colorful *hanbok*. They dance with large fans that (A)_____ in bright colors. The dancers move the fans gracefully to show different kinds of beauty. Their movements look as beautiful as flowers or flying birds. In Korea, *Buchaechum* is so popular that people can see it in many traditional festivals.

09 단어 paint를 어법에 맞게 빈칸 (A)에 쓰시오.

➡ _____

10 According to the passage, what is *Buchaechum*?

➡ _____

11 Write the reason why the dancers move the fans gracefully. Use the phrase below.

> (It's because / want)

➡ _____
_____

[12~14] 다음 글을 읽고 물음에 답하시오.

> *Tarantella*, Italy
>
> In the past, people danced the *tarantella* for sick people. Nowadays, it is a couple's dance. People dance the *tarantella* on happy days such as weddings.
>
> *Adumu*, Kenya
>
> This dance is performed before a fight. It is also called a jumping dance. Dancers jump high in the air. When a dancer jumps, other dancers cheer him on with loud noises.

12 Why did people dance the *tarantella* in the past? Answer in English with a full sentence.

➡ _____

13 According to the passage, what can we see when we attend an Italian friend's wedding?

➡ _____

14 When is the dance *Adumu* performed?

➡ _____

해석

Listen and Speak 2 - C

A: I'm going to a culture event in our town next week. Do you want to join me?

to부정사의 명사적 용법

B: Sounds interesting.

A: We can enjoy dancing from many countries. I'm sure we'll have a lot of

enjoy+동명사　　　　　　　　　　= certain　　　= much

fun.

구문해설　• have fun: 즐거운 시간을 보내다

A: 나는 다음 주말에 우리 마을에서 열리는 문화 행사에 갈 거야. 나와 같이 갈래?

B: 재미있겠다.

A: 우리는 많은 국가에서 온 춤들을 즐길 수 있어. 우리는 매우 즐거울 거라고 확신해.

Culture & Life

Tarantella, Italy

In the past, people danced the *tarantella* for sick people.

~을 위해

Nowadays, it is a couple's dance. People dance the *tarantella* on happy days

Tarantella 지칭　　　　　　　　특정 날짜 앞에 전치사 on

such as weddings.

=like

구문해설　• past: 과거　• nowadays: 요즈음　• such as: ~와 같은

Tarantella − 이탈리아

과거에, 사람들은 아픈 사람들을 위해 tarantella를 추었다. 요즈음, 이 춤은 커플 춤이다. 사람들은 결혼식 같은 행복한 날에 tarantella를 춘다.

Culture & Life

Adumu, Kenya

This dance is performed before a fight. It is also called a jumping dance.

dance는 perform의 대상이므로 수동태　　　People also call it a jumping dance.

Dancers jump high in the air. When a dancer jumps, other dancers cheer him

높이　　　　　　　　　　　　타동사+대명사 목적어+부사

on with loud noises.

구문해설　• perform: 행하다, 수행하다　• cheer ~ on: ~을 응원하다　• noise: 소음

Adumu − 케냐

이 춤은 전투하기 전에 춘다. 이것은 점핑 댄스라고도 불린다. 춤꾼들은 공중에 높이 뛰어오른다. 한 춤꾼이 점프하면, 다른 사람들은 큰 소리를 내며 그를 응원한다.

영역별 핵심문제

Words & Expressions

01 다음 짝지어진 단어의 관계가 같도록 빈칸에 알맞은 말을 쓰시오.

> sure : unsure = comfortable : _____

02 다음 문장에 공통으로 들어갈 말을 고르시오.

> • I don't want to give up _____ achieving my goal.
> • I took a taxi to arrive at the meeting _____ time.

① to   ② from   ③ by
④ on   ⑤ of

03 다음 영영풀이가 가리키는 것을 고르시오.

> a flat object that you wave with your hand which makes the air cooler

① field   ② pan
③ fight   ④ fan
⑤ uniform

04 다음 중 밑줄 친 부분의 뜻풀이가 바르지 않은 것은?

① Have you ever played <u>rugby</u>? 럭비
② What are you going to <u>perform</u> on the school dancing contest? 공연하다
③ Through dancing, you can <u>communicate</u> with people around the world. 의사소통하다
④ When Irene danced <u>gracefully</u>, I fell in love with her. 신나게
⑤ It's <u>windy</u> outside, so bring your sweater. 바람이 센

05 다음 문장의 빈칸에 들어갈 말을 〈보기〉에서 골라 쓰시오.

> ┤ 보기 ├
> bright / scared / wild / hide / popular

(1) It is not easy to tame _____ animals.
(2) I'll _____ this letter in a drawer.
(3) Picasso didn't use _____ colors.
(4) He is very _____ among students.
(5) I was so _____ that I hid under my bed.

06 다음 주어진 문장의 밑줄 친 express와 다른 의미로 쓰인 것은?

> Teachers <u>express</u> their concerns about the changes in school.

① Singing is one of the ways to <u>express</u> my feelings.
② Her face <u>expresses</u> how happy she is.
③ I didn't have enough time, so I decided to travel by <u>express</u>.
④ I was so nervous that I couldn't <u>express</u> what I meant.
⑤ How can I <u>express</u> all my thoughts in one page?

07 다음 우리말을 주어진 단어를 이용하여 영작하시오.

(1) 그들은 적에게 그들의 힘을 보여 주고 싶었다. (show, strength)

➡ _____

(2) 다른 춤꾼들은 그를 큰 소리로 응원한다. (noises, up, other)

➡ _____

(3) 수진이는 사자만큼 용감하다. (as, is)

➡ _____

Conversation

08 다음 대화가 자연스럽게 이어지도록 순서대로 배열하시오.

> (A) In my opinion, it's interesting. I smiled when I first saw it.
> (B) Me, too. The dancers in the painting look happy.
> (C) Jimin, what do you think about this painting?

➡ _____

[09~11] 다음 대화를 읽고 물음에 답하시오.

Jenny: (A) Look at the dancing girls, Dongjun. Aren't they amazing?
Dongjun: (B) Girls? I can only see one dancer.
Jenny: (C) Do you see many arms behind her?
Dongjun: (D) Wow. I didn't know that there were other dancers behind her.
Jenny: (E) That's right. I'm sure there are more than 10 dancers.

09 위 대화의 (A)~(E) 중 주어진 문장이 들어가기에 적절한 곳은?

> Look more closely.

① (A)　② (B)　③ (C)　④ (D)　⑤ (E)

10 위 대화를 읽고 동준이의 감정으로 적절한 것은?

① nervous　　② disappointed
③ lonely　　④ surprised
⑤ terrible

11 위 대화의 내용과 일치하지 <u>않는</u> 것은?

① Jenny와 동준이는 춤추는 여자들을 보고 있다.
② 동준이는 처음에 한 명의 무용수만 발견했다.
③ 많은 팔을 가진 한 명의 무용수를 발견할 수 있다.
④ 동준은 한 명의 무용수 뒤에 다른 무용수들이 있다는 것을 몰랐었다.
⑤ Jenny는 10명 이상의 무용수들이 있다는 것을 확신한다.

12 다음 대화에서 (A)~(E)가 자연스럽게 이어지도록 순서대로 배열하시오.

Junsu: You know what? The school dance contest will be held soon.
Emily: That's right. I heard Jimin's class is going to perform a taekwondo dance and Tim's class is going to do a K-pop dance.
(A) How about a *Buchaechum*? In my opinion, it is easy to learn, and it's also beautiful.
(B) Of course, I will. I'm sure we'll have a lot of fun.
(C) That sounds like a good idea. But who will teach us?
(D) We should also decide what to do.
(E) Mina is good at traditional dances. Can you help us, Mina?

➡ _____

[13~15] 다음 대화를 읽고 물음에 답하시오.

Emily: Hojun, did you know that some male birds dance?
Hojun: No. Why do they dance?
Emily: They dance to show their love to female birds.
Hojun: That's interesting. Do you know any other animals that can dance?
Emily: Yes, some bees dance to show (A)_____.
Hojun: That's cool! In my opinion, dancing is a great way to communicate.
Emily: (B)<u>I'm with you on that.</u> (agree)

13 위 대화의 빈칸 (A)에 '먹이를 찾을 수 있는 곳'을 뜻하도록 〈보기〉에 주어진 단어들 중 필요한 4단어만을 사용하여 완성하시오.

┌─── 보기 ────────────────┐
│ find / to / of / where / how / them / food │
└─────────────────────────┘

➡ _____

14 위 대화의 밑줄 친 (B)와 의미가 같도록 주어진 단어를 사용하여 다시 쓰시오.

➡ _____

15 위 대화를 읽고 대답할 수 없는 것은?

① Why do some male birds dance?
② What do some male birds want to show to female birds by dancing?
③ Why do some bees dance?
④ What does Hojun think about animals' dancing?
⑤ How do some animals communicate while dancing?

Grammar

16 다음 빈칸에 들어갈 말로 가장 적절한 것은?

┌─────────────────────────┐
│ The earrings are so precious _____ she always wears them. │
└─────────────────────────┘

① what   ② which   ③ too
④ that   ⑤ if

17 다음 문장과 같은 의미의 문장으로 가장 적절한 것은?

┌─────────────────────────┐
│ This river is the longest river in the world. │
└─────────────────────────┘

① No other river in the world is as short as this river.
② This river is not as long as the other rivers in the world.
③ No other river in the world is as long as this river.
④ This river is shorter than any other river in the world.
⑤ This river is not as short as the other rivers in the world.

18 주어진 단어를 활용하여 다음 우리말을 영어로 쓰시오.

┌─────────────────────────┐
│ 그녀는 매우 현명해. (as / owl) │
└─────────────────────────┘

➡ _____

19 다음 우리말을 영어로 바르게 옮긴 것을 모두 고르시오.

┌─────────────────────────┐
│ 그는 너무 어려서 그 책을 이해할 수 없었다. │
└─────────────────────────┘

① He is very young that he can't understand the book.
② He was so young that he couldn't understand the book.
③ He was young enough to understand the book.
④ He was so young that he could understand the book.
⑤ He was too young to understand the book.

20 다음 중 어법상 바르지 않은 것은?

① She reads as many books as I do.
② The boy is smart enough to speak five languages.
③ The train runs two times as fast as this train.
④ These shoes are too tight that I can't wear them.
⑤ I was happy enough to hold a party.

21 다음 중 빈칸에 들어갈 말로 가장 적절한 것은?

> The room is _____ that it can hold a hundred people.

① very big ② too big
③ so big ④ big enough
⑤ bigger than

22 다음 두 문장의 의미가 같도록 빈칸에 알맞은 말을 쓰시오.

> Tom is the tallest basketball player in America.
> = _____ _____ _____ _____
> in America _____ _____ _____
> _____ Tom.

23 다음 대화의 빈칸에 들어갈 말로 가장 적절한 것은?

> A: Did you drink the water?
> B: No, _____.
> A: Oh, let me warm up the water.

① it was too dangerous to eat
② it was so cold that I couldn't drink it
③ it was cold enough to drink
④ it was as cold as mine
⑤ it was too hot to drink

24 다음 표의 내용과 일치하지 않는 것은?

Rope A	Rope B	Rope C	Rope D
100cm	200cm	100cm	210cm

① Rope A is not as long as Rope B.
② Rope C is not as long as Rope D.
③ No other rope is as long as Rope B.
④ Rope A is as long as Rope C.
⑤ Rope B is not as long as Rope D.

25 주어진 단어를 활용하여 다음 우리말을 영어로 쓰시오.

> 나는 너무 행복해서 하루 종일 노래를 불렀어. (that / all day)

➡ _____

26 주어진 단어를 활용하여 다음 대화의 빈칸에 알맞은 말을 쓰시오.

> A: Is Sumin brave?
> B: Sure, she _____.
>   (as / a lion)

27 주어진 문장과 같은 의미의 문장을 쓰시오.

> He is too talkative to listen to others.

➡ _____

Reading

[28~32] 다음 글을 읽고 물음에 답하시오.

Why do people dance? They dance to express feelings, give happiness (A)_____ others, or enjoy themselves. Let's take a look at different (B)kinds of dance around the world.

India: *Kathakali*

Kathakali tells a story. The dancers tell stories through their body movements. These stories are usually about a fight between good and evil. Dancers who are playing good characters paint their faces green. Those who are playing evil characters wear black make-up. Interestingly, in *Kathakali*, only men are allowed to dance. The body movements are so powerful that the dancers need to train for many years.

28 다음 중 빈칸 (A)에 들어갈 말로 가장 적절한 것은?

① in   ② to   ③ at

④ on   ⑤ for

29 다음 중 밑줄 친 (B)와 쓰임이 같은 것은?

① James is very kind to animals.

② Exercises of this kind are very well known.

③ The weather was very kind to us.

④ Would you be kind enough to turn off the radio?

⑤ It's very kind of you to say so!

30 다음 중 위 글의 내용과 일치하지 <u>않는</u> 것은?

① By dancing, people can express their feelings.

② There are many types of dance around the world.

③ If you see someone wear black make-up in *Kathakali*, it means he is playing an evil character.

④ Performing *Kathakali* is limited to only men.

⑤ There is no need to train hard to perform a *Kathakali*.

31 What kind of story does *Kathakali* try to tell? Answer in English with a full sentence.

➡ _____

_____

32 According to the passage, how do the body movements of the dancers look? Answer in English with a full sentence.

➡ _____

[33~35] 다음 글을 읽고 물음에 답하시오.

Korea: *Buchaechum*

Buchaechum is a traditional Korean fan dance. The dancers wear colorful *hanbok*. They dance with large fans that are painted in bright colors. The dancers move the fans gracefully to show different kinds of beauty. Their movements look as beautiful as flowers or flying birds. In Korea, *Buchaechum* is so popular that people can see it in many traditional festivals.

33 다음 중 부채춤 공연에서 찾아볼 수 <u>없는</u> 것은?

① dancers wearing *hanbok*

② dancers moving gracefully

③ flowers and flying birds

④ fans painted in bright colors

⑤ beautiful movements of fans

34 다음 중 위 글을 읽고 답할 수 있는 것은?

① Who made *Buchaechum*?

② When was *Buchaechum* performed first?

③ How many fans are there in *Buchaechum*?

④ Why do the dancers move the fans gracefully?

⑤ How many people are needed to perform *Buchaechum*?

35 Write the reason why people can see *Buchaechum* in many traditional festivals in Korea. Use the word 'because.'

➡ _____

단원별 예상문제

[01~02] 다음 대화를 읽고 물음에 답하시오.

> Jane: Minsu, (a)저 그림에 대해 어떻게 생각해?
>
> Minsu: Umm ... The people look like they're having fun.
>
> Jane: (A)_____ In my opinion, the dancing boy really enjoys dancing.

출제율 90%

01 위 대화의 빈칸 (A)에 들어갈 말로 나머지와 의미가 다른 것은?

① I think so, too.

② I agree with you.

③ I believe so, too.

④ I disagree with you.

⑤ I see it that way, too.

출제율 100%

02 위 대화의 밑줄 친 (a)의 우리말을 〈보기〉에 주어진 단어를 배열하여 영작하시오.

> ┌─ 보기 ─┐
>
> about / painting / what / that / do / think / you

➡ _____

[03~05] 다음 대화를 읽고 물음에 답하시오.

> Emily: Hojun, did you know that some male birds dance?
>
> Hojun: No. Why do they dance?
>
> Emily: They dance to show their love to female birds.
>
> Hojun: That's interesting. Do you know any other animals that can dance?
>
> Emily: Yes, some bees dance to show where to find food.
>
> Hojun: That's cool! (A)_____, dancing is a great way to communicate.
>
> Emily: I totally agree with you.

출제율 90%

03 위 대화의 빈칸 (A)에 '내 의견으로는'을 의미하도록 3단어로 영작하시오.

➡ _____

출제율 95%

04 What do some male birds show by dancing?

➡ _____

출제율 90%

05 What information do some bees show by dancing?

➡ _____

[06~07] 다음 대화를 읽고 물음에 답하시오.

> Jenny: Look at the dancing girls, Dongjun. Aren't they (A)[amazed / amazing]?
>
> Dongjun: Girls? I can only see one dancer.
>
> Jenny: Look more closely. Do you see many arms behind her?
>
> Dongjun: Wow. I didn't know (B)[that / which] there were other dancers behind her.
>
> Jenny: That's right. I'm sure there (C)[is / are] more than 10 dancers.

출제율 95%

06 위 대화의 (A)~(C)에 들어갈 말이 바르게 짝지어진 것은?

	(A)	(B)	(C)
①	amazed	that	is
②	amazed	which	are
③	amazing	that	are
④	amazing	which	is
⑤	amazing	that	is

07 위 대화의 내용과 일치하도록 빈칸을 완성하시오.

> Dongjun: When I saw the dancing girls at first, I thought there was only one dancer. However, looking more closely again, I found that (A) _____ behind her. Because of many arms, I could guess that (B) _____ .

[08~10] 다음 대화를 읽고 물음에 답하시오.

> Junsu: You know what? The school dance contest will ⓐhold soon.
> Emily: That's right. I heard Jimin's class is going to perform a taekwondo dance and Tim's class is going to do a K-pop dance.
> Brian: We should also decide ⓑwhat to do.
> Mina: How about a *Buchaechum*? In my opinion, it is easy to learn, and it's also beautiful.
> Emily: That ⓒsounds like a good idea. But who will teach us?
> Brian: Mina ⓓis good at traditional dances. (A) Can you help us, Mina?
> Mina: Of course, I will. I'm sure we'll have a lot of fun.
> Junsu: Great. Let's ⓔgive it a try.

08 위 대화의 밑줄 친 ⓐ~ⓔ 중 어법상 어색한 것을 찾아 바르게 고치시오.

➡ _____

09 위 대화의 밑줄 친 (A)와 바꾸어 쓸 수 있는 것은?

① What can I do for you, Mina?
② Can you give us a hand, Mina?
③ How can I help you, Mina?
④ Do you need my help, Mina?
⑤ May I help you, Mina?

10 위 대화의 내용과 일치하지 않는 것은?

① 곧 학교 춤 대회가 열릴 것이다.
② 지민이네 반은 태권도 춤을 공연할 것이다.
③ Tim네 반은 K-pop 춤을 선보일 것이다.
④ 미나는 전통 춤을 잘 춘다.
⑤ 부채춤은 아름답지만 배우기가 어렵다.

11 주어진 단어를 사용하여 다음 문장과 같은 의미의 문장을 쓰시오.

> He is so funny that he can be a comedian. (to)

➡ _____

12 다음 중 의미하는 것이 다른 하나는?

① She is beautiful enough to be a movie star.
② She is so beautiful that she can be a movie star.
③ She can be a movie star because she is very beautiful.
④ She is very beautiful, so she can be a movie star.
⑤ She can be a movie star although she is beautiful.

13 다음 빈칸에 알맞은 말을 쓰시오.

> A: I heard that Leo has red hair, right?
> B: Yes. His hair is _____ _____ _____ a tomato.

14 다음 중 어법상 옳은 문장은?

① He is strong enough to moving it.

② She is too sad that she said nothing.

③ Your kite is as colorful as mine.

④ Ann was is as lighter as air when he danced with her.

⑤ This pond is too dangerous swim in.

15 주어진 단어를 이용하여 다음 두 문장을 하나의 문장으로 쓰시오.

> The dancer is so beautiful. I can't take my eyes off her. (that)

➡ _____

_____

16 다음 중 빈칸에 들어갈 말로 가장 적절한 것은?

> I am so sick _____ .

① because I want to go to school

② that I can't get up

③ so I enjoy my holiday

④ that I play with my friends

⑤ that I am excited

17 다음 우리말을 영어로 바르게 옮기지 않은 것은?

① 너는 나보다 두 배만큼 많이 잔다.

→ You sleep two times as much as I do.

② 그 도서관은 쥐 죽은 듯이 조용해.

→ The library is as quiet as a mouse.

③ 나는 가능한 한 빨리 네가 이곳에 도착하길 바란다.

→ I hope you arrive here as soon as possible.

④ 그 자동차는 그 나라에서 가장 빠르다.

→ No other cars in the country is as fast as the car.

⑤ 네 방은 내 방만큼 지저분하지 않아.

→ Your room is not as messy as my room.

[18~21] 다음 글을 읽고 물음에 답하시오.

New Zealand: *Haka*

When people visit New Zealand, they may meet a group of *haka* dancers. The dancers ①perform this traditional dance with ②scared faces. This dance was ③originally performed by the Maori before a fight. They wanted to show ④their strength to the enemy. The dancers looked as scary as ⑤wild animals before fighting. (A)Nowadays, in New Zealand, rugby players usually perform a *haka* before a game to show their strength to the other team.

18 밑줄 친 (A)를 대신하여 쓰일 수 있는 것으로 가장 적절한 것은?

① At last   ② Suddenly

③ These days   ④ All at once

⑤ Fortunately

19 ①~⑤ 중 글의 흐름상 어색한 것은?

①   ②   ③   ④   ⑤

20 다음 중 글의 내용과 일치하는 것은?

① It is hard to see people perform a *haka* in New Zealand.

② The Maori learned how to perform a *haka* from other tribes.

③ Before performing a *haka*, the Maori fought the enemy.

④ You can see the *haka* at rugby matches nowadays.

⑤ The Maori performed the *haka* to find better mates.

21 What did the Maori want to do by performing a *haka*?

➡ _____

[22~23] 다음 글을 읽고 물음에 답하시오.

Tarantella, Italy

In the past, people danced the *tarantella* for sick people. Nowadays, it is a couple's dance. People dance the *tarantella* (A)_____ happy days such as weddings.

Adumu, Kenya

This dance is performed before a fight. It is also called a jumping dance. Dancers jump high in the air. When a dancer jumps, other dancers cheer him on with loud noises.

22 빈칸 (A)에 들어갈 말로 가장 적절한 것은?

① in   ② about   ③ at
④ to   ⑤ on

23 다음 중 위 글을 읽고 답할 수 <u>없는</u> 것은?

① Why did people dance the *tarantella* in the past?
② Who dances the *tarantella* these days?
③ Where can we see people dance the *tarantella*?
④ What do other dancers do when dancers jump high while dancing *Adumu*?
⑤ What do dancers need to perform the *adumu*?

[24~25] 다음 글을 읽고 물음에 답하시오.

Korea: *Buchaechum*

Buchaechum is a traditional Korean fan dance. The dancers wear colorful *hanbok*. They dance with large fans that are painted in bright colors. The dancers move the fans gracefully to show different kinds of beauty. Their movements look as beautiful as flowers or flying birds. In Korea, *Buchaechum* is so popular that people can see it in many traditional festivals.

24 What do the dancers' movements look like? Answer in English with a full sentence.

➡ _____

25 위 글의 내용에 맞게 빈칸에 알맞은 말을 쓰시오.

According to the passage, we need _____ _____ and _____ _____ _____ _____ bright colors to dance *Buchaechum*.

[01~03] 다음 대화를 읽고 물음에 답하시오.

> Junsu: You know what? The school dance contest will be held soon.
>
> Emily: That's right. I heard Jimin's class is going to perform a taekwondo dance and Tim's class is going to do a K-pop dance.
>
> Brian: We should also decide what to do.
>
> Mina: How about a *Buchaechum*? In my opinion, it is easy to learn, and it's also beautiful.
>
> Emily: That sounds like a good idea. But who will teach us?
>
> Brian: Mina is good at traditional dances. Can you help us, Mina?
>
> Mina: Of course, I will. I'm sure we'll have a lot of fun.
>
> Junsu: Great. Let's give it a try.

01 What is Jimin's class going to perform at the school dance contest?

➡ _____

02 What is Mina good at?

➡ _____

03 What does Mina think about a *Buchaechum*?

➡ _____

_____

04 다음 주어진 문장과 같은 의미의 문장을 쓰시오.

> I can't dance in front of many people because I am too shy.

(1) to부정사를 사용하여

➡ _____

(2) that절을 사용하여

➡ _____

05 다음 대화를 읽고 빈칸에 알맞은 말을 쓰시오.

> A: I'm planning to buy a bike. How about you, Brian?
>
> B: I don't need one. It's because my bike still works well.

➡ Brian's bike _____ he doesn't want to buy another one.

06 다음 글을 하나의 문장으로 표현하시오.

> The diamond ring is 20,000 dollars. It is expensive. The car is the same price.

➡ _____

07 다음 주어진 단어를 이용해 우리말을 영어로 쓰시오.

> 그녀는 거북이만큼 느려. (turtle)

➡ _____

08 주어진 어구를 바르게 배열하여 다음 우리말을 영어로 쓰시오.

> 그 파티는 너무 즐거워서 누구도 떠나길 원치 않았다.
> (leave / the party / so / enjoyable / was / to / nobody / that / wanted)

➡ _____

_____

[09~10] 다음 글을 읽고 물음에 답하시오.

India: *Kathakali*

Kathakali tells a story. The dancers tell stories through their body movements. These stories are usually about a fight between good and evil. Dancers who are playing good characters paint their faces green. Those who are playing evil characters wear black make-up. Interestingly, in *Kathakali*, only men are allowed to dance. The body movements are so powerful that the dancers need to train for many years.

09 다음은 카타할리 공연을 보고 있는 친구들의 대화이다. 빈칸에 알맞은 말을 쓰시오.

> A: I don't understand what the dance tries to say.
> B: Let me explain. Do you see the man whose face is _____? He is playing a good character.
> A: Really? That's interesting. Then, what about the man who is _____ _____ _____?
> B: He is playing an _____ _____.

10 위 글의 내용을 바탕으로 *Kathakali*를 소개하는 홍보 글을 완성하시오.

> *Kathakali* is a traditional dance in _____. The dancers tell _____ about a fight between _____. Interestingly, only _____ are allowed to dance. The body movements are so _____ that the dancers need to train for many years.

[11~12] 다음 글을 읽고 물음에 답하시오.

Come and Enjoy the Step Dance

A step dance is a traditional dance in Ireland. The dancers wear colorful costumes. In my opinion, (A)_____. The dancers move their feet so fast that they look like they're flying!

11 원급 비교 표현을 이용하여 다음 두 문장을 하나의 문장으로 빈칸 (A)에 쓰시오.

> The dancers look cute. They are like dolls.

➡ _____

12 위 글의 내용에 맞게 빈칸에 알맞은 말을 쓰시오.

> The dancers who do a step dance move their feet _____ _____ _____ it is hard to see their feet!

01 다음 대화의 내용과 일치하도록 Kelly의 일기를 완성하시오.

> **Tom:** What are you reading, Kelly?
> **Kelly:** I'm reading a story about Michaela DePrince.
> **Tom:** Michaela DePrince? Can you tell me more about her?
> **Kelly:** Sure. Michaela lost her parents when she was three. After that, she had a lot of difficulties. But she never gave up on her dream of becoming a dancer.
> **Tom:** Wow, she worked very hard to be a good dancer. Kelly, you also have a dream to be a dancer, right?
> **Kelly:** Yes. I will try my best to be a great dancer like her.
> **Tom:** Keep up the good work. I'm sure you can make it.

Mon, Oct 7th, 2019

Today, I read a story about Michaela DePrince. The reason why I chose this book is that I want to be (A)_____ like her. The story was so impressive that I shared it with Tom. I explained Michaela's story to Tom including her difficulties and her great efforts to become (B)_____. After reading her story, I decided to (C)_____. Tom also encouraged me a lot, so I appreciated him.

02 'so ~ that' 구문을 이용하여 두 문장을 의미에 맞게 연결하시오.

The wind was very strong.	It blew my hat off my head.
The soup was very hot.	I couldn't eat it.
She is very friendly.	She will throw a party for us.

(1) _____

(2) _____

(3) _____

03 다음은 아일랜드 전통 춤에 관한 사실과 의견이다. 이를 참고하여 아일랜드 전통 춤을 소개하는 글을 완성하시오.

> Step Dance, Ireland
> Fact 1 – wear colorful costumes
> Opinion 1 – look like cute dolls
> Fact 2 – move their feet fast
> Opinion 2 – look like they're flying

A step dance is a traditional dance in _____. The dancers _____. In my opinion, the dancers look _____. The dancers _____ that they look _____!

단원별 모의고사

01 다음 영영풀이가 가리키는 것을 고르시오.

> a particular type of clothing worn by all the members of a group or organization such as the police, the army, etc.

① dress
② uniform
③ movement
④ culture
⑤ costume

02 다음 문장의 빈칸에 들어갈 말을 〈보기〉에서 골라 쓰시오. (필요하면 변형할 것.)

> ┤ 보기 ├
> be good at / good and evil / have fun /
> take a look / give up on

(1) Why don't you go out and _____ at the festival?

(2) Let's _____ at some traditional games in Scotland.

(3) It's the story of a fight between _____.

(4) She _____ dancing.

(5) Don't _____ your dream.

[03~04] 다음 대화를 읽고 물음에 답하시오.

Junsu: You know what? The school dance contest will be held soon.

Emily: That's right. I heard Jimin's class is going to perform a taekwondo dance and Tim's class is going to do a K-pop dance.

Brian: We should also decide what to do.

Mina: How about a *Buchaechum*? In my opinion, it is easy to learn, and it's also beautiful.

Emily: That sounds like a good idea. But who will teach us?

Brian: Mina is good at traditional dances. Can you help us, Mina?

Mina: Of course, I will. (A)_____

Junsu: Great. Let's give it a try.

03 위 대화의 빈칸 (A)에 들어갈 말을 〈보기〉에 주어진 단어들을 모두 배열하여 완성하시오.

> ┤ 보기 ├
> we'll / I'm / of / have / fun / sure / lot / a

➡ _____

04 위 대화를 읽고 대답할 수 <u>없는</u> 것은?

① What is Jimin's class going to perform?
② What does Mina think about a *Buchaechum*?
③ What kind of dance is Tim's class going to perform?
④ What is Mina good at?
⑤ Why did Jimin's class choose a taekwondo dance?

[05~07] 다음 대화를 읽고 물음에 답하시오.

Tom: What are you reading, Kelly?

Kelly: (A) I'm reading a story about Michaela DePrince.

Tom: (B) Michaela DePrince? Can you tell me more about her?

Kelly: (C) After that, she had a lot of difficulties. But she never gave up on her dream of becoming a dancer.

Tom: (D) Wow, she worked very hard to be a good dancer. Kelly, you also have a dream to be a dancer, right?

Kelly: (E) Yes. I will ⓐtry my best to be a great dancer like her.

Tom: Keep up the good work. I'm sure you can make it.

05 위 대화의 (A)~(E) 중 주어진 문장이 들어가기에 적절한 곳은?

> Sure. Michaela lost her parents when she was three.

① (A) ② (B) ③ (C) ④ (D) ⑤ (E)

06 위 대화의 밑줄 친 ⓐ와 바꾸어 쓸 수 있는 것은?

① do ② work ③ take
④ make ⑤ have

07 위 대화의 내용과 일치하지 <u>않는</u> 것은?

① Michaela는 3살 때 부모님을 잃었다.
② Michaela는 부모님을 잃은 후 많은 역경을 겪었다.
③ Michaela는 무용수가 되겠다는 꿈을 절대 포기하지 않았다.
④ Michaela는 훌륭한 무용수가 되기 위해 굉장히 열심히 노력했다.
⑤ Michaela는 무용수로 계속 좋은 일들을 하고 있다.

08 다음 대화의 (A)~(C)에 들어갈 말이 바르게 짝지어진 것은?

> Minji: I use my voice to make music. Listen to my music. My voice is soft and cool. I'm sure you will like it.
>
> Jimin: I move my body to (A)[impress / express] my feelings. Look at my movements. Why don't you jump like me? I'm (B)[certain / unsure] you'll feel great.
>
> Sujin: I use my hands to make sounds. Come and listen to my music. I'm sure you'll want to dance (C)[what / when] you listen to it.

	(A)	(B)	(C)
①	impress	certain	what
②	impress	unsure	when
③	express	certain	when
④	express	unsure	when
⑤	express	certain	what

09 다음 대화가 자연스럽게 이어지도록 순서대로 배열하시오.

> Emily: Hojun, did you know that some male birds dance?
>
> Hojun: No. Why do they dance?
>
> (A) Yes, some bees dance to show where to find food.
>
> (B) They dance to show their love to female birds.
>
> (C) I totally agree with you.
>
> (D) That's interesting. Do you know any other animals that can dance?
>
> (E) That's cool! In my opinion, dancing is a great way to communicate.

➡ _____

[10~11] 다음 대화를 읽고 물음에 답하시오.

> Minji: I use my voice to make music. Listen to my music. My voice is soft and cool. I'm sure you will like it.
>
> Jimin: I move my body to express my feelings. Look at my movements. Why don't you jump like me? I'm sure you'll feel great.
>
> Sujin: I use my hands to make sounds. Come and listen to my music. I'm sure you'll want to dance when you listen to it.

10 What does Minji use to make music?

➡ _____

11 Why does Jimin move her body?

➡ _____

12 다음 중 어법상 바르지 <u>않은</u> 것은?

① She was not as lazy as my sister.
② The coffee tastes so great that I will have another cup.
③ No other city in Korea is as big as Seoul.
④ Mina and Sujin is the same age. Mina is as old as Sujin.
⑤ Your nail is twice longer as mine.

13 다음 우리말을 영어로 바르게 옮긴 것은?

나는 그녀만큼 빠르게 달릴 수 없어.

① I can run not as fast as she.
② I can't run as faster as she.
③ I can't run as fast as she.
④ I can run as fast as she.
⑤ She can run as fast as I.

14 다음 문장과 같은 의미의 문장으로 가장 적절한 것은?

It was raining heavily. So we canceled the field trip.

① It was raining heavily enough to cancel the field trip.
② It was raining too heavily that we canceled the field trip.
③ We canceled the field trip although it was raining heavily.
④ It was raining so heavily that we canceled the field trip.
⑤ It was raining heavily because we canceled the field trip.

15 주어진 단어를 활용하여 다음 우리말을 영어로 쓰시오.

그녀는 매우 바빠. (as / bee)

➡ _____

16 주어진 단어를 활용하여 다음 우리말을 영어로 쓰시오.

그 영화는 너무 감동적이어서 나는 많이 울었어. (moving / a lot)

➡ _____

[17~18] 다음 글을 읽고 물음에 답하시오.

Why do people dance? ①They dance ②to express feelings, give happiness ③to others, or ④enjoying themselves. Let's take a look ⑤at different kinds of dance around the world.

17 위 글에 이어질 내용으로 가장 적절한 것은?

① various kinds of feelings
② why people like to dance
③ various kinds of dance around the world
④ what people do when they are happy
⑤ some reasons why people enjoy watching dances

18 ①~⑤ 중 어법상 바르지 <u>않은</u> 것은?

①   ②   ③   ④   ⑤

[19~20] 다음 글을 읽고 물음에 답하시오.

Korea: *Buchaechum*

 Buchaechum is a traditional Korean fan dance. The dancers wear colorful *hanbok*. They dance with large fans that are painted in bright colors. The dancers move the fans gracefully to show different kinds of beauty. Their movements look as (A)_____ as flowers or flying birds. In Korea, *Buchaechum* is so popular that people can see it in many traditional festivals.

19 빈칸 (A)에 들어갈 말로 가장 적절한 것은?

① difficult   ② beautiful
③ boring   ④ annoying
⑤ embarrassing

20 위 글의 제목으로 가장 적절한 것은?

① Come and Dance *Buchaechum* with Us
② *Buchaechum*, Most Loved Dance in Korea
③ Korean Traditional Dance, *Buchaechum*
④ Useful Tool, A Korean Fan
⑤ Enjoy the Beauty of Korea with Flowers

[21~24] 다음 글을 읽고 물음에 답하시오.

New Zealand: *Haka*

 When people visit New Zealand, they may meet a group of *haka* dancers. The dancers ① perform this traditional dance with ②scary faces. This dance was originally performed by the Maori before a fight. (A)They wanted to show their ③strength to the ④enemy. The dancers looked as scary as ⑤wild animals before fighting. Nowadays, in New Zealand, rugby players usually perform a *haka* before a game to show (B)their strength to the other team.

21 밑줄 친 (A)와 (B)가 가리키는 것을 각각 쓰시오.

➡ (A) _____   (B) _____

22 Why do rugby players in New Zealand usually perform a *haka* before a game? Answer in English with a full sentence.

➡ _____
   _____

23 위 글의 내용에 맞게 다음 물음에 완전한 문장의 영어로 답하시오.

Q: When did the Maori originally perform a *haka*?

➡ _____

24 다음 중 ①~⑤의 풀이로 적절하지 않은 것은?

① to entertain an audience by singing or acting
② rather frightening
③ the state of being weak
④ someone who attacks or tries to harm another
⑤ living in nature without human control or care

Lesson 7

Magic or Science?

 의사소통 기능

- 질문하기
  Which sport do you want to learn?
- 희망·기대 표현하기
  I can't wait to see the difference.

 언어 형식

- 가주어 It
  It is exciting **to watch** a magic show.
- How come ...?
  How come the water rose into the glass?

Words & Expressions

Key Words

- **abracadabra** [æbrəkədǽbrə] 몡 수리수리마수리 (주문)
- **absorb** [æbsɔ́ːrb] 동 흡수하다
- **balloon** [bəlúːn] 몡 풍선
- **behind** [biháind] 전 ~ 뒤에
- **candle** [kǽndl] 몡 양초
- **coin** [kɔin] 몡 동전
- **compare** [kəmpɛ́ər] 동 비교하다
- **confuse** [kənfjúːz] 동 혼동하게 하다
- **contract** [kəntrǽkt] 동 수축하다
- **difference** [dífərəns] 몡 차이, 차이점
- **disappear** [dìsəpíər] 동 사라지다
- **dry** [drai] 형 마른, 비가 오지 않는
- **escape** [iskéip] 동 탈출하다, (액체, 가스가) 새다
- **expand** [ikspǽnd] 동 팽창하다
- **experiment** [ikspérəmənt] 몡 실험
- **fill** [fil] 동 채우다
- **flame** [fleim] 몡 불꽃
- **flavor** [fléivər] 몡 맛
- **float** [flout] 동 뜨다
- **freezer** [fríːzər] 몡 냉동고
- **hold** [hould] 동 잡다, 쥐다

- **instead** [instéd] 부 대신에
- **lightning** [láitniŋ] 몡 번개
- **magic** [mǽdʒik] 몡 마술, 마법
- **material** [mətíəriəl] 몡 재료, 물질
- **mix** [miks] 동 섞다
- **move** [muːv] 동 움직이다
- **necessary** [nésəsèri] 형 필요한
- **ocean** [óuʃən] 몡 대양, 바다
- **practice** [prǽktis] 몡 연습
- **prepare** [pripɛ́ər] 동 준비하다
- **pressure** [préʃər] 몡 압력
- **push** [puʃ] 동 밀다
- **rise** [raiz] 동 오르다, 올라가다
- **rose** [rouz] 몡 장미
- **safe** [seif] 형 안전한
- **secret** [síːkrit] 몡 비밀
- **sink** [siŋk] 동 가라앉다
- **sunburn** [sʌ́nbərn] 몡 볕에 탐
- **sunscreen** [sʌ́nskrìːn] 몡 자외선 차단제
- **trick** [trik] 몡 마술, 속임수
- **weigh** [wei] 동 무게를 재다

Key Expressions

- **a glass of** 한 잔의
- **burn out** 타 버리다
- **cool down** 차가워지다
- **dry season** 건기
- **for a long time** 오랫동안
- **give it a try** 시도해 보다

- **pick out** 골라내다
- **see through** 속을 들여다 보다
- **sign up for** ~을 신청하다
- **some day** 언젠가, 머지않아
- **stick to** ~을 (바꾸지 않고) 고수하다
- **turn A into B** A가 B로 변하다

Word Power

※ 서로 반대되는 뜻을 가진 어휘

- □ **contract** 수축하다 ↔ **expand** 팽창하다
- □ **dry** 건조한 ↔ **wet** 젖은
- □ **behind** ~ 뒤에 ↔ **in front of** ~ 앞에
- □ **necessary** 필요한 ↔ **unnecessary** 불필요한
- □ **safe** 안전한 ↔ **dangerous** 위험한
- □ **sink** 가라앉다 ↔ **float** 뜨다

- □ **fill** 채우다 ↔ **empty** 비우다
- □ **mix** 섞다 ↔ **separate** 분리하다
- □ **appear** 나타나다 ↔ **disappear** 사라지다
- □ **rise** 올라가다 ↔ **drop** 떨어지다
- □ **careful** 주의 깊은 ↔ **careless** 부주의한
- □ **absorb** 흡수하다 ↔ **release** 방출하다

English Dictionary

- □ **absorb** 흡수하다
  → to take in something in a natural or gradual way
  자연스럽거나 점차적인 방식으로 무언가를 받아들이다

- □ **confuse** 혼동하다
  → to mistake one person or thing for another
  누군가 또는 어떤 것을 다른 것으로 잘못 알다

- □ **contract** 수축하다
  → to become smaller
  더 작아지다

- □ **expand** 팽창하다
  → to increase in size, range, or amount
  크기, 범위, 또는 양에서 증가하다

- □ **float** 뜨다
  → to rest on top of a liquid or in the air
  액체 맨 윗부분에 또는 공기 중에 있다

- □ **freezer** 냉동고
  → a device or room for freezing food or keeping it frozen
  음식을 얼리거나 언 채로 유지되도록 하기 위한 장치 또는 공간

- □ **magic** 마술의
  → having the power to make impossible things happen
  불가능한 일들이 일어나게 만드는 힘을 가진

- □ **material** 물질, 재료
  → a substance that things can be made from
  무언가가 그로부터 만들 수 있는 재료

- □ **mix** 섞다
  → to combine two or more substances so that they become a single substance
  두 개 이상의 물질을 결합하여 하나의 물질이 되게 하다

- □ **practice** 연습
  → the activity of doing something again and again in order to become better at it
  더 잘하기 위해 무언가를 계속해서 하는 활동

- □ **secret** 비밀
  → a piece of information that is kept hidden from other people 다른 사람들에게 숨겨진 정보

- □ **sink** 가라앉다
  → to go down below the surface of water
  물의 표면 아래로 내려가다

- □ **trick** 속임수, 마술
  → something done to surprise or confuse someone
  누군가를 놀라게 하거나 혼란시키기 위해 행해지는 것

- □ **weigh** 무게를 재다
  → to find how heavy someone or something is
  누군가 또는 무언가가 얼마나 무거운지 알아내다

서답형

01 다음 짝지어진 단어의 관계가 같도록 빈칸에 알맞은 말을 쓰시오.

> increase : decrease = appear : _____

02 다음 영영풀이가 가리키는 것을 고르시오.

> to increase in size, range, or amount

① expand　　　② sink
③ float　　　　④ weigh
⑤ hold

중요

03 다음 중 밑줄 친 부분의 뜻풀이가 바르지 <u>않은</u> 것은?

① The material doesn't <u>absorb</u> the water. 흡수하다
② Which things will Ms. Jeong <u>weigh</u> for the test? 무게를 재다
③ I want to learn how to hold a <u>flame</u> without burning my hands. 불꽃
④ I always <u>confuse</u> your bag and mine. 비교하다
⑤ Can you tell me the <u>secret</u> of success? 비밀

04 다음 문장에 공통으로 들어갈 말을 고르시오.

> • It is _____ to prepare something for a dry season.
> • This machine is _____ for treating disease.
> • Exercise is _____ to keep your health.

① safe　　　　② necessary
③ confusing　　④ amazing
⑤ dry

중요

05 다음 주어진 문장의 밑줄 친 rose와 같은 의미로 쓰인 것은?

> The sales <u>rose</u> by 20 percent last week.

① The cloud of smoke <u>rose</u> suddenly.
② She drew a <u>rose</u> on her note.
③ Some flowers, like <u>roses</u>, need special care.
④ The prince was looking for a <u>rose</u>.
⑤ When I smelled the <u>rose</u>, I felt so happy.

서답형

06 다음 우리말에 맞게 빈칸에 알맞은 말을 쓰시오.

(1) 우리는 경비원들을 속이고 지나가기 위해 속임수를 생각해 내야 했다.
➡ We had to think of _____ to get past the guards.

(2) 나는 특별한 물질을 컵 하나에 넣어 두었다.
➡ I put a special _____ into one of the cups.

(3) 우리 아빠는 나를 위해 매일 아침을 준비하신다.
➡ My father always _____ breakfast for me every day.

(4) 당신은 속을 들여다볼 수 없는 컵을 사용하는 것이 필요하다.
➡ It's _____ to use cups that you can't see through.

(5) 공기는 더 높은 압력을 생성한다.
➡ Air creates higher _____.

(6) 회사의 확장 계획에 대해 어떻게 생각하세요?
➡ What do you think of the company's plans to _____?

01 다음 짝지어진 단어의 관계가 같도록 빈칸에 알맞은 말을 쓰시오.

> contract : expand = sink : _____

02 다음 문장의 빈칸에 들어갈 말을 〈보기〉에서 골라 쓰시오.

┌─ 보기 ─┐
stick to / cooled down / see through /
turn ~ into / burned out
└─────┘

(1) I can't _____ _____ the window.
(2) The magician can _____ rain _____ snow.
(3) After an hour, the candle _____ _____.
(4) The weather has _____ _____ a little.
(5) I _____ _____ what I think I am good at.

03 다음 우리말을 주어진 단어를 이용하여 영작하시오.

(1) 우리는 물고기 대신에 손가락을 사용할 수 있다.
➡ We can use a finger _____ of a fish.

(2) 달걀이 물에 뜰 때, 그것들은 신선하지 않다.
➡ When eggs _____ in water, they're not fresh.

(3) 마술 공연을 보는 것은 흥미롭다.
➡ It's exciting to watch a _____ show.

(4) 그것이 물을 유리컵 속으로 밀었다.
➡ It _____ the water into the glass.

04 다음 우리말과 일치하도록 주어진 어구를 모두 배열하여 영작하시오.

(1) 네가 싫어하는 채소들을 골라내는 것은 좋지 않다.
(that / good / to / it / don't / is / pick out / not / you / like / vegetables)
➡ _____
_____

(2) 내가 시도해 볼게.
(it / I'll / a / give / try)
➡ _____

(3) 졸리면, 차가운 물 한 잔을 마셔라.
(drink / if / sleepy / are / you / water / cold / a glass / of)
➡ _____

(4) 나는 배드민턴 수업을 신청했다.
(the / class / badminton / signed / for / up / I)
➡ _____

05 다음 문장의 빈칸에 들어갈 말을 〈보기〉에서 골라 쓰시오.

┌─ 보기 ─┐
hold / coin / sunburn / expands /
escape / contract
└─────┘

(1) It is necessary to wear sunscreen to prevent _____.
(2) _____ the bottle in your hands for a while.
(3) As the air gets warm, it _____.
(4) You can see how a _____ dances in a bottle.
(5) The expanding air tries to _____ from the bottle.
(6) When you bend your arms, your muscles _____.

1 질문하기

Which sport do you want to learn? 너는 어느 운동을 배우고 싶니?

- 'Which …?'는 '어느[어떤] …?'라는 뜻으로, 어떤 것을 선택하고자 하는지 묻는 표현이다. Which 뒤에는 sport, flavor, activity 등의 표현이 온다.

질문하기

- Which sport do you like? Badminton or soccer? 너는 어느 운동을 좋아하니? 배드민턴 또는 축구?
- What's your favorite color? 가장 좋아하는 색이 무엇이니?

선호 말하기

- I like soccer most[best]. 나는 축구를 가장 좋아한다.
- I love playing basketball. 나는 농구하기를 매우 좋아한다.
- I'm fond of ~. 나는 ~을 좋아한다.
- My favorite sport is dodge ball. 내가 가장 좋아하는 운동은 피구이다.
- I enjoy playing baseball (very much). 나는 야구하기를 (매우) 즐긴다.

핵심 Check

1. 다음 우리말과 일치하도록 빈칸에 알맞은 말을 쓰시오.

(1) **A:** _____ _____ do you want to visit the most? (너는 어느 나라를 가장 방문하고 싶니?)

   B: I want to visit Indonesia. (나는 인도네시아를 방문하고 싶어.)

(2) **A:** _____ _____ does Sejun want to play? (세준이는 어느 운동을 하고 싶어 하니?)

   B: He wants to play basketball. (그는 농구를 하고 싶어 해.)

(3) **A:** _____ _____ _____ _____, a straw or a potato?

   (짚과 감자 중 어느 것이 더 강하니?)

   B: It's a potato, isn't it? (감자야, 그렇지 않니?)

② 희망·기대 표현하기

I can't wait to see the difference. 나는 빨리 그 차이를 보고 싶어.

- "I can't wait to …'는 '나는 …이 무척 기다려져.'라는 뜻으로, 희망이나 기대를 말할 때 쓰는 표현이다. to 뒤에는 동사원형이 온다. 이 표현은 'I'm looking forward to -ing'로 바꿔 쓸 수 있다.

바라거나 기대하는 일 표현하기

- I can't wait for the cooking class. 나는 요리 수업이 매우 기대가 된다.
- I can't wait to go on a picnic. 나는 소풍가는 것이 매우 기대된다.
- I'm looking forward to meeting my friend. 나는 내 친구를 만나기를 기대하고 있다.
- I really want to visit the museum. 나는 정말로 박물관에 가고 싶다.

핵심 Check

2. 다음 우리말과 일치하도록 빈칸에 알맞은 말을 쓰시오.

(1) **A:** We are going to visit the science museum. (우리는 과학 박물관에 방문할 거야.)

   B: I _____ _____ to go there. (나는 빨리 그곳에 가고 싶어.)

(2) **A:** What are you going to do this Sunday? (이번 주 일요일에 무엇을 할 예정이니?)

   B: I'm going to visit my grandparents. I'm _____ _____ _____ _____ them. (나는 그들을 만나기를 무척 기대하고 있어.)

(3) **A:** I _____ _____ _____ _____ _____ _____.

   (나는 너를 다시 빨리 보고 싶어.)

   B: Me too.

Conversation 교과서 대화문 익히기

Listen and Speak 1 A

W: Today we'll make ice cream. ❶Which ❷flavor do you want to make? ❸How about strawberry? First, mix two cups of milk, two cups of heavy cream, and half a cup of sugar. ❹Next, cut five strawberries into small pieces. Then, mix everything together and put it in the freezer. That's it. It's easy to make, isn't it? Why don't you ❺try making it at home?

W: 오늘 우리는 아이스크림을 만들 거예요. 여러분은 어느 맛을 만들고 싶은가요? 딸기는 어때요? 첫째로, 우유 2컵, 헤비 크림 2컵, 설탕 1/2컵을 섞으세요. 다음, 딸기 5개를 작은 조각으로 자르세요. 그 다음에, 모든 것을 섞어서 냉동실에 넣으세요. 이게 다예요. 만들기 쉽죠, 그렇지 않나요? 집에서 아이스크림을 만들어 보는 게 어때요?

❶ 'Which ~?'는 '어느[어떤] ~?'라는 뜻으로 어느 것을 선택하고자 하는지 묻는 표현이다.
❷ flavor: 맛
❸ How about ~? = What about ~?: '~는 어때?'라는 제안을 나타낸다.
❹ Next = Second
❺ try -ing: ~해 보다, cf. try to ~: ~하려고 노력하다

Check(√) True or False

(1) The woman explains how to make strawberry ice cream.　　　T ☐ F ☐

(2) The woman needs a cup of sugar to make ice cream.　　　T ☐ F ☐

Listen and Speak 2 A

B: Ms. Jeong, does ❶a glass of water ❷weigh more when there's a fish in it?
W: Yes, it does. We can test it now.
B: But how? We don't have a fish.
W: We can use a finger ❸instead of a fish.
B: How will that work?
W: I'll weigh a glass of water first. Then I will put my finger in the water and weigh it to ❹compare.
B: Oh, ❺I can't wait to see the difference.

B: 정 선생님, 물속에 물고기가 있을 때 물 1잔의 무게가 더 무겁나요?
W: 응, 그렇단다. 우리는 지금 실험해 볼 수 있어.
B: 하지만 어떻게요? 물고기가 없는데요.
W: 우리는 물고기 대신 손가락을 사용할 수 있단다.
B: 어떻게 할 수 있어요?
W: 먼저 물 1잔의 무게를 잴 거야. 그 다음에 비교하기 위해 물속에 손가락을 넣고 무게를 잴 거란다.
B: 아, 차이를 빨리 알고 싶어요.

❶ a glass of: 한 잔의
❷ weigh: 무게를 재다, cf. weight: 무게
❸ instead of: ~ 대신에
❹ compare: 비교하다
❺ I can't wait to ~ = I'm looking forward to -ing: 매우 ~하고 싶다, ~을 기대하다

Check(√) True or False

(3) They don't have a fish now.　　　T ☐ F ☐

(4) The finger will be used to do an experiment.　　　T ☐ F ☐

Listen and Speak 1 B

B: Yujin, why did you ❶put the eggs in water?

G: I'm ❷picking out the bad eggs.

B: Which eggs are fresh, and which ❸ones are not?

G: Eggs ❹that ❺sink in water are fresh. When eggs ❻float in water, they're not fresh. You shouldn't eat them.

B: That's interesting. Why do the bad eggs float?

G: Because they have gas inside. The gas acts like the air in a balloon.

B: Oh, I see.

❶ put A in B: A를 B에 넣다
❷ pick out: 골라내다
❸ ones = eggs
❹ 주격 관계대명사로 which로 바꾸어 쓸 수 있다.
❺ sink: 가라앉다
❻ float: 뜨다

Listen and Speak 2 B

King Sejong: It ❶hasn't rained ❷for a long time.

Jang Yeongsil: Yes. The ❸dry season is ❹lasting too long. The farmers are very worried.

King Sejong: We should do something to help ❺ them.

Jang Yeongsil: How about making a special clock?

King Sejong: A clock? How will that help?

Jang Yeongsil: The clock will show the time and the seasons. We can use ❻it to prepare for the dry season.

King Sejong: That sounds like a good idea. But who's going to make it?

Jang Yeongsil: I'll ❼give it a try. I know a lot about time and the seasons.

King Sejong: Okay, I can't wait to see your clock.

❶ 현재완료 시제가 쓰였다.
❷ for a long time: 오랫동안
❸ dry season 건기
❹ last: 지속되다
❺ them = farmers
❻ it = the clock
❼ give it a try: 시도해 보다

Real Life Communication A

Brian: Mina, will you join our tennis club?

Mina: It sounds interesting, but I ❶signed up for a special class this fall.

Brian: Which class did you sign up for?

Mina: I signed up for a magic class. ❷I can't wait to learn new magic ❸tricks there.

Brian: That sounds cool! ❹Have you learned magic tricks before?

Mina: Yes, I learned some before, but I need more practice.

Brian: I hope I can see your magic tricks some day.

❶ sign up for: ~을 신청하다
❷ 'I'm looking forward to learning new magic tricks there.'로 바꾸어 쓸 수 있다.
❸ trick: 마술, 속임수
❹ 현재완료 시제로 경험을 묻고 있다.

Let's Check

B: What are you reading, Jiwon?

G: I'm reading a book about magic and science.

B: That sounds interesting.

G: Yes. This book ❶introduces 100 magic tricks ❷that use science. I've learned about half of them.

B: That's cool. Can you show me some of the tricks?

G: Sure. I can show you a ❸balloon trick now.

B: Great! I can't wait to see ❹it.

❶ introduce: 소개하다
❷ 관계대명사로 which로 바꾸어 쓸 수 있다.
❸ ballon: 풍선
❹ it = a balloon trick

● 다음 우리말과 일치하도록 빈칸에 알맞은 말을 쓰시오.

Listen & Speak 1 A

W: Today we'll make ice cream. _____ _____ do you want to make? How about strawberry? _____, mix two cups of milk, two cups of heavy cream, and _____ _____ _____ of sugar. _____, cut five strawberries into small pieces. Then, _____ everything together and put it in the _____. That's it. It's easy to make, isn't it? Why don't you _____ _____ it at home?

W: 오늘 우리는 아이스크림을 만들 거예요. 여러분은 어느 맛을 만들고 싶은가요? 딸기는 어때요? 첫째로, 우유 2컵, 헤비 크림 2컵, 설탕 1/2컵을 섞으세요. 다음, 딸기 5개를 작은 조각으로 자르세요. 그 다음에, 모든 것을 섞어서 냉동실에 넣으세요. 이게 다예요. 만들기 쉽죠, 그렇지 않나요? 집에서 아이스크림을 만들어 보는 게 어때요?

Listen & Speak 1 B

B: Yujin, why did you _____ the eggs in water?

G: I'm _____ _____ the bad eggs.

B: _____ eggs are fresh, and _____ ones are not?

G: Eggs _____ _____ _____ _____ are fresh. When eggs _____ in water, they're not fresh. You shouldn't eat them.

B: That's _____. Why do the bad eggs _____?

G: Because they have gas _____. The gas acts _____ the air in a _____.

B: Oh, I see.

B: 유진아, 왜 달걀을 물속에 넣었니?
G: 나는 상한 달걀을 골라내는 중이야.
B: 어느 달걀이 신선하고 어느 것이 신선하지 않은 거야?
G: 물에 가라앉는 달걀은 신선해. 달걀이 물에 뜨면, 그건 신선하지 않아. 그것들을 먹으면 안 돼.
B: 그거 재미있다. 상한 달걀은 왜 물에 뜨는 거니?
G: 상한 달걀은 속에 가스가 차기 때문이야. 가스가 풍선 속의 공기 같은 역할을 하거든.
B: 아, 이제 이해했다.

Listen & Speak 2 A

B: Ms. Jeong, does _____ _____ _____ water _____ more when there's a fish in it?

W: Yes, it does. We can _____ it now.

B: But how? We don't have a fish.

W: We can use a finger _____ _____ a fish.

B: How will that work?

W: I'll _____ a glass of water first. Then I will _____ my finger in the water and weigh it to _____.

B: Oh, I _____ _____ _____ see the difference.

B: 정 선생님, 물속에 물고기가 있을 때 물 1잔의 무게가 더 무겁나요?
W: 응, 그렇단다. 우리는 지금 실험해 볼 수 있어.
B: 하지만 어떻게요? 물고기가 없는데요.
W: 우리는 물고기 대신 손가락을 사용할 수 있단다.
B: 어떻게 할 수 있어요?
W: 먼저 물 1잔의 무게를 잴 거야. 그 다음에 비교하기 위해 물속에 손가락을 넣고 무게를 잴 거란다.
B: 아, 차이를 빨리 알고 싶어요.

Listen & Speak 2 B

King Sejong: It _____ _____ for a long time.

Jang Yeongsil: Yes. The dry season is _____ too long. The farmers are very _____.

King Sejong: We _____ do something to help them.

Jang Yeongsil: How about making a special _____?

King Sejong: A clock? How will that help?

Jang Yeongsil: The clock will show the time and the _____. We can use it _____ _____ _____ the _____ _____.

King Sejong: That sounds _____ a good idea. But who's going to make it?

Jang Yeongsil: I'll _____ _____ _____ _____. I know a lot about time and the seasons.

King Sejong: Okay, I _____ _____ _____ _____ _____ _____.

Real Life Communication A

Brian: Mina, will you _____ our tennis club?

Mina: It sounds interesting, but I _____ _____ _____ a special class this _____.

Brian: Which class did you sign up for?

Mina: I signed up for a magic class. I can't _____ _____ learn new magic _____ there.

Brian: That sounds _____! _____ _____ _____ magic tricks before?

Mina: Yes, I learned some before, but I need more _____.

Brian: I hope I can see your magic tricks _____ _____.

Let's Check

B: What are you reading, Jiwon?

G: I'm reading a book about _____ and _____.

B: That sounds _____.

G: Yes. This book _____ 100 magic tricks that _____ _____. I've learned about _____ of them.

B: That's _____. Can you show me _____ of the tricks?

G: Sure. I can show you a _____ trick now.

B: Great! I can't _____ _____ see it.

해석

King Sejong: 오랫동안 비가 오지 않는구나.

Jang Yeongsil: 그렇습니다. 건기가 너무 오래 계속되고 있습니다. 농부들이 아주 걱정하고 있습니다.

King Sejong: 그들을 돕기 위해 뭔가 해야 한다.

Jang Yeongsil: 특별한 시계를 만드는 것은 어떨까요?

King Sejong: 시계? 그것이 어떻게 도움이 되겠느냐?

Jang Yeongsil: 시계는 시간과 계절을 알려줄 겁니다. 건기를 준비하기 위해 시계를 사용할 수 있습니다.

King Sejong: 그거 좋은 생각 같구나. 하지만 누가 시계를 만들겠느냐?

Jang Yeongsil: 제가 한번 해 보겠습니다. 저는 시간과 계절에 대해 많이 알고 있습니다.

King Sejong: 좋다, 네 시계를 빨리 보고 싶구나.

Brian: 미나야, 우리 테니스 동아리에 가입할래?

Mina: 재미있겠다. 하지만 나는 이번 가을에 특별 수업에 등록했어.

Brian: 무슨 수업에 등록했니?

Mina: 마술 수업에 등록했어. 거기서 새로운 마술 묘기를 빨리 배우고 싶어.

Brian: 그거 재미있겠다! 전에 마술 묘기를 배운 적이 있니?

Mina: 응, 전에 몇 가지 배웠어, 하지만 더 연습을 해야 해.

Brian: 언젠가 네 마술 묘기를 볼 수 있길 바라.

B: 지원아, 뭘 읽고 있니?

G: 마술과 과학에 관한 책을 읽고 있어.

B: 그거 재미있겠다.

G: 응. 이 책은 과학을 사용하는 100가지 마술을 소개하고 있어. 나는 그 중에 절반 정도를 익혔어.

B: 멋지다. 마술 중 몇 가지를 보여줄 수 있니?

G: 물론이지. 지금 풍선 마술을 보여줄 수 있어.

B: 멋지다! 빨리 보고 싶어.

[01~02] 다음 대화를 읽고 물음에 답하시오.

> Jaemin: Ms. Jeong, does a glass of water ⓐweigh more when there's a fish in it?
> Ms. Jeong: Yes, it ⓑdoes. We can test it now.
> Jaemin: But how? We don't have a fish.
> Ms. Jeong: We can use a finger ⓒinstead of a fish.
> Jaemin: How will that work?
> Ms. Jeong: I'll weigh a glass of water first. Then I will put my finger in the water and weigh it ⓓto compare.
> Jaemin: Oh, I can't wait to ⓔseeing the difference.

01 위 대화의 밑줄 친 ⓐ~ⓔ 중 어법상 어색한 것을 찾아 바르게 고치시오.

➡ _____

02 위 대화의 내용과 일치하지 <u>않는</u> 것은?

① 물속에 물고기가 있을 때 물 한 잔의 무게는 더 무겁다.
② 정 선생님과 재민이는 물고기 대신 손가락으로 실험하려고 한다.
③ 정 선생님은 물 한 잔의 무게를 잴 것이다.
④ 물 한 잔의 무게를 잰 후 물속에 손가락을 넣고 무게를 잴 것이다.
⑤ 재민이는 그 실험의 결과를 이미 알고 있다.

[03~04] 다음 대화를 읽고 물음에 답하시오.

> Brian: Mina, will you join our tennis club?
> Mina: It sounds interesting, but I signed up for a special class this fall.
> Brian: (A)무슨 수업에 등록했니? (for, which)
> Mina: I signed up for a magic class. I can't wait to learn new magic tricks there.
> Brian: That sounds cool! Have you learned magic tricks before?
> Mina: Yes, I learned some before, but I need more practice.
> Brian: I hope I can see your magic tricks some day.

03 위 대화의 밑줄 친 (A)의 우리말을 주어진 단어를 사용하여 영작하시오.

➡ _____

04 위 대화에서 알 수 있는 Mina의 심경으로 적절한 것은?

① excited   ② worried   ③ lonely
④ upset   ⑤ depressed

[01~03] 다음 글을 읽고 물음에 답하시오.

Jane: Today we'll make ice cream. Which flavor do you want to make? How about strawberry? First, mix two cups of milk, two cups of heavy cream, and half a cup of sugar. Next, cut five strawberries into small pieces. Then, mix everything together and put it in the freezer. That's it. It's easy to make, (A)그렇지 않나요? Why don't you try making it at home?

서답형

01 위 글의 밑줄 친 (A)의 우리말을 두 단어를 사용하여 영작하시오.

➡ _____

서답형

02 위 글에서 언급한 아이스크림을 만들기 위한 준비물로서 바르지 않은 것은?

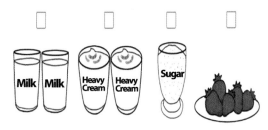

중요

03 위 글의 내용과 일치하지 <u>않는</u> 것은?

① Jane은 딸기 아이스크림 만드는 법을 설명하고 있다.
② 아이스크림을 만들기 위해 우유, 헤비 크림, 설탕, 딸기가 필요하다.
③ 딸기 5개를 작은 조각으로 잘라야 한다.
④ 모든 재료를 섞어서 냉동실에 넣어야 한다.
⑤ Jane은 집에서는 아이스크림을 만들지 않는다.

[04~06] 다음 대화를 읽고 물음에 답하시오.

Brian: Yujin, why did you put the eggs in water?
Yujin: I'm picking out the bad eggs.
Brian: Which eggs are fresh, and (A)[which / what] ones are not?
Yujin: Eggs that sink in water (B)[is / are] fresh. When eggs float in water, they're not fresh. You shouldn't eat (D)them.
Brian: That's interesting. Why do the bad eggs float?
Yujin: (C)[Because / Because of] they have gas inside. The gas acts like the air in a balloon.
Brian: Oh, I see.

04 위 대화의 괄호 (A)~(C)에 들어갈 말로 바르게 짝지어진 것은?

① which – is – Because
② which – are – Because of
③ which – are – Because
④ what – are – Because of
⑤ what – is – Because

서답형

05 위 대화의 밑줄 친 (D)them이 가리키는 것을 우리말로 쓰시오.

➡ _____

중요

06 위 대화의 내용과 일치하지 <u>않는</u> 것은?

① 유진이는 상한 달걀을 골라내는 중이다.
② 물에 가라앉는 달걀은 신선한 것이다.
③ 달걀이 물에 뜨면 신선하지 않은 것이다.
④ 상한 달걀은 가스를 내뿜는다.
⑤ 가스가 풍선 속의 공기 같은 역할을 한다.

[07~08] 다음 대화를 읽고 물음에 답하시오.

King Sejong: It hasn't rained for a long time.

Jang Yeongsil: Yes. The dry season is lasting too long. The farmers are very worried.

King Sejong: (A) We should do something to help them.

Jang Yeongsil: (B) How about making a special clock?

King Sejong: (C) A clock? How will that help?

Jang Yeongsil: (D) We can use it to prepare for the dry season.

King Sejong: (E) That sounds like a good idea. But who's going to make it?

Jang Yeongsil: I'll give it a try. I know a lot about time and the seasons.

King Sejong: Okay, I can't wait to see your clock.

07 위 대화의 (A)~(E) 중 주어진 문장이 들어가기에 적절한 곳은?

> The clock will show the time and the seasons.

① (A)　② (B)　③ (C)　④ (D)　⑤ (E)

08 위 대화를 읽고 대답할 수 없는 것은?

① What's the matter?

② What does Jang Yeongsil suggest?

③ Why does Jang Yeongsil want to make a special clock?

④ What does Jang Yeongsil know about a lot?

⑤ What does King Sejong do to finish the dry season?

[09~10] 다음 대화를 읽고 물음에 답하시오.

Brian: Mina, will you join our tennis club?

Mina: It sounds interesting, but I signed up for a special class this fall.

Brian: Which class did you sign up for?

Mina: I signed up for a magic class. I can't wait to learn new magic tricks there.

Brian: _____(A)_____ Have you learned magic tricks before?

Mina: Yes, I learned some before, but I need more practice.

Brian: I hope I can see your magic tricks some day.

09 위 대화의 빈칸 (A)에 들어갈 말로 적절한 것은?

① I'm sorry to hear that.

② That sounds cool!

③ Take it easy.

④ I don't think so.

⑤ It's not your fault.

10 위 대화를 읽고 대답할 수 없는 것은?

① Which class did Mina sign up for this fall?

② Why couldn't Mina join the tennis club?

③ What does Mina want to learn in the magic class?

④ Has Mina learned magic tricks before?

⑤ How long has Mina practiced magic tricks?

[01~03] 다음 대화를 읽고 물음에 답하시오.

Jaemin: Ms. Jeong, does a glass of water weigh more when there's a fish in it?

Ms. Jeong: Yes, it does. We can test it now.

Jaemin: But how? We don't have a fish.

Ms. Jeong: We can use a finger instead of a fish.

Jaemin: How will that work?

Ms. Jeong: I'll weigh a glass of water first. Then I will put my finger in the water and weigh it to compare.

Jaemin: Oh, (A)차이를 빨리 알고 싶어요.

중요

01 위 대화의 밑줄 친 (A)의 우리말을 <보기>에 주어진 모든 단어들을 배열하여 영작하시오.

┌─ 보기 ─┐
to / I / difference / wait / can't / see / the
└─────────┘

➡ _____

02 What will Ms. Jeong use instead of a fish?

➡ _____

고난이도

03 What do Ms. Jeong and Jaemin want to see through the experiment?

A: They want to see whether _____
_____.

04 다음 대화에서 (A)~(E)를 자연스럽게 이어지도록 순서대로 배열하시오.

King Sejong: It hasn't rained for a long time.

Jang Yeongsil: Yes. The dry season is lasting too long. The farmers are very worried.

King Sejong: We should do something to help them.

(A) I'll give it a try. I know a lot about time and the seasons.

(B) A clock? How will that help?

(C) That sounds like a good idea. But who's going to make it?

(D) How about making a special clock?

(E) The clock will show the time and the seasons. We can use it to prepare for the dry season.

King Sejong: Okay, I can't wait to see your clock.

➡ _____

[05~06] 다음 글을 읽고 물음에 답하시오.

Jane: Today we'll make ice cream. Which flavor do you want to make? How about strawberry? First, mix two cups of milk, two cups of heavy cream, and half a cup of sugar. Next, cut five strawberries into small pieces. Then, mix everything together and put it in the freezer. That's it. It's easy to make, isn't it? Why don't you try making it at home?

05 According to Jane, what do you need to prepare for making strawberry ice cream?

➡ _____
_____

고난이도

06 What should you do after cutting the strawberries into small pieces?

➡ _____
_____

Conversation **123**

Grammar

교과서

① 가주어 It

- **It** is good **to meet** him. 그를 만나는 것은 좋다.
- **It** is wrong **to speak** ill of your friends. 친구에 관해 나쁘게 말하는 것은 옳지 않다.

■ to부정사구가 주어로 쓰여 주어가 길어진 경우, 주어부를 문장의 맨 뒤로 보내고 이 자리에 It을 쓰는 것이 가주어 It이다. 명사절 접속사가 이끄는 that절 역시 이에 해당한다.

- · **To keep** your promise is important.
  = **It** is important **to keep** your promise. 너의 약속을 지키는 것은 중요하다.
- · **That he broke his leg** was surprising.
  = **It** was surprising **that** he broke his leg. 그의 다리가 부러졌다는 것은 놀라웠다.

■ 가주어 It은 따로 해석하지 않으며 to부정사구를 주어로 해석해야 한다. to부정사구의 부정은 'not+to V'로 표기한다.

- **It** is good **not to make** noises in the library. 도서관에서는 소음을 내지 않는 것이 좋다.
- **It** is bad **not to say** sorry when you do wrong. 네가 잘못을 했을 때 미안하다고 말하지 않는 것은 나빠.

■ 진주어 to부정사의 행위 주체를 명시하고 싶은 경우, 의미상의 주어로 'for/of+목적격'을 사용한다. 'for+목적격'은 '상황에 대한 의견'을 나타내는 형용사 뒤에서, 'of+목적격'은 '사람의 성격'을 나타내는 형용사 뒤에서 쓰인다.

- **It** is kind **of** her **to help** you. 그녀가 너를 도와주는 것은 친절해.
- **It** is not safe **for** you **to go** outside alone. 네가 혼자 밖으로 나가는 것은 안전하지 않아.

핵심 Check

1. 다음 우리말과 일치하도록 빈칸에 알맞은 말을 쓰시오.

(1) 식물을 돌보는 것은 쉽지 않다.
➡ It is not easy _____ _____ _____ of plants.

(2) 너를 매일 만나는 것은 좋아.
➡ It is nice _____ _____ you every day.

(3) 우리가 침착함을 유지하는 것은 중요해.
➡ It is important _____ _____ _____ _____ calm.

2 How come ...?

- **How come** you are angry with me? 도대체 너는 왜 내게 화가 났니?
- **How come** she came late? 그녀는 도대체 왜 늦었니?

■ 의문사 why와 how come은 의미는 비슷하지만 어순상의 차이를 보인다. 'How come+주어+동사 …?'
로 쓰여 '도대체 왜 …?'라는 의미이지만, why는 'Why+동사+주어 …?'의 어순으로 쓰인다.

- **How come** you bought this? 도대체 이걸 왜 산 거야?

  Why did you buy this? 이것을 왜 산 거니?

  How come he made this cake? 도대체 왜 그가 이 케이크를 만든 거야?

  Why did he make this cake? 그는 왜 이 케이크를 만든 거야?

  How come she looked disappointed? 그녀는 도대체 왜 실망한 것처럼 보였니?

  Why did she look disappointed? 그녀는 왜 실망한 것처럼 보였니?

  How come you are here? 도대체 네가 왜 여기에 있는 거야?

  Why are you here? 너는 왜 여기에 있니?

  How come you sent the message like that? 도대체 너는 왜 그런 메시지를 보낸 거야?

  Why did you send the message like that? 왜 너는 그런 메시지를 보냈니?

핵심 Check

2. 다음 우리말을 영어로 쓰시오.

(1) 도대체 왜 내게 거짓말을 했니?

➡ _____ _____ you lied to me?

(2) 왜 그 소년이 울고 있니?

➡ _____ is the boy crying?

(3) 도대체 왜 그가 그런 말을 했니?

➡ _____ _____ he said things like that?

(4) 도대체 왜 그를 초대했니?

➡ _____ _____ you invited him?

01 다음 문장에서 어법상 <u>어색한</u> 부분을 바르게 고쳐 쓰시오.

(1) It was difficult stop my bad habit.

_____ ➡ _____

(2) It is impossible of you to finish the project.

_____ ➡ _____

(3) How come did you meet her?

_____ ➡ _____

(4) How came he was with you?

_____ ➡ _____

02 다음 우리말과 일치하도록 빈칸에 알맞은 말을 쓰시오.

(1) 도대체 왜 그는 물을 그렇게 많이 마시는 거야?

➡ How come _____ _____ so much water?

(2) 왜 너는 운동을 열심히 하니?

➡ Why _____ _____ _____ hard?

(3) 도대체 왜 그녀가 슬퍼 보이는 거지?

➡ How come _____ _____ sad?

(4) 왜 너는 그렇게 빨리 달렸니?

➡ Why _____ _____ _____ so fast?

03 주어진 단어를 바르게 배열하여 다음 우리말을 영어로 쓰시오. 필요하다면 단어를 추가하시오.

(1) 운동을 규칙적으로 하는 것은 매우 중요해.

(exercise / regularly / important / is / it / very)

➡ _____

(2) 놀이공원에 가는 것은 신난다.

(it / the amusement park / exciting / to / go / is)

➡ _____

(3) 친구들에게 정직한 것은 중요해.

(your friends / important / honest / be / is / it / with)

➡ _____

(4) 그것을 설명하는 것은 나의 일이야. (it / it / explain / my job / is)

➡ _____

01 다음 빈칸에 들어갈 말로 가장 적절한 것은?

> It is good _____ early in the morning.

① wake up ② to wake up
③ woke up ④ to waking up
⑤ woken up

02 다음 우리말을 영어로 바르게 옮긴 것은?

> 도대체 왜 그녀는 우리에게 다시 돌아온 거야?

① Why is she coming back to us?
② Why is she returning to us?
③ How come she came back to us?
④ How come did she come back to us?
⑤ How came she came back to us?

03 다음 중 빈칸에 들어갈 말이 다른 하나는?

① It was wise _____ him to say sorry.
② It is generous _____ her to lend us money.
③ It is rude _____ you to talk like that to your elders.
④ It is easy _____ me to solve this problem.
⑤ It was careful _____ them to keep their valuables in the safe.

서답형

04 주어진 단어를 활용하여 다음 우리말을 영어로 쓰시오.

> 외국어를 배우는 것은 재미있다.
> (fun / it)

➡ _____

05 다음 주어진 문장의 밑줄 친 부분과 쓰임이 같은 것은?

> It is exciting to ride a bike with friends.

① The dog was barking at us to protect his house.
② It is surprising to see you here.
③ Is there anything to wear?
④ The man went into his room to take a rest.
⑤ We want you to do your best.

06 다음 빈칸에 들어갈 말이 바르게 짝지어진 것은?

> • It is amazing _____ the plants grow in our garden.
> • _____ he jogs every morning?

① see – Why ② to see – Why
③ saw – Why ④ to see – How come
⑤ to seeing – How come

07 다음 중 빈칸에 들어갈 말이 다른 하나는?

① _____ she took him to the store?
② _____ he broke his promise?
③ _____ we didn't take a bus?
④ _____ they didn't come?
⑤ _____ are we going to visit them?

서답형

08 다음 빈칸에 알맞은 말을 쓰시오.

> To read books is very fun.
> ➡ It is very fun _____ _____ _____.

09 주어진 단어를 바르게 배열하여 다음 우리말을 영어로 쓸 때 다섯 번째로 오는 단어는?

> 인사하는 방법을 아는 것은 좋다.
> (hello / nice / how / it / to / is / say / to / know)

① to　　　　② nice　　　　③ say
④ know　　　⑤ hello

10 다음 중 밑줄 친 부분의 쓰임이 다른 하나는?

① <u>It</u> is true that he succeeded in climbing the mountain.
② <u>It</u> was good to hear the news from her.
③ <u>It</u> is cloudy and windy.
④ <u>It</u> is fun to see movies.
⑤ <u>It</u> was wrong to make fun of your friend.

11 다음 중 어법상 바르지 <u>않은</u> 것은?

① How come you woke up so late?
② It is true that he made the robot.
③ That is surprising to see you play the piano.
④ It will be difficult for you to understand the book.
⑤ It was not easy to talk with her.

12 다음 중 어법상 바르지 않은 것은?

> ①It was ②careless ③for them ④to tell their children something ⑤like that.

①　　②　　③　　④　　⑤

13 주어진 단어를 활용하여 다음 우리말을 영어로 쓰시오.

> 도대체 그녀는 왜 그 재킷을 산 거야?
> (how / the jacket)

➡ _____

14 다음 중 우리말로 옮긴 것이 바르지 <u>않은</u> 것은?

① 도대체 왜 너는 내 말을 안 들은 거니?
　→ How come you didn't listen to me?
② 네가 그 음악을 듣는 것은 놀랍다.
　→ It is surprising for you to hear the music.
③ 그 단어들의 의미를 찾는 것은 도움이 될 거야.
　→ It will be helpful to find the meanings of the words.
④ 그 일에 너를 추천하는 것은 나의 생각이 아니었어.
　→ To recommend you for the job was not my idea.
⑤ 내가 너를 막는 것은 불가능했어.
　→ It was impossible of me to stop you.

15 다음 빈칸에 들어갈 말로 가장 적절한 것은?

> _____ he broke into someone's house?

① Why　　② What　　③ When
④ How come　⑤ Where

16 주어진 단어를 바르게 배열하여 다음 우리말을 영어로 쓰시오. 필요하다면 단어를 추가하시오.

> 걷는 동안 휴대 전화기를 사용하지 않는 것이 중요하다.
> (important / your phone / walking / to / it / use / is / while)

➡ _____

서답형

17 다음 빈칸에 알맞은 말을 쓰시오.

> 도대체 그녀는 왜 어제 떠난 거야?
> ➡ How come _____ _____ yesterday?

중요

18 다음 중 빈칸에 들어갈 말이 바르게 짝지어진 것은?

> • It is wise _____ her to go with you to the hospital.
> • It is necessary _____ they come here on time.

① to – to
② for – to
③ of – that
④ of – to
⑤ for – that

19 다음 우리말을 영어로 바르게 옮긴 것을 <u>모두</u> 고르시오.

> 부주의하게 운전하는 것은 위험하다.

① It is careless to drive dangerously.
② It is dangerous drive carelessly.
③ To drive carelessly is dangerous.
④ It is dangerous to drive carelessly.
⑤ It is careless drive dangerously.

중요

20 다음 괄호 안의 단어를 어법에 맞게 쓸 때 형태가 <u>다른</u> 하나는?

① It is kind of him (help) you.
② It is rude of you (say) such words.
③ It is good at (build) nests on trees.
④ It is bad for you (use) someone's stuff without asking.
⑤ It is necessary for me (do) my homework.

서답형

21 다음 문장과 같은 의미의 문장을 쓰시오.

> To tell a stranger where you live is dangerous.

➡ _____

22 다음 중 빈칸에 들어갈 말이 바르게 짝지어진 것은?

> A: Your room is so messy. _____ you didn't clean your room?
> B: It's because I was too busy. It was impossible _____ me to clean the room.

① Why – that
② Why – of
③ How come – for
④ How come – of
⑤ How come – that

중요

23 다음 중 어법상 옳은 것은?

① It is fun hear him talking about interesting stories.
② How come did you lose your weight?
③ It is brave for you to make the decision.
④ Why you weren't doing the laundry?
⑤ It is stupid of her to behave like that in front of so many people.

서답형

24 다음 주어진 단어를 활용하여 다음 문장과 같은 의미의 문장을 쓰시오.

> Why did you call me? (how)

➡ _____

01 주어진 단어를 활용하여 다음 우리말을 영어로 쓰시오.

> 헬멧을 쓰지 않는 것은 위험하다.
> (it / your / wear)

➡ _____

02 다음 빈칸에 알맞은 말을 쓰시오.

(1) 왜 그녀는 지금 너를 쳐다보고 있는 거야?
  ➡ How come _____ _____ _____
    at you now?

(2) 왜 너는 그 아이들을 초대한 거니?
  ➡ Why _____ _____ _____ the
    children?

(3) 도대체 왜 그 선생님은 우리에게 할 일을 그렇게 많이 주시는 거야?
  ➡ How come _____ _____ _____
    us so many things to do?

(4) 왜 우리는 그 식당으로 가고 있는 거야?
  ➡ How come _____ _____ _____
    to the restaurant?

(5) 왜 너는 모자를 쓰고 있는 거니?
  ➡ Why _____ _____ _____ a hat?

03 다음 문장과 같은 의미의 문장을 완성하시오.

(1) To travel abroad is exciting.
  ➡ It _____.

(2) To read this novel is not easy.
  ➡ It _____.

(3) It is useful to know how to use this machine.
  ➡ To _____.

04 주어진 단어를 바르게 배열하여 다음 우리말을 영어로 쓰시오. 필요하다면 단어를 추가하시오.

> 네가 그렇게 말한 것은 어리석었어.
> (you / it / say / stupid / was / so / to)

➡ _____

05 주어진 단어를 활용하여 다음 문장과 같은 의미의 문장을 쓰시오.

> Why did you put your wallet on the table?
> (how)

➡ _____

06 다음 빈칸에 알맞은 말을 쓰시오.

> 내가 그 산을 오르는 것이 가능해?
> ➡ Is it possible _____ _____ _____
>   _____ up the mountain?

07 주어진 단어를 활용하여 다음 대화를 영어로 쓰시오.

> A: _____ (how / today)
> B: I am going to meet her today because I don't have any free time tomorrow.

➡ _____

08 다음 빈칸에 알맞은 말을 쓰시오.

> It is surprising _____ he didn't call you.

09 다음 빈칸에 적절한 말을 쓰시오.

> _____ _____ you made her do the dishes?
>
> = _____ did you make her do the dishes?

10 다음 대화의 빈칸에 알맞은 말을 쓰시오.

> A: Is it easy _____?
> B: I don't think so. To form good habits is not easy.

➡ _____

11 주어진 단어를 활용하여 다음 대화를 영어로 쓰시오.

> A: 도대체 왜 그녀는 나에게 사과하지 않는 거야? (how / say sorry)
> B: 그녀가 너에게 미안하다고 말하는 것은 쉽지 않다고 생각해. (it / think)

A: _____

B: _____

12 다음 빈칸에 들어갈 알맞은 말을 쓰시오.

> It was nice _____ you to send me a birthday card.

13 다음 문장에서 어법상 틀린 것을 바르게 고쳐 문장을 다시 쓰시오.

> How come did you forget to bring the book?

➡ _____

14 주어진 단어를 바르게 배열하여 다음 우리말을 영어로 쓰시오. 필요하다면 단어를 추가하시오.

> 그가 너에게 자기의 옷을 빌려준 것은 정말 관대했어.
> (his clothes / him / lend / generous / was / to / it / you)

➡ _____

15 주어진 단어를 활용하여 다음 문장과 같은 의미의 문장을 쓰시오.

> Why did you book the restaurant?
> (how)

➡ _____

16 다음 빈칸에 알맞은 말을 쓰시오.

> A: Was it fun to watch the movie?
> B: Yes. _____ was really fun.

➡ _____

17 다음 빈칸에 알맞은 말을 쓰시오.

> 너는 왜 John을 돕지 않았니?
> = _____ you didn't help John?
> = _____ _____ _____ help John?

18 주어진 단어를 활용하여 다음 대화의 우리말을 영어로 쓰시오.

> A: 너는 왜 공부를 열심히 하는 거야? (how)
> B: 공부를 열심히 하는 것은 나를 행복하게 해.
> (make me happy / it)

A: _____

B: _____

The Super Science Magic Show

Jina: Welcome to the Super Science Magic Show! It's always exciting
~에 오신 것을 환영합니다 · 가주어 It
to see magic tricks. And it's more exciting to find out the secrets
진주어 to부정사 · 가주어 It · 진주어 to부정사
behind them. Some people think the secret of magic is science.
magic tricks
Today, Ken, a member of the School Magic Club, will use science

to perform his tricks. Which tricks will he show us? I can't wait to
to부정사의 부사적 용법 중 목적(~하기 위해서) · = I am looking forward to seeing them.
see them.

The Amazing Rising Water
현재분사(솟아오르는)

Ken: Hello, everyone. Today, I'm going to show you something
부정대명사는 형용사의 수식을 뒤에서 받음
amazing. Here's a dish with water in it. Now, I'll put a candle in
~을 ···에 두다
the middle of the dish. Next, I'll light the candle and cover it with
cover A with B: A를 B로 덮다
a glass. "Abracadabra!"

Jina: Look at the water! How come it rose into the glass?
How come+주어+동사 ~?

Ken: Air expands when it gets hot and creates higher pressure. When it

gets cold, air contracts and creates lower pressure. When the flame

burnt out, the air inside the glass cooled down. As the air cooled
~할 때 (= When)
down, the air pressure dropped. So the air outside the glass was at
형용사구
a higher pressure. It pushed the water into the glass.
= the air outside the glass · push A into B: A를 B 안으로 밀다

글자:
magic 마술의
trick 속임수, 마술, 묘기
secret 비밀
candle 초, 양초
abracadabra 아브라카다브라 (주문)
expand 팽창하다
pressure 압력
contract 수축하다
flame 불꽃
burn out 타 버리다
cool down 식다, 차가워지다

확인문제

● 다음 문장이 본문의 내용과 일치하면 T, 일치하지 않으면 F를 쓰시오.

1 Ken belongs to the School Magic Club. ☐

2 Ken will show students some tricks without using science. ☐

3 Air expands when it gets hot and creates lower pressure. ☐

4 As the air cooled down, the air pressure rose. ☐

5 The air inside the glass cooled down because the flame burnt out. ☐

The Secret of the Disappearing Water
현재분사(사라지는)

Ken: Now, I'm going to fill one of these cups with water. I will move
fill A with B: A를 B로 채우다
them around to confuse you. Jina, which cup has the water in it?
cups   to부정사의 부사적 용법 중 목적(~하기 위해서)

Jina: That's easy! It's the middle one.

Ken: Okay, let's check. See? No water.
= There is no water

Jina: Show me the other cups.
4형식 (show+사람+사물)

Ken: See? There's no water.

Jina: Wow! How come the water disappeared?
How come+주어+동사 ~?

Ken: Before the trick, I put a special material into one of the cups. The
put A into B: A를 B 안에 넣다
material absorbed the water and turned it into jelly. Then the jelly
the water
stuck to the bottom. If you want to try this trick, it's necessary to
stick(들러붙다)의 과거   진주어 to부정사
use cups that you can't see through.
목적격 관계대명사

Jina: Thank you for your great performance. It was really amazing!
현재분사(놀라움을 유발하는)

confuse 혼동하게 하다
material 물질, 재료
absorb 흡수하다
turn A into B A를 B로 바꾸다
bottom 바닥
necessary 필요한, 필연적인
see through 속을 들여다보다, 꿰뚫어 보다

확인문제

● 다음 문장이 본문의 내용과 일치하면 T, 일치하지 않으면 F를 쓰시오.

1 Ken moved cups around including the one which had water in it. ☐

2 Jina thought that the cup which was in the middle had water. ☐

3 There was no water in all of the cups. ☐

4 The jelly didn't stick to the bottom of the cup. ☐

5 You need cups that can't be seen through to do the trick. ☐

6 Jina thought the performance that Ken showed was amazing. ☐

● 우리말을 참고하여 빈칸에 알맞은 말을 쓰시오.

1 Jina: _____ _____ the Super Science Magic Show!

2 _____ always _____ _____ _____ magic tricks.

3 And it's more exciting _____ _____ _____ the secrets _____ them.

4 Some people think the secret of magic _____ _____.

5 Today, Ken, a member of the School Magic Club, _____ _____ _____ _____ _____ his tricks.

6 Which tricks _____ he _____ _____? I can't wait _____ _____.

7 Ken: Hello, everyone. Today, I'm going _____ _____ _____ something amazing.

8 Here's a dish _____ _____ _____ _____.

9 Now, I'll _____ _____ in the middle of the dish.

10 Next, I'll _____ the candle and _____ _____ _____ a glass. "Abracadabra!"

11 Jina: Look _____ the water! _____ _____ it _____ _____ the glass?

12 Ken: Air _____ when it gets _____ and creates _____ _____.

13 When it _____ _____, air _____ and creates _____ _____.

14 When the flame _____ _____, the air inside the glass _____ _____.

15 As the air _____ _____, the air pressure _____.

1 지나: 특별 과학 마술 쇼에 오신 것을 환영합니다!

2 마술을 보는 것은 항상 신나는 일입니다.

3 그리고 마술 뒤에 숨겨진 비밀을 알아내는 것은 더 신나는 일입니다.

4 어떤 사람들은 마술의 비밀이 과학이라고 생각합니다.

5 오늘 학교 마술 동아리 회원인 Ken은 마술을 수행하기 위해 과학을 사용할 것입니다.

6 그는 우리에게 어떤 마술을 보여줄까요? 무척 기다려지는군요.

7 Ken: 안녕하세요, 여러분. 오늘, 저는 여러분에게 놀라운 무언가를 보여 주려고 합니다.

8 여기에 물이 담긴 접시가 있습니다.

9 이제, 저는 접시 한가운데에 초를 놓을 것입니다.

10 그다음에 초를 켜고 유리컵으로 초를 덮어 보겠습니다. "아브라카다브라!"

11 지나: 물을 보세요! 어째서 물이 유리컵 속으로 올라간 거지요?

12 Ken: 공기가 뜨거워지면 팽창해서, 더 높은 압력을 만듭니다.

13 공기가 차가워지면 수축해서, 더 낮은 압력을 만듭니다.

14 불꽃이 다 타 버렸을 때, 유리컵 속의 공기는 식어 버렸습니다.

15 공기가 식었으므로, 기압이 낮아졌습니다.

16 So the air outside the glass _____ _____ _____ _____ _____.

17 It _____ the water _____ the glass.

18 Ken: Now, I'm going _____ _____ _____ _____ _____ with water.

19 I will move _____ _____ _____ _____ you.

20 Jina, _____ _____ has the water in it?

21 Jina: That's easy! _____ the middle _____.

22 Ken: Okay, _____ _____. See? No water.

23 Jina: Show _____ _____ _____ _____.

24 Ken: See? There's _____ _____.

25 Jina: Wow! _____ _____ the water _____?

26 Ken: _____ the trick, I _____ a special material _____ one of _____ _____.

27 The material _____ the water and _____ _____ _____ jelly.

28 Then the jelly _____ _____ _____ _____.

29 If you want to try this trick, it's _____ _____ _____ cups _____ you can't see through.

30 Jina: Thank you _____ your great _____. It was really _____!

16 그래서 유리컵 밖의 공기 압력
이 더 높아졌습니다.

17 높아진 압력의 공기가 물을 밀
어서 유리컵으로 들어가게 된
것입니다.

18 Ken: 이제, 이 컵들 중 하나를
물로 채워 보겠습니다.

19 여러분을 헷갈리게 하려고 이
컵들을 섞어 보겠습니다.

20 지나, 어떤 컵에 물이 있을까요?

21 지나: 쉽네요! 가운데 컵이에요.

22 Ken: 좋습니다, 확인해 봅시다.
보셨죠? 물이 없군요.

23 지나: 다른 컵들도 보여 주세요.

24 Ken: 보셨죠? 물이 없네요.

25 지나: 왜! 어째서 물이 사라진 거죠?

26 Ken: 마술 전에, 저는 특별한 물
질을 컵 하나에 넣어 두었습니다.

27 그 물질은 물을 흡수하고, 그것
을 젤리로 변하게 했습니다.

28 그러고 나서 젤리는 컵 바닥에
달라붙었습니다.

29 여러분이 이 마술을 해 보고자
한다면, 속을 들여다볼 수 없는
컵을 사용해야 합니다.

30 지나: 멋진 공연 고맙습니다. 정
말 놀라웠어요!

● 우리말을 참고하여 본문을 영작하시오.

1 지나: 특별 과학 마술 쇼에 오신 것을 환영합니다!

➡ _____

2 마술을 보는 것은 항상 신나는 일입니다.

➡ _____

3 그리고 마술 뒤에 숨겨진 비밀을 알아내는 것은 더 신나는 일입니다.

➡ _____

4 어떤 사람들은 마술의 비밀이 과학이라고 생각합니다.

➡ _____

5 오늘 학교 마술 동아리 회원인 Ken은 마술을 수행하기 위해 과학을 사용할 것입니다.

➡ _____

6 그는 우리에게 어떤 마술을 보여 줄까요? 무척 기다려지는군요.

➡ _____

7 Ken: 안녕하세요, 여러분. 오늘, 저는 여러분에게 놀라운 무언가를 보여 주려고 합니다.

➡ _____

8 여기에 물이 담긴 접시가 있습니다.

➡ _____

9 이제, 저는 접시 한가운데에 초를 놓을 것입니다.

➡ _____

10 그다음에 초를 켜고 유리컵으로 초를 덮어 보겠습니다. "아브라카다브라!"

➡ _____

11 지나: 물을 보세요! 어째서 물이 유리컵 속으로 올라간 거지요?

➡ _____

12 Ken: 공기가 뜨거워지면 팽창해서, 더 높은 압력을 만듭니다.

➡ _____

13 공기가 차가워지면 수축해서, 더 낮은 압력을 만듭니다.

➡ _____

14 불꽃이 다 타 버렸을 때, 유리컵 속의 공기는 식어 버렸습니다.

➡ _____

15 공기가 식었으므로, 기압이 낮아졌습니다.

➡ _____

16 그래서 유리컵 밖의 공기 압력이 더 높아졌습니다.

➡ _____

17 높아진 압력의 공기가 물을 밀어서 유리컵으로 들어가게 된 것입니다.

➡ _____

18 Ken: 이제, 이 컵들 중 하나를 물로 채워 보겠습니다.

➡ _____

19 여러분을 헷갈리게 하려고 이 컵들을 섞어 보겠습니다.

➡ _____

20 지나, 어떤 컵에 물이 있을까요?

➡ _____

21 지나: 쉽네요! 가운데 컵이에요.

➡ _____

22 Ken: 좋습니다, 확인해 봅시다. 보셨죠? 물이 없군요.

➡ _____

23 지나: 다른 컵들도 보여 주세요.

➡ _____

24 Ken: 보셨죠? 물이 없네요.

➡ _____

25 지나: 와! 어째서 물이 사라진 거죠?

➡ _____

26 Ken: 마술 전에, 저는 특별한 물질을 컵 하나에 넣어 두었습니다.

➡ _____

27 그 물질은 물을 흡수하고, 그것을 젤리로 변하게 했습니다.

➡ _____

28 그러고 나서 젤리는 컵 바닥에 달라붙었습니다.

➡ _____

29 여러분이 이 마술을 해 보고자 한다면, 속을 들여다볼 수 없는 컵을 사용해야 합니다.

➡ _____

30 지나: 멋진 공연 고맙습니다. 정말 놀라웠어요!

➡ _____

[01~03] 다음 글을 읽고 물음에 답하시오.

Jina: Welcome (A)_____ the Super Science Magic Show! It's always exciting to see magic tricks. And it's more exciting to find out the secrets behind them. Some people think the secret of magic is science. Today, Ken, a member of the School Magic Club, will use science to perform his tricks. Which tricks will he show us? I can't wait to see them.

01 다음 중 빈칸 (A)에 들어갈 말로 가장 적절한 것은?

① for ② to ③ in
④ at ⑤ about

02 What does Jina want to talk about?

① Science that uses magic.
② Magic used by scientists.
③ Magic using science.
④ Magical things around us.
⑤ The most surprising thing in the world.

서답형

03 Who is Ken? Answer in English with a full sentence.

➡ _____

[04~09] 다음 글을 읽고 물음에 답하시오.

Ken: Hello, everyone. Today, I'm going to show you something amazing. Here's a dish with water in it. Now, I'll put a candle in the middle of the dish. Next, I'll light the candle and cover it with a glass. "Abracadabra!"
Jina: Look at the water! How come it ①rose into the glass?

Ken: Air expands when it gets hot and creates higher pressure. When it gets cold, air contracts and creates ___(A)___ pressure. When the flame burnt out, the air inside the glass ②heated up. As the air ③cooled down, the air pressure ④dropped. So the air ⑤outside the glass was at a higher pressure. It pushed the water into the glass.

04 다음 중 빈칸 (A)에 들어갈 말로 가장 적절한 것은?

① higher ② the same ③ lower
④ no ⑤ strong

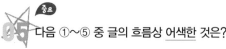

05 다음 ①~⑤ 중 글의 흐름상 어색한 것은?

①   ②   ③   ④   ⑤

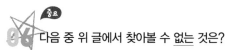

06 다음 중 위 글에서 찾아볼 수 없는 것은?

① a boy who is showing a magic
② a girl watching a magic show
③ a dish which has water in it
④ a candle covered with a towel
⑤ water pushed into the glass from outside of the dish

서답형

07 What happened when Kevin covered the candle with a glass? Answer in English with a full sentence.

➡ _____

08 다음 중 위 글을 읽고 답할 수 있는 것은?

① How much water is there in the dish?
② What does Ken want to show?
③ How did Ken learn the magic?
④ Where did Ken show the magic?
⑤ When did Ken show the magic?

09 위 글의 내용에 맞게 빈칸에 알맞은 말을 쓰시오.

> Pressure _____ causes the water to move into the glass.

[10~15] 다음 글을 읽고 물음에 답하시오.

Ken: Now, I'm going to fill one of these cups with water. I will move them around to confuse you. Jina, which cup has the water in it?

Jina: That's easy! It's the middle one.

Ken: Okay, let's check. See? No water.

Jina: Show me (A) cups.

Ken: See? There's no water.

Jina: Wow! How come the water disappeared?

Ken: ① Before the trick, I put a special material into one of the cups. ② The material absorbed the water and turned it into jelly. ③ If you want to try this trick, it's necessary to use cups that you can't see through. ④

Jina: ⑤ Thank you for your great performance. It was really amazing!

10 다음 중 빈칸 (A)에 들어갈 말로 가장 적절한 것은?

① the others　　② another
③ other　　④ the other
⑤ others

11 다음 ①~⑤ 중 주어진 문장이 들어가기에 가장 적절한 곳은?

> Then the jelly stuck to the bottom.

①　　②　　③　　④　　⑤

서답형

12 다음과 같이 풀이되는 단어를 위 글에서 찾아 쓰시오.

> to take in something in a natural or gradual way

➡ _____

서답형

13 What did Ken do after he filled one of cups with water? Answer in English with four words.

➡ _____

서답형

14 According to Ken, what is necessary if we want to try the trick?

➡ _____
_____

15 다음 중 위 글의 내용을 바르게 이해한 사람은?

① Teo: If there is no mysterious power, we can't perform the magic.
② Jenny: I will need only two cups to try the magic.
③ Chris: Ken made the water disappear by drinking it when no one saw him.
④ Paul: To try the magic, I will buy the special material which can take in water and turn it into jelly.
⑤ Nick: I need to buy a special material and some glasses which people can see through.

[16~18] 다음 글을 읽고 물음에 답하시오.

Jina: Welcome to the Super Science Magic Show! (A)It's always exciting to see magic tricks. And it's more exciting to find out the secrets behind (B)them. Some people think the secret of magic is science. Today, Ken, a member of the School Magic Club, will use science to perform his tricks. Which tricks will he show us? I can't wait to see them.

16 다음 중 밑줄 친 (A)와 쓰임이 같은 것은?

① It is rainy and windy.
② It is not what I said.
③ It is clear that you can't drive.
④ It is dark outside.
⑤ It is flowing under the bridge.

17 다음 밑줄 친 (B)가 가리키는 것을 위 글에서 찾아 쓰시오.

➡ _____

18 다음 중 위 글에 이어질 내용으로 가장 적절한 것은?

① Ken의 자기소개
② Ken의 과학을 이용한 발명품
③ Jina의 과학 동아리 소개
④ Ken의 과학을 이용한 마술 쇼
⑤ 마술에 숨겨진 비밀

[19~23] 다음 글을 읽고 물음에 답하시오.

Jina: Hello, everyone. Today, I'm going to show you ①amazing something.
(A) Next, I'll light the candle and cover it with a glass. "Abracadabra!"
(B) Now, I'll put a candle ②in the middle of the dish.
(C) Here's a dish with water in it.

Jina: Look at the water! _____ ⓐ
Ken: Air expands when it gets hot and creates higher pressure. When it ③gets cold, air contracts and creates lower pressure. When the flame ④burnt out, the air inside the glass cooled down. As the air cooled down, the air pressure dropped. So the air outside the glass was at a higher pressure. It pushed the water ⑤into the glass.

19 다음 중 빈칸 ⓐ에 들어갈 말로 가장 적절한 것은?

① Why did you cover it with a glass?
② How come you pour more water?
③ How come there is no water?
④ Why did you light the candle?
⑤ How come it rose into the glass?

20 자연스러운 글이 되도록 (A)~(C)를 바르게 배열한 것은?

① (A) – (C) – (B)   ② (B) – (A) – (C)
③ (B) – (C) – (A)   ④ (C) – (B) – (A)
⑤ (C) – (A) – (B)

서답형

21 According to the passage, which side of the air is at a higher pressure while the candle is still burning? Answer in English with a full sentence.

➡ _____

22 다음 ①~⑤ 중 어법상 바르지 않은 것은?

①   ②   ③   ④   ⑤

서답형

23 주어진 단어를 활용하여 Ken의 마술 쇼 제목을 쓰시오.

> The _____ Water (amaze, rise)

➡ _____

[24~27] 다음 글을 읽고 물음에 답하시오.

Ken: Now, I'm going to fill one of these cups with water. I will move them around to confuse you. Jina, which cup has the water in it?

Jina: That's easy! It's the middle one.

Ken: Okay, let's check. See? No water.

Jina: Show me the other cups.

Ken: See? There's no water.

Jina: Wow! (A)어째서 물이 사라진 거죠?

Ken: Before the trick, I put (B)a special material into one of the cups. The material absorbed the water and turned it into jelly. Then the jelly stuck to the bottom. If you want to try this trick, it's necessary to use cups (C)that you can't see through.

Jina: Thank you for your great performance. It was really amazing!

서답형

24 주어진 단어를 활용하여 밑줄 친 우리말 (A)를 영어로 쓰시오.

> (how)

➡ _____

25 다음 중 밑줄 친 (B)에 관한 설명으로 옳은 것은?

① Ken put it into one of the cups after the show.

② It can't take in water.

③ It turns water into jelly after absorbing water.

④ It is easy to remove it from the cup.

⑤ You should put it into all of the cups when trying the magic.

26 다음 중 밑줄 친 (C)와 쓰임이 같은 것은?

① I thought that we were lost.

② It was surprising that he accepted their apology.

③ The fact that he spread the news shocked everyone.

④ Did he say that he didn't serve the table?

⑤ The boy that you shook hands with is my cousin, Alan.

서답형

27 Write the reason why Ken moved around the cups after filling one of them with water. Answer in English with a full sentence.

➡ _____

[28~29] 다음 글을 읽고 물음에 답하시오.

> USA – The moving rocks in Death Valley
> How come the rocks move ___(A)___ their own? They weigh up to 300 kilograms each. Some scientists have watched their movements closely for a long time. Now we know that ice and wind move the rocks.

중요

28 다음 중 빈칸 (A)에 들어갈 말로 가장 적절한 것은?

① in ② about ③ at

④ on ⑤ out

서답형

29 위 글의 내용에 맞게 빈칸에 알맞은 말을 쓰시오.

> According to the research of the scientists, _____ make the rocks look like they move by themselves.

[01~03] 다음 글을 읽고 물음에 답하시오.

Jina: Welcome to the Super Science Magic Show! (A)It's always exciting to see magic tricks. And it's more exciting to find out the secrets behind them. Some people think the secret of magic is science. Today, Ken, a member of the School Magic Club, will use science to perform his tricks. Which tricks will he show us? I can't wait to see them.

01 According to Jina, what is more exciting about magic tricks? Answer in English with a full sentence.

➡ _____

_____

02 What will Ken perform? Answer in English with seven words.

➡ _____

03 밑줄 친 (A)가 의미하는 것을 위 글에서 찾아 쓰시오.

➡ _____

[04~08] 다음 글을 읽고 물음에 답하시오.

Ken: Hello, everyone. Today, I'm going to show you something amazing. Here's a dish with water in it. Now, I'll put a candle in the middle of the dish. Next, I'll light the candle and cover it with a glass. "Abracadabra!"

Jina: Look at the water! ___(A)___ it rose into the glass?

Ken: Air expands when it gets hot and creates higher pressure. When it gets cold, air contracts and creates lower pressure.

When the flame burnt out, the air inside the glass cooled down. As the air cooled down, the air pressure dropped. So the air outside the glass was at a higher pressure. It pushed the water into the glass.

04 빈칸 (A)에 알맞은 말을 쓰시오.

➡ _____

05 Where did Ken put the candle? Answer in English with a full sentence.

➡ _____

06 When air gets hot, what happens? Answer in English with a full sentence.

➡ _____

07 위 글의 내용에 맞게 빈칸에 알맞은 말을 쓰시오.

> When air gets cold, it becomes smaller in size and creates _____ _____.

08 위 글의 내용에 맞게 빈칸에 알맞은 말을 쓰시오.

> _____ Water Trick
> When the flame _____ _____, the air inside the glass _____ down and the air pressure _____. The _____ air pressure _____ the glass _____ the water into the glass.

[09~12] 다음 글을 읽고 물음에 답하시오.

Ken: Now, I'm going to fill one of these cups with water. I will move them around to confuse you. Jina, which cup has the water in it?

Jina: That's easy! It's the middle one.

Ken: Okay, let's check. See? No water.

Jina: Show me the other cups.

Ken: See? There's no water.

Jina: Wow! How come the water disappeared?

Ken: Before the trick, I put a special material into one of the cups. The material absorbed the water and turned it into jelly. Then the jelly stuck to the bottom. If you want to try this trick, (A)to use cups that you can't see through is necessary.

Jina: Thank you for your great performance. (B)It was really amazing!

09 위 글의 내용에 맞게 다음 빈칸에 알맞은 말을 쓰시오.

> Jina thought that the cup _____ _____ _____ _____ is the middle one.

10 What happens when the special material turns water into jelly? Answer in English and use the phrase 'of the cup.'

➡ _____

11 밑줄 친 (A)와 같은 의미의 문장을 쓰시오.

➡ _____

12 밑줄 친 (B)가 가리키는 것을 위 글에서 찾아 쓰시오.

➡ _____

[13~15] 다음 글을 읽고 물음에 답하시오.

A Dancing Coin

Can a coin dance? Let's test it. You need a coin and a bottle. Before you start, (A)병을 차갑게 하는 것이 중요합니다.(it)

Q: How do you do it?
A: First, put a coin on the mouth of the bottle. Then, hold the bottle in your hands for a while.

Q: What happens?
A: The coin moves up and down

Q: How come the coin moves?
A: Your hands warm the cold air inside the bottle. As the air gets warm, it expands. The expanding air tries to escape from the bottle.

13 What do we need to prepare to try the trick? Answer in English with a full sentence.

➡ _____

14 주어진 단어를 활용하여 밑줄 친 우리말 (A)를 영어로 쓰시오.

➡ _____

15 다음은 위 글을 요약한 것이다. 글의 내용과 일치하지 않는 것을 두 개 찾아 바르게 고쳐 쓰시오.

> There is a simple trick you can do if you have a coin and a bottle. First, prepare a cool bottle. Second, put a coin on the bottom of the bottle. Third, hold the bottle with your hands for some time. Then, the coin will spin.

➡ _____

➡ _____

해석

Real Life Communication B

A: Which class do you want to sign up for?

B: I want to take the badminton class. I like playing badminton. How about
you?
= What about you?

A: I want to take the computer class. I can't wait to make a computer program
= look forward to making
there.
= at the computer class

B: That sounds cool!

구문해설 • sign up for: ～을 신청하다, 등록하다

A: 무슨 수업을 등록하고 싶니?
B: 난 배드민턴 수업을 듣고 싶어. 나는 배드민턴 치는 것을 좋아하거든. 너는?
A: 난 컴퓨터 수업을 듣고 싶어. 나는 빨리 거기에서 컴퓨터 프로그램을 만들고 싶어.
B: 멋진 것 같다!

Culture & Life

North Atlantic Ocean – The Bermuda Triangle

A number of airplanes and ships have disappeared in the Bermuda Triangle.
a number of+복수명사   자동사 (수동태 불가)
How come? It's still a mystery.
= Why?

구문해설 • a number of: 많은 • disappear: 사라지다 • still: 여전히

북대서양 – 버뮤다 삼각 지대
많은 비행기와 선박이 버뮤다 삼각 지대에서 사라졌다. 이유가 무엇일까? 그것은 여전히 미스터리이다.

Culture & Life

Egypt – The pyramids

Some of the rocks that were used to build the pyramids weigh about 70 tons.
주격 관계대명사 be used to V: V 하는 데 사용되다   대략(전치사)
How was it possible to move such heavy rocks back then? It's still a mystery.
가주어   진주어 to부정사

구문해설 • rock: 바위 • build: 짓다 • weigh: 무게가 나가다 • possible: 가능한

이집트 – 피라미드
피라미드를 만드는 데 사용된 몇몇 바위들은 무게가 70톤 정도인 것들이 있다. 어떻게 그 시대에 그렇게 무거운 바위를 옮기는 것이 가능했을까? 그것은 여전히 미스터리이다.

영역별 핵심문제

Words & Expressions

01 다음 영영풀이가 가리키는 것을 고르시오.

> having the power to make impossible things happen

① necessary   ② magic
③ instead   ④ dry
⑤ safe

02 다음 중 밑줄 친 부분의 뜻풀이가 바르지 <u>않은</u> 것은?

① Would you <u>push</u> the window up? 밀다
② There is a huge <u>difference</u> between them. 차이
③ <u>Mix</u> some water with the flour. 섞다
④ Don't forget to put the ice cream back in the <u>freezer</u>. 냉동실
⑤ The boat was beginning to <u>sink</u> fast. 세면대

03 다음 우리말에 맞게 빈칸에 알맞은 말을 쓰시오.

(1) 타 버리고 꽃으로 변해라!
➡ Burn out and _____ _____ a flower!

(2) 유리컵 속의 공기는 차가워졌다.
➡ The air inside the glass _____ _____.

(3) 어째서 Ken은 당신이 속을 들여다 볼 수 없는 컵을 사용했는가?
➡ How come Ken used cups that you can't _____ _____.

(4) 그 물질은 물을 흡수하고 그것을 젤리로 변화시켰다.
➡ The material absorbed the water and _____ it _____ jelly.

04 다음 주어진 문장의 밑줄 친 sink와 <u>다른</u> 의미로 쓰인 것은?

> Don't leave your dirty plates in the <u>sink</u>.

① He is washing cups in the <u>sink</u>.
② The boat began to <u>sink</u> like a stone.
③ The <u>sink</u> is filled with water.
④ The sponge absorbed water from the <u>sink</u>.
⑤ The <u>sink</u> should be fixed to be used again.

05 다음 문장에 공통으로 들어갈 말을 고르시오.

> • Would you _____ the milk with the flour?
> • The cook is adding something to the _____.
> • Water and oil do not _____.

① practice   ② mix   ③ move
④ contract   ⑤ absorb

06 우리말과 일치하도록 주어진 어구를 모두 배열하여 영작하시오.

(1) 어느 불꽃이 먼저 꺼질까요?
(out / first / which / will / flame / burn)
➡ _____

(2) 나의 딸이 케이크 위에 촛불을 불었다.
(her / on / cake / my / blew / daughter / the candles / out)
➡ _____

(3) 물은 기온의 변화에 따라 팽창하고 수축한다.
(and / with / changes / temperature / in / expands / water / contracts)
➡ _____

07 다음 짝지어진 대화가 어색한 것은?

① A: Which trick do you want to learn?
　B: The ballon trick looks interesting. I want to learn how to move a can without touching it.

② A: Look at that girl. She's driving a robot.
　B: That looks really fun. I can't wait to try it.

③ A: Which eggs are fresh, and which ones are not?
　B: I can't wait to tell the difference.

④ A: Which program do you want to do at the science museum, Mira?
　B: I want to make lightning.

⑤ A: Which movie do you want to see?
　B: I want to see a 4D movie.

[08~10] 다음 대화를 읽고 물음에 답하시오.

King Sejong: It ⓐhasn't rained for a long time.
Jang Yeongsil: Yes. The dry season is lasting too long. The farmers are very worried.
King Sejong: We should do something ⓑto help them.
Jang Yeongsil: How about making a special clock?
King Sejong: A clock? How will that help?
Jang Yeongsil: The clock will show the time and the seasons. We can use it ⓒto prepare for the dry season.
King Sejong: That ⓓsound like a good idea. But who's going to make it?
Jang Yeongsil: I'll give it a try. I know a lot about time and the seasons.
King Sejong: Okay, I can't wait ⓔto see your clock.

08 위 대화의 밑줄 친 ⓐ~ⓔ 중 어법상 어색한 것을 찾아 바르게 고치시오.

➡ _____

09 위 대화에서 나타난 세종대왕의 기분 변화로 적절한 것은?

① worried → disappointed
② worried → pleased
③ disappointed → nervous
④ disappointed → worried
⑤ pleased → worried

10 위 대화의 내용과 일치하지 않는 것은?

① 비가 오랫동안 내리지 않았다.
② 건기가 너무 오래 계속 되고 있어 농부들이 매우 걱정하고 있다.
③ 장영실은 농부들을 돕기 위해 특별한 시계를 만들 것을 제안하였다.
④ 장영실은 시간과 계절에 대해 많이 알고 있다.
⑤ 장영실은 비가 내리게 하기 위해 시계를 만들고자 한다.

[11~12] 다음 대화를 읽고 물음에 답하시오.

Brian: Yujin, why did you put the eggs in water?
Yujin: I'm picking out the bad eggs.
Brian: Which eggs are fresh, and which ones are not?
Yujin: Eggs that sink in water are fresh. When eggs float in water, they're not fresh. You shouldn't eat them.
Brian: That's interesting. Why do the bad eggs float?
Yujin: Because they have gas inside. The gas acts like the air in a balloon.
Brian: Oh, I see.

11 위 대화에서 다음의 영영풀이가 가리키는 것을 찾아 쓰시오.

> to go down below the surface of water

➡ _____

12 위 대화를 읽고 대답할 수 없는 것은?

① What is Yujin doing with the eggs?
② How can Yujin tell the fresh eggs from the bad ones?
③ What do the bad eggs have inside?
④ What does the gas act like?
⑤ What is Yujin going to do with a balloon?

13 〈보기〉에 주어진 단어를 다음 글의 빈칸에 알맞게 쓰시오.

┌─── 보기 ───┐
strawberry / try / put / mix / cut / flavor
└───────────┘

Jane: Today we'll make ice cream. Which (A)_____ do you want to make? How about (B)_____? First, (C)_____ two cups of milk, two cups of heavy cream, and half a cup of sugar. Next, (D)_____ five strawberries into small pieces. Then, mix everything together and (E)_____ it in the freezer. That's it. It's easy to make, isn't it? Why don't you (F)_____ making it at home?

14 다음 우리말을 영어로 바르게 옮긴 것은?

> 네가 우리를 위해 나서 준 것은 정말 용감했어.

① It was brave you to step forward for us.
② It was brave for you to step forward for you.
③ It was brave of you step forward for us.
④ It was brave of you to step forward for us.
⑤ It was brave with you to step forward for us.

15 다음 빈칸에 들어갈 말로 적절하지 않은 것은?

> It is _____ for me to share my room with her.

① difficult   ② wise   ③ easy
④ hard   ⑤ necessary

16 다음 중 어법상 바르지 않은 것은?

① It is important to listen to others.
② It is foolish of you to behave like that.
③ How come you didn't take the umbrella?
④ Is it possible of her to stop biting her nail?
⑤ To see is to believe.

17 다음 중 밑줄 친 부분의 쓰임이 다른 하나는?

① It is okay for you to wear my clothes.
② To keep this place safe is important.
③ The bird is building a nest to lay eggs.
④ It is good to go out with you tonight.
⑤ To meet him in person is amazing.

18 주어진 단어를 활용하여 다음 우리말을 영어로 쓰시오.

> 그녀가 그 상자들을 옮기는 것은 쉽지 않아요.
> (it / move)

➡ _____

19 다음 빈칸에 들어갈 말이 바르게 짝지어진 것은?

> _____ is boring _____ he keeps saying the same thing over and over.

① That – that   ② It – to
③ It – that   ④ To – to
⑤ That – to

20 다음 중 빈칸에 들어갈 말이 <u>다른</u> 하나는?

① _____ she told you to go?
② _____ they didn't make it?
③ _____ he didn't want to see us?
④ _____ was there no one in the room?
⑤ _____ you didn't have your dinner?

21 다음 빈칸에 들어갈 말로 가장 적절한 것은?

> 왜 그는 매번 우리를 비난하는 거야?
> ➡ _____ he blames us every time?

① Why   ② What   ③ When
④ Who   ⑤ How come

22 다음 중 어법상 옳은 문장은?

① That is necessary to tell the truth.
② It is kind for her to read a book to us.
③ Why do you look unsatisfied?
④ It is fun play tennis with friends.
⑤ How come did he drink the coffee?

23 주어진 단어를 활용하여 다음 문장과 같은 의미의 문장을 쓰시오.

> Why did she make an appointment?
> (come)

➡ _____

24 다음 빈칸에 알맞은 말을 쓰시오.

> Was it strange that he said so?
> ➡ Was it strange _____ _____ to say so?

Reading

[25~27] 다음 글을 읽고 물음에 답하시오.

Ken: Hello, everyone. Today, I'm going to show you something amazing. Here's a dish with water in it. Now, I'll put a candle in the middle of the dish. Next, I'll (A)light the candle and cover it with a glass. "Abracadabra!"

Jina: Look at the water! How come it rose into the glass?

25 다음 중 밑줄 친 (A)와 같은 의미로 쓰인 것은?

① This is a room with natural <u>light</u>.
② Did you turn the <u>light</u> on?
③ Julia has <u>light</u> blue eyes.
④ I need to buy <u>light</u> summer clothes.
⑤ She wanted to <u>light</u> a cooking stove.

26 위 글에 이어질 내용으로 가장 적절한 것은?

① the reason why Ken likes to do magic
② the time when Ken first started to do magic
③ the next magic that Ken prepared
④ the reason why the water rose into the glass
⑤ how Ken made the water disappear

27 위 마술의 원리를 바르게 배열하시오.

Air expands when it gets hot and creates higher pressure. And when it gets cold, air contracts and creates lower pressure.
ⓐ So the air outside the glass was at a higher pressure.
ⓑ It pushed the water into the glass.
ⓒ As the air cooled down, the air pressure dropped.
ⓓ When the flame burnt out, the air inside the glass cooled down.

➡ _____

[28~30] 다음 글을 읽고 물음에 답하시오.

Ken: Air expands when it gets hot and creates ①<u>higher</u> pressure. When it gets cold, air ②<u>contracts</u> and creates lower pressure. When the flame burnt out, the air inside the glass cooled down. As the air ③ <u>cooled down</u>, the air pressure ④<u>dropped</u>. So the air outside the glass was at a higher pressure. (A)It ⑤<u>pulled</u> the water into the glass.

28 다음 밑줄 친 (A)가 가리키는 말을 위 글에서 찾아 쓰시오.

➡ _____

29 위 글의 ①~⑤ 중 글의 흐름상 어색한 것은?

① ② ③ ④ ⑤

30 다음과 같이 풀이할 수 있는 말을 위 글에서 찾아 쓰시오.

to increase in size, range, or amount

➡ _____

[31~32] 다음 대화를 읽고 물음에 답하시오.

Ken: Now, I'm going to fill one of these cups ____(A)____ . I will move them around to confuse you. Jina, which cup has the water in it?
Jina: That's easy! It's the middle one.
Ken: Okay, let's check. See? No water.
Jina: Show me the other cups.
Ken: See? There's no water.
Jina: Wow! How come the water disappeared?

31 다음 중 빈칸 (A)에 들어갈 말로 가장 적절한 것은?

① with sand   ② with water
③ with oil   ④ with another cup
⑤ with balls

32 다음 중 위 대화의 제목으로 가장 적절한 것은?

① The Magic of a Disappearing Cup
② The Amazing Science Experiment
③ The Secret of the Special Material
④ The Man Who Disappeared
⑤ The Secret of the Disappearing Water

[01~02] 다음 글을 읽고 물음에 답하시오.

> **Jane:** Today we'll make ice cream. (A)여러분은 어떤 맛을 만들고 싶은가요? How about strawberry? First, mix two cups of milk, two cups of heavy cream, and half a cup of sugar. Next, cut five strawberries into small pieces. Then, mix everything together and put it in the freezer. That's it. It's easy to make, isn't it? Why don't you try making it at home?

출제율 90%

01 위 글의 밑줄 친 (A)의 우리말을 주어진 단어를 이용하여 영작하시오. (which, flavor, make)

➡ _____

출제율 85%

02 위 글에서 다음 영영풀이가 나타내는 말을 찾아 쓰시오.

> to combine two or more substances so that they become a single substance

➡ _____

[03~04] 다음 대화를 읽고 물음에 답하시오.

> **Brian:** Yujin, why did you put the eggs in water?
> **Yujin:** (A) I'm picking out the bad eggs.
> **Brian:** (B) Which eggs are fresh, and which ones are not?
> **Yujin:** (C) When eggs float in water, they're not fresh. You shouldn't eat them.
> **Brian:** (D) That's interesting. Why do the bad eggs float?
> **Yujin:** (E) Because they have gas inside. The gas acts like the air in a balloon.
> **Brian:** Oh, I see.

출제율 100%

03 위 대화의 (A)~(E) 중 주어진 문장이 들어가기에 적절한 곳은?

> Eggs that sink in water are fresh.

① (A)   ② (B)   ③ (C)   ④ (D)   ⑤ (E)

출제율 85%

04 위 대화의 내용과 일치하도록 빈칸에 알맞은 말을 쓰시오.

> When eggs _____ in water, they're fresh. On the other hand, the eggs that _____ in water are not fresh. Bad eggs have _____ inside. It acts like the _____ in a balloon.

[05~06] 다음 대화를 읽고 물음에 답하시오.

> **Minsu:** What are you reading, Jiwon?
> **Jiwon:** I'm reading a book ⓐabout magic and science.
> **Minsu:** That sounds ⓑinteresting.
> **Jiwon:** Yes. This book introduces 100 magic tricks that ⓒuses science. I've ⓓlearned about half of them.
> **Minsu:** That's cool. Can you show me some of the tricks?
> **Jiwon:** Sure. I can show you a balloon trick now.
> **Minsu:** Great! I can't wait ⓔto see it.

출제율 90%

05 위 대화의 밑줄 친 ⓐ~ⓔ 중 어법상 어색한 것을 찾아 바르게 고치시오.

➡ _____

출제율 95%

06 위 대화를 읽고 대답할 수 없는 것은?

① What is Jiwon reading?
② What does the book introduce?
③ How many tricks has Jiwon learned from the book?
④ Which trick can Jiwon show to Minsu?
⑤ How long has Jiwon practiced a balloon trick?

[07~08] 다음 대화를 읽고 물음에 답하시오.

Brian: Mina, will you join our tennis club?

Mina: It sounds interesting, but I signed up for a special class this fall.

Brian: Which class did you sign up for?

Mina: I signed up for a magic class. I can't wait to learn new magic tricks there.

Brian: That sounds cool! Have you learned magic tricks before?

Mina: Yes, I learned some before, but I need more practice.

Brian: I hope I can see your magic tricks some day.

출제율 90%

07 Which class did Mina sign up for this fall?

➡ _____

출제율 95%

08 What is Mina looking forward to?

➡ _____

[09~10] 다음 대화를 읽고 물음에 답하시오.

Jaemin: Ms. Jeong, does a glass of water weigh more when there's a fish in it?

Ms. Jeong: (A) Yes, it does. We can test it now.

Jaemin: (B) But how? We don't have a fish.

Ms. Jeong: (C) We can use a finger instead of a fish.

Jaemin: (D) How will that work?

Ms. Jeong: (E) Then I will put my finger in the water and weigh it to compare.

Jaemin: Oh, (F)I can't wait to see the difference.

(to, looking)

출제율 100%

09 위 대화의 (A)~(E) 중 주어진 문장이 들어가기에 적절한 곳은?

I'll weigh a glass of water first.

① (A)　② (B)　③ (C)　④ (D)　⑤ (E)

출제율 85%

10 위 대화의 밑줄 친 (F)와 의미가 같도록 주어진 단어들을 사용하여 다시 쓰시오.

➡ _____

출제율 90%

11 다음 빈칸에 들어갈 말로 가장 적절한 것은?

How come _____ the flower?

① did she send　② does he cut
③ she brought　④ did you bring
⑤ did I send

출제율 100%

12 다음 빈칸에 들어갈 말이 나머지와 다른 하나는?

① It is difficult _____ us to know who wrote the letter.

② Is it hard _____ you to focus on what you are doing?

③ It is necessary _____ him to drink eight glasses of water every day.

④ It is careful _____ her to bring her purse all the time.

⑤ Is it important _____ them to be on time here?

출제율 80%

13 다음 우리말을 영어로 옮길 때 빈칸에 알맞은 말을 쓰시오.

네가 그러한 결정을 내린 것은 정말 현명했어.

➡ _____ _____ _____ _____ _____
_____ make such a decision.

14 다음 중 어법상 옳은 문장은?

① Is it possible to finding something meaningful in your life?

② How come is she complaining about it?

③ It is rude of you to not follow the advice.

④ Why he is sitting over there?

⑤ It is dangerous for us to swim in the river.

15 다음 중 어법상 옳은 것끼리 바르게 짝지은 것은?

(A) [That / It] is impossible to meet Ann on Sunday afternoon.

(B) It is important [to / that] he takes part in the race.

(C) [Why / How come] you lost the cap?

① That – to – Why

② That – that – How come

③ That – to – How come

④ It – that – How come

⑤ It – to – Why

16 주어진 어구를 활용하여 다음 우리말을 영어로 쓰시오.

그가 그 대회에서 우승했다는 것은 놀랍다.
(surprising / the competition / that / it)

➡ _____

17 일곱 개의 단어를 사용하여 다음 문장과 같은 의미의 문장을 쓰시오.

Why are you home so early?

➡ _____

[18~21] 다음 글을 읽고 물음에 답하시오.

Ken: Now, I'm going to fill one of these cups with water. I will move them around (A) to confuse you. Jina, which cup has the water in it?

Jina: That's easy! It's the middle one.

Ken: Okay, let's check. See? No water.

Jina: Show me the other cups.

Ken: See? There's no water.

Jina: Wow! How come the water disappeared?

Ken: Before the trick, I put a special material into one of the cups. The material absorbed the water and turned it into jelly. Then the jelly stuck to the bottom. If you want to try this trick, (B)it's necessary to use cups that you can't see through.

Jina: Thank you for your great performance. It was really amazing!

18 다음 중 밑줄 친 (A)와 쓰임이 같은 것은?

① I want you to tidy your room.

② He tried hard to succeed.

③ Is there any chance to win the race?

④ It is nice to hear it from you.

⑤ She planned to open a new office.

19 다음 중 위 글의 내용과 일치하는 것은?

① Ken prepared two cups.

② Jina thought it was difficult to find which cup had the water in it.

③ Ken moved around the cups to make Jina confused.

④ Jina didn't want to see if the other cups had the water in it.

⑤ Jina wasn't interested in the reason why the water disappeared.

출제율 90%

20 Ken이 밑줄 친 (B)와 같이 말한 이유를 우리말로 쓰시오.

➡ _____

출제율 95%

21 다음 중 Ken이 마술을 보여 주기 위하여 가장 먼저 한 일은?

① moving around the cups to confuse people
② pouring water into one of the cups
③ putting a special material into one of the cups
④ buying some jelly to treat people
⑤ preparing a cup which has a hole

[22~25] 다음 글을 읽고 물음에 답하시오.

A Dancing Coin

Can a coin dance? Let's test it. You need a coin and a bottle. Before you start, it is important to cool the bottle.

Q: _____ ⓐ _____
A: First, put a coin on the mouth of the bottle. Then, hold the bottle in your hands for a while.

Q: _____ ⓑ _____
A: The coin moves up and down.

Q: _____ ⓒ _____
A: Your hands warm the cold air inside the bottle. As the air gets warm, it expands. The (A) air tries to escape from the bottle.

출제율 95%

22 다음 빈칸 ⓐ~ⓒ에 주어진 문장을 내용에 맞게 쓰시오.

• What happens?
• How come the coin moves?
• How do you do it?

ⓐ _____
ⓑ _____
ⓒ _____

출제율 90%

23 위 글의 단어를 활용하여 빈칸 (A)에 알맞은 말을 쓰시오.

➡ _____

출제율 100%

24 What is important to do before we do the magic?

① We should prepare an empty bottle.
② We need to prepare as many coins as possible.
③ Cooling the bottle is important.
④ It is important to keep the bottle open.
⑤ We should prepare a clean bottle.

출제율 85%

25 글의 내용에 맞게 빈칸에 알맞은 말을 쓰시오.

Because of the air _____ _____ _____ _____ _____ _____, the coin on the mouth of the bottle moves up and down.

[01~03] 다음 대화를 읽고 물음에 답하시오.

Jang Yeongsil: Yes. The dry season is lasting too long. The farmers are very worried.

King Sejong: We should do something to help them.

Jang Yeongsil: How about making a special clock?

King Sejong: A clock? How will that help?

Jang Yeongsil: The clock will show the time and the seasons. We can use it to prepare for the dry season.

King Sejong: That sounds like a good idea. But who's going to make it?

Jang Yeongsil: I'll give it a try. I know a lot about time and the seasons.

King Sejong: Okay, I can't wait to see your clock.

01 What's the problem with King Sejong and Jang Yeongsil?

➡ _____

02 What does Jang Yeongsil suggest doing?

➡ _____

03 Why does Jang Yeongsil think the clock will help the farmers?

➡ _____
_____
_____

04 주어진 어구를 바르게 배열하여 다음 우리말을 영어로 쓰시오. 두 개의 단어를 추가하시오.

그녀의 허락 없이 그녀의 사진을 찍다니 그는 무례해.

(her permission / it / without / rude / her / is / him / take / of / pictures)

➡ _____
_____

05 다음 빈칸에 알맞은 말을 쓰시오.

It is amazing that he exercises regularly.
= It is amazing _____ _____ _____ exercise regularly.

06 다음 대화의 빈칸에 들어갈 말을 일곱 단어로 쓰시오.

A: _____

B: I couldn't catch the bus because he woke up late.

07 다음 주어진 문장과 같은 의미의 문장을 쓰시오.

To keep a diary is important.
= _____ a diary.

08 주어진 단어를 활용하여 다음 우리말을 영어로 쓰시오.

도대체 왜 그들은 피곤한 거야? (how)

➡ _____

Jina: Wow! (A)How come the water disappeared?

Ken: Before the trick, I put a special material into one of the cups. The material absorbed the water and turned it into jelly. Then the jelly stuck to the bottom. If you want to try this trick, it's necessary to use cups that you can't see through.

Jina: Thank you for your great performance. It was really amazing!

09 What did Ken put into one of the cups? Answer in English with a full sentence.

➡ _____

10 How come the water in the cup turned into jelly? Answer in English with a full sentence.

➡ _____

_____

11 주어진 단어를 활용하여 문장 (A)와 같은 의미의 문장을 쓰시오.

(why)

➡ _____

[12~13] 다음 글을 읽고 물음에 답하시오.

A Dancing Coin

Can a coin dance? Let's test it. You need a coin and a bottle. Before you start, it is important to cool the bottle.

Q: How do you do it?

A: First, put a coin on the mouth of the bottle. Then, hold the bottle in your hands for a while.

Q: What happens?

A: The coin moves up and down.

Q: How come the coin moves?

A: Your hands ____(A)____ the cold air inside the bottle. As the air ____(B)____ warm, it ____(C)____ . The expanding air tries to ____(D)____ from the bottle.

12 주어진 단어를 내용에 맞게 빈칸 (A)~(D)에 쓰시오. 필요하다면 어형을 바꾸시오.

escape / warm / expand / get

(A) _____ (B) _____

(C) _____ (D) _____

13 위 마술의 순서를 바르게 배열하시오.

ⓐ Hold the bottle in your hands.
ⓑ Cool a bottle.
ⓒ After a while, the coin will move.
ⓓ Put a coin on the mouth of the bottle.

➡ _____

01 다음 대화의 내용과 일치하도록 빈칸을 완성하시오.

King Sejong: It hasn't rained for a long time.

Jang Yeongsil: Yes. The dry season is lasting too long. The farmers are very worried.

King Sejong: We should do something to help them.

Jang Yeongsil: How about making a special clock?

King Sejong: A clock? How will that help?

Jang Yeongsil: The clock will show the time and the seasons. We can use it to prepare for the dry season.

King Sejong: That sounds like a good idea. But who's going to make it?

Jang Yeongsil: I'll give it a try. I know a lot about time and the seasons.

King Sejong: Okay, I can't wait to see your clock.

↓

King Sejong was worried about farmers because (A)_____ was lasting too long. When he looked for the way to help them, Jang Yeonsil suggested making (B)_____. King Sejong wondered how that clock could help farmers. Jang Yeonsil explained that the clock would show (C)_____, so it could be used (D)_____. Fortunately, Jang Yeongsli knew a lot about (E)_____, so he tried to invent it.

---

02 가주어 it과 주어진 to부정사구를 활용하여 여러 가지 문장을 쓰시오.

---

to make many friends / to love your pet / to save your allowance / to think others first

---

(1) _____

(2) _____

(3) _____

(4) _____

단원별 모의고사

01 다음 영영풀이가 가리키는 것을 고르시오.

> a device or room for freezing food or keeping it frozen

① coin　　　　② balloon
③ freezer　　　④ candle
⑤ pressure

02 다음 우리말에 맞게 빈칸에 알맞은 말을 쓰시오.

(1) 가스는 풍선 안의 공기처럼 작용한다.
　➡ The gas acts like the air in a _____.
(2) 나는 접시 한 가운데에 양초를 놓을 것이다.
　➡ I'll put a _____ in the middle of the dish.
(3) 나는 비교하기 위해서 물속에 내 손가락을 넣을 것이다.
　➡ I will put my finger in the water to _____.

03 다음 문장의 빈칸에 들어갈 말을 〈보기〉에서 골라 쓰시오.

> ┤ 보기 ├
> flames / material / absorbs /
> pressure / experiment

(1) Apply _____ to the wound to stop the bleeding.
(2) They tried to put out the fire, but the _____ grew higher.
(3) The sponge _____ water.
(4) Steel is an essential _____ in building.
(5) Students are doing a science _____ with a candle.

[04~05] 다음 대화를 읽고 물음에 답하시오.

Minsu: What are you reading, Jiwon?
Jiwon: I'm reading a book about magic and science.
Minsu: That sounds interesting.
Jiwon: Yes. This book introduces 100 magic tricks that use science. I've learned about half of (A)them.
Minsu: That's cool. Can you show me some of the tricks?
Jiwon: Sure. I can show you a balloon trick now.
Minsu: Great! I can't wait to see it.

04 위 대화의 밑줄 친 (A)them이 가리키는 것을 찾아 쓰시오.

➡ _____

05 위 대화의 내용과 일치하지 않는 것은?

① 지원이는 마술과 과학에 관한 책을 읽고 있다.
② 책은 과학을 사용하는 100가지 마술을 소개하고 있다.
③ 지원이는 책에서 소개한 마술 중 절반 정도를 익혔다.
④ 지원이는 풍선 마술을 보여 줄 수 있다.
⑤ 민수는 지원이가 소개한 책을 빨리 읽고 싶다.

[06~07] 다음 대화를 읽고 물음에 답하시오.

Brian: Mina, will you join our tennis club?
Mina: It sounds interesting, but I signed up for a special class this fall.
Brian: Which class did you sign up for?
Mina: I signed up for a magic class. ____(A)____
Brian: That sounds cool! Have you learned magic tricks before?
Mina: Yes, I learned some before, but I need more practice.
Brian: I hope I can see your magic tricks some day.

06 〈보기〉에 주어진 단어들을 모두 배열하여 위 대화의 빈칸 (A)에 쓰시오.

┌─── 보기
tricks / new / there / can't / to / I / wait / learn / magic
└────────────

➡ _____

07 위 대화의 내용과 일치하지 <u>않는</u> 것은?

① 미나는 이번 가을에 특별 수업에 등록했다.
② 미나는 마술 수업에 등록했다.
③ 미나는 새로운 마술 묘기를 빨리 배우고 싶어 한다.
④ 미나는 전에 마술 묘기를 배운 적이 없다.
⑤ Brian은 언젠가 미나의 마술 묘기를 볼 수 있기를 바란다.

08 다음 대화의 밑줄 친 (A)와 바꾸어 쓸 수 있는 것은?

> Jaemin: Ms. Jeong, does a glass of water weigh more when there's a fish in it?
> Ms. Jeong: Yes, it does. We can test it now.
> Jaemin: But how? We don't have a fish.
> Ms. Jeong: We can use a finger instead of a fish.
> Jaemin: How will that work?
> Ms. Jeong: I'll weigh a glass of water first. Then I will put my finger in the water and weigh it to compare.
> Jaemin: Oh, (A)I can't wait to see the difference.

① I don't have time to wait to see the difference.
② I'm not able to see the difference.
③ I'm looking forward to seeing the difference.
④ I'm doubtful if there is the difference.
⑤ I don't know how to tell the difference.

[09~10] 다음 글을 읽고 물음에 답하시오.

> Jane: Today we'll make ice cream. ⓐWhich flavor do you want to make? How about strawberry? First, ⓑmix two cups of milk, two cups of heavy cream, and half a cup of sugar. Next, cut five strawberries into small pieces. Then, mix everything together and ⓒputting it in the freezer. That's it. It's easy ⓓto make, isn't it? Why don't you try ⓔmaking it at home?

09 위 대화의 밑줄 친 ⓐ~ⓔ 중 어법상 어색한 것을 찾아 바르게 고치시오.

➡ _____

10 위 글을 읽고 대답할 수 <u>없는</u> 것은?

① Which flavor ice cream is Jane going to make?
② What should Jane prepare to make the ice cream?
③ How much milk does Jane need to make the ice cream?
④ What should Jane do after cutting five strawberries into small pieces?
⑤ How long should Jane keep the mix in the freezer?

[11~12] 다음 대화를 읽고 물음에 답하시오.

> Brian: Yujin, why did you put the eggs in water?
> Yujin: I'm picking out the bad eggs.
> Brian: Which eggs are fresh, and which ones are not?
> Yujin: Eggs that sink in water are fresh. When eggs float in water, they're not fresh. You shouldn't eat them.
> Brian: That's interesting. Why do the bad eggs float?
> Yujin: Because they have gas inside. The gas acts like the air in a balloon.
> Brian: Oh, I see.

11 Which eggs are not fresh?

➡ _____

12 What makes the bad eggs float in the water?

➡ _____

13 다음 빈칸에 들어갈 말이 바르게 짝지어진 것은?

(A) _____ it is so cold here?

(B) It is clever _____ her to know the answer.

① Why – to   ② Why – for
③ How come – in   ④ How come – of
⑤ How come – to

14 다음 중 어법상 바르지 <u>않은</u> 것은?

① It is nice of her to give you a candy.
② How come you are so busy these days?
③ It is considerate of her to do the volunteer work.
④ Why did you throw away the paper?
⑤ It is possible of him to ride a bike alone.

15 다음 중 밑줄 친 부분의 쓰임이 <u>다른</u> 하나는?

① <u>It</u> is dangerous for you to be alone in the playground.
② <u>It</u> is foolish of her to believe such a thing.
③ <u>It</u> is my duty to protect you.
④ <u>It</u> is a great idea to invent something to make your life comfortable.
⑤ <u>It</u> was very dark in the forest and the girl couldn't find the way.

16 다음 빈칸에 알맞은 말을 쓰시오.

그가 너의 생일에 축하하지 않은 것은 인색했어.

➡ It was mean _____ _____ _____ _____ say congratulations on your birthday.

17 주어진 단어를 활용하여 다음 우리말을 영어로 쓰시오.

도대체 왜 그는 파티에 오지 않는 거야?
(how / to the party)

➡ _____

[18~19] 다음 글을 읽고 물음에 답하시오.

Jina: Wow! How come the water disappeared?

Ken: (A) Then the jelly stuck to the bottom.

(B) Before the trick, I put a special material into one of the cups.

(C) Therefore, if you want to try this trick, it's necessary to use cups that you can't see through.

(D) The material absorbed the water and turned it into jelly.

Jina: Thank you for your great performance. It was really amazing!

18 자연스러운 글이 되도록 (A)~(D)를 바르게 배열하시오.

➡ _____

19 다음은 위 마술의 원리를 요약한 것이다. 빈칸에 알맞은 말을 쓰시오.

> The special material in the cup _____ the water and turned it into jelly. Then the jelly _____ to _____ _____.

[20~21] 다음 글을 읽고 물음에 답하시오.

Jina: Welcome to the Super Science Magic Show! It's always exciting to see magic tricks. And it's more exciting to find out the secrets behind them. Some people think the secret of magic is science. Today, Ken, a member of the School Magic Club, will use science to perform his tricks. Which tricks will he show us? (A)I can't wait to see them.

20 According to Jina, what will Ken use to perform his tricks? Answer in English with a full sentence.

➡ _____

21 다음 중 밑줄 친 (A)가 의미하는 것으로 가장 적절한 것은?

① I have been waiting for Ken for a long time.
② I don't have any interest in seeing a magic show.
③ I am really looking forward to seeing them.
④ I want Ken to show us many tricks more often.
⑤ I can't help seeing the show as soon as possible.

[22~25] 다음 글을 읽고 물음에 답하시오.

Ken: Hello, everyone. Today, I'm going to ① show you something amazing. ②Here's a dish with water in it. Now, I'll put a candle in the middle of the dish. Next, I'll light the candle and cover ③it with a glass. "Abracadabra!"
Jina: Look at the water! ④Why it rose into the glass?
Ken: Air expands when it gets hot and creates ⑤higher pressure. When it gets cold, air contracts and creates lower pressure. When the flame burnt out, the air inside the glass cooled down. As the air cooled down, the air pressure dropped. So the air outside the glass was at a higher pressure. It pushed the water into the glass.

22 위 글의 ①~⑤ 중 어법상 바르지 <u>않은</u> 것은?

①   ②   ③   ④   ⑤

23 What happened to the water after the flame in the glass burnt out?

➡ _____

24 위 글을 읽고 답할 수 <u>없는</u> 것은?

① What happens when air gets cold?
② What should we do if we want air to contract?
③ When does air expand?
④ Why did the air pressure inside the glass drop?
⑤ How long did the candle burn?

25 What did Ken do after lighting the candle? Answer in English with a full sentence.

➡ _____

INSIGHT
on the textbook

교과서 파헤치기

※ 다음 영어를 우리말로 쓰시오.

01 block	22 scene
02 half	23 strange
03 delete	24 thief
04 accident	25 prize
05 throw	26 safely
06 somewhere	27 explain
07 dragon	28 straight
08 bottom	29 finally
09 suspect	30 disappear
10 lie	31 fold
11 escape	32 none
12 outside	33 solve
13 clue	34 riddle
14 hide	35 button
15 detective	36 help yourself
16 luckily	37 write down
17 bean	38 turn over
18 twice	39 catch a thief
19 space	40 fill A with B
20 inside	41 for free
21 congratulation	42 at the time of
	43 make it to ~

※ 다음 우리말을 영어로 쓰시오.

01 단추

02 장면

03 단서, 실마리

04 던지다

05 맨 아래 (부분)

06 이상한

07 설명하다

08 접다

09 건너다

10 반, 절반

11 어딘가에

12 삭제하다

13 두 번

14 마침내

15 숨기다, 숨다

16 거짓말하다

17 똑바로, 일직선으로

18 사고

19 해결하다

20 사라지다

21 콩

22 용의자

23 탈출하다

24 다행히

25 축하

26 공간

27 ~ 밖에, 밖으로

28 상

29 수수께끼

30 안전하게

31 탐정, 형사

32 양초

33 도둑

34 우표

35 용

36 A를 B로 채우다

37 뒤집다

38 ~에 이르는데 성공하다

39 공짜로

40 ~이 일어나던 때에

41 적다

42 도둑을 잡다

43 마음껏 드세요

※ 다음 영영풀이에 알맞은 단어를 <보기>에서 골라 쓴 후, 우리말 뜻을 쓰시오.

1 _____ : to go or come into a place: _____

2 _____ : someone who is thought to be guilty of a crime: _____

3 _____ : a seed or a pod that comes from a climbing plant and is cooked as food: _____

4 _____ : the flat surface on the lowest side of an object: _____

5 _____ : someone who steals things from another person or place: _____

6 _____ : exactly or about 50% of an amount, time, distance, number etc.: _____

7 _____ : an object or piece of information that helps someone solve a crime or mystery: _____

8 _____ : to go from one side of something such as a road, river, room, etc. to the other: _____

9 _____ : to remove something that has been written down or stored in a computer: _____

10 _____ : a long wooden stick with a special shape that is used in some sports and games: _____

11 _____ : an event in which a car, train, plane, etc. is damaged and often someone is hurt: _____

12 _____ : someone who is paid to discover information about someone or something: _____

13 _____ : a question that is deliberately very confusing and has a humorous or clever answer: _____

14 _____ : to leave a place when someone is trying to catch you or stop you, or when there is a dangerous situation: _____

15 _____ : to put or keep someone or something in a place where they/it cannot be seen or found: _____

16 _____ : a small piece of paper with a design on it that you buy and stick on an envelope or a package before you post it: _____

보기			
riddle	suspect	detective	delete
bean	escape	hide	clue
accident	thief	bat	cross
enter	bottom	stamp	half

※ 다음 우리말과 일치하도록 빈칸에 알맞은 말을 쓰시오.

Listen & Speak 1-A

Jimin: Do you _____ _____ _____ the new game _____ I
_____?

Brian: Sure, _____ is _____, Jimin?

Jimin: It's _____ a soccer game but the players are _____ and
_____. You _____ _____ _____ these buttons
_____ _____.

Brian: That _____ _____. _____ _____ _____ _____
_____ _____ the buttons?

Jimin: Sure.

Jimin: 내가 산 새로운 게임을 하고 싶니?

Brian: 물론이야. 그게 뭐니, 지민아?

Jimin: 축구 시합 같은 것인데 선수들이 용과 해마야. 게임을 하려면 이 버튼들을 사용해야 해.

Brian: 재밌을 거 같아. 버튼 사용법을 설명해 줄 수 있니?

Jimin: 물론이지.

Listen & Speak 1-B

Jack: Kelly, here's a _____. You can see this _____
_____ _____, _____ in a year, but _____
_____ _____. What is this?

Kelly: _____ _____ _____ _____ _____.

Jack: It's the letter "E."

Kelly: I don't _____ _____. _____ _____ _____ _____?

Jack: Well, there are two "E"s in the word "week," one "E" in the
word "_____" but _____ "E"s in the word "_____."

Kelly: Aha! Now I _____ _____.

Jack: Kelly, 수수께끼가 있어. 넌 이것을 1주에 두 번, 1년에 한 번 볼 수 있어, 하지만 1일에는 전혀 볼 수가 없어. 이게 뭐게?

Kelly: 전혀 모르겠어.

Jack: 알파벳 'E'야.

Kelly: 이해가 안 가. 이유를 설명해 줄 수 있니?

Jack: 음, 단어 week에는 'E'가 2개 있고, 단어 year에는 'E'가 1개 있고, 단어 day에는 'E'가 없잖아.

Kelly: 아! 이제 이해했다.

Listen & Speak 2-A

Tom: Yujin, _____ _____ my paper fox.

Yujin: That's cute. _____ _____ _____ _____ _____ _____?

Tom: _____, fold a paper _____ _____ to _____ _____
_____. _____, _____ _____ of the triangle
to the _____ _____. _____, fold _____ _____ of
the bottom line to the top _____ _____ _____. _____,
_____ it _____ and draw a face.

Yujin: That _____ _____.

Tom: 유진아, 내 종이 여우를 봐.

Yujin: 귀엽다. 어떻게 만들었니?

Tom: 먼저, 종이를 반으로 접어서 세모를 만들어. 두 번째로, 세모의 꼭대기를 맨 아랫선 쪽으로 접어. 세 번째로, 맨 아랫선 양쪽 끝을 위로 접어서 귀를 만들어. 그러고 나서, 그것을 뒤집어서 얼굴을 그려.

Yujin: 쉽구나.

Listen & Speak 2-B

Jane: Minsu, do you know the TV show about the student _____?

Minsu: Yes. I love that show, but I _____ _____ it _____ _____. What was it _____?

Jane: Well, _____ _____ the bikes at school _____.

Minsu: So, what _____ he _____?

Jane: _____, he _____ _____ the school. _____, he met some _____ and asked questions. _____, he _____ the _____. The thief was ....

Minsu: No, _____ _____ me! I'll _____ it _____.

Real Life Communication

Emily: Junsu, do you want to _____ a riddle?

Junsu: Sure, what is it?

Emily: There is a farmer. _____, the farmer buys a fox, a duck, and _____ _____ _____ _____ _____. Then, the farmer _____ _____ _____ _____ _____ _____.

Junsu: What's the problem?

Emily: The boat _____ _____ _____ the farmer and _____ _____ thing.

Junsu: _____ _____ _____ that the farmer can _____ only one thing _____ _____ _____?

Emily: Yes. Also, the fox will eat the duck or the duck will eat the beans if the farmer isn't there. _____ _____ _____ _____ _____ _____ _____ the river _____?

Junsu: Hmm ....

Let's Check

Minjun: Wow! Something _____ really _____, Mom. What is it?

Mom: We're _____ _____ have tacos _____ _____. _____ _____.

Minjun: _____ _____ _____ _____ _____ _____ _____ _____ _____ _____ a taco?

Mom: _____, _____ your tortilla _____ vegetables and meat. _____, _____ some sauce _____ _____ _____.

Minjun: Sounds _____!

Mom: _____ you _____ some cheese?

Minjun: No, _____.

Jane: 민수야, 학생 탐정이 나오는 TV 쇼를 아니?

Minsu: 응, 나는 그 쇼를 아주 좋아하지만 이번 주에는 못 봤어. 무슨 내용이었어?

Jane: 음, 학교의 모든 자전거들이 사라졌어.

Minsu: 그래서 그가 무엇을 했어?

Jane: 첫째로, 그는 학교를 둘러 봤어. 그러고 나서, 몇몇의 용의자를 만나서 질문을 했지. 마침내, 그는 도둑을 찾았어. 도둑은....

Minsu: 안 돼, 말하지 마! 내가 나중에 볼 거야.

Emily: 준수야, 수수께끼 하나 풀어볼래?

Junsu: 물론이지, 뭔데?

Emily: 한 농부가 있어. 먼저 농부는 여우, 오리, 콩 자루를 하나씩 사. 그러고 나서, 농부는 강을 건너야 해.

Junsu: 뭐가 문제인데?

Emily: 보트는 단지 농부와 한 가지만 더 옮길 수 있어.

Junsu: 농부가 한 번에 오직 한 가지만 옮길 수 있다는 말이니?

Emily: 응. 또한 만약 농부가 없다면 여우가 오리를 먹거나, 오리가 콩을 먹을 거야. 전부를 강 건너로 안전하게 옮길 방법을 설명할 수 있겠니?

Junsu: 음....

Minjun: 와! 뭔가 정말 좋은 냄새가 나요, 엄마. 뭐예요?

Mom: 우리는 저녁 식사로 타코를 먹을 거야. 맘껏 먹으렴.

Minjun: 타코 만드는 법을 설명해 주실 수 있어요?

Mom: 먼저, 토르티야를 채소와 코기로 채워. 그 다음, 위에 약간의 소스를 추가하렴.

Minjun: 맛있을 것 같아요!

Mom: 치즈 좀 줄까?

Minjun: 아뇨, 괜찮아요.

※ 다음 우리말에 맞도록 대화를 영어로 쓰시오.

Listen & Speak 1-A

Jimin: _____

Brian: _____

Jimin: _____

_____

Brian: _____

Jimin: _____

Jimin: 내가 산 새로운 게임을 하고 싶니?

Brian: 물론이야. 그게 뭐니, 지민아?

Jimin: 축구 시합 같은 것인데 선수들이 용과 해마야. 게임을 하려면 이 버튼들을 사용해야 해.

Brian: 재밌을 거 같아. 버튼 사용법을 설명해 줄 수 있니?

Jimin: 물론이지.

Listen & Speak 1-B

Jack: _____

_____

Kelly: _____

Jack: _____

Kelly: _____

Jack: _____

_____

Kelly: _____

Jack: Kelly, 수수께끼가 있어. 넌 이것을 1주에 두 번, 1년에 한 번 볼 수 있어, 하지만 1일에는 전혀 볼 수가 없어. 이게 뭐게?

Kelly: 전혀 모르겠어.

Jack: 알파벳 'E'야.

Kelly: 이해가 안 가. 이유를 설명해 줄 수 있니?

Jack: 음, 단어 week에는 'E'가 2개 있고, 단어 year에는 'E'가 1개 있고, 단어 day에는 'E'가 없잖아.

Kelly: 아! 이제 이해했다.

Listen & Speak 2-A

Tom: _____

Yujin: _____

Tom: _____

_____

Yujin: _____

Tom: 유진아, 내 종이 여우를 봐.

Yujin: 귀엽다. 어떻게 만들었니?

Tom: 먼저, 종이를 반으로 접어서 세모를 만들어. 두 번째로, 세모의 꼭대기를 맨 아랫선 쪽으로 접어. 세 번째로, 맨 아랫선 양쪽 끝을 위로 접어서 귀를 만들어. 그리고 나서, 그것을 뒤집어서 얼굴을 그려.

Yujin: 쉽구나.

Listen & Speak 2-B

Jane: _____

Minsu: _____

Jane: _____

Minsu: _____

Jane: _____

_____

Minsu: _____

Real Life Communication

Emily: _____

Junsu: _____

Emily: _____

_____

Junsu: _____

Emily: _____

Junsu: _____

Emily: _____

_____

Junsu: _____

Let's Check

Minjun: _____

Mom: _____

Minjun: _____

Mom: _____

_____

Minjun: _____

Mom: _____

Minjun: _____

Jane: 민수야, 학생 탐정이 나오는 TV 쇼를 아니?

Minsu: 응, 나는 그 쇼를 아주 좋아하지만 이번 주에는 못 봤어. 무슨 내용이었어?

Jane: 음, 학교의 모든 자전거들이 사라졌어.

Minsu: 그래서 그가 무엇을 했어?

Jane: 첫째로, 그는 학교를 둘러 봤어. 그러고 나서, 몇몇의 용의자를 만나서 질문을 했지. 마침내, 그는 도둑을 찾았어. 도둑은....

Minsu: 안 돼, 말하지 마! 내가 나중에 볼 거야.

Emily: 준수야, 수수께끼 하나 풀어볼래?

Junsu: 물론이지, 뭔데?

Emily: 한 농부가 있어. 먼저 농부는 여우, 오리, 콩 자루를 하나씩 사. 그러고 나서, 농부는 강을 건너야 해.

Junsu: 뭐가 문제인데?

Emily: 보트는 단지 농부와 한 가지만 더 옮길 수 있어.

Junsu: 농부가 한 번에 오직 한 가지만 옮길 수 있다는 말이니?

Emily: 응. 또한 만약 농부가 없다면 여우가 오리를 먹거나, 오리가 콩을 먹을 거야. 전부를 강 건너로 안전하게 옮길 방법을 설명할 수 있겠니?

Junsu: 음....

Minjun: 와! 뭔가 정말 좋은 냄새가 나요, 엄마. 뭐예요?

Mom: 우리는 저녁 식사로 타코를 먹을 거야. 맘껏 먹으렴.

Minjun: 타코 만드는 법을 설명해 주실 수 있어요?

Mom: 먼저, 토르티야를 채소와 코기로 채워. 그 다음, 위에 약간의 소스를 추가하렴.

Minjun: 맛있을 것 같아요!

Mom: 치즈 좀 줄까?

Minjun: 아뇨, 괜찮아요.

※ 다음 우리말과 일치하도록 빈칸에 알맞은 것을 골라 쓰시오.

The Great Escape

1 _____ _____ the _____ Tower.
A. Escape   B. to   C. Welcome

2 You will _____ the _____ room in _____ tower.
A. first   B. our   C. enter

3 You need to _____ some _____ to _____ .
A. riddles   B. solve   C. escape

4 Clues can _____ _____ somewhere _____ the room.
A. inside   B. found   C. be

5 So, _____ you _____ to _____ like Sherlock Holmes?
A. think   B. are   C. ready

Room # 1

6 Mr. Doodle was _____ _____ a car _____ Sunday afternoon.
A. by   B. on   C. hit

7 _____ , he wasn't _____ _____ , but he didn't _____ the driver.
A. see   B. badly   C. hurt   D. luckily

8 Three _____ were _____ _____ a police officer.
A. by   B. suspects   C. questioned

9 Ms. A said she was _____ a book at the _____ of the _____ .
A. accident   B. time   C. reading

10 Mr. B _____ he _____ _____ his dog.
A. was   B. said   C. walking

11 Ms. C said she _____ _____ _____ .
A. making   B. breakfast   C. was

12 _____ _____ Mr. Doodle? Can you _____ why?
A. hit   B. explain   C. who

13 Do you _____ the answer? _____ it _____ .
A. have   B. down   C. write

14 Then you can _____ the _____ room.
A. next   B. to   C. move

15 **Clue** The _____ _____ _____ the afternoon.
A. in   B. happened   C. accident

16 Congratulations! You _____ _____ _____ the second room.
A. to   B. made   C. it

대탈출

1 '탈출탑'에 오신 것을 환영합니다.

2 당신은 저희 탑의 첫 번째 방에 들어갈 것입니다.

3 당신은 탈출하기 위하여 몇 개의 수수께끼를 풀어야 합니다.

4 단서들은 방 어딘가에서 발견될 수 있습니다.

5 그러면 당신은 셜록 홈스처럼 생각할 준비가 되었나요?

방 # 1

6 Doodle씨는 일요일 오후에 차에 치였습니다.

7 다행히 그는 심하게 다치지 않았으나 그는 운전자를 보지 못했습니다.

8 세 명의 용의자들이 경찰에게 심문을 받았습니다.

9 A씨는 사고가 일어난 시간에 책을 읽고 있었다고 말했습니다.

10 B씨는 그의 개를 산책시키고 있었다고 말했습니다.

11 C씨는 아침을 만들고 있었다고 말했습니다.

12 누가 Doodle씨를 치었을까요? 왜 그런지 설명할 수 있나요?

13 답을 가지고 있나요? 적어 보세요.

14 그런 다음, 당신은 다음 방으로 갈 수 있습니다.

15 단서: 사건은 오후에 일어났습니다.

16 축하합니다! 당신은 두 번째 방에 오는 데 성공하셨습니다.

17 However, the second room is _____ _____ to _____ than the first one. Good luck!

    A. escape   B. harder   C. much

Room #2

18 Jay _____ an email _____ his favorite _____ store.

    A. clothing   B. from   C. gets

19 The title _____ "You _____ our Lucky Day _____!"

    A. won   B. reads   C. event

20 Jay is _____. He _____ _____ it.

    A. quickly   B. surprised   C. opens

21 JayJr@kmail.com

You _____ _____ 'Lucky Day' _____!

    A. our   B. event   C. won

22 Congratulations! You _____ _____ a special _____.

    A. prize   B. won   C. have

23 _____ our Lucky Day event, you can _____ any seven _____ from our store for _____!

    A. free   B. choose   C. items   D. during

24 Come _____ our store _____ November 31.

    A. on   B. to

25 We _____ _____ _____ see you.

    A. wait   B. to   C. can't

26 _____ _____, Kay Brown

    A. yours   B. truly

27 _____, Jay thinks that the event isn't _____ and _____ the email.

    A. deletes   B. real   C. however

28 _____ you _____ _____?

    A. explain   B. why   C. can

29 **Clue** _____ are _____ 30 or 31 _____ in a month.

    A. usually   B. days   C. there

30 Do you _____ the _____?

    A. answer   B. have

31 _____ it _____ and then you are _____ to go!

    A. down   B. free   C. write

17 그러나 두 번째 방은 첫 번째 방보다 탈출하기 훨씬 더 어렵습니다. 행운을 빕니다!

방 # 2

18 Jay는 그가 가장 좋아하는 옷 가게로부터 이메일을 받습니다.

19 제목은 "당신은 '행운의 날' 행사에 당첨되었습니다!"라고 적혀 있습니다.

20 Jay는 놀랍니다. 그는 재빨리 그것을 엽니다.

21 JayJr@kmail.com
당신은 우리의 '행운의 날' 행사에 당첨되었습니다!

22 축하합니다! 당신은 특별한 상품을 받게 되었습니다.

23 '행운의 날' 행사 동안, 당신은 우리 가게에서 일곱 가지 상품을 아무거나 무료로 선택할 수 있습니다!

24 11월 31일에 우리 가게로 오세요.

25 우리는 몹시 당신을 보기를 기대합니다.

26 안녕히 계십시오, Kay Brown

27 그러나 Jay는 그 행사가 사실이 아니라고 생각하고 이메일을 삭제합니다.

28 왜 그런지 설명할 수 있나요?

29 단서: 한 달은 주로 30일 또는 31일이 있습니다.

30 답을 가지고 계신가요?

31 그것을 적으면, 당신은 자유롭게 가실 수 있습니다!

※ 다음 우리말과 일치하도록 빈칸에 알맞은 말을 쓰시오.

The Great Escape

1 _____ _____ the Escape Tower.

2 You will _____ _____ _____ _____ in our tower.

3 You _____ _____ _____ _____ to escape.

4 Clues can _____ _____ somewhere _____ the room.

5 So, _____ you _____ _____ _____ _____ Sherlock Holmes?

Room # 1

6 Mr. Doodle _____ _____ _____ a car _____ Sunday afternoon.

7 _____ , he _____ _____ _____ , but he _____ _____ the driver.

8 Three suspects _____ _____ _____ a police officer.

9 Ms. A said she was _____ _____ _____ _____ _____ _____ _____ _____ _____ .

10 Mr. B _____ he _____ _____ his dog.

11 Ms. C said she _____ _____ _____ .

12 _____ _____ Mr. Doodle? Can you _____ _____ ?

13 Do you have the answer? _____ _____ _____ .

14 Then you _____ _____ _____ the next room.

15 Clue The _____ _____ _____ the afternoon.

16 Congratulations! You _____ _____ _____ the second room.

대탈출

1 '탈출탑'에 오신 것을 환영합니다.

2 당신은 저희 탑의 첫 번째 방에 들어갈 것입니다.

3 당신은 탈출하기 위하여 몇 개의 수수께끼를 풀어야 합니다.

4 단서들은 방 어딘가에서 발견될 수 있습니다.

5 그러면 당신은 셜록 홈스처럼 생각할 준비가 되었나요?

방 # 1

6 Doodle씨는 일요일 오후에 차에 치였습니다.

7 다행히 그는 심하게 다치지 않았으나 그는 운전자를 보지 못했습니다.

8 세 명의 용의자들이 경찰에게 심문을 받았습니다.

9 A씨는 사고가 일어난 시간에 책을 읽고 있었다고 말했습니다.

10 B씨는 그의 개를 산책시키고 있었다고 말했습니다.

11 C씨는 아침을 만들고 있었다고 말했습니다.

12 누가 Doodle씨를 치었을까요? 왜 그런지 설명할 수 있나요?

13 답을 가지고 있나요? 적어 보세요.

14 그런 다음, 당신은 다음 방으로 갈 수 있습니다.

15 단서: 사건은 오후에 일어났습니다.

16 축하합니다! 당신은 두 번째 방에 오는 데 성공하셨습니다.

17 _____, the second room is _____ _____ _____
_____ _____ the first one. Good luck!

Room #2

18 Jay _____ an email _____ his favorite _____ _____.

19 The title _____ "You _____ our Lucky Day event!"

20 Jay is _____. He _____ _____ it.

21 JayJr@kmail.com
You _____ _____ 'Lucky Day' event!

22 _____! You _____ _____ a special _____.

23 _____ our Lucky Day event, you can _____ any seven items
_____ our store _____ _____!

24 _____ _____ _____ our store _____ November 31.

25 We _____ _____ _____ _____ you.

26 _____ _____, Kay Brown

27 _____, Jay _____ _____ the event _____ _____ and
_____ the email.

28 _____ you _____ _____ ?

29 **Clue** _____ _____ _____ 30 or 31 _____ in a month.

30 Do you _____ _____ _____ ?

31 _____ _____ _____ and then you _____ _____
_____ _____!

17 그러나 두 번째 방은 첫 번째 방보다 탈출하기 훨씬 더 어렵습니다. 행운을 빕니다!

방 # 2

18 Jay는 그가 가장 좋아하는 옷 가게로부터 이메일을 받습니다.

19 제목은 "당신은 '행운의 날' 행사에 당첨되었습니다!"라고 적혀 있습니다.

20 Jay는 놀랍니다. 그는 재빨리 그것을 엽니다.

21 JayJr@kmail.com
당신은 우리의 '행운의 날' 행사에 당첨되었습니다!

22 축하합니다! 당신은 특별한 상품을 받게 되었습니다.

23 '행운의 날' 행사 동안, 당신은 우리 가게에서 일곱 가지 상품을 아무거나 무료로 선택할 수 있습니다!

24 11월 31일에 우리 가게로 오세요.

25 우리는 몹시 당신을 보기를 기대합니다.

26 안녕히 계십시오, Kay Brown

27 그러나 Jay는 그 행사가 사실이 아니라고 생각하고 이메일을 삭제합니다.

28 왜 그런지 설명할 수 있나요?

29 단서: 한 달은 주로 30일 또는 31일이 있습니다.

30 답을 가지고 계신가요?

31 그것을 적으면, 당신은 자유롭게 가실 수 있습니다!

※ 다음 문장을 우리말로 쓰시오.

The Great Escape

1 Welcome to the Escape Tower.

➡ _____

2 You will enter the first room in our tower.

➡ _____

3 You need to solve some riddles to escape.

➡ _____

4 Clues can be found somewhere inside the room.

➡ _____

5 So, are you ready to think like Sherlock Holmes?

➡ _____

Room #1

6 Mr. Doodle was hit by a car on Sunday afternoon.

➡ _____

7 Luckily, he wasn't badly hurt, but he didn't see the driver.

➡ _____

8 Three suspects were questioned by a police officer.

➡ _____

9 Ms. A said she was reading a book at the time of the accident.

➡ _____

10 Mr. B said he was walking his dog.

➡ _____

11 Ms. C said she was making breakfast.

➡ _____

12 Who hit Mr. Doodle? Can you explain why?

➡ _____

13 Do you have the answer? Write it down.

➡ _____

14 Then you can move to the next room.

➡ _____

15 Clue The accident happened in the afternoon.

➡ _____

16 Congratulations! You made it to the second room.

➡ _____

17 However, the second room is much harder to escape than the first one. Good luck!

➡ _____

Room #2

18 Jay gets an email from his favorite clothing store.

➡ _____

19 The title reads "You won our Lucky Day event!"

➡ _____

20 Jay is surprised. He quickly opens it.

➡ _____

21 JayJr@kmail.com
You won our 'Lucky Day' event!

➡ _____

22 Congratulations! You have won a special prize.

➡ _____

23 During our Lucky Day event, you can choose any seven items from our store for free!

➡ _____

24 Come to our store on November 31.

➡ _____

25 We can't wait to see you.

➡ _____

26 Truly yours, Kay Brown

➡ _____

27 However, Jay thinks that the event isn't real and deletes the email.

➡ _____

28 Can you explain why?

➡ _____

29 Clue There are usually 30 or 31 days in a month.

➡ _____

30 Do you have the answer?

➡ _____

31 Write it down and then you are free to go!

➡ _____

※ 다음 괄호 안의 단어들을 우리말에 맞도록 바르게 배열하시오.

The Great Escape

1 (to / Welcome / Tower. / Escape / the)
➡ _____

2 (will / you / the / enter / room / first / tower. / our / in)
➡ _____

3 (need / you / solve / to / riddles / some / escape. / to)
➡ _____

4 (can / clues / found / be / inside / somewhere / room. / the)
➡ _____

5 (are / so, / ready / you / think / to / Sherlock / like / Holmes?)
➡ _____

Room #1

6 (Doodle / Mr. / hit / was / a / by / car / afternoon. / Sunday / on)
➡ _____

7 (he / luckily, / wasn't / hurt, / badly / but / didn't / he / driver. / the / see)
➡ _____

8 (suspects / three / questioned / were / a / by / officer. / police)
➡ _____

9 (A / Ms. / she / said / redaing / was / book / a / the / at / time / accident. / the / of)
➡ _____

10 (B / Mr. / he / said / walking / was / dog. / his)
➡ _____

11 (C / Ms. / she / said / making / was / breakfast.)
➡ _____

12 (hit / who / Doodle? / Mr. // you / can / why? / explain)
➡ _____

13 (you / do / have / answer? / the // down. / it / write)
➡ _____

14 (you / then / move / can / the / to / room. / next)
➡ _____

15 (clue // accident / the / in / happened / afternoon. / the)
➡ _____

16 (congratulations! // made / you / to / it / room. / second / the)
➡ _____

대탈출

1 '탈출탑'에 오신 것을 환영합니다.

2 당신은 저희 탑의 첫 번째 방에 들어갈 것입니다.

3 당신은 탈출하기 위하여 몇 개의 수수께끼를 풀어야 합니다.

4 단서들은 방 어딘가에서 발견될 수 있습니다.

5 그러면 당신은 셜록 홈스처럼 생각할 준비가 되었나요?

방 # 1

6 Doodle씨는 일요일 오후에 차에 치였습니다.

7 다행히 그는 심하게 다치지 않았으나 그는 운전자를 보지 못했습니다.

8 세 명의 용의자들이 경찰에게 심문을 받았습니다.

9 A씨는 사고가 일어난 시간에 책을 읽고 있었다고 말했습니다.

10 B씨는 그의 개를 산책시키고 있었다고 말했습니다.

11 C씨는 아침을 만들고 있었다고 말했습니다.

12 누가 Doodle씨를 치었을까요? 왜 그런지 설명할 수 있나요?

13 답을 가지고 있나요? 적어 보세요.

14 그런 다음, 당신은 다음 방으로 갈 수 있습니다.

15 단서: 사건은 오후에 일어났습니다.

16 축하합니다! 당신은 두 번째 방에 오는 데 성공하셨습니다.

17 (however, / second / the / is / room / harder / much / escape / to / than / first / the / one. // luck! / good)

➡ _____

_____

Room #2

18 (gets / Jay / email / an / his / from / store. / clothing / favorite)

➡ _____

19 (title / the / reads / "you / our / won / Day / event!" / Lucky)

➡ _____

20 (is / Jay / surprised. // he / quickly / it. / opens)

➡ _____

21 JayJr@kmail.com

(won / you / event! / our / Day' / 'Lucky)

➡ JayJr@kmail.com _____

22 (congratulations! // have / you / a / prize. / special / won)

➡ _____

23 (our / during / event, / Day / Lucky / can / you / any / choose / items / seven / from / store / our / free! / for)

➡ _____

_____

24 (to / come / store / our / 31. / November / on)

➡ _____

25 (can't / we / see / wait / you. / to)

➡ _____

26 (yours, / truly / Brown / Kay)

➡ _____

27 (however, / thinks / Jay / the / that / isn't / event / deletes / and / real / email. / the)

➡ _____

28 (you / can / why? / explain)

➡ _____

29 (clue // are / there / 30 / usually / 31 / or / month. / a / in / days)

➡ _____

30 (you / do / have / answer? / the)

➡ _____

31 (down / it / write / then / and / are / you / go! / to / free)

➡ _____

---

17 그러나 두 번째 방은 첫 번째 방보다 탈출하기 훨씬 더 어렵습니다. 행운을 빕니다!

방 # 2

18 Jay는 그가 가장 좋아하는 옷 가게로부터 이메일을 받습니다.

19 제목은 "당신은 '행운의 날' 행사에 당첨되었습니다!"라고 적혀 있습니다.

20 Jay는 놀랍니다. 그는 재빨리 그것을 엽니다.

21 JayJr@kmail.com
당신은 우리의 '행운의 날' 행사에 당첨되었습니다!

22 축하합니다! 당신은 특별한 상품을 받게 되었습니다.

23 '행운의 날' 행사 동안, 당신은 우리 가게에서 일곱 가지 상품을 아무거나 무료로 선택할 수 있습니다!

24 11월 31일에 우리 가게로 오세요.

25 우리는 몹시 당신을 보기를 기대합니다.

26 안녕히 계십시오, Kay Brown

27 그러나 Jay는 그 행사가 사실이 아니라고 생각하고 이메일을 삭제합니다.

28 왜 그런지 설명할 수 있나요?

29 단서: 한 달은 주로 30일 또는 31일이 있습니다.

30 답을 가지고 계신가요?

31 그것을 적으면, 당신은 자유롭게 가실 수 있습니다!

※ 다음 우리말을 영어로 쓰시오.

The Great Escape

1 '탈출 탑'에 오신 것을 환영합니다.

➡ _____

2 당신은 저희 탑의 첫 번째 방에 들어갈 것입니다.

➡ _____

3 당신은 탈출하기 위하여 몇 개의 수수께끼를 풀어야 합니다.

➡ _____

4 단서들은 방 어딘가에서 발견될 수 있습니다.

➡ _____

5 그러면 당신은 셜록 홈스처럼 생각할 준비가 되었나요?

➡ _____

Room #1

6 Doodle씨는 일요일 오후에 차에 치였습니다.

➡ _____

7 다행히 그는 심하게 다치지 않았으나 그는 운전자를 보지 못했습니다.

➡ _____

8 세 명의 용의자들이 경찰에게 심문을 받았습니다.

➡ _____

9 A씨는 사고가 일어난 시간에 책을 읽고 있었다고 말했습니다.

➡ _____

10 B씨는 그의 개를 산책시키고 있었다고 말했습니다.

➡ _____

11 C씨는 아침을 만들고 있었다고 말했습니다.

➡ _____

12 누가 Doodle씨를 치었을까요? 왜 그런지 설명할 수 있나요?

➡ _____

13 답을 가지고 있나요? 적어 보세요.

➡ _____

14 그런 다음, 당신은 다음 방으로 갈 수 있습니다.

➡ _____

15 단서: 사건은 오후에 일어났습니다.

➡ _____

16 축하합니다! 당신은 두 번째 방에 오는 데 성공하셨습니다.

➡ _____

17 그러나 두 번째 방은 첫 번째 방보다 탈출하기 훨씬 더 어렵습니다. 행운을 빕니다!

➡ _____

Room #2

18 Jay는 그가 가장 좋아하는 옷 가게로부터 이메일을 받습니다.

➡ _____

19 제목은 "당신은 '행운의 날' 행사에 당첨되었습니다!"라고 적혀 있습니다.

➡ _____

20 Jay는 놀랍니다. 그는 재빨리 그것을 엽니다.

➡ _____

21 JayJr@kmail.com
당신은 우리의 '행운의 날' 행사에 당첨되었습니다!

➡ JayJr@kmail.com _____

22 축하합니다! 당신은 특별한 상품을 받게 되었습니다.

➡ _____

23 '행운의 날' 행사 동안, 당신은 우리 가게에서 일곱 가지 상품을 아무거나 공짜로 선택할 수 있습니다!

➡ _____

24 11월 31일에 우리 가게로 오세요.

➡ _____

25 우리는 몹시 당신을 보기를 기대합니다.

➡ _____

26 안녕히 계십시오, Kay Brown

➡ _____

27 그러나 Jay는 그 행사가 사실이 아니라고 생각하고 이메일을 삭제합니다.

➡ _____

28 왜 그런지 설명할 수 있나요?

➡ _____

29 단서: 한 달은 주로 30일 또는 31일이 있습니다.

➡ _____

30 답을 가지고 계신가요?

➡ _____

31 그것을 적으면, 당신은 자유롭게 가실 수 있습니다!

➡ _____

※ 다음 우리말과 일치하도록 빈칸에 알맞은 말을 쓰시오.

Listen and Speak 1-C

1. A: _____ _____ _____ this riddle.

2. B: Sure.

3. A: Four people _____ _____ one umbrella, but nobody _____ _____. Can you _____ _____?

4. B: Yes! It's _____ it's _____ _____ _____!

1. A: 이 수수께끼를 풀어봐.
2. B: 그래.
3. A: 4명의 사람들이 하나의 우산 아래 있는데 아무도 젖지 않아. 이유를 설명할 수 있겠니?
4. B: 응! 왜냐하면 맑은 날이기 때문이야.

Let's Write

1. _____ was _____ Sunday.

2. Dohun was _____ _____.

3. _____, he _____ _____ _____ in the next room.

4. When he _____ _____ the room, the window _____ _____.

5. When he _____ _____, Sujin _____ _____ a baseball bat and Ted _____ _____ a ball to his dog.

6. Who _____ the window?

7. How _____ it be _____?

1. 지난 일요일이었다.
2. 도훈이는 집에 있었다.
3. 갑자기, 그는 옆방에서 나는 어떤 소리를 들었다.
4. 그가 그 방으로 갔을 때, 창문이 깨져 있었다.
5. 도훈이가 밖을 보았을 때, 수진이는 야구 방망이를 들고 있었고 Ted는 그의 개에게 공을 던지고 있었다.
6. 누가 창문을 깼을까?
7. 그것은 어떻게 설명될 수 있을까?

Culture & Life

1. This is the _____ _____ of the Sphinx.

2. Oedipus _____ _____ it to _____ Thebes.

3. This is the question _____ the Sphinx _____ _____.

4. _____ creature _____ _____ _____ _____ in the morning, two legs in the afternoon, and three legs in the evening?

1. 이것은 스핑크스의 유명한 수수께끼이다.
2. 오이디푸스는 Thebes에 들어가기 위해 그것을 풀어야 한다.
3. 이것은 스핑크스가 그에게 묻는 질문이다.
4. 어느 생명체가 아침에는 네 다리로 걷고, 오후에는 두 다리로 걷고, 저녁에는 세 다리로 걷는가?

※ 다음 우리말을 영어로 쓰시오.

Listen and Speak 1-C

1. A: 이 수수께끼를 풀어봐.

➔ _____

2. B: 그래.

➔ _____

3. A: 4명의 사람들이 하나의 우산 아래 있는데 아무도 젖지 않아. 이유를 설명할 수 있겠니?

➔ _____

4. B: 응! 왜냐하면 맑은 날이기 때문이야.

➔ _____

Let's Write

1. 지난 일요일이었다.

➔ _____

2. 도훈이는 집에 있었다.

➔ _____

3. 갑자기, 그는 옆방에서 나는 어떤 소리를 들었다.

➔ _____

4. 그가 그 방으로 갔을 때, 창문이 깨져 있었다.

➔ _____

5. 도훈가 밖을 보았을 때, 수진이는 야구 방망이를 들고 있었고 Ted는 그의 개에게 공을 던지고 있었다.

➔ _____

6. 누가 창문을 깼을까?

➔ _____

7. 그것은 어떻게 설명될 수 있을까?

➔ _____

Culture & Life

1. 이것은 스핑크스의 유명한 수수께끼이다.

➔ _____

2. 오이디푸스는 Thebes에 들어가기 위해 그것을 풀어야 한다.

➔ _____

3. 이것은 스핑크스가 그에게 묻는 질문이다.

➔ _____

4. 어느 생명체가 아침에는 네 다리로 걷고, 오후에는 두 다리로 걷고, 저녁에는 세 다리로 걷는가?

➔ _____
_____

※ 다음 영어를 우리말로 쓰시오.

01 between

02 character

03 strength

04 brave

05 through

06 bright

07 powerful

08 enemy

09 express

10 fight

11 fan

12 hide

13 cheer

14 scared

15 communicate

16 behind

17 scary

18 hold

19 popular

20 costume

21 interestingly

22 female

23 windy

24 traditional

25 nowadays

26 opinion

27 originally

28 male

29 perform

30 comfortable

31 totally

32 wild

33 couple

34 gracefully

35 in my opinion

36 be allowed to

37 take a look

38 give up on

39 on time

40 try one's best

41 look like

42 make a sound

43 keep up the good work

※ 다음 우리말을 영어로 쓰시오.

01	등장인물	
02	암컷의, 여성의	
03	인기 있는	
04	용감한	
05	의사소통하다	
06	(색상이) 밝은	
07	적	
08	표현하다	
09	부채	
10	확실한	
11	야생의	
12	두 사람, 남녀	
13	전통적인	
14	~ 사이에	
15	바람이 많이 부는	
16	우아하게	
17	의상, 복장	
18	~ 뒤에	
19	흥미 있게도	
20	~을 통해	
21	수컷의, 남성의	

22	완전히	
23	오늘날에는	
24	무서운	
25	의견	
26	숨다	
27	원래, 본래	
28	움직임, 동작	
29	공연하다	
30	싸움, 다툼	
31	강한, 힘 있는	
32	응원하다	
33	편안한	
34	힘	
35	살펴보다	
36	최선을 다하다	
37	내 의견으로는	
38	~을 포기하다	
39	정시에	
40	소리를 내다	
41	~처럼 들리다, ~일 것 같다	
42	~을 잘하다	
43	~이 허용되다	

※ 다음 영영풀이에 알맞은 단어를 <보기>에서 골라 쓴 후, 우리말 뜻을 쓰시오.

1. _____ : liked by a lot of people: _____

2. _____ : at or towards the back of a thing or person: _____

3. _____ : an act of moving: _____

4. _____ : to stop holding or carrying something so that it falls: _____

5. _____ : living in a natural state, not changed or controlled by people: _____

6. _____ : the physical power and energy that makes someone strong: _____

7. _____ : dealing with danger, pain, or difficult situations with courage and confidence: _____

8. _____ : a flat object that you wave with your hand which makes the air cooler: _____

9. _____ : in the beginning, before other things happened or before things changed: _____

10. _____ : to put or keep someone or something in a place where they/it cannot be seen or found: _____

11. _____ : to tell or show what you are feeling or thinking by using words, looks, or action: _____

12. _____ : an area of land in the country, especially one where crops are grown or animals feed on grass: _____

13. _____ : to do something to entertain people, for example by acting a play or playing a piece of music: _____

14. _____ : a particular type of clothing worn by all the members of a group or organization such as the police, the army, etc.: _____

15. _____ : to shout as a way of showing happiness, praise, approval, or support of someone or something: _____

16. _____ : making you feel physically relaxed, without any pain or without being too hot, cold, etc.: _____

보기			
cheer	comfortable	popular	strength
originally	behind	express	field
drop	wild	brave	hide
uniform	fan	movement	perform

※ 다음 우리말과 일치하도록 빈칸에 알맞은 말을 쓰시오.

Listen & Speak 1 A-1

Jane: Minsu, _____ do you _____ _____ that _____?

Minsu: Umm … The people _____ _____ they're _____ _____.

Jane: I agree. _____ _____ _____, the dancing boy really _____ _____.

Listen & Speak 1 A-2

Brian: Jimin, _____ do you think _____ _____ _____?

Jimin: In my opinion, it's _____. I _____ _____ I _____ _____ it.

Brian: _____, _____. The dancers in the painting _____ _____.

Listen & Speak 1 B

Emily: Hojun, did you know that _____ _____ _____ _____?

Hojun: No. _____ do they _____?

Emily: They dance _____ _____ their _____ to _____ _____.

Hojun: That's interesting. Do you know _____ _____ _____ that can dance?

Emily: Yes, some _____ dance to show _____ _____ _____.

Hojun: That's cool! In my opinion, dancing is a great _____ _____ _____.

Emily: I _____ _____ _____ _____.

Listen & Speak 2 A-1

Minji: I use _____ _____ to make music. _____ _____ my music. My voice is _____ and _____. I'm _____ you will like it.

Jimin: I move _____ _____ _____ _____ my feelings. Look at my _____. _____ _____ you jump _____ me? I'm _____ you'll _____ _____.

Sujin: I use my hands to _____ _____. Come and listen to my music. I'm sure you'll want to _____ when you listen to it.

Jane: 민수야, 저 그림에 대해 어떻게 생각해?

Minsu: 음… 사람들이 재미있게 노는 것처럼 보여.

Jane: 나도 동의해. 내 의견으로는, 춤추는 소년이 춤추는 것을 정말로 즐기는 것 같아.

Brian: 지민아, 이 그림에 대해 어떻게 생각해?

Jimin: 내 의견으로는 흥미로워. 처음 이것을 봤을 때 난 미소 지었어.

Brian: 나도 그래. 그림 속 춤추는 사람들은 행복해 보여.

Emily: 호준아, 너는 일부 수컷 새들이 춤을 춘다는 것을 알고 있었니?

Hojun: 아니. 왜 춤을 추지?

Emily: 그들은 암컷 새들에게 그들의 사랑을 보여주기 위해 춤을 춰.

Hojun: 그거 흥미로운 걸. 춤을 출 수 있는 또 다른 동물들을 알고 있니?

Emily: 응, 일부 벌들은 먹이를 찾을 수 있는 곳을 보여주기 위해 춤을 춰.

Hojun: 멋지다! 내 의견으로는, 춤을 추는 것은 의사소통을 위한 굉장한 방법인 것 같아.

Emily: 전적으로 너에게 동의해.

Minji: 나는 음악을 만들기 위해 내 목소리를 사용합니다. 내 음악을 들어보세요. 내 목소리는 부드럽고 멋지죠. 나는 당신이 그것을 좋아할 거라고 확신해요.

Jimin: 나는 내 감정을 표현하기 위해 내 몸을 움직입니다. 내 동작을 보세요. 나처럼 뛰어올라 보는 게 어때요? 나는 당신이 멋진 기분이 들 거라고 확신해요.

Sujin: 나는 소리를 만들기 위해 내 손을 사용합니다. 와서 내 음악을 들어 보세요. 나는 당신이 이것을 들을 때 춤을 추고 싶을 거라고 확신해요.

Listen & Speak 2 B

Tom: _____ are you _____, Kelly?

Kelly: I'm reading a _____ _____ Michaela DePrince.

Tom: Michaela DePrince? Can you _____ me _____ about her?

Kelly: Sure. Michaela _____ her parents _____ she was three. _____ _____, she had a lot of _____. But she never _____ _____ _____ her dream of becoming a dancer.

Tom: Wow, she _____ very _____ _____ _____ a good dancer. Kelly, you also have a dream _____ _____ a dancer, _____?

Kelly: Yes. I will _____ _____ _____ to be a great dancer like her.

Tom: _____ _____ the good _____. I'm _____ you can _____ _____.

Real Life Communication

Junsu: You know _____? The school dance contest _____ _____ _____ soon.

Emily: That's right. I heard Jimin's class is going to _____ a taekwondo dance and Tim's class is going to do a K-pop dance.

Brian: We should also _____ _____ _____ _____.

Mina: _____ _____ a Buchaechum? In my _____, it is _____ _____ _____, and it's also _____.

Emily: That _____ a good idea. But who will teach us?

Brian: Mina _____ _____ _____ traditional dances. Can you help us, Mina?

Mina: Of course, I will. _____ _____ we'll have a lot of fun.

Junsu: Great. Let's _____ _____ _____ _____.

Let's Check

Jenny: Look at the _____ _____, Dongjun. Aren't they _____?

Dongjun: Girls? I can _____ _____ one dancer.

Jenny: _____ _____ _____. Do you see many arms _____ her?

Dongjun: Wow. I _____ _____ that there were _____ _____ _____ _____.

Jenny: That's _____. _____ _____ there are _____ _____ 10 dancers.

Tom: 무엇을 읽고 있니, Kelly?

Kelly: Michaela DePrince에 대한 이야기를 읽고 있어.

Tom: Michaela DePrince? 그녀에 대해 좀 더 얘기해 줄 수 있니?

Kelly: 그래. Michaela는 세 살 때 부모를 잃었어. 그 후 그녀는 많은 역경을 겪었지. 그러나 그녀는 무용수가 되겠다는 꿈을 절대 포기하지 않았어.

Tom: 와, 그녀는 훌륭한 무용수가 되기 위해 굉장히 열심히 노력했구나. Kelly, 너도 무용수가 되려는 꿈이 있지, 그렇지?

Kelly: 응. 그녀처럼 멋진 무용수가 되기 위해 최선을 다할 거야.

Tom: 계속 노력해 봐. 난 네가 해낼 거라고 확신해.

Junsu: 있잖아. 학교 춤 경연 대회가 곧 열릴 거야.

Emily: 맞아. 지민이네 반은 태권도 춤을 공연하고, Tim네 반은 K-pop 춤을 출 거라고 들었어.

Brian: 우리도 무엇을 할지 결정해야 해.

Mina: 부채춤은 어때? 내 의견으로는, 그것은 배우기 쉽고 또한 아름다워.

Emily: 좋은 생각인 것 같아. 하지만 누가 우리를 가르치지?

Brian: 미나가 전통 춤을 잘 춰. 우리를 도울 수 있니, 미나야?

Mina: 물론, 그럴 거야. 우리는 매우 즐거울 거라고 확신해.

Junsu: 아주 좋아. 시도해 보자.

Jenny: 춤추는 여자들을 봐, 동준아. 대단하지 않니?

Donjun: 여자들? 난 단지 한 명의 무용수만 보이는 걸.

Jenny: 좀 더 가까이 봐. 그녀 뒤에 많은 팔들이 보이니?

Donjun: 와. 그녀 뒤에 다른 무용수들이 있는지 몰랐어.

Jenny: 맞아. 나는 10명 이상의 무용수들이 있다고 확신해.

※ 다음 우리말에 맞도록 대화를 영어로 쓰시오.

Listen & Speak 1 A-1

Jane: _____

Minsu: _____

Jane: _____

Listen & Speak 1 A-2

Brian: _____

Jimin: _____

Brian: _____

Listen & Speak 1 B

Emily: _____

Hojun: _____

Emily: _____

Hojun: _____

Emily: _____

Hojun: _____

Emily: _____

Listen & Speak 2 A-1

Minji: _____

_____

Jimin: _____

_____

Sujin: _____

_____

해석

Jane: 민수야, 저 그림에 대해 어떻게 생각해?
Minsu: 음… 사람들이 재미있게 노는 것처럼 보여.
Jane: 나도 동의해. 내 의견으로는, 춤추는 소년이 춤추는 것을 정말로 즐기는 것 같아.

Brian: 지민아, 이 그림에 대해 어떻게 생각해?
Jimin: 내 의견으로는 흥미로워. 처음 이것을 봤을 때 난 미소 지었어.
Brian: 나도 그래. 그림 속 춤추는 사람들은 행복해 보여.

Emily: 호준아, 너는 일부 수컷 새들이 춤을 춘다는 것을 알고 있었니?
Hojun: 아니. 왜 춤을 추지?
Emily: 그들은 암컷 새들에게 그들의 사랑을 보여주기 위해 춤을 춰.
Hojun: 그거 흥미로운 걸. 춤을 출 수 있는 또 다른 동물들을 알고 있니?
Emily: 응, 일부 벌들은 먹이를 찾을 수 있는 곳을 보여주기 위해 춤을 춰.
Hojun: 멋지다! 내 의견으로는, 춤을 추는 것은 의사소통을 위한 굉장한 방법인 것 같아.
Emily: 전적으로 너에게 동의해.

Minji: 나는 음악을 만들기 위해 내 목소리를 사용합니다. 내 음악을 들어보세요. 내 목소리는 부드럽고 멋지죠. 나는 당신이 그것을 좋아할 거라고 확신해요.
Jimin: 나는 내 감정을 표현하기 위해 내 몸을 움직입니다. 내 동작을 보세요. 나처럼 뛰어올라 보는 게 어때요? 나는 당신이 멋진 기분이 들 거라고 확신해요.
Sujin: 나는 소리를 만들기 위해 내 손을 사용합니다. 와서 내 음악을 들어 보세요. 나는 당신이 이것을 들을 때 춤을 추고 싶을 거라고 확신해요.

Listen & Speak 2 B

Tom: _____

Kelly: _____

Tom: _____

Kelly: _____

_____

Tom: _____

_____

Kelly: _____

Tom: _____

Tom: 무엇을 읽고 있니, Kelly?

Kelly: Michaela DePrince에 대한 이야기를 읽고 있어.

Tom: Michaela DePrince? 그녀에 대해 좀 더 얘기해 줄 수 있니?

Kelly: 그래. Michaela는 세 살 때 부모를 잃었어. 그 후 그녀는 많은 역경을 겪었지. 그러나 그녀는 무용수가 되겠다는 꿈을 절대 포기하지 않았어.

Tom: 와, 그녀는 훌륭한 무용수가 되기 위해 굉장히 열심히 노력했구나. Kelly, 너도 무용수가 되려는 꿈이 있지, 그렇지?

Kelly: 응. 그녀처럼 멋진 무용수가 되기 위해 최선을 다할 거야.

Tom: 계속 노력해 봐. 난 네가 해낼 거라고 확신해.

Real Life Communication

Junsu: _____

Emily: _____

_____

Brian: _____

Mina _____

_____

Emily: _____

Brian: _____

Mina: _____

Junsu: _____

Junsu: 있잖아. 학교 춤 경연 대회가 곧 열릴 거야.

Emily: 맞아. 지민이네 반은 태권도 춤을 공연하고, Tim네 반은 K-pop 춤을 출 거라고 들었어.

Brian: 우리도 무엇을 할지 결정해야 해.

Mina: 부채춤은 어때? 내 의견으로는, 그것은 배우기 쉽고 또한 아름다워.

Emily: 좋은 생각인 것 같아. 하지만 누가 우리를 가르치지?

Brian: 미나가 전통 춤을 잘 춰. 우리를 도울 수 있니, 미나야?

Mina: 물론, 그럴 거야. 우리는 매우 즐거울 거라고 확신해.

Junsu: 아주 좋아. 시도해 보자.

Let's Check

Jenny: _____

Dongjun: _____

Jenny: _____

Dongjun: _____

Jenny: _____

Jenny: 춤추는 여자들을 봐, 동준아. 대단하지 않니?

Donjun: 여자들? 난 단지 한 명의 무용수만 보이는 걸.

Jenny: 좀 더 가까이 봐. 그녀 뒤에 많은 팔들이 보이니?

Donjun: 와. 그녀 뒤에 다른 무용수들이 있는지 몰랐어.

Jenny: 맞아. 나는 10명 이상의 무용수들이 있다고 확신해.

※ 다음 우리말과 일치하도록 빈칸에 알맞은 것을 골라 쓰시오.

Dance with a Story

1 _____ do people _____?

A. dance   B. why

2 They dance to _____ feelings, give _____ to others, or
_____ _____.

A. enjoy   B. express   C. themselves   D. happiness

3 Let's _____ a look at _____ _____ of dance _____
the world.

A. kinds   B. take   C. around   D. different

India: *Kathakali*

4 *Kathakali* _____ a _____.

A. story   B. tells

5 The dancers tell _____ _____ their _____ _____.

A. body   B. stories   C. movements   D. through

6 These stories are usually about a _____ between _____
and _____.

A. good   B. fight   C. evil

7 Dancers who are _____ good _____ paint their faces
_____.

A. green   B. playing   C. characters

8 Those who are playing _____ characters _____ black
_____.

A. wear   B. evil   C. make-up

9 _____, in *Kathakali*, only men are _____ _____ dance.

A. allowed   B. interestingly   C. to

10 The body _____ are so _____ that the dancers need to
_____ for many years.

A. train   B. powerful   C. movements

New Zealand: *Haka*

11 _____ people _____ New Zealand, they _____ _____
a group of *haka* dancers.

A. may   B. visit   C. when   D. meet

12 The dancers _____ this _____ dance with _____ faces.

A. traditional   B. perform   C. scary

이야기가 있는 춤

1 사람들은 왜 춤을 추는 걸까요?

2 사람들은 감정을 표현하고, 다른
사람들에게 행복감을 주거나 스
스로 즐기기 위해 춤을 춥니다.

3 세계의 여러 가지 춤을 살펴봅
시다.

인도: *Kathakali*

4 *Kathakali*에는 이야기가 있습니다.

5 춤꾼들은 몸동작을 통해 이야기
합니다.

6 이러한 이야기들은 대개 선과
악의 싸움에 관한 것입니다.

7 선한 역할을 맡은 춤꾼들은 자
신의 얼굴을 초록색으로 칠합니
다.

8 악한 역할을 맡은 춤꾼들은 검
은색 화장을 합니다.

9 재미있는 것은 *Kathakali* 춤에
서 남자들만 춤추는 것이 허락
된다는 사실입니다.

10 몸동작이 매우 힘이 넘쳐서 춤
꾼들은 수년 동안 연습을 해야
합니다.

뉴질랜드: *Haka*

11 사람들이 뉴질랜드를 방문할
때, 그들은 *haka* 춤꾼들의 무리
를 만날지도 모릅니다.

12 그 춤꾼들은 무서운 얼굴로 이
전통 춤을 춥니다.

13 This dance was _____ _____ by the Maori before a _____.

A. performed   B. fight   C. originally

14 They wanted to _____ their _____ to the _____.

A. enemy   B. show   C. strength

15 The dancers _____ as _____ _____ wild animals _____ fighting.

A. before   B. scary   C. looked   D. as

16 _____, in New Zealand, rugby players usually _____ a *haka* before a game to _____ their strength to the _____ team.

A. perform   B. nowadays   C. other   D. show

Korea: *Buchaechum*

17 *Buchaechum* is a _____ Korean _____ _____.

A. fan   B. traditional   C. dance

18 The dancers _____ _____ *hanbok*.

A. colorful   B. wear

19 They dance _____ large fans that are _____ in _____ colors.

A. bright   B. with   C. painted

20 The dancers _____ the fans _____ to show _____ kinds of _____.

A. gracefully   B. beauty   C. move   D. different

21 Their _____ look _____ _____ as flowers or _____ birds.

A. as   B. flying   C. beautiful   D. movements

22 In Korea, *Buchaechum* is _____ _____ _____ people can see it in many _____ festivals.

A. that   B. popular   C. so   D. traditional

---

13 이 춤은 원래 마오리족에 의해 싸움 전에 행해졌습니다.

14 그들은 적에게 그들의 힘을 보여 주고 싶었습니다.

15 춤꾼들은 싸움하기 전의 야생 동물들만큼 무섭게 보였습니다.

16 요즈음, 뉴질랜드에서는 럭비 선수들이 다른 팀에게 그들의 힘을 보여 주기 위해 게임 전에 주로 *haka*를 보여 줍니다.

한국: 부채춤

17 부채춤은 한국 전통 부채춤입니다.

18 춤꾼들은 다채로운 한복을 입습니다.

19 그들은 밝은 색으로 칠해진 커다란 부채를 가지고 춤을 춥니다.

20 그 춤꾼들은 다양한 종류의 미를 보여 주기 위해 부채를 우아하게 움직입니다.

21 그들의 움직임은 꽃 또는 날아다니는 새들처럼 우아하게 보입니다.

22 한국에서, 부채춤은 너무 인기가 있어서 사람들은 많은 전통 축제에서 그것을 볼 수 있습니다.

※ 다음 우리말과 일치하도록 빈칸에 알맞은 말을 쓰시오.

Dance with a Story

1 _____ do people _____ ?

2 They dance _____ _____ _____ , give happiness _____ _____ , or _____ _____ .

3 _____ _____ a look at _____ _____ _____ _____ around the world

India: *Kathakali*

4 *Kathakali* _____ a _____ .

5 The dancers tell _____ _____ their _____ _____ .

6 These stories are usually about _____ _____ _____ _____ _____ _____ .

7 Dancers _____ _____ _____ _____ _____ paint their faces _____ .

8 Those _____ _____ _____ evil characters _____ _____ _____ .

9 _____ , in *Kathakali*, only men _____ _____ _____ .

10 The body movements are _____ _____ _____ the dancers _____ _____ train _____ many years.

New Zealand: *Haka*

11 When people visit New Zealand, they _____ _____ a group of _____ _____ .

12 The dancers _____ this _____ dance _____ _____ .

이야기가 있는 춤

1 사람들은 왜 춤을 추는 걸까요?

2 사람들은 감정을 표현하고, 다른 사람들에게 행복감을 주거나 스스로 즐기기 위해 춤을 춥니다.

3 세계의 여러 가지 춤을 살펴봅시다.

인도: *Kathakali*

4 *Kathakali*에는 이야기가 있습니다.

5 춤꾼들은 몸동작을 통해 이야기합니다.

6 이러한 이야기들은 대개 선과 악의 싸움에 관한 것입니다.

7 선한 역할을 맡은 춤꾼들은 자신의 얼굴을 초록색으로 칠합니다.

8 악한 역할을 맡은 춤꾼들은 검은색 화장을 합니다.

9 재미있는 것은 *Kathakali* 춤에서 남자들만 춤추는 것이 허락된다는 사실입니다.

10 몸동작이 매우 힘이 넘쳐서 춤꾼들은 수년 동안 연습을 해야 합니다.

뉴질랜드: *Haka*

11 사람들이 뉴질랜드를 방문할 때, 그들은 *haka* 춤꾼들의 무리를 만날지도 모릅니다.

12 그 춤꾼들은 무서운 얼굴로 이 전통 춤을 춥니다.

13 This dance was _____ _____ _____ the Maori before a _____.

14 They wanted _____ _____ _____ _____ to the _____.

15 The dancers _____ _____ _____ _____ wild animals _____ _____.

16 _____, in New Zealand, rugby players _____ _____ a *haka* before a game _____ _____ their strength _____ _____ _____ _____.

Korea: *Buchaechum*

17 *Buchaechum* is a _____ _____ _____ _____.

18 The dancers _____ _____ _____.

19 They dance _____ large fans _____ _____ _____ in bright colors.

20 The dancers _____ the fans _____ to show _____ _____ _____ _____.

21 Their movements _____ _____ _____ _____ _____ flowers or _____ _____.

22 In Korea, *Buchaechum* is _____ _____ _____ people _____ _____ _____ in many traditional festivals.

13 이 춤은 원래 마오리족에 의해 싸움 전에 행해졌습니다.

14 그들은 적에게 그들의 힘을 보여 주고 싶었습니다.

15 춤꾼들은 싸움하기 전의 야생 동물들만큼 무섭게 보였습니다.

16 요즈음, 뉴질랜드에서는 럭비 선수들이 다른 팀에게 그들의 힘을 보여 주기 위해 게임 전에 주로 *haka*를 보여 줍니다.

한국: 부채춤

17 부채춤은 한국 전통 부채춤입니다.

18 춤꾼들은 다채로운 한복을 입습니다.

19 그들은 밝은 색으로 칠해진 커다란 부채를 가지고 춤을 춥니다.

20 그 춤꾼들은 다양한 종류의 미를 보여 주기 위해 부채를 우아하게 움직입니다.

21 그들의 움직임은 꽃 또는 날아다니는 새들처럼 우아하게 보입니다.

22 한국에서, 부채춤은 너무 인기가 있어서 사람들은 많은 전통 축제에서 그것을 볼 수 있습니다.

※ 다음 문장을 우리말로 쓰시오.

Dance with a Story

1 Why do people dance?

➡ _____

2 They dance to express feelings, give happiness to others, or enjoy themselves.

➡ _____

3 Let's take a look at different kinds of dance around the world.

➡ _____

India: *Kathakali*

4 *Kathakali* tells a story.

➡ _____

5 The dancers tell stories through their body movements.

➡ _____

6 These stories are usually about a fight between good and evil.

➡ _____

7 Dancers who are playing good characters paint their faces green.

➡ _____

8 Those who are playing evil characters wear black make-up.

➡ _____

9 Interestingly, in *Kathakali*, only men are allowed to dance.

➡ _____

10 The body movements are so powerful that the dancers need to train for many years.

➡ _____

New Zealand: *Haka*

11 When people visit New Zealand, they may meet a group of haka dancers.

➡ _____

12 The dancers perform this traditional dance with scary faces.

➡ _____

13 This dance was originally performed by the Maori before a fight.

➡ _____

14 They wanted to show their strength to the enemy.

➡ _____

15 The dancers looked as scary as wild animals before fighting.

➡ _____

16 Nowadays, in New Zealand, rugby players usually perform a *haka* before a game to show their strength to the other team.

➡ _____

Korea: *Buchaechum*

17 *Buchaechum* is a traditional Korean fan dance.

➡ _____

18 The dancers wear colorful *hanbok*.

➡ _____

19 They dance with large fans that are painted in bright colors.

➡ _____

20 The dancers move the fans gracefully to show different kinds of beauty.

➡ _____

21 Their movements look as beautiful as flowers or flying birds.

➡ _____

22 In Korea, *Buchaechum* is so popular that people can see it in many traditional festivals.

➡ _____

※ 다음 괄호 안의 단어들을 우리말에 맞도록 바르게 배열하시오.

Dance with a Story

1 (do / why / dance? / people)

➡ _____

2 (dance / they / express / to / feelings, / happiness / give / others, / to / or / themselves. / enjoy)

➡ _____

3 (take / let's / look / a / different / at / kinds / dance / of / around / world. / the)

➡ _____

India: *Kathakali*

4 (tells / *Kathakali* / story. / a)

➡ _____

5 (dancers / the / stories / tell / through / body / their / movements.)

➡ _____

6 (stories / these / are / about / usually / fight / a / between / evil. / and / good)

➡ _____

7 (who / dancers / are / good / playing / characters / their / paint / green. / faces)

➡ _____

8 (those / are / who / playing / evil / wear / characters / make-up. / black)

➡ _____

9 (in / interestingly, / *Kathakali*, / men / only / allowed / are / dance. / to)

➡ _____

10 (body / the / are / movements / so / that / powerful / dancers / the / to / need / train / many / for / years.)

➡ _____

New Zealand: *Haka*

11 (people / when / New / visit / Zealand, / may / they / meet / a / *haka* / of / group / dancers.)

➡ _____

12 (dancers / the / this / perform / traditional / with / dance / scary / faces.)

➡ _____

이야기가 있는 춤

1 사람들은 왜 춤을 추는 걸까요?

2 사람들은 감정을 표현하고, 다른 사람들에게 행복감을 주거나 스스로 즐기기 위해 춤을 춥니다.

3 세계의 여러 가지 춤을 살펴봅시다.

인도: *Kathakali*

4 *Kathakali*에는 이야기가 있습니다.

5 춤꾼들은 몸동작을 통해 이야기합니다.

6 이러한 이야기들은 대개 선과 악의 싸움에 관한 것입니다.

7 선한 역할을 맡은 춤꾼들은 자신의 얼굴을 초록색으로 칠합니다.

8 악한 역할을 맡은 춤꾼들은 검은색 화장을 합니다.

9 재미있는 것은 *Kathakali* 춤에서 남자들만 춤추는 것이 허락된다는 사실입니다.

10 몸동작이 매우 힘이 넘쳐서 춤꾼들은 수년 동안 연습을 해야 합니다.

뉴질랜드: *Haka*

11 사람들이 뉴질랜드를 방문할 때, 그들은 *haka* 춤꾼들의 무리를 만날지도 모릅니다.

12 그 춤꾼들은 무서운 얼굴로 이 전통 춤을 춥니다.

13 (dance / this / originally / was / by / performed / the / before / Maori / fight. / a)

➡ _____

14 (wanted / they / show / to / strength / their / to / enemy. / the)

➡ _____

15 (dancers / the / as / looked / scary / as / animals / wild / fighting. / before)

➡ _____

16 (in / nowadays, / Zealand, / New / players / rugby / perform / usually / *haka* / a / before / game / a / show / to / strength / their / the / to / team. / other)

➡ _____

Korea: *Buchaechum*

17 (is / *Buchaechum* / a / Korean / traditional / dance. / fan)

➡ _____

18 (dancers / the / colorful / wear / *hanbok*.)

➡ _____

19 (dance / they / large / with / that / fans / are / in / printed / colors. / bright)

➡ _____

20 (dancers / the / move / fans / the / to / gracefully / show / kinds / different / beauty. / of)

➡ _____

21 (movements / their / as / look / beautiful / flowers / as / birds. / or / flying)

➡ _____

22 (Korea, / in / *Buchaechum* / so / is / popular / people / that / see / can / in / many / it / festivals. / traditional)

➡ _____
_____

13 이 춤은 원래 마오리족에 의해 싸움 전에 행해졌습니다.

14 그들은 적에게 그들의 힘을 보여 주고 싶었습니다.

15 춤꾼들은 싸움하기 전의 야생 동물들만큼 무섭게 보였습니다.

16 요즈음, 뉴질랜드에서는 럭비 선수들이 다른 팀에게 그들의 힘을 보여 주기 위해 게임 전에 주로 *haka*를 보여 줍니다.

한국: 부채춤

17 부채춤은 한국 전통 부채춤입니다.

18 춤꾼들은 다채로운 한복을 입습니다.

19 그들은 밝은 색으로 칠해진 커다란 부채를 가지고 춤을 춥니다.

20 그 춤꾼들은 다양한 종류의 미를 보여 주기 위해 부채를 우아하게 움직입니다.

21 그들의 움직임은 꽃 또는 날아다니는 새들처럼 우아하게 보입니다.

22 한국에서, 부채춤은 너무 인기가 있어서 사람들은 많은 전통 축제에서 그것을 볼 수 있습니다.

※ 다음 우리말을 영어로 쓰시오.

Dance with a Story

1 사람들은 왜 춤을 추는 걸까요?

➡ _____

2 사람들은 감정을 표현하고, 다른 사람들에게 행복감을 주거나 스스로 즐기기 위해 춤을 춥니다.

➡ _____

3 세계의 여러 가지 춤을 살펴봅시다.

➡ _____

India: *Kathakali*

4 *Kathakali*에는 이야기가 있습니다.

➡ _____

5 춤꾼들은 몸동작을 통해 이야기합니다.

➡ _____

6 이러한 이야기들은 대개 선과 악의 싸움에 관한 것입니다.

➡ _____

7 선한 역할을 맡은 춤꾼들은 자신의 얼굴을 초록색으로 칠합니다.

➡ _____

8 악한 역할을 맡은 춤꾼들은 검은색 화장을 합니다.

➡ _____

9 재미있는 것은 *Kathakali* 춤에서 남자들만 춤추는 것이 허락된다는 사실입니다.

➡ _____

10 몸동작이 매우 힘이 넘쳐서 춤꾼들은 수년 동안 연습을 해야 합니다.

➡ _____

New Zealand: *Haka*

11 사람들이 뉴질랜드를 방문할 때, 그들은 *haka* 춤꾼들의 무리를 만날지도 모릅니다.

➡ _____

12 그 춤꾼들은 무서운 얼굴로 이 전통 춤을 춥니다.

➡ _____

13 이 춤은 원래 마오리족에 의해 싸움 전에 행해졌습니다.

➡ _____

14 그들은 적에게 그들의 힘을 보여 주고 싶었습니다.

➡ _____

15 그 춤꾼들은 싸움하기 전의 야생 동물들만큼 무섭게 보였습니다.

➡ _____

16 요즈음, 뉴질랜드에서는 럭비 선수들이 다른 팀에게 그들의 힘을 보여 주기 위해 게임 전에 주로 *haka*를 보여 줍니다.

➡ _____

_____

Korea: *Buchaechum*

17 부채춤은 한국 전통 부채춤입니다.

➡ _____

18 춤꾼들은 다채로운 한복을 입습니다.

➡ _____

19 그들은 밝은 색으로 칠해진 커다란 부채를 가지고 춤을 춥니다.

➡ _____

20 그 춤꾼들은 다양한 종류의 미를 보여 주기 위해 부채를 우아하게 움직입니다.

➡ _____

21 그들의 움직임은 꽃 또는 날아다니는 새들처럼 우아하게 보입니다.

➡ _____

22 한국에서, 부채춤은 너무 인기가 있어서 사람들은 많은 전통 축제에서 그것을 볼 수 있습니다.

➡ _____

※ 다음 우리말과 일치하도록 빈칸에 알맞은 말을 쓰시오.

Listen and Speak 2 - C

1. A: I'm _____ _____ a _____ _____ in our town next
   week. Do you _____ _____ _____ me?

2. B: _____ interesting.

3. A: We can _____ _____ from many countries. I'm _____
   we'll have _____ _____ _____ _____.

1. A: 나는 다음 주말에 우리 마을에서 열리는 문화 행사에 갈 거야. 나와 같이 갈래?
2. B: 재미있겠다.
3. A: 우리는 많은 국가에서 온 춤들을 즐길 수 있어. 우리는 매우 즐거울 거라고 확신해.

Culture & Life

1. *Tarantella*, _____

2. _____ _____ _____, people danced the *tarantella* for
   _____ _____.

3. _____, it is a _____ _____.

4. People dance the *tarantella* _____ happy days _____ _____
   _____.

1. Tarantella – 이탈리아
2. 과거에, 사람들은 아픈 사람들을 위해 tarantella를 추었다.
3. 요즈음, 이 춤은 커플 춤이다.
4. 사람들은 결혼식 같은 행복한 날에 tarantella를 춘다.

Culture & Life

1. *Adumu*, _____

2. This dance _____ _____ before a _____.

3. It _____ _____ _____ a jumping dance.

4. Dancers _____ _____ in the air.

5. _____ a dancer jumps, other dancers _____ him _____ with
   _____ _____.

1. Adumu – 케냐
2. 이 춤은 전투하기 전에 춘다.
3. 이것은 점핑 댄스라고도 불린다.
4. 춤꾼들은 공중에 높이 뛰어오른다.
5. 한 춤꾼이 점프하면, 다른 사람들은 큰 소리를 내며 그를 응원한다.

Step2

※ 다음 우리말을 영어로 쓰시오.

Listen and Speak 2 - C

1. A: 나는 다음 주말에 우리 마을에서 열리는 문화 행사에 갈 거야. 나와 같이 갈래?

   ➡ _____

2. B: 재미있겠다.

   ➡ _____

3. A: 우리는 많은 국가에서 온 춤들을 즐길 수 있어. 우리는 매우 즐거울 거라고 확신해.

   ➡ _____

Culture & Life

1. Tarantella – 이탈리아

   ➡ _____

2. 과거에, 사람들은 아픈 사람들을 위해 tarantella를 추었다.

   ➡ _____

3. 요즈음, 이 춤은 커플 춤이다.

   ➡ _____

4. 사람들은 결혼식 같은 행복한 날에 tarantella를 춘다.

   ➡ _____

Culture & Life

1. Adumu – 케냐

   ➡ _____

2. 이 춤은 전투하기 전에 춘다.

   ➡ _____

3. 이것은 점핑 댄스라고도 불린다.

   ➡ _____

4. 춤꾼들은 공중에 높이 뛰어오른다.

   ➡ _____

5. 한 춤꾼이 점프하면, 다른 사람들은 큰 소리를 내며 그를 응원한다.

   ➡ _____

※ 다음 영어를 우리말로 쓰시오.

01 flavor		22 contract
02 safe		23 disappear
03 difference		24 experiment
04 escape		25 dry
05 fill		26 confuse
06 freezer		27 rise
07 instead		28 weigh
08 sink		29 magic
09 float		30 sunscreen
10 lightning		31 hold
11 pressure		32 candle
12 secret		33 practice
13 behind		34 necessary
14 prepare		35 for a long time
15 sunburn		36 cool down
16 expand		37 sign up for
17 trick		38 give it a try
18 material		39 stick to
19 compare		40 burn out
20 absorb		41 pick out
21 flame		42 see through
		43 turn A into B

※ 다음 우리말을 영어로 쓰시오.

01	동전		22	필요한
02	채우다		23	안전한
03	연습		24	마술, 속임수
04	마술, 마법		25	불꽃
05	사라지다		26	준비하다
06	마른, 비가 오지 않는		27	혼동하게 하다
07	팽창하다		28	뜨다
08	양초		29	탈출하다, (액체, 가스가) 새다
09	볕에 탐		30	비교하다
10	맛		31	압력
11	가라앉다		32	무게를 재다
12	흡수하다		33	오르다, 올라가다
13	비밀		34	냉동고
14	대신에		35	골라내다
15	번개		36	타 버리다
16	재료, 물질		37	~을 (바꾸지 않고) 고수하다
17	자외선 차단제		38	오랫동안
18	차이, 차이점		39	차가워지다
19	수축하다		40	A가 B로 변하다
20	섞다		41	~을 신청하다
21	실험		42	시도해 보다
			43	속을 들여다 보다

※ 다음 영영풀이에 알맞은 단어를 <보기>에서 골라 쓴 후, 우리말 뜻을 쓰시오.

1 _____ : to become impossible to see: _____

2 _____ : to become smaller: _____

3 _____ : to combine two or more substances so that they become a single
   substance: _____

4 _____ : to go down below the surface of water: _____

5 _____ : to increase in size, range, or amount: _____

6 _____ : to rest on top of a liquid or in the air: _____

7 _____ : to mistake one person or thing for another: _____

8 _____ : a substance that things can be made from: _____

9 _____ : something done to surprise or confuse someone: _____

10 _____ : a device or room for freezing food or keeping it frozen: _____

11 _____ : to find how heavy someone or something is: _____

12 _____ : to take in something in a natural or gradual way: _____

13 _____ : having the power to make impossible things happen: _____

14 _____ : a scientific test that is done in order to study what happens and to gain
   new knowledge: _____

15 _____ : a piece of information that is kept hidden from other people: _____

16 _____ : the activity of doing something again and again in order to become
   better at it: _____

보기			
secret	expand	contract	absorb
trick	magic	weigh	confuse
practice	float	sink	experiment
freezer	disappear	material	mix

※ 다음 우리말과 일치하도록 빈칸에 알맞은 말을 쓰시오.

해석

Listen & Speak 1 A

W: Today we'll make ice cream. _____ _____ do you want to make? _____ _____ strawberry? _____, mix two cups of milk, two cups of heavy cream, and _____ _____ _____ of sugar. _____, _____ five strawberries _____ small pieces. Then, _____ everything together and put it in the _____. That's it. It's _____ _____ _____, _____ it? _____ _____ you _____ _____ it at home?

W: 오늘 우리는 아이스크림을 만들 거예요. 여러분은 어느 맛을 만들고 싶은가요? 딸기는 어때요? 첫째로, 우유 2컵, 헤비 크림 2컵, 설탕 1/2컵을 섞으세요. 다음, 딸기 5개를 작은 조각으로 자르세요. 그 다음에, 모든 것을 섞어서 냉동실에 넣으세요. 이게 다예요. 만들기 쉽죠, 그렇지 않나요? 집에서 아이스크림을 만들어 보는 게 어때요?

Listen & Speak 1 B

B: Yujin, _____ did you _____ the eggs in water?

G: I'm _____ _____ the bad eggs.

B: _____ _____ are fresh, and _____ ones are not?

G: Eggs _____ _____ _____ _____ are fresh. When eggs _____ in water, they're not fresh. You _____ _____ them.

B: That's _____. Why do the bad eggs _____?

G: _____ they have gas _____. The gas _____ _____ the air in a _____.

B: Oh, I see.

B: 유진아, 왜 달걀을 물속에 넣었니?

G: 나는 상한 달걀을 골라내는 중이야.

B: 어느 달걀이 신선하고 어느 것이 신선하지 않은 거야?

G: 물에 가라앉는 달걀은 신선해. 달걀이 물에 뜨면, 그건 신선하지 않아. 그것들을 먹으면 안 돼.

B: 그거 재미있다. 상한 달걀은 왜 물에 뜨는 거니?

G: 상한 달걀은 속에 가스가 차기 때문이야. 가스가 풍선 속의 공기 같은 역할을 하거든.

B: 아, 이제 이해했다.

Listen & Speak 2 A

B: Ms. Jeong, does _____ _____ _____ water _____ more when there's a fish in it?

W: Yes, it does. We _____ _____ it now.

B: But how? We don't have a _____.

W: We _____ _____ a finger _____ _____ a fish.

B: _____ will that _____?

W: I'll _____ a glass of water first. Then I will _____ my finger in the water and _____ it to _____.

B: Oh, I _____ _____ _____ see the _____.

B: 정 선생님, 물속에 물고기가 있을 때 물 1잔의 무게가 더 무겁나요?

W: 응, 그렇단다. 우리는 지금 실험해 볼 수 있어.

B: 하지만 어떻게요? 물고기가 없는데요.

W: 우리는 물고기 대신 손가락을 사용할 수 있단다.

B: 어떻게 할 수 있어요?

W: 먼저 물 1잔의 무게를 잴 거야. 그 다음에 비교하기 위해 물속에 손가락을 넣고 무게를 잴 거란다.

B: 아, 차이를 빨리 알고 싶어요.

Listen & Speak 2 B

King Sejong: It _____ _____ _____ a long time.

Jang Yeongsil: Yes. The _____ _____ is _____ too long. The farmers are very _____.

King Sejong: We _____ do something _____ _____ them.

Jang Yeongsil: How about making a _____ _____?

King Sejong: A clock? _____ will that _____?

Jang Yeongsil: The clock will show the time and the _____. We can use it _____ _____ _____ the _____ _____.

King Sejong: That _____ _____ a good idea. But who's _____ _____ make it?

Jang Yeongsil: I'll _____ _____ _____ _____. I know _____ _____ about time and the seasons.

King Sejong: Okay, I _____ _____ _____ _____ _____ _____.

Real Life Communication A

Brian: Mina, will you _____ our tennis club?

Mina: It _____ _____, but I _____ _____ _____ a special class this _____.

Brian: _____ _____ did you sign up for?

Mina: I signed up for a _____ _____. I _____ _____ _____ learn new magic _____ there.

Brian: That sounds _____! _____ _____ _____ magic tricks before?

Mina: Yes, I learned some before, but I need _____ _____.

Brian: I hope I can see your magic tricks _____ _____.

Let's Check

B: What _____ you _____, Jiwon?

G: I'm reading a book about _____ and _____.

B: That _____ _____.

G: Yes. This book _____ 100 magic tricks that _____ _____. I've _____ _____ _____ of them.

B: That's _____. Can you show me _____ of the tricks?

G: Sure. I can show you a _____ _____ now.

B: Great! I _____ _____ _____ _____ it.

King Sejong: 오랫동안 비가 오지 않는구나.

Jang Yeongsil: 그렇습니다. 건기가 너무 오래 계속되고 있습니다. 농부들이 아주 걱정하고 있습니다.

King Sejong: 그들을 돕기 위해 뭔든 해야 한다.

Jang Yeongsil: 특별한 시계를 만드는 것은 어떨까요?

King Sejong: 시계? 그것이 어떻게 도움이 되겠느냐?

Jang Yeongsil: 시계는 시간과 계절을 알려줄 겁니다. 건기를 준비하기 위해 시계를 사용할 수 있습니다.

King Sejong: 그거 좋은 생각 같구나. 하지만 누가 시계를 만들겠느냐?

Jang Yeongsil: 제가 한번 해 보겠습니다. 저는 시간과 계절에 대해 많이 알고 있습니다.

King Sejong: 좋다, 네 시계를 빨리 보고 싶구나.

Brian: 미나야, 우리 테니스 동아리에 가입할래?

Mina: 재미있겠다. 하지만 나는 이번 가을에 특별 수업에 등록했어.

Brian: 무슨 수업에 등록했니?

Mina: 마술 수업에 등록했어. 거기서 새로운 마술 묘기를 빨리 배우고 싶어.

Brian: 그거 재미있겠다! 전에 마술 묘기를 배운 적이 있니?

Mina: 응, 전에 몇 가지 배웠어, 하지만 더 연습을 해야 해.

Brian: 언젠가 네 마술 묘기를 볼 수 있길 바라.

B: 지원아, 뭘 읽고 있니?

G: 마술과 과학에 관한 책을 읽고 있어.

B: 그거 재미있겠다.

G: 응. 이 책은 과학을 사용하는 100가지 마술을 소개하고 있어. 나는 그 중에 절반 정도를 익혔어.

B: 멋지다. 마술 중 몇 가지를 보여줄 수 있니?

G: 물론이지. 지금 풍선 마술을 보여줄 수 있어.

B: 멋지다! 빨리 보고 싶어.

※ 다음 우리말에 맞도록 대화를 영어로 쓰시오.

Listen & Speak 1 A

W: _____

_____

_____

_____

_____

W: 오늘 우리는 아이스크림을 만들 거예요. 여러분은 어느 맛을 만들고 싶은가요? 딸기는 어때요? 첫째로, 우유 2컵, 헤비 크림 2컵, 설탕 1/2컵을 섞으세요. 다음, 딸기 5개를 작은 조각으로 자르세요. 그 다음에, 모든 것을 섞어서 냉동실에 넣으세요. 이게 다예요. 만들기 쉽죠, 그렇지 않나요? 집에서 아이스크림을 만들어 보는 게 어때요?

Listen & Speak 1 B

B: _____

G: _____

B: _____

G: _____

B: _____

G: _____

B: _____

B: 유진아, 왜 달걀을 물속에 넣었니?
G: 나는 상한 달걀을 골라내는 중이야.
B: 어느 달걀이 신선하고 어느 것이 신선하지 않은 거야?
G: 물에 가라앉는 달걀은 신선해. 달걀이 물에 뜨면, 그건 신선하지 않아. 그것들을 먹으면 안 돼.
B: 그거 재미있다. 상한 달걀은 왜 물에 뜨는 거니?
G: 상한 달걀은 속에 가스가 차기 때문이야. 가스가 풍선 속의 공기 같은 역할을 하거든.
B: 아, 이제 이해했다.

Listen & Speak 2 A

B: _____

W: _____

B: _____

W: _____

B: _____

W: _____

B: _____

B: 정 선생님, 물속에 물고기가 있을 때 물 1잔의 무게가 더 무겁나요?
W: 응, 그렇단다. 우리는 지금 실험해 볼 수 있어.
B: 하지만 어떻게요? 물고기가 없는데요.
W: 우리는 물고기 대신 손가락을 사용할 수 있단다.
B: 어떻게 할 수 있어요?
W: 먼저 물 1잔의 무게를 잴 거야. 그 다음에 비교하기 위해 물속에 손가락을 넣고 무게를 잴 거란다.
B: 아, 차이를 빨리 알고 싶어요.

Listen & Speak 2 B

King Sejong: _____

Jang Yeongsil: _____

King Sejong: _____

Jang Yeongsil: _____

King Sejong: _____

Jang Yeongsil: _____

_____

King Sejong: _____

Jang Yeongsil: _____

King Sejong: _____

Real Life Communication A

Brian: _____

Mina: _____

Brian: _____

Mina: _____

Brian: _____

Mina: _____

Brian: _____

Let's Check

B: _____

G: _____

B: _____

G: _____

_____

B: _____

G: _____

B: _____

King Sejong: 오랫동안 비가 오지 않는구나.

Jang Yeongsil: 그렇습니다. 건기가 너무 오래 계속되고 있습니다. 농부들이 아주 걱정하고 있습니다.

King Sejong: 그들을 돕기 위해 뭐든 해야 한다.

Jang Yeongsil: 특별한 시계를 만드는 것은 어떨까요?

King Sejong: 시계? 그것이 어떻게 도움이 되겠느냐?

Jang Yeongsil: 시계는 시간과 계절을 알려줄 겁니다. 건기를 준비하기 위해 시계를 사용할 수 있습니다.

King Sejong: 그거 좋은 생각 같구나. 하지만 누가 시계를 만들겠느냐?

Jang Yeongsil: 제가 한번 해 보겠습니다. 저는 시간과 계절에 대해 많이 알고 있습니다.

King Sejong: 좋다, 네 시계를 빨리 보고 싶구나.

Brian: 미나야, 우리 테니스 동아리에 가입할래?

Mina: 재미있겠다. 하지만 나는 이번 가을에 특별 수업에 등록했어.

Brian: 무슨 수업에 등록했니?

Mina: 마술 수업에 등록했어. 거기서 새로운 마술 묘기를 빨리 배우고 싶어.

Brian: 그거 재미있겠다! 전에 마술 묘기를 배운 적이 있니?

Mina: 응, 전에 몇 가지 배웠어, 하지만 더 연습을 해야 해.

Brian: 언젠가 네 마술 묘기를 볼 수 있길 바라.

B: 지원아, 뭘 읽고 있니?

G: 마술과 과학에 관한 책을 읽고 있어.

B: 그거 재미있겠다.

G: 응. 이 책은 과학을 사용하는 100가지 마술을 소개하고 있어. 나는 그 중에 절반 정도를 익혔어.

B: 멋지다. 마술 중 몇 가지를 보여줄 수 있니?

G: 물론이지. 지금 풍선 마술을 보여줄 수 있어.

B: 멋지다! 빨리 보고 싶어.

※ 다음 우리말과 일치하도록 빈칸에 알맞은 것을 골라 쓰시오.

1 Jina: _____ _____ the _____ Science _____ Show!
    A. Magic   B. to   C. welcome   D. Super

2 _____ always _____ to _____ magic _____ .
    A. exciting   B. tricks   C. see   D. it's

3 And it's _____ exciting to _____ _____ the secrets _____ them.
    A. find   B. behind   C. out   D. more

4 Some people think the _____ of _____ is _____ .
    A. magic   B. science   C. secret

5 Today, Ken, a _____ of the School Magic Club, will use _____ to _____ his _____ .
    A. perform   B. member   C. tricks   D. science

6 Which tricks will he _____ us? I _____ to see them.
    A. wait   B. show   C. can't

7 Ken: Hello, everyone. Today, I'm going to _____ you _____ .
    A. something   B. show   C. amazing

8 Here's a _____ _____ _____ in it.
    A. with   B. dish   C. water

9 Now, I'll _____ a candle in the _____ of the _____ .
    A. middle   B. put   C. dish

10 Next, I'll _____ the candle and _____ it _____ a glass. "Abracadabra!"
    A. cover   B. light   C. with

11 Jina: Look at the water! _____ _____ it _____ the glass?
    A. come   B. into   C. how   D. rose

12 Ken: Air _____ when it gets _____ and creates _____ _____ .
    A. hot   B. pressure   C. expands   D. higher

13 When it _____ cold, air _____ and creates _____ _____ .
    A. contracts   B. pressure   C. gets   D. lower

14 When the flame _____ _____ , the air inside the glass _____ _____ .
    A. pressure   B. out   C. lower   D. burnt

15 As the air _____ down, the air _____ _____ .
    A. pressure   B. cooled   C. dropped

1 지나: 특별 과학 마술 쇼에 오신 것을 환영합니다!

2 마술을 보는 것은 항상 신나는 일입니다.

3 그리고 마술 뒤에 숨겨진 비밀을 알아내는 것은 더 신나는 일입니다.

4 어떤 사람들은 마술의 비밀이 과학이라고 생각합니다.

5 오늘 학교 마술 동아리 회원인 Ken은 마술을 수행하기 위해 과학을 사용할 것입니다.

6 그는 우리에게 어떤 마술을 보여 줄까요? 무척 기다려지는군요.

7 Ken: 안녕하세요, 여러분. 오늘, 저는 여러분에게 놀라운 무언가를 보여 주려고 합니다.

8 여기에 물이 담긴 접시가 있습니다.

9 이제, 저는 접시 한가운데에 초를 놓을 것입니다.

10 그다음에 초를 켜고 유리컵으로 초를 덮어 보겠습니다. "아브라카다브라!"

11 지나: 물을 보세요! 어째서 물이 유리컵 속으로 올라간 거지요?

12 Ken: 공기가 뜨거워지면 팽창해서, 더 높은 압력을 만듭니다.

13 공기가 차가워지면 수축해서, 더 낮은 압력을 만듭니다.

14 불꽃이 다 타 버렸을 때, 유리컵 속의 공기는 식어 버렸습니다.

15 공기가 식었으므로, 기압이 낮아졌습니다.

16 So the air _____ the glass was at a _____ _____.

    A. higher   B. outside   C. pressure

17 It _____ the _____ into the _____.

    A. water   B. pushed   C. glass

18 Ken: Now, I'm going to _____ _____ of these cups _____ _____.

    A. fill   B. water   C. with   D. one

19 I will _____ them _____ to _____ you.

    A. around   B. move   C. confuse

20 Jina, _____ _____ has the _____ in it?

    A. cup   B. which   C. water

21 Jina: That's _____! It's the _____ _____.

    A. one   B. easy   C. middle

22 Ken: Okay, _____ _____. See? No water.

    A. check   B. let's

23 Jina: Show _____ _____ _____ _____.

    A. other   B. me   C. cups   D. the

24 Ken: See? _____ _____ _____.

    A. no   B. there's   C. water

25 Jina: Wow! _____ the water _____?

    A. come   B. how   C. disappeared

26 Ken: _____ the trick, I _____ a special material _____ one of the _____.

    A. put   B. into   C. before   D. cups

27 The material _____ the water and _____ it jelly.

    A. turned   B. absorbed   C. into

28 Then the jelly _____ _____ the _____.

    A. bottom   B. to   C. stuck

29 If you want to _____ this trick, it's _____ to _____ cups that you can't see _____.

    A. necessary   B. try   C. through   D. use

30 Jina: Thank you _____ your great _____. It was really _____!

    A. performance   B. for   C. amazing

---

16 그래서 유리컵 밖의 공기 압력이 더 높아졌습니다.

17 높아진 압력의 공기가 물을 밀어서 유리컵으로 들어가게 된 것입니다.

18 Ken: 이제, 이 컵들 중 하나를 물로 채워 보겠습니다.

19 여러분을 헷갈리게 하려고 이 컵들을 섞어 보겠습니다.

20 지나, 어떤 컵에 물이 있을까요?

21 지나: 쉽네요! 가운데 컵이에요.

22 Ken: 좋습니다, 확인해 봅시다. 보셨죠? 물이 없군요.

23 지나: 다른 컵들도 보여 주세요.

24 Ken: 보셨죠? 물이 없네요.

25 지나: 왜! 어째서 물이 사라진 거죠?

26 Ken: 마술 전에, 저는 특별한 물질을 컵 하나에 넣어 두었습니다.

27 그 물질은 물을 흡수하고, 그것을 젤리로 변하게 했습니다.

28 그러고 나서 젤리는 컵 바닥에 달라붙었습니다.

29 여러분이 이 마술을 해 보고자 한다면, 속을 들여다볼 수 없는 컵을 사용해야 합니다.

30 지나: 멋진 공연 고맙습니다. 정말 놀라웠어요!

※ 다음 우리말과 일치하도록 빈칸에 알맞은 말을 쓰시오.

1 Jina: _____ _____ the Super _____ _____ Show!

2 _____ always _____ _____ _____ magic tricks.

3 And it's more exciting _____ _____ _____ the secrets _____ them.

4 Some people think the _____ of magic _____ _____ .

5 Today, Ken, a member of the School Magic Club, _____ _____ _____ _____ _____ his _____ .

6 Which tricks _____ he _____ _____ ? I can't _____ _____ _____ _____ .

7 Ken: Hello, everyone. Today, I'm going _____ _____ _____ _____ _____ .

8 Here's a dish _____ _____ _____ _____ .

9 Now, I'll _____ _____ _____ in the _____ of the dish.

10 Next, I'll _____ the candle and _____ _____ _____ a glass. "Abracadabra!"

11 Jina: _____ _____ the water! _____ _____ it _____ the glass?

12 Ken: Air _____ when it _____ _____ and _____ _____ _____ .

13 When it _____ _____ , air _____ and _____ _____ .

14 When the flame _____ _____ , the air inside the glass _____ _____ .

15 As the air _____ _____ , the air pressure _____ .

1 지나: 특별 과학 마술 쇼에 오신 것을 환영합니다!

2 마술을 보는 것은 항상 신나는 일입니다.

3 그리고 마술 뒤에 숨겨진 비밀을 알아내는 것은 더 신나는 일입니다.

4 어떤 사람들은 마술의 비밀이 과학이라고 생각합니다.

5 오늘 학교 마술 동아리 회원인 Ken은 마술을 수행하기 위해 과학을 사용할 것입니다.

6 그는 우리에게 어떤 마술을 보여줄까요? 무척 기다려지는군요.

7 Ken: 안녕하세요, 여러분. 오늘, 저는 여러분에게 놀라운 무언가를 보여 주려고 합니다.

8 여기에 물이 담긴 접시가 있습니다.

9 이제, 저는 접시 한가운데에 초를 놓을 것입니다.

10 그다음에 초를 켜고 유리컵으로 초를 덮어 보겠습니다. "아브라카다브라!"

11 지나: 물을 보세요! 어째서 물이 유리컵 속으로 올라간 거지요?

12 Ken: 공기가 뜨거워지면 팽창해서, 더 높은 압력을 만듭니다.

13 공기가 차가워지면 수축해서, 더 낮은 압력을 만듭니다.

14 불꽃이 다 타 버렸을 때, 유리컵 속의 공기는 식어 버렸습니다.

15 공기가 식었으므로, 기압이 낮아졌습니다.

16 So the air _____ the glass _____ _____ _____ _____ _____.

17 It _____ the water _____ the glass.

18 Ken: Now, I'm _____ _____ _____ _____ _____ _____ _____ water.

19 I will move _____ _____ _____ _____ you.

20 Jina, _____ _____ has the water in it?

21 Jina: That's easy! _____ the _____ _____.

22 Ken: Okay, _____ _____. See? No water.

23 Jina: Show _____ _____ _____ _____.

24 Ken: See? There's _____ _____.

25 Jina: Wow! _____ _____ the water _____?

26 Ken: _____ the trick, I _____ a special material _____ _____ _____ _____ _____.

27 The material _____ the water and _____ _____ _____ jelly.

28 Then the jelly _____ _____ _____ _____.

29 If you _____ _____ _____ this trick, it's _____ _____ _____ cups _____ you can't _____ _____.

30 Jina: Thank you _____ your great _____. It was really _____!

16 그래서 유리컵 밖의 공기 압력이 더 높아졌습니다.

17 높아진 압력의 공기가 물을 밀어서 유리컵으로 들어가게 된 것입니다.

18 Ken: 이제, 이 컵들 중 하나를 물로 채워 보겠습니다.

19 여러분을 헷갈리게 하려고 이 컵들을 섞어 보겠습니다.

20 지나, 어떤 컵에 물이 있을까요?

21 지나: 쉽네요! 가운데 컵이에요.

22 Ken: 좋습니다, 확인해 봅시다. 보셨죠? 물이 없군요.

23 지나: 다른 컵들도 보여 주세요.

24 Ken: 보셨죠? 물이 없네요.

25 지나: 왜 어째서 물이 사라진 거죠?

26 Ken: 마술 전에, 저는 특별한 물질을 컵 하나에 넣어 두었습니다.

27 그 물질은 물을 흡수하고, 그것을 젤리로 변하게 했습니다.

28 그리고 나서 젤리는 컵 바닥에 달라붙었습니다.

29 여러분이 이 마술을 해 보고자 한다면, 속을 들여다볼 수 없는 컵을 사용해야 합니다.

30 지나: 멋진 공연 고맙습니다. 정말 놀라웠어요!

※ 다음 문장을 우리말로 쓰시오.

1 Jina: Welcome to the Super Science Magic Show!

➡ _____

2 It's always exciting to see magic tricks.

➡ _____

3 And it's more exciting to find out the secrets behind them.

➡ _____

4 Some people think the secret of magic is science.

➡ _____

5 Today, Ken, a member of the School Magic Club, will use science to perform his tricks.

➡ _____

6 Which tricks will he show us? I can't wait to see them.

➡ _____

7 Ken: Hello, everyone. Today, I'm going to show you something amazing.

➡ _____

8 Here's a dish with water in it.

➡ _____

9 Now, I'll put a candle in the middle of the dish.

➡ _____

10 Next, I'll light the candle and cover it with a glass. "Abracadabra!"

➡ _____

11 Jina: Look at the water! How come it rose into the glass?

➡ _____

12 Ken: Air expands when it gets hot and creates higher pressure.

➡ _____

13 When it gets cold, air contracts and creates lower pressure.

➡ _____

14 When the flame burnt out, the air inside the glass cooled down.

➡ _____

15 As the air cooled down, the air pressure dropped.

➡ _____

16 ▶ So the air outside the glass was at a higher pressure.

➡ _____

17 ▶ It pushed the water into the glass.

➡ _____

18 ▶ Ken: Now, I'm going to fill one of these cups with water.

➡ _____

19 ▶ I will move them around to confuse you.

➡ _____

20 ▶ Jina, which cup has the water in it?

➡ _____

21 ▶ Jina: That's easy! It's the middle one.

➡ _____

22 ▶ Ken: Okay, let's check. See? No water.

➡ _____

23 ▶ Jina: Show me the other cups.

➡ _____

24 ▶ Ken: See? There's no water.

➡ _____

25 ▶ Jina: Wow! How come the water disappeared?

➡ _____

26 ▶ Ken: Before the trick, I put a special material into one of the cups.

➡ _____

27 ▶ The material absorbed the water and turned it into jelly.

➡ _____

28 ▶ Then the jelly stuck to the bottom.

➡ _____

29 ▶ If you want to try this trick, it's necessary to use cups that you can't see through.

➡ _____

30 ▶ Jina: Thank you for your great performance. It was really amazing!

➡ _____

Step4

※ 다음 괄호 안의 단어들을 우리말에 맞도록 바르게 배열하시오.

1 (Jina: / to / welcome / the / Science / Super / Show! / Magic)
➡ _____

2 (always / it's / to / exciting / see / tricks. / magic)
➡ _____

3 (it's / and / exciting / more / find / to / out / secrets / the / them. / behind)
➡ _____

4 (people / some / the / think / of / secret / is / magic / science.)
➡ _____

5 (Ken, / today, / member / a / of / School / the / Club, / Magic / use / will / to / science / perform / tricks. / his)
➡ _____
_____

6 (tricks / which / he / will / us? / show // I / wait / can't / see / them. / to)
➡ _____

7 (Ken: / everyone. / hello, // today, / going / I'm / show / to / something / you / amazing.)
➡ _____

8 (a / here's / with / dish / in / water / it.)
➡ _____

9 (now, / put / I'll / candle / a / the / in / of / middle / dish. / the)
➡ _____

10 (next, / light / I'll / candle / the / and / it / cover / with / glass. / a // "Abracadabra!")
➡ _____

11 (Jina: / at / look / water! / the // come / how / rose / it / the / into / glass?)
➡ _____

12 (Ken: / expands / air / it / when / gets / and / hot / higher / creates / pressure.)
➡ _____

13 (it / when / cold, / gets / contracts / air / and / lower / creates / pressure.)
➡ _____

14 (the / when / burnt / flame / out, / air / the / inside / glass / the / down. / cooled)
➡ _____

15 (the / as / cooled / air / down, / air / the / dropped. / pressure)
➡ _____

1 지나: 특별 과학 마술 쇼에 오신 것을 환영합니다!

2 마술을 보는 것은 항상 신나는 일입니다.

3 그리고 마술 뒤에 숨겨진 비밀을 알아내는 것은 더 신나는 일입니다.

4 어떤 사람들은 마술의 비밀이 과학이라고 생각합니다.

5 오늘 학교 마술 동아리 회원인 Ken은 마술을 수행하기 위해 과학을 사용할 것입니다.

6 그는 우리에게 어떤 마술을 보여 줄까요? 무척 기다려지는군요.

7 Ken: 안녕하세요, 여러분. 오늘, 저는 여러분에게 놀라운 무언가를 보여 주려고 합니다.

8 여기에 물이 담긴 접시가 있습니다.

9 이제, 저는 접시 한가운데에 초를 놓을 것입니다.

10 그다음에 초를 켜고 유리컵으로 초를 덮어 보겠습니다. "아브라카다브라!"

11 지나: 물을 보세요! 어째서 물이 유리컵 속으로 올라간 거지요?

12 Ken: 공기가 뜨거워지면 팽창해서, 더 높은 압력을 만듭니다.

13 공기가 차가워지면 수축해서, 더 낮은 압력을 만듭니다.

14 불꽃이 다 타 버렸을 때, 유리컵 속의 공기는 식어 버렸습니다.

15 공기가 식었으므로, 기압이 낮아졌습니다.

16 (the / so / outside / air / glass / the / at / was / a / pressure. / higher)

➡ _____

17 (pushed / it / water / the / the / glass. / into)

➡ _____

18 (Ken: / now, / going / I'm / fill / to / of / one / cups / these / water. / with)

➡ _____

19 (I / move / will / around / them / confuse / you. / to)

➡ _____

20 (Jina, / cup / which / the / has / in / it? / water)

➡ _____

21 (Jina / easy! / that's // the / it's / one. / middle)

➡ _____

22 (Ken: / okay, / check. / let's // see? // water. / no)

➡ _____

23 (Ken: / me / show / other / the / cups.)

➡ _____

24 (Ken: / see? // no / there's / water.)

➡ _____

25 (Jina: / wow! // come / how / water / the / disappeared?)

➡ _____

26 (Ken: / the / before / trick, / put / I / a / material / special / one / into / cups. / the / of)

➡ _____

27 (material / the / absorbed / water / the / and / it / turned / jelly. / into)

➡ _____

28 (the / then / stuck / jelly / to / bottom. / the)

➡ _____

29 (you / if / to / want / try / trick, / this / necessary / it's / use / to / cups / you / that / see / can't / through.)

➡ _____

30 (Jina: / you / thank / your / for / performance. / great // was / it / amazing! / really)

➡ _____

---

16 그래서 유리컵 밖의 공기 압력이 더 높아졌습니다.

17 높아진 압력의 공기가 물을 밀어서 유리컵으로 들어가게 된 것입니다.

18 Ken: 이제, 이 컵들 중 하나를 물로 채워 보겠습니다.

19 여러분을 헷갈리게 하려고 이 컵들을 섞어 보겠습니다.

20 지나, 어떤 컵에 물이 있을까요?

21 지나: 쉽네요! 가운데 컵이에요.

22 Ken: 좋습니다, 확인해 봅시다. 보셨죠? 물이 없군요.

23 지나: 다른 컵들도 보여 주세요.

24 Ken: 보셨죠? 물이 없네요.

25 지나: 왜! 어째서 물이 사라진 거죠?

26 Ken: 마술 전에, 저는 특별한 물질을 컵 하나에 넣어 두었습니다.

27 그 물질은 물을 흡수하고, 그것을 젤리로 변하게 했습니다.

28 그리고 나서 젤리는 컵 바닥에 달라붙었습니다.

29 여러분이 이 마술을 해 보고자 한다면, 속을 들여다볼 수 없는 컵을 사용해야 합니다.

30 지나: 멋진 공연 고맙습니다. 정말 놀라웠어요!

※ 다음 우리말을 영어로 쓰시오.

1 지나: 특별 과학 마술 쇼에 오신 것을 환영합니다!

➡ _____

2 마술을 보는 것은 항상 신나는 일입니다.

➡ _____

3 그리고 마술 뒤에 숨겨진 비밀을 알아내는 것은 더 신나는 일입니다.

➡ _____

4 어떤 사람들은 마술의 비밀이 과학이라고 생각합니다.

➡ _____

5 오늘 학교 마술 동아리 회원인 Ken은 마술을 수행하기 위해 과학을 사용할 것입니다.

➡ _____

6 그는 우리에게 어떤 마술을 보여 줄까요? 무척 기다려지는군요.

➡ _____

7 Ken: 안녕하세요, 여러분. 오늘, 저는 여러분에게 놀라운 무언가를 보여 주려고 합니다.

➡ _____

8 여기에 물이 담긴 접시가 있습니다.

➡ _____

9 이제, 저는 접시 한가운데에 초를 놓을 것입니다.

➡ _____

10 그다음에 초를 켜고 유리컵으로 초를 덮어 보겠습니다. "아브라카다브라!"

➡ _____

11 지나: 물을 보세요! 어째서 물이 유리컵 속으로 올라간 거지요?

➡ _____

12 Ken: 공기가 뜨거워지면 팽창해서, 더 높은 압력을 만듭니다.

➡ _____

13 공기가 차가워지면 수축해서, 더 낮은 압력을 만듭니다.

➡ _____

14 불꽃이 다 타 버렸을 때, 유리컵 속의 공기는 식어 버렸습니다.

➡ _____

15 공기가 식었으므로, 기압이 낮아졌습니다.

➡ _____

16 그래서 유리컵 밖의 공기 압력이 더 높아졌습니다.

➡ _____

17 높아진 압력의 공기가 물을 밀어서 유리컵으로 들어가게 된 것입니다.

➡ _____

18 Ken: 이제, 이 컵들 중 하나를 물로 채워 보겠습니다.

➡ _____

19 여러분을 헷갈리게 하려고 이 컵들을 섞어 보겠습니다.

➡ _____

20 지나, 어떤 컵에 물이 있을까요?

➡ _____

21 지나: 쉽네요! 가운데 컵이에요.

➡ _____

22 Ken: 좋습니다, 확인해 봅시다. 보셨죠? 물이 없군요.

➡ _____

23 지나: 다른 컵들도 보여 주세요.

➡ _____

24 Ken: 보셨죠? 물이 없네요.

➡ _____

25 지나: 와! 어째서 물이 사라진 거죠?

➡ _____

26 Ken: 마술 전에, 저는 특별한 물질을 컵 하나에 넣어 두었습니다.

➡ _____

27 그 물질은 물을 흡수하고, 그것을 젤리로 변하게 했습니다.

➡ _____

28 그리고 나서 젤리는 컵 바닥에 달라붙었습니다.

➡ _____

29 여러분이 이 마술을 해 보고자 한다면, 속을 들여다볼 수 없는 컵을 사용해야 합니다.

➡ _____

30 지나: 멋진 공연 고맙습니다. 정말 놀라웠어요!

➡ _____

※ 다음 우리말과 일치하도록 빈칸에 알맞은 말을 쓰시오.

Real Life Communication B

1. A: _____ _____ do you want to _____ _____ _____?

2. B: I want to _____ the badminton _____. I _____ _____ badminton. How _____ you?

3. A: I want to _____ _____ _____ _____. I _____ _____ _____ make a computer program there.

4. B: That _____ cool!

1. A: 무슨 수업을 등록하고 싶니?
2. B: 난 배드민턴 수업을 듣고 싶어. 나는 배드민턴 치는 것을 좋아하거든. 너는?
3. A: 난 컴퓨터 수업을 듣고 싶어. 나는 빨리 거기에서 컴퓨터 프로그램을 만들고 싶어.
4. B: 맛진 것 같다!

Culture & Life

1. North _____ _____ – The Bermuda _____

2. _____ _____ _____ airplanes and ships _____ _____ in the Bermuda Triangle.

3. How _____?

4. It's _____ a mystery.

1. 북대서양 – 버뮤다 삼각 지대
2. 많은 비행기와 선박이 버뮤다 삼각 지대에서 사라졌다.
3. 이유가 무엇일까?
4. 그것은 여전히 미스터리이다.

Culture & Life

1. _____ – The pyramids

2. Some of the rocks _____ _____ _____ _____ _____ the pyramids _____ _____ 70 tons.

3. How was _____ _____ _____ _____ such heavy rocks back then?

4. It's _____ _____ _____.

1. 이집트 – 피라미드
2. 피라미드를 만드는 데 사용된 몇몇 바위들은 무게가 70톤 정도인 것들이 있다.
3. 어떻게 그 시대에 그렇게 무거운 바위를 옮기는 것이 가능했을까?
4. 그것은 여전히 미스터리이다.

※ 다음 우리말을 영어로 쓰시오.

Real Life Communication B

1. A: 무슨 수업을 등록하고 싶니?

   ➡ _____

2. B: 난 배드민턴 수업을 듣고 싶어. 나는 배드민턴 치는 것을 좋아하거든. 너는?

   ➡ _____

3. A: 난 컴퓨터 수업을 듣고 싶어. 나는 빨리 거기에서 컴퓨터 프로그램을 만들고 싶어.

   ➡ _____

4. B: 멋진 것 같다!

   ➡ _____

Culture & Life

1. 북대서양 – 버뮤다 삼각 지대

   ➡ _____

2. 많은 비행기와 선박이 버뮤다 삼각 지대에서 사라졌다.

   ➡ _____

3. 이유가 무엇일까?

   ➡ _____

4. 그것은 여전히 미스터리이다.

   ➡ _____

Culture & Life

1. 이집트 – 피라미드

   ➡ _____

2. 피라미드를 만드는 데 사용된 몇몇 바위들은 무게가 70톤 정도인 것들이 있다.

   ➡ _____

3. 어떻게 그 시대에 그렇게 무거운 바위를 옮기는 것이 가능했을까?

   ➡ _____

4. 그것은 여전히 미스터리이다.

   ➡ _____

MEMO

영어 기출 문제집

적중100

2학기

정답 및 해설

지학 | 민찬규

중 2

적중100

I Don't Have a Clue

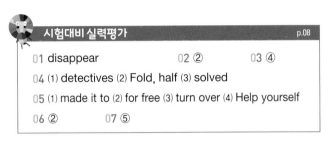

시험대비 실력평가 p.08

01 disappear 02 ② 03 ④

04 (1) detectives (2) Fold, half (3) solved

05 (1) made it to (2) for free (3) turn over (4) Help yourself

06 ② 07 ⑤

01 주어진 단어의 관계는 반의어 관계이다. appear: 나타나다, disappear: 사라지다

02 '적어 놓았거나 컴퓨터에 저장해 놓은 무언가를 제거하다'를 나타내는 것은 delete(삭제하다)이다.

03 hide는 '숨기다'를 뜻한다.

04 detective: 탐정, fold: 접다, solve: 해결하다

05 make it to: ~에 이르는 데 성공하다, for free: 무료로, turn over: 뒤집다, help yourself: 마음껏 드세요

06 주어진 문장에서 suspect는 '용의자'를 뜻하며 이와 같은 의미로 쓰인 것은 ②번이다. 나머지는 모두 '의심하다'라는 의미로 사용되었다. food poisoning: 식중독

07 첫 번째 문장에서 lie는 '눕다'를 뜻하지만 두 번째, 세 번째 문장에서는 '거짓말하다'를 의미한다.

서술형 시험대비 p.09

01 outside

02 (1) twice (2) at the time (3) for free

03 (1) Can you explain the story to me?

 (2) You should take the pills twice a day.

 (3) I cut the bread into triangles.

04 (1) accident (2) hurt (3) question (4) delete

05 (1) The police were sure (that) they could catch the thief.

 (2) Turn over the page and look at the picture.

 (3) Would you fill this bottle with water?

06 table

01 주어진 단어의 관계는 반의어 관계이다. inside: ~ 안에, outside: ~ 밖에

02 twice: 두 번, at the time of: ~이 일어나던 때에, for free: 무료로

03 explain A to B: A를 B에게 설명하다 ('explain A B'의 형식으로 쓰이지 않음에 유의한다.) pill: 환약, 알약 triangle: 삼각형

06 세 개 또는 네 개의 다리가 있지만 걸을 수 없는 것은 table을 가리킨다.

Conversation

핵심 Check p.10~11

1 (1) explain

 (2) Let me know

 (3) Can you tell me what happened yesterday

2 (1) First / Then (2) First / Then (3) First / Second / Third / Then

교과서 대화문 익히기

Check(√) True or False p.12

1 T 2 T 3 T 4 F

교과서 확인학습 p.14~15

Listen & Speak 1 - A

that, bought / like, dragons, seahorses / need to use, to play / sounds, Can you explain how to use

Listen & Speak 1 - B

riddle, twice, once, never in a day / I have no idea / get it, Can you explain why / get it

Listen & Speak 2 - A

look at / How did you make it / First, in half / Second, bottom line / Third, both ends / Then, turn, over / easy

Listen & Talk 2 - B

detective / didn't see, this week, about / all of, disappeared / did, do / First, looked around / Then, suspects / Finally, thief / don't tell, watch, later

Real Life Communication

solve / First, a bag of beans / needs to cross a river / hold, one more / take, at a time / Can you explain how to move everything across

Let's Check

smells, good / going to, for dinner / Help yourself /

Can you explain how to make / First, fill, with / Then,
on the top / delicious / Would, like / thanks

01 (D) → (A) → (C) → (B)   02 triangle
03 (A) Second (B) Third   04 ③

01 (D) 제안 → (A) 수용 및 질문 → (C) 게임 설명 → (B) 반응
02 3개의 선과 3개의 각으로 구성된 모양을 가리키는 말은
   triangle(삼각형)이다.
04 ③ 두 번째 단계에서 세모의 꼭대기를 맨 아랫선 쪽으로 접어야
   한다.

01 ②, ⑤   02 ②   03 E   04 ②
05 the paper fox   06 She should fold the
   top of the triangle to the bottom line.
07 She should make the ears first.   08 ④
09 ③   10 맘껏 먹으렴.
11 Can you explain how to make a taco? 12 ①
13 (a) with (b) delicious

01 (A)는 설명을 요청하는 표현이다. ②번은 상대방의 이해를 점
   검하는 표현이며 ⑤번은 제안을 나타낸다.
02 ② Brian이 Jimin과 운동장에서 축구하고 싶어한다는 설명은 대
   화의 내용과 일치하지 않는다.
03 'week'이라는 단어에는 'E'가 2번, 'year'라는 단어에는 한 번
   나오지만 'day'라는 단어에는 한 번도 나오지 않는다.
06 유진은 종이를 반으로 접어 삼각형을 만든 후에 세모의 꼭대기
   를 맨 아랫선 쪽으로 접어야 한다.
07 유진은 얼굴을 그리기 전에 귀를 먼저 만들어야 한다.
08 이어지는 대화에서 Then ~ 그리고 Finally로 절차를 열거하고
   있으므로 (D)가 적절하다.
09 대화를 통해 학교에서 모든 자전거를 훔친 도둑이 누구인지는 알
   수 없다.
10 Help yourself.: 마음껏 드세요.
11 explain: 설명하다
12 (C)는 음식을 권유하는 표현으로 ①번과 바꾸어 쓸 수 있다.
13 (a) fill A with B: A를 B로 채우다, (b) sound+형용사 보어:
   ~일 것 같다

01 He bought a fox, a duck, and a bag of beans.
02 He could load only one thing at a time.
03 The fox will eat the duck.
04 how to move
05 (D) → (B) → (A) → (C)
06 (A) Fold the top of the triangle to the bottom line.
   (B) Fold both ends of the bottom line to the top to
       make ears.
   (C) Turn it over and draw a face.

01 농부는 강을 건너기 전에 여우, 오리, 한 자루의 콩을 샀다.
02 농부는 한 번에 하나씩만 배에 실을 수 있다.
03 농부가 없다면 여우가 오리를 먹을 것이다.
04 how to+동사원형: ~하는 방법
05 (D) 좋은 냄새가 무엇인지 질문 → (B) 저녁 메뉴 설명 → (A)
   만드는 법 질문 → (C) 만드는 과정 설명

Grammar

1 (1) was painted by   (2) was taught
2 (1) will clean the room / will be cleaned by me
  (2) must do our homework / must be done by us
  (3) will help her / will be helped by him

01 (1) made → was made
   (2) will complete → will be completed
   (3) is caused → causes
   (4) can't open → can't be opened
02 (1) was stolen (2) be sent (3) visit (4) are held
   (5) is looked up to (6) play (7) be played
03 (1) The classroom is cleaned every day.
   (2) When was this building built?
   (3) We were not given tickets by him.
   (4) This must be done before tonight.
   (5) The door will be closed in 10 minutes.

01 (1), (2) 스웨터는 만들어지는 것이고, 건물 역시 완공되어지는
   것이므로 수동태를 쓰는 것이 옳다. (3) 부주의한 운전이 사고를
   유발하는 것이므로 능동태를 써야 한다. (4) 창문은 스스로 여는
   것이 아니므로 수동태를 쓰는 것이 옳다.

02 주어가 동사의 행위의 주체가 될 수 있으면 능동태를, 동사의 행위의 대상이 될 경우 수동태를 쓴다.

03 동사의 행위의 주체가 될 수 없는 주어들이므로 수동태를 쓰는 것이 옳다. 수동태의 형태는 'be 동사+p.p.' 형태임에 유의한다.

시험대비 실력평가
p.23~25

01 ⑤ 02 ④ 03 ③
04 was not woken up 05 ④ 06 ③
07 ⑤ 08 The fish will be cooked by her.
09 ③
10 Will the letter be sent to the right address?
11 ②
12 You will be punished by the teacher. 13 ④
14 ③ 15 ⑤ 16 ③
17 are taken care of by 18 ⑤
19 Stamps are sold in a post office (by them).
20 seen 21 (1) He was seen dancing by me.
(2) The cake will be bought by Jack.
(3) Was the juice drunk by you? 22 ②
23 ⑤ 24 ①
25 will be taken care of by me
26 This bridge must be repaired.

01 사고 발생이 과거이며 주어가 복수이므로 ⑤번이 옳다.
02 고기는 '보관되는 것'이므로 수동태를 쓰는 것이 옳다.
03 목적어가 these books이므로 이를 주어로 하고 동사 should return을 수동태로 만든 ③번이 같은 의미의 문장이다.
04 능동태에서 일반동사의 부정형이 쓰였으므로 수동태 역시 부정문으로 쓰는 것에 유의한다.
05 ④ '노래'가 주어이므로 수동태를 써서 was sung이라고 쓰는 것이 옳다.
06 모든 시점이 과거이며 주어가 동사의 행위의 대상이므로 수동태를 쓰는 것이 옳다. find(찾다)-found-found
07 동작의 주체가 일반인이거나 막연한 사람일 때, 그리고 명확하지 않을 때 'by+행위자'를 생략한다.
08 목적어가 the fish이므로 이를 주어로 하고 조동사의 수동태는 '조동사+be+p.p.'를 쓰는 것에 유의하여 문장을 만든다.
09 shut은 3단 변화가 동일한 형태인 shut-shut-shut임에 유의한다. shut down: 문을 닫다
10 편지는 '보내지는' 것이므로 will be sent를 쓰되 의문문임에 유의하여 will the letter be sent의 어순으로 쓴다.
11 모두 동사의 행위의 대상이 되어 played가 들어가지만 ②번은 행위의 주체이므로 playing이 들어간다.
12 너희들이 벌을 받는 대상이 되므로 수동태를 쓰는 것이 옳다.
13 speak well of: ~에 대해 좋게 말하다

14 바깥이 추웠으므로 히터를 틀었다고 보는 것이 옳으며, 'by+행위자'를 써야 한다. 구동사의 수동태의 경우 동사만 p.p형으로 변화시켜 수동태를 만들 수 있다.
15 by 이외의 다른 전치사를 쓰는 수동태에 유의하자. be interested in: ~에 흥미가 있다
16 run의 3단 변화는 run-ran-run이다.
17 take care of의 수동태는 be taken care of를 써야 하며 주어가 복수 명사이므로 are taken care of를 쓴다. 'by+행위자'를 쓰는 것을 잊지 않는다.
18 be crowded with: ~으로 붐비다, be satisfied with: ~에 만족하다
19 sell-sold-sold: ~을 팔다, 팔리다
20 주어진 우리말을 수동태를 활용하여 영어로 쓰면 'This performance will be seen by many people.'이다.
21 (1) 5형식 동사의 수동태에서 목적격 보어가 원형부정사가 아닌 경우 그대로 쓸 수 있다. (2) 조동사가 있는 수동태는 '조동사+be+p.p.'를 쓴다. (3) 의문문이므로 수동태 의문문을 쓴다.
22 ② happen은 자동사이므로 수동태로 쓸 수 없다.
23 'Your brothers help you.'를 수동태로 고쳐 'You are helped by your brothers.'를 쓰고 의문문을 만들기 위하여 주어와 동사 자리를 바꾸면 된다.
24 buy와 make는 4형식 동사로, 직접목적어를 주어로 한 수동태에서 간접목적어에 전치사 for를 쓴다.
25 조동사의 수동태는 '조동사+be+p.p.' 형태임에 유의한다.
26 의무를 나타내는 조동사 must를 대신하여 should를 써도 무방하다. 다리는 수리되는 대상이므로 수동태를 쓰는 것에 유의하자.

서술형 시험대비
p.26~27

01 The project will not be given up by us.
02 My parents will use the treadmill.
03 will be offered 04 were put on by David
05 be made, be bought, be invited
06 (1) was laughed at (2) be arrested (3) ate (4) be cut
(5) serves
07 will be written
08 When was this house built?
09 should be told the news
10 (1) Chris may be offered a job by the company. / A job may be offered to Chris by the company.
(2) This letter must be sent by you before June 1.
(3) Thomas Edison invented the electric light bulb in 1879.
(4) The class will be divided into two sections by me.
(5) People grow rice in many countries.

11 must be worn

12 should be finished

13 is married

14 originated, are grown, were introduced

15 are required to wear uniforms

16 was dropped by Timmy after dinner last night

17 (1) Food must not be brought into the lab (by you).

   (2) Cell phones should be turned off (by you).

   (3) UFO sightings cannot be explained (by us).

01 조동사가 있는 문장의 수동태는 '조동사+be+p.p.' 형태를 쓰며 부정어는 조동사 뒤에 위치시킨다.

02 주어가 동사의 행위의 주체가 되므로 능동태를 쓰는 것이 옳다. The treadmill will be used by my parents.로 고칠 수도 있다. treadmill: 러닝머신

03 주어가 행위의 대상이 되는 사물이므로 수동태를 쓰는 것이 옳다.

04 3인칭 단수 주어에서 동사 put이 쓰인 것으로 보아 과거시제임을 알 수 있다. 따라서 수동태로 바꿀 경우 복수 주어 The pants에 맞추어 were put on을 쓴다.

05 케이크가 만들어지고, 풍선이 구매되며, 친구들이 초대되는 것이므로 모두 수동태를 쓰는 것이 옳다.

06 (1) Julia는 반 친구들에 의해 웃음거리가 되었다. 그녀는 매우 당황했다. (2) 걱정 마. 그 용의자는 경찰에 의해 반드시 체포될 거야. (3) 내 개가 어젯밤에 탁자 위에 있던 모든 피자를 먹었다. (4) 등록금이 절반으로 삭감될 것이라는 소식은 나를 행복하게 한다. (5) 주방장은 직접 고객을 응대한다. 그래서 고객들은 만족을 느낀다.

07 주어인 '대본(a script)'은 행위의 대상이므로 수동태를 쓰는 것이 옳다.

08 집이 지어지는 것이므로 수동태를 쓰고, 시점은 과거이므로 was를 쓰는 것이 옳다.

09 4형식 동사의 간접목적어가 주어로 쓰인 수동태에서, 직접목적어에는 전치사를 쓰지 않는다.

10 (1) 4형식 동사는 목적어가 두 개이므로 두 개의 수동태를 만들 수 있다. 직접목적어가 주어로 쓰인 경우 간접목적어에 전치사를 붙이는 것에 유의하자. (2), (4) 조동사의 수동태는 '조동사+be+p.p.' 형태이다. (3) 과거에 발생한 일이므로 과거시제를 쓰는 것에 유의한다. (5) 능동태의 주어가 복수이므로 동사의 수를 일치시키는 것에 유의한다.

11 능동태의 목적어가 주어 자리에 있으므로 수동태로 쓰인 문장임을 알 수 있다.

12 주어가 동사의 행위의 대상이 되므로 수동태를 쓰는 것이 옳다. chore: 허드렛일, 하기 싫은 일

13 결혼한 상태를 말할 때에는 'be married'를 쓴다.

14 바나나는 아시아에서 유래했지만 지금은 전 세계 사람들에 의해 재배되고 있다. 바나나는 1516년에 미국에 소개되었다.

originate은 '비롯되다, 유래하다'는 의미로 쓰일 경우 자동사로 수동태로 쓰이지 않는다.

15 교복을 입도록 요구받는다는 의미가 자연스럽다. 따라서 수동태를 활용하여 문장을 완성할 수 있다.

16 능동태의 목적어가 주어로 쓰이고 있으므로 수동태를 쓰는 것이 옳다.

17 조동사가 있는 수동태는 '조동사+be+p.p.'이다.

교과서
Reading

확인문제   p.28

1 T   2 F   3 T   4 F

확인문제   p.29

1 F   2 T   3 F   4 F   5 T   6 F

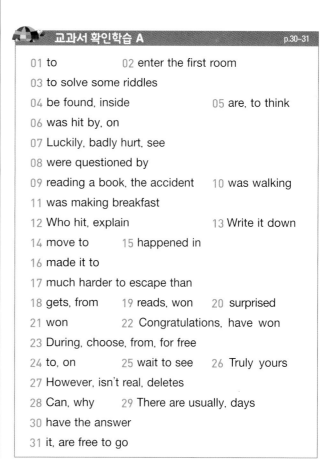

교과서 확인학습 A   p.30~31

01 to   02 enter the first room

03 to solve some riddles

04 be found, inside   05 are, to think

06 was hit by, on

07 Luckily, badly hurt, see

08 were questioned by

09 reading a book, the accident   10 was walking

11 was making breakfast

12 Who hit, explain   13 Write it down

14 move to   15 happened in

16 made it to

17 much harder to escape than

18 gets, from   19 reads, won   20 surprised

21 won   22 Congratulations, have won

23 During, choose, from, for free

24 to, on   25 wait to see   26 Truly yours

27 However, isn't real, deletes

28 Can, why   29 There are usually, days

30 have the answer

31 it, are free to go

1 Welcome to the Escape Tower.

2 You will enter the first room in our tower.

3 You need to solve some riddles to escape.

4 Clues can be found somewhere inside the room.

5 So, are you ready to think like Sherlock Holmes?

6 Mr. Doodle was hit by a car on Sunday afternoon.

7 Luckily, he wasn't badly hurt, but he didn't see the driver.

8 Three suspects were questioned by a police officer.

9 Ms. A said she was reading a book at the time of the accident.

10 Mr. B said he was walking his dog.

11 Ms. C said she was making breakfast.

12 Who hit Mr. Doodle? Can you explain why?

13 Do you have the answer? Write it down.

14 Then you can move to the next room.

15 Clue The accident happened in the afternoon.

16 Congratulations! You made it to the second room.

17 However, the second room is much harder to escape than the first one. Good luck!

18 Jay gets an email from his favorite clothing store.

19 The title reads "You won our Lucky Day event!"

20 Jay is surprised. He quickly opens it.

21 You won our 'Lucky Day' event!

22 Congratulations! You have won a special prize.

23 During our Lucky Day event, you can choose any seven items from our store for free!

24 Come to our store on November 31.

25 We can't wait to see you.

26 Truly yours, Kay Brown

27 However, Jay thinks that the event isn't real and deletes the email.

28 Can you explain why?

29 Clue There are usually 30 or 31 days in a month.

30 Do you have the answer?

31 Write it down and then you are free to go!

01 clue   02 ⑤   03 ②   04 ④

05 ②   06 ①

07 There are three suspects.

08 We have to go to the second room.

09 is surprised   10 the email   11 ③

12 ④

13 He can choose any seven items from their store for free.   14 ②

15 can find clues somewhere inside the room

16 ②   17 ①   18 was not seen by

19 She was reading a book (when Mr. Doodle was hit by a car).   20 ③

21 is written down   22 accident   23 ③

24 ④   25 ③   26 you are free to go

27 is deleted by Jay   28 ⑤

29 on November 31, 30 days

30 easy to escape

01 무언가를 발견하고, 이해하고 또는 미스터리나 수수께끼를 풀도록 돕는 것은 '단서(clue)'이다.

02 ⑤ 셜록 홈즈처럼 생각할 준비가 되었느냐고 물었을 뿐 그가 이 타워에서 많은 것을 생각하곤 했다는 말은 없다.

03 밑줄 친 (A)는 동사 need의 목적어로 쓰인 to부정사이다. ① anything을 수식하는 형용사 ② hopes의 목적어 ③ 부사적 용법 중 목적 ④ 부사적 용법 중 감정의 원인 ⑤ 부사적 용법 중 판단의 근거

04 과거에 발생한 일이며 차에 치였다는 의미이므로 ④번이 옳다.

05 ② Mr. Doodle이 운전자를 보지 못한 이유는 위 글에 나와 있지 않다.

06 심하게 다치지 않았다고 하였으므로 Luckily라고 쓰는 것이 옳다.

07 용의자는 세 명이라고 하였다.

08 첫 번째 방에서 탈출하고 나면 두 번째 방으로 가야 한다.

09 시점은 현재이며, 이메일 제목이 Jay를 놀라게 한 것이다. Jay가 주어로 쓰였으므로 수동태로 빈칸을 채워야 한다.

10 옷 가게에서 온 이메일을 가리키는 인칭대명사이다.

11 특정 날짜 앞에는 전치사 on을 쓴다.

12 밑줄 친 (D)는 명사절 접속사로 완전한 문장을 이끈다. ④번은 불완전한 문장을 이끄는 관계대명사이다.

13 행운의 날 행사 동안 그들의 가게에서 아무거나 일곱 가지 상품을 공짜로 선택할 수 있다고 하였다.

14 이메일의 제목은 'You won our Lucky Day event!'였다.

15 수동태를 능동태로 바꾸는 문제이다. 수동태에 쓰인 주어를 능동태의 목적어로 만든다.

16 특정한 순간이나 시각 앞에 쓰이는 전치사는 at이다.

17 (A) 주어가 동사의 행위의 주체가 되므로 수동태를 쓸 수 없다. (B) 지칭하는 것이 the answer이므로 단수 명사를 지칭하는 it이 알맞다. (C) happen은 자동사이므로 수동태로 쓰일 수 없다.

18 Mr. Doodle은 운전자를 보지 못했다고 하였다. 운전자가 주어이므로 수동태를 쓰는 것이 옳다.

19 Ms. A는 Mr. Doodle이 차에 치였을 때 책을 읽고 있었다고

20 hardly는 '거의 ~하지 않은'이란 의미의 부사이다. Mr. Doodle이 거의 다치지 않았다는 것은 글의 내용과 일치하지 않는다.

21 답을 쓰면 다음 방으로 갈 수 있다고 하였다. 사물이 주어이므로 수동태를 쓰는 것이 옳다.

22 예고되지 않고 피해나 부상을 유발하는 갑작스러운 사건은 '사고(accident)'이다.

23 두 번째 방으로 온 것을 축하하지만 두 번째 방은 첫 번째 방보다 탈출하기 더 어렵다고 하였으므로 '그러나'가 가장 적절하다.

24 '~로부터'라는 의미의 전치사 from이 들어가는 것이 옳다.

25 for free는 '무료로'라는 의미이다. 따라서 ③번이 옳다.

26 free: 자유로운, 자유의

27 Jay가 이메일을 지운다고 하였다. 주어가 사물이며 시점은 현재이므로 is deleted를 쓴다.

28 Jay가 이메일을 언제 받았는지는 위 글을 읽고 알 수 없다.

29 Jay가 이메일을 믿지 않은 이유는, 11월은 30일까지 있는데 행사 날짜가 11월 31일이라고 표기되어 있었기 때문이다.

30 두 번째 방은 첫 번째 방보다 탈출하기 훨씬 더 어렵다고 하였으므로, 두 번째 방은 첫 번째 방만큼 탈출하기 쉽지 않다는 말을 쓸 수 있다.

서술형 시험대비 p.38~39

01 We need to solve some riddles.

02 You will enter the first room in our tower.

03 escape, like Sherlock Holmes

04 A car hit Mr. Doodle on Sunday afternoon.

05 wasn't seen by him

06 He was walking his dog.

07 He was hit by a car (on Sunday afternoon).

08 The second room is much harder to escape than the first one.

09 is opened quickly by Jay

10 There are usually 30 or 31 days in a month.

11 He won their 'Lucky Day' event.

12 He thinks that the event isn't real and deletes the email.

13 is surprised at[by]

14 a sound in the next room was heard by him.

15 It was broken last Sunday.

16 was the window broken

17 Sujin was holding a baseball bat.

---

01 방을 탈출하기 위하여 몇 개의 수수께끼를 풀어야 한다고 하였다.

02 enter는 타동사이므로 목적어 앞에 전치사 into가 불필요하다.

03 해석: 방을 탈출하기 위해서는 셜록 홈즈처럼 생각해야 한다.

04 by a car가 쓰인 것으로 보아 행위의 주체가 a car임을 알 수 있다. 과거시제이므로 hit을 쓴다.

05 목적어가 주어로 쓰였으므로 능동태를 수동태로 전환하는 문제이다.

06 두 번째 용의자인 Mr. B는 개를 산책시키던 중이라고 하였다.

07 Mr. Doodle은 일요일 오후에 차에 치였다고 하였다.

08 much는 비교급을 강조하는 부사로 '훨씬'이라고 해석된다.

09 목적어를 주어 자리에 배치하였으므로 능동태를 수동태로 전환하는 문제임을 알 수 있다.

10 '~이 있다'는 표현은 There is/are로 쓴다. 빈도부사 usually의 위치는 be동사 뒤이다.

11 이메일에 따르면 Jay는 옷가게의 '행운의 날' 행사에 당첨되었다고 하였다.

12 이메일을 읽은 후 Jay는 그 행사가 사실이 아니라고 생각하고 이메일을 삭제한다고 하였다.

13 Jay는 이메일 제목을 읽고 놀란다고 하였다. surprise는 수동태로 쓰일 때 by 대신에 at을 주로 쓴다. by를 써도 좋다.

14 과거동사이므로 수동태로 전환할 때 was heard로 쓴다.

15 지난 일요일에 창문이 깨졌다고 하였다.

16 의문문이 있는 문장의 수동태이다. 우선 'The window was broken by whom.'을 쓴 후 전치사와 의문사를 문두에 배치하면 된다.

17 수진이는 야구 방망이를 들고 있었다고 하였다.

영역별 핵심문제 p.41~45

01 ③   02 ⑤

03 (1) Frist, draw a circle.
   (2) Second, put a star inside the circle.
   (3) Then, put a triangle on top of the circle.

04 (1) escaped   (2) suspect   (3) clues   (4) Delete

05 (1) ready to   (2) at the time of   (3) Write down

06 ①   07 ⓐ → that (또는 which)   08 ⑤

09 riddle   10 ③   11 ⓔ → draw 12 ①

13 ③   14 ⑤   15 ④   16 ⑤

17 ⑤   18 When will the food be delivered?

19 ③   20 ④   21 ②

22 We are interested in studying English.   23 ②, ④

24 ②   25 ④

26 (1) Trash must be picked up by us.
   (2) Peter looks down on Kelly.   27 ①

28 ②   29 It happened in the afternoon.

30 a bike → a car / dinner → breakfast   31 title

32 Our Lucky Day event was won by you.

33 ⑤   34 ③

01 '다른 사람이나 장소로부터 물건들을 훔치는 사람'을 가리키는 말은 thief(도둑)이다.

02 hold: 잡다, 쥐다, by oneself: 도움을 받지 않고, 혼자서, detective: 탐정

03 circle: 원, inside: ~의 안에, on top of: ~의 위에, triangle: 삼각형

04 escape: 탈출하다, suspect: 용의자, clue: 단서, delete: 삭제하다

06 주어진 문장에서 cross는 '건너다'를 뜻하며 이와 같은 의미로 쓰인 것은 ①번이다. 나머지는 모두 '십자가, X표'를 의미한다.

07 the new game을 수식하는 목적격 관계대명사 that이나 which가 적절하다.

09 '게임으로 질문하고 놀랍거나 재미있는 대답을 갖는 질문'을 가리키는 말은 riddle(수수께끼)이다.

10 이어지는 문장에서 이해되지 않은 답에 대해 설명을 요청하고 있으므로 (C)가 적절하다.

11 명령문의 동사 turn과 병렬 구조로 draw가 적절하다.

12 열거를 나타내고 있으므로 next 등으로 열거를 이어나갈 수 있다.

13 주어진 문장은 타코를 만드는 과정의 일부를 Then으로 이어서 설명하고 있으므로 (C)가 적절하다.

15 by 이외에 다른 전치사를 쓰는 수동태 문제이다. 모두 전치사 with를 쓰지만 surprised는 전치사 at을 쓴다.

16 die는 자동사이므로 수동태로 쓸 수 없다.

17 make를 p.p.로 바꾸고 나머지는 그대로 쓴다. 행위자 앞에 전치사 by를 쓰는 것을 기억하자.

18 음식이 배달되는 것이므로 수동태를 쓴다. 미래의 일이므로 will을 쓰고 의문사는 문장 맨 앞에 놓는다.

19 ③ 4형식 동사 ask가 직접목적어를 수동태의 주어로 사용할 경우 간접목적어에 전치사 of를 쓴다.

20 be located: ~에 위치해 있다, '존재하다'는 의미의 exist는 자동사로 수동태가 불가능하다.

21 작문이 쓰여지는 것이므로 should be written이라고 써야 한다. composition: 작문, 작곡

22 interest는 by 이외의 전치사를 쓰는 수동태이다.

23 4형식 동사의 수동태에서 직접목적어가 주어로 쓰인 경우 간접목적어에 특정 전치사를 부여한다. teach는 to를 쓰는 동사이다.

24 ⓐ will be sharpened ⓑ Were the flowers picked up? ⓒ is played

25 *Romeo and Juliet*은 책 이름으로 단수 취급하며 시점이 과거이므로 was written by를 쓰는 것이 옳다.

26 (1) 조동사의 수동태는 '조동사+be+p.p.' 형태이다. (2) look down on: 무시하다, 경멸하다

27 많이 다치지는 않았지만 운전자를 보지 못했다는 내용이 가장

자연스럽다. 따라서 ①번에 들어가는 것이 옳다.

28 (A)는 to부정사의 부사적 용법 중 '목적'으로 쓰였다. ① 명사적 용법(목적격 보어) ② 부사적 용법 '목적' ③ 형용사적 용법 ④ 명사적 용법(진주어) ⑤ 부사적 용법 '감정의 원인'

29 그 사건은 오후에 발생하였다.

30 Mr. Doodle은 자전거가 아닌 차에 치였으며, Ms. C는 아침을 만들고 있었다고 하였다.

31 책, 노래, 혹은 영화 같은 것에 식별하거나 묘사하기 위해서 주어지는 이름은 '제목'이다.

32 능동태의 목적어인 our Lucky Day event가 주어가 되고 시제는 과거이므로 was won으로 쓰는 것에 유의한다.

33 답을 알면 적으라고 하였다. 따라서 ⑤번은 답할 수 있다.

34 ③ Jay가 이메일을 지운 이유는 행사가 사실이 아니라고 생각해서이다.

단원별 예상문제 p.46~49

01 ①　　02 ④　　03 ②　　04 ②, ④
05 Can you explain why?　　06 ③
07 Help yourself.　　08 (A) tacos (B) I should fill my tortilla with vegetables and meat (C) add some sauce on the top
09 (B) → (C) → (D) → (A)
10 E'는 'week'이라는 단어에는 2번, 'year'라는 단어에는 한 번 나오지만, 'day'라는 단어에는 한 번도 나오지 않기 때문이다.
11 ③　　12 ④
13 The table was set and the candles were lit.
14 ⑤　　15 ①, ⑤　　16 will be delivered
17 (1) The kids were told to leave.
　 (2) I was heard singing in my room by Thomas.
18 ⑤　　19 ③
20 You made it to the second room.
21 three suspects / questioned them
22 ⑤　　23 ⑤
24 He was throwing a ball to his dog.　　25 ③

01 (A)는 자신의 이해를 점검하는 표현이므로 이해를 점검하는 ①번과 바꾸어 쓸 수 있다.

03 '어떤 범죄의 죄가 있다고 생각되는 사람'을 가리키는 말은 suspect(용의자)이다.

04 Finally는 '마침내'를 뜻하며 이와 바꾸어 쓸 수 있는 표현은 'Eventually(결국), At last(마침내)'이다. Though: 비록 ~일지라도, Nevertheless: 그럼에도 불구하고, Initially: 처음에는

06 Kelly는 처음에 답을 이해하지 못했다는 설명이 대화의 내용과 일치한다.

08 나는 엄마와 저녁식사로 타코를 먹었다. 매우 맛있었다. 나는 타코를 어떻게 만드는지 궁금했다. 엄마는 내게 먼저 토르티야에 야채와 고기를 넣고 그 다음에 위에 소스를 추가해야 한다고 말해 주셨다. 다음에 나는 그것을 혼자 만들어볼 것이다.

09 (B) 관심 끌기 → (C) 만드는 방법 질문 → (D) 만드는 방법 설명 → (A) 반응

11 행위자가 불분명하거나 일반 사람들일 때 'by+행위자'를 생략할 수 있다.

12 disappoint는 수동태로 쓰일 때 by 대신에 전치사 with를 쓰는 동사이다.

13 식탁이 차려지고 양초들에 불이 켜지는 것은 모두 수동태를 쓰는 것이 옳다

14 건물은 손상을 입는 것이므로 수동태로 쓰는 것이 옳으며, disappear는 자동사이므로 수동태로 쓰일 수 없다.

15 그 소녀가 공에 맞았다는 것은 공이 그 소녀를 쳤다는 의미이다. 따라서 ①, ⑤번이 옳다.

16 조동사가 있는 수동태의 형태는 '조동사+be+p.p.'이다.

17 5형식 동사의 수동태에서 목적격 보어가 원형부정사가 아닌 경우는 그대로 쓰일 수 있다.

18 Mr. Doodle이 일요일 오후에 차에 치임 - (C) 다행히도 많이 다치지 않았지만 운전자를 보지 못하고 경찰은 용의자 세 명을 심문함 - (B) 용의자 셋을 심문한 이야기가 나오고 - (A) 누가 범인인지 답을 쓰면 다음 방으로 갈 수 있다는 순서가 가장 자연스럽다.

19 (A)는 '다행히도'라는 의미이다. 따라서 ③번이 옳다. ① 특히 ② 최근에 ④ 갑자기 ⑤ 특히

20 make it to: ~에 이르다

21 용의자는 세 명이라고 하였으며, 경찰이 그들을 심문했다고 하였다. 경찰이 주어로 있으므로 능동태를 써서 표현한다.

22 두 번째 방은 첫 번째 방보다 탈출하기 훨씬 더 어렵다고 하였다. 따라서 ⑤번은 옳지 않다.

23 주어가 동사의 행위의 주체가 되는지 유무를 판단하여 답을 고를 수 있다.

24 도훈이 창밖을 보았을 때 Ted는 개에게 공을 던지는 중이었다.

25 ③ 도훈이가 있던 옆방의 창문이 깨졌다.

🦉 서술형 실전문제
p.50~51

01 Can you explain how to use the buttons?

02 They are going to play the new game that Jimin bought.

03 They can play the game by using the buttons.

04 all of the bikes at school disappeared

05 He looked around the school. Then, he met some suspects and asked questions.

---

06 (1) The coffee was already made.
 (2) Was the book returned by you?
 (3) My friends will be invited by me.

07 were attacked by

08 will be made by

09 The missing girl was found by the police yesterday.

10 is expected

11 Luckily

12 were questioned by a police officer

13 I[We] can find them inside the room.

14 broke the window

15 He was at home last Sunday.

16 explain

---

01 how to+동사원형: ~하는 방법

02 Jimin과 Brain은 Jimin이 산 새로운 게임을 함께 할 것이다.

03 Jimin과 Brian은 버튼을 사용해서 게임을 할 수 있다.

04 민수가 놓친 TV쇼는 학교에 있던 모든 자전거가 사라진 사건에 대한 것이다. case: 사건

05 학생 탐정은 도둑을 찾기 위해 학교를 둘러보았다. 그러고 나서 그는 몇 명의 용의자들을 만나 질문을 하였다.

06 (1) 행위의 주체가 불분명할 때에는 'by+행위자'를 생략할 수 있다. (3) 조동사가 있는 문장의 수동태는 '조동사+be+p.p.' 형태를 쓰는 것에 유의한다.

07 attack: ~을 공격하다

08 사물이 주어이므로 수동태를 써서 문장을 완성할 수 있다.

09 발견된 것이므로 수동태를 써야 하며, 어제 일어난 일이므로 과거 시제를 쓴다.

10 정시에 올 것으로 예상된다는 의미가 적절하므로 수동태를 써야 한다.

11 문맥상 문장을 수식하는 부사로 바꾼다.

12 목적어 three suspects가 주어로 쓰이고 있으므로 수동태 문장을 완성하는 문제임을 알 수 있다.

14 행위의 주체가 불분명할 때에는 'by+행위자'를 생략하여 수동태를 만들며 문장 (A)는 이에 해당한다. 불분명한 주어로 시작하는 문장이므로 능동태를 쓰는 것이 옳다.

15 도훈이는 지난주 일요일에 집에 있었다.

16 수동태 문장을 능동태로 전환한 것이다. 주어가 동사의 행위의 주체가 될 수 있으므로 explain을 쓰는 것이 옳다.

01 (A) all of the bikes at school disappeared

   (B) had missed[hadn't seen]

   (C) the student detective

   (D) the thief

02 (A) was the book read

   (B) were not[weren't] seen

   (C) was made by

|모범답안|

03 (1) The flowers will be sent to her on Monday

   (2) The mountain can be seen from here.

   (3) The performance was shown last month.

   (4) The food can't be eaten inside the building.

   (5) Only three books can be borrowed by a person at a time.

01 나는 학생 탐정이 나오는 TV 쇼에 매료되었다. 나는 민수 또한 그 TV 쇼를 아주 좋아한다는 이야기를 듣고 기뻤다. 이번 주, 방송분은 매우 흥미로웠다. 쇼는 학교의 모든 자전거들이 사라진 범죄에 관한 것이었다. 나 또한 자전거를 잃어버린 경험이 있었기 때문에 그것은 더 재미있었다. 내가 이것에 대해 민수에게 이야기했을 때, 그는 이 방송분을 보지 못했다고 이야기했다. 나는 그에게 범인을 잡기 위해 학생 탐정이 한 것에 대해 이야기했다. 나는 누가 범인인지 알지만 민수는 알고 싶어 하지 않았다. 그는 나중에 그것을 볼 것이라고 말했다.

02 경찰이 용의자 A에게 책을 어디에서 읽었느냐고 묻는 말이다. by you가 있으므로 수동태를 쓸 수 있다. (B) 누구도 용의자 B가 개를 산책시키는 것을 보지 못했다고 하였고, 이것은 누구에 의해서도 목격되지 않았다는 의미이므로 마찬가지로 수동태를 쓸 수 있다. (C) 대답으로 미루어 보아 무엇이 만들어졌는지를 묻는 말이 들어가는 것이 옳다.

단원별 모의고사   p.53~56

01 (s)afe   02 ①

03 (1) hide   (2) case   (3) candle   (4) triangle

04 ②   05 detective   06 ⑤   07 ⑤

08 Can you explain how to move everything across the river safely?

09 ③

10 (A) the fox (B) the duck (C) the beans (D) the duck

11 (E) → (B) → (A) → (C) → (D)   12 ⑤

13 ⑤   14 ②

15 The rock star was surrounded by hundreds of fans outside the theater.

16 ④   17 was caused by lightning

18 당신은 우리 가게에서 일곱 가지 상품을 아무거나 무료로

선택할 수 있습니다.   19 ④   20 ④

21 November 31 / deleted his email

22 Seven items are free during the event.   23 ③

24 ③   25 How can it be explained?

01 주어진 단어의 관계는 반의어 관계이다. safe: 안전한, dangerous: 위험한

02 '누군가가 범죄나 미스터리를 풀도록 도와주는 물체나 정보'를 가리키는 말은 clue(단서)이다.

03 case: 사건 opposite: 맞은편의, 반대쪽의

04 scene은 '현장, 장면, 풍경' 등을 뜻한다.

05 범죄를 조사하고 범죄자를 잡는 경찰을 가리키는 말은 detective(형사)이다. detective: 탐정, 형사

06 appear: 나타나다, disappear: 사라지다, suspect: 용의자, suspend: 매달다, thief: 도둑, chief: 장(長), 우두머리

07 Minsu는 Jane에게 도둑이 누구인지 이야기하지 말라고 했으므로 ⑤번 설명은 대화의 내용과 일치하지 않는다. deal with: 다루다 investigate: 조사하다

09 ③ 농부가 왜 강을 건너야 하는지는 알 수 없다.

11 (E) 수수께끼 제시 → (B) 모르겠다고 말함 → (A) 정답 제시 → (C) 설명 요청 → (D) 정답에 대한 이유 설명

13 조동사 부정형의 수동태이므로 '조동사+not+be+p.p.' 형태를 써야 한다.

14 belong to는 상태를 나타내는 동사이므로 수동태로 쓰일 수 없다. symptom: 증상

15 목적어가 the rock star이므로 이를 주어로 하여 수동태를 만들 수 있다.

16 annoy는 수동태로 쓰일 경우 전치사 with, about, at과 주로 함께 쓰인다.

17 '불은 번개에 의해 야기되었다'는 문장을 완성하는 것이 적절하다.

18 any는 긍정문에서 '무엇이든, 아무것이든'의 뜻이다.

19 thinks와 병렬 관계에 있으므로 deletes라고 쓰는 것이 옳다.

20 Jay는 이메일 제목을 보고 놀라 빠르게 그것을 열어보았다고 하였으므로 ④번이 글의 내용과 일치한다.

21 행사 날짜는 11월 31일이라고 하였고, Jay는 이메일 내용이 사실이 아니라고 생각하여 메일을 지운다고 하였다.

22 행사 동안 일곱 가지 상품을 무료로 선택할 수 있다고 하였다.

23 Jay 외에 몇 명의 사람들이 이메일을 받았는지는 위 글을 읽고 알 수 없다.

24 도훈이네 집으로 던져진 공은 위 글에서 찾아볼 수 없다.

25 주어로 쓸 수 있는 것은 it밖에 없으므로 행위의 대상으로 보아 수동태를 써서 나타내는 것이 옳다.

Lesson 6

We're Here to Dance

시험대비 실력평가
p.60

01 female   02 ①   03 ⑤
04 (1) behind (2) strength (3) graceful (4) traditional
05 ③   06 ①

01 주어진 관계는 반의어 관계를 나타낸다. male 수컷의, 남성의, female 암컷의, 여성의

02 '용기와 자신감을 갖고 위험, 고통 또는 어려운 상황을 다루는'을 뜻하는 말은 brave(용감한)이다.

03 opinion: 의견

04 graceful: 우아한, strength: 힘, behind: ~ 뒤에, traditional:전통적인

05 주어진 문장에서 character는 '등장인물'을 뜻하며 이와 같은 의미로 쓰인 것은 ③번이다. 나머지는 모두 '성격, 기질'을 뜻한다.

06 good and evil: 선과 악, be good at: ~을 잘하다

서술형 시험대비
p.61

01 enemy
02 (1) expressed (2) perform (3) originally
   (4) strength (5) enemy
03 (1) are allowed to (2) make sounds
   (3) try(또는 do) your best
04 (1) In my opinion, dancers look as cute as dolls.
   (2) The boy's shoes are so comfortable that he can wear them all day.
   (3) Do you see many people behind the actors?
05 (1) The dance is so popular that everybody learns it.
   (2) Don't miss this great show which was originally performed in Hungary.
   (3) I move my body to express my feelings.

01 주어진 관계는 반의어 관계를 나타낸다. enemy: 적, friend: 친구

02 enemy: 적, express: 표현하다, originally: 원래, 본래, strength: 힘, perform: 공연하다

03 be allowed to: ~이 허용되다, make sounds: 소리를 내다, try[do] one's best: 최선을 다하다

04 in my opinion: 내 의견으로는, comfortable: 편안한, behind: ~ 뒤에

05 popular: 인기 있는, originally: 원래, 본래, express: 표현하다

교과서
Conversation

핵심 Check
p.62~63

1 (1) What do you think about / In my opinion
  (2) wearing a school uniform / I think that, should not wear a school uniform
2 (1) culture event / interesting / I'm sure
  (2) I'm certain

교과서 대화문 익히기

Check(√) True or False
p.64

1 T 2 F 3 T 4 F

교과서 확인학습
p.66~67

Listen & Speak 1 A-1

painting / like, having fun / In my opinion, enjoys dancing

Listen & Speak 1 A-2

what, about this painting / interesting, smiled / look happy

Listen & Speak 1 B

some male birds dance / Why / love, female birds / any other animals / bees, where to find food / communicate / agree with you

Listen & Speak 2 A-1

my voice, soft, cool, sure / my body, movements, Why don't, sure / make sounds, dance

Listen & Speak 2 B

What, reading / story about / tell, more / lost, when , After that, gave up on / to be, to be, right / try my best / Keep up, make it

Real Life Communication

what, held / perform / decide what to do / How about,

opinion, beautiful / sounds like / is good at / I'm sure /
give it a try

Let's Check

dancing girls, amazing / Look more, behind / other
dancers behind her / right, I'm sure, more

---

01 ⑤   02 dancing   03 ⑤
04 He thinks that the dancers in the painting look
   happy.

01 나머지는 모두 '내 의견으로는'이라는 뜻으로 쓰였지만 ⑤번은
   '요약해서 말하면'을 나타낸다.

02 enjoy는 동명사를 목적어로 취한다.

03 (A)에는 '흥미로운'을 뜻하는 interesting, (B)는 동사
   smiled, (C)는 'look+형용사= ~처럼 보이다'를 나타내므로
   happy가 적절하다.

04 Brian은 그림에서 춤추는 사람들이 행복해 보인다고 생각한다.

---

01 ①   02 communicate   03 ⑤
04 ①, ⑤   05 ④   06 ⑤   07 ③
08 Keep up the good work. 09 ③
10 She lost her parents.
11 She didn't give up on her dream of becoming a
   dancer.
12 She is going to try her best.

01 나머지는 모두 상대방의 설명에 흥미를 나타내지만 ①번은 '나
   는 새들에 흥미를 갖고 있다.'를 나타낸다.

02 '말하기, 글쓰기, 손 움직이기 등에 의해 누군가에게 무언가에 대
   해 정보를 주다'를 뜻하는 말은 communicate(의사소통하다)이
   다.

04 (A)는 확신을 나타내는 표현으로 ①, ⑤번과 바꾸어 쓸 수 있
   다.

05 (A)는 본인처럼 뛰어 올라볼 것을 권유하는 표현이므로 ④번과
   바꾸어 쓸 수 있다.

06 수진은 소리를 만들기 위해 손을 사용한다.

07 (A)는 동사 lost, (B)는 try one's best(최선을 다하다)이므로
   best, (C)는 make it(해내다)이므로 ③번이 적절하다.

08 keep up the good work: 계속 열심히 하다

09 Michaela가 무용수가 된 후 어떤 어려움을 겪었는지는 대화를

통해 알 수 없다.

10 Michaela는 3살 때 그녀의 부모님을 잃었다.

11 Michaela는 많은 어려움에도 불구하고 무용수가 되고자 하는
   꿈을 포기 하지 않았다.

12 Kelly는 그녀의 꿈을 이루기 위해 최선을 다할 것이다.

---

01 (A) show their love to female birds
   (B) show where to find food
   (C) communicate
02 (A) a Buchaechum
   (B) It is easy to learn, and it's also beautiful
03 (B) → (E) → (D) → (A) → (C)

01 오늘 나는 Emily로부터 동물들의 춤에 대해 배웠다. 그녀는 내
   게 몇몇 수컷 새들이 암컷 새들에게 그들의 사랑을 보여주기 위
   해 춤을 춘다고 말했다. 게다가 일부 벌들이 먹이를 찾을 수 있
   는 곳을 보여주기 위해 춤을 춘다고 들었다. 이것은 매우 흥미로
   웠다. 나는 춤이 동물들 사이에 의사소통을 위한 굉장한 방법이
   라고 생각했다.

03 (B) Michaela DePrince에 대한 설명 요청 → (E)
   Michaela DePrince에 대한 설명 → (D) 반응 및 Kelly의
   장래 희망 확인 → (A) 대답 및 다짐 나타내기 → (C) 격려

교과서

Grammar

1 (1) so nice[kind] that   (2) so big[large] that
   (3) so rich that
2 (1) not as[so] hot as   (2) as handsome as

---

01 (1) very → so   (2) taller → tall   (3) so → too
   (4) two time → two times
02 (1) so tough that   (2) too thin to   (3) so happy
   that   (4) generous enough to   (5) too much to
03 (1) No other song in this album is as beautiful as
       this song.
   (2) Your cookies are not as delicious as his.
   (3) This mountain is three times as high as Namsan.
   (4) Call me as often as possible.

---

01 (1) 원인과 결과를 나타내는 어구는 so ~ that이다. (2) as ~ as 사이에는 형용사나 부사의 원급이 온다. (3) '너무 ~해서 … 할 수 없는'은 'too ~ to V' 혹은 'so ~ that 주어 can't'로 표현한다. (4) 비교급을 이용하여 배수 표현을 나타낼 때에는 times 를 쓰는 것에 유의한다.

02 'so ~ that 주어 동사'는 원인과 결과를 나타내는 어구이다. that 절에서 can't가 쓰이면 '너무 ~해서 …할 수 없는'이란 의미로 쓰이며, 이는 'too ~ to V'와 같다. that절에서 can이 쓰이면 '~ 하기에 충분히 …한'이란 의미가 되며 'so ~ that 주어 can' 혹은 '~ enough to V'로 표현할 수 있다.

03 (1) 원급을 이용하여 최상급을 표현할 수 있다. (2) 원급 비교의 부정인 'not as[so]+원급+as ~'는 '~만큼 …하지 않은[않게]' 라는 의미로, 비교하는 두 대상의 정도가 같지 않을 때 쓸 수 있다. (3) 원급으로 나타낼 수 있는 비교 표현은 '배수사+as+원급 +as'이다. (4) as ~ as possible: 가능한 한 ~하게

시험대비 실력평가 p.75~77

01 ③　　02 ④　　03 ③

04 She is so busy that she can't talk with us now.

05 ④　　06 ④　　07 Your room is as clean as mine.　08 ⑤　　09 ③

10 (1) I was too busy to do my homework.

(2) I was so busy that I couldn't do my homework.

11 ③　　12 ②, ④　　13 ④

14 I was so young that I couldn't see the movie.

15 ④　　16 ⑤　　17 ②

18 They are not as[so] poor as we are.　　19 ②, ⑤

20 ③

21 She was so upset that she went home early.

22 (1) not as[so] tall as　(2) as expensive as

01 원인과 결과를 이끄는 구문은 'so ~ that 주어 동사'이다.

02 배수사(twice, two times)를 사용하여 비교급을 나타낼 때에는 '배수사 as 원급 as'로 표현한다.

03 ③ 원인은 Kelly가 성가신 것이고 그 결과 휴대전화기를 끈 것이다.

04 'so ~ that 주어 동사'는 원인과 결과를 나타내는 어구이다. that절에서 can't가 쓰이면 '너무 ~해서 …할 수 없는'이란 의미로 쓰인다.

05 약속은 1시였지만 you와 Julia 모두 2시에 왔으므로 동등비교 표현을 쓰는 것이 적절하다.

06 'so ~ that 주어 can't'와 같은 표현은 'too ~ to V'이다.

07 mine을 대신하여 my room을 써도 좋다. 동등비교 표현이므로 'as 원급 as'를 사용한다.

08 목이 마른 것이 원인이고 생수 한 병을 모두 마신 것이 결과이므

로 'so ~ that' 구문을 이용하는 것이 적절하다.

09 원인과 결과를 나타내는 것은 'so ~ that' 구문이고, '그는 우리 를 위해 싸워줄 만큼 충분히 용감하다.'는 의미이므로 enough 가 적절하다. 동등 비교는 'as 형용사나 부사의 원급 as'를 사용 한다.

10 '너무 ~해서 …할 수 없는'은 'too ~ to V' 혹은 'so ~ that 주어 can't 동사원형'으로 표현할 수 있다.

11 '~ enough to V'이다.

12 '내가 매우 바쁘기 때문에 너와 함께 놀 수 없다.'는 의미이므로 'too ~ to V' 혹은 'so ~ that 주어 can't 동사원형'으로 나타낼 수 있다.

13 동등비교 표현인 'as ~ as' 사이에는 형용사나 부사의 원급이 오 는 것이 적절하다.

14 'too ~ to V'는 'so ~ that 주어 can't 동사원형'과 같다.

15 Necklaces were so expensive that we couldn't buy them.

16 '~하기에 충분히 …한'이라고 하였으므로 'strong enough to move the desk'라고 쓰는 것이 적절하다.

17 'so ~ that 주어 can 동사원형'은 '~ enough to V'와 같다.

18 동등비교의 부정이므로 'not as[so] ~ as'를 쓴다.

19 '너무 ~해서 …할 수 없는'은 'too ~ to V' 혹은 'so ~ that 주어 can't 동사원형'으로 표현할 수 있다.

20 동등비교이므로 'as ~ as'를 써서 나타낸다. taste: ~한 맛이 나 다

21 원인과 결과를 나타내는 어구는 'so ~ that'이다.

22 James는 Parker만큼 크지 않으며, 장미와 백합은 한 송이에 만 원이므로 장미는 백합만큼 비싸다고 말할 수 있다.

서술형 시험대비 p.78~79

01 (1) She is bright enough to solve all the puzzles.

(2) He runs so fast that he can win the race.

(3) It was too hot for me to go out.

(4) They were too poor to buy books as much as they wanted.

(5) They studied hard enough to pass the test.

02 Are you as clever as your sister?

03 so difficult that

04 (1) as old as, not as[so] old as

(2) as[so] short as

(3) not as[so] tall as, as much as

(4) not as[so] heavy as

05 The food was so hot that I burned my tongue.

06 Emily gets up as early as Judy.

07 (1) I woke up too late to attend the meeting.

(2) I woke up so late that I couldn't attend the meeting.

08 The dog is as heavy as the cat.

09 She drives so well that she always picks me up.

10 as busy as a bee

11 as far as

12 you were so rude that I was disappointed with you

13 Did you eat pizza as much as Tom

14 I know June so well that I can ask for help.

15 The book is three times as thick as this book.

01 '너무 ~해서 …할 수 없는'이란 의미의 'so ~ that 주어 can't 동사원형'은 'too ~ to V'와 같다. that절에서 can이 쓰이면 '~하기에 충분히 …한'이란 의미가 되며 'so ~ that 주어 can' 혹은 '~ enough to V'로 표현할 수 있다.

02 '~만큼 …한'은 동등비교 표현을 사용하여 나타낼 수 있다.

03 어려운 것이 원인이고 책 읽기를 포기한 것이 결과이므로 'so ~ that' 구문을 활용하여 문장을 완성한다.

04 Kevin은 Daisy와 나이가 같지만 Peter만큼 나이가 들지 않았다. 세 학생 중 Daisy가 가장 키가 작으며, 가장 가볍다. Peter는 Kevin만큼 크지 않지만 Kevin과 체중이 같다.

05 너무 뜨거운 것이 원인이 되어 혀를 데인 것이 결과이므로 'so ~ that' 구문을 활용하여 문장을 쓸 수 있다.

06 두 사람은 모두 오전 7시에 일어나며, 두 학생 모두 아침 일찍 일어난다고 하였으므로 동등비교 표현을 사용하여 나타낼 수 있다.

07 늦게 일어난 것이 원인이 되어 회의에 참석할 수 없는 결과를 낳았으므로 '너무 ~해서 …할 수 없는'이란 의미의 'too ~ to V' 혹은 'so ~ that 주어 can't 동사원형'으로 표현할 수 있다.

08 개와 고양이의 무게가 같으므로 동등비교 표현을 활용한다.

09 운전을 잘하는 것이 원인이고 나를 데리러 오는 것이 결과이므로 'so ~ that' 구문으로 나타낼 수 있다.

10 as busy as a bee: 매우 바쁜

11 서점과 도서관이 이곳에서 모두 3킬로미터 떨어진 곳에 있으므로, 도서관은 서점만큼 멀다고 말할 수 있다.

12 was를 대신하여 felt를 써도 좋다.

13 얼마나 먹었는지를 답하고 있으므로 '너는 피자를 Tom만큼 많이 먹었니?'라는 질문을 할 수 있다.

14 '~할 만큼 충분히 …한'이란 의미의 '~ enough to V'는 'so ~ that 주어 can 동사원형'과 같다.

15 원급으로 비교 표현을 할 때에는 '배수사+as 원급 as'를 사용한다.

Reading

확인문제   p.80

1 F 2 T 3 T 4 F 5 F 6 T

확인문제   p.81

1 F 2 F 3 T 4 F 5 F 6 F

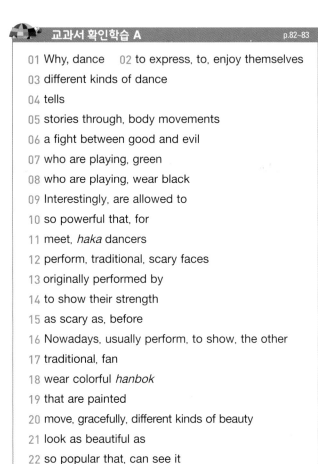

교과서 확인학습 A   p.82~83

01 Why, dance   02 to express, to, enjoy themselves

03 different kinds of dance

04 tells

05 stories through, body movements

06 a fight between good and evil

07 who are playing, green

08 who are playing, wear black

09 Interestingly, are allowed to

10 so powerful that, for

11 meet, *haka* dancers

12 perform, traditional, scary faces

13 originally performed by

14 to show their strength

15 as scary as, before

16 Nowadays, usually perform, to show, the other

17 traditional, fan

18 wear colorful *hanbok*

19 that are painted

20 move, gracefully, different kinds of beauty

21 look as beautiful as

22 so popular that, can see it

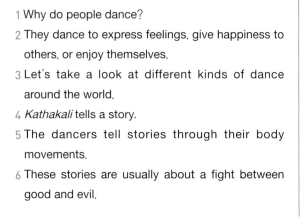

교과서 확인학습 B   p.84~85

1 Why do people dance?

2 They dance to express feelings, give happiness to others, or enjoy themselves.

3 Let's take a look at different kinds of dance around the world.

4 *Kathakali* tells a story.

5 The dancers tell stories through their body movements.

6 These stories are usually about a fight between good and evil.

7 Dancers who are playing good characters paint their faces green.

8 Those who are playing evil characters wear black make-up.

9 Interestingly, in *Kathakali*, only men are allowed to dance.

10 The body movements are so powerful that the dancers need to train for many years.

11 When people visit New Zealand, they may meet a group of *haka* dancers.

12 The dancers perform this traditional dance with scary faces.

13 This dance was originally performed by the Maori before a fight.

14 They wanted to show their strength to the enemy.

15 The dancers looked as scary as wild animals before fighting.

16 Nowadays, in New Zealand, rugby players usually perform a haka before a game to show their strength to the other team.

17 *Buchaechum* is a traditional Korean fan dance.

18 The dancers wear colorful *hanbok*.

19 They dance with large fans that are painted in bright colors.

20 The dancers move the fans gracefully to show different kinds of beauty.

21 Their movements look as beautiful as flowers or flying birds.

22 In Korea, *Buchaechum* is so popular that people can see it in many traditional festivals.

시험대비 실력평가 p.86~89

01 ① 　　　　02 ④ 　　　　03 ①, ③
04 movement 05 ③
06 They wear black make-up to express that they are playing evil characters.
07 ⑤ 　　　　08 ③ 　　　　09 show their strength
10 ⑤
11 People can see Buchaechum in many traditional festivals in Korea. 　　12 ③ 　　13 ④
14 ③ 　　　　15 ③ 　　　　16 good character
17 It's because the body movements are so powerful that the dancers need to train for many years.
18 by 　　　　19 ⑤
20 the traditional dance in New Zealand 　　21 ④

22 ④ 　　　　23 부채춤 　　24 ④ 　　　　25 cute
26 ⑤

01 이어지는 말로 보아 사람들이 왜 춤을 추는지를 묻는 말이 들어가는 것이 적절하다.

02 빈칸 (B)에는 전치사 at이 들어간다. ① take care of: ~을 돌보다 ② become interested in: ~에 흥미를 갖게 되다 ③ agree with: ~에 동의하다 ④ be good at: ~을 잘하다 ⑤ be full of: ~으로 가득 차다

03 사람을 선행사로 받는 주격 관계대명사가 쓰인다. 따라서 who 또는 that이 적절하다.

04 몸을 움직이는 행위나 몸의 일부를 움직이는 행위는 '움직임, 동작(movement)'이다.

05 ③ 춤꾼들은 몸동작을 통해 이야기한다고 하였다.

06 춤꾼들은 악한 역할을 맡은 것을 표현하기 위해 검은색 화장을 한다고 하였다.

07 적에게 힘을 보여 주고자 춘 춤에서 기인한 것이라고 하였으므로 scary faces가 가장 적절하다.

08 ③ 마오리족이 haka 춤을 춘 이유는 적들에게 그들의 힘을 보여주고 싶어서라고 하였다. attraction: 관광지, 관광명소

09 럭비 선수들이 다른 팀에게 그들의 힘을 보여주기 위해 게임 전에 haka를 보여준다고 하였다.

10 (A)는 birds를 수식하는 현재분사로 쓰이고 있다. 모두 동명사이지만 ⑤번은 현재분사이다.

11 한국의 많은 전통 축제에서 부채춤을 볼 수 있다고 하였다.

12 부채춤을 추는 춤꾼들은 다채로운 한복을 입고 우아하게 부채를 움직인다고 하였다. 부채춤은 너무 인기가 있어서 많은 전통 축제에서 그것을 볼 수 있다.

13 선과 악에 관한 이야기를 들려주고자 하는 춤이고 앞 문장에서는 선한 역할을 맡은 춤꾼들이 얼굴을 무슨 색으로 칠하는지가 나와 있으므로 evil이 가장 적절하다.

14 재귀대명사의 재귀적 용법으로 주어와 목적어가 같을 때 쓰인 재귀대명사이다. ③번은 강조 용법으로 쓰였으며 생략해도 무방하다.

15 ③ 오직 남성만이 춤을 추도록 허용되었다고 하였다.

16 선한 역할을 맡은 춤꾼들은 얼굴을 초록색으로 칠한다고 하였다.

17 춤꾼들이 수 년 동안 연습을 해야 하는 이유는 몸동작이 매우 힘이 넘쳐서이다.

18 수동태의 행위 주체를 표현하는 by가 적절하다.

19 뉴질랜드에서 만날 수 있는 haka 춤꾼 무리들 - [C] 이들은 전통 춤을 추는 것으로 원래 마오리 족에 의해 행해지던 것임 -

[B] 마오리족들은 적에게 그들의 힘을 보여주고 싶어서 춤을 춤
- [A] 요즘에는 럭비 선수들이 이 춤을 춤

20 *haka*는 뉴질랜드의 전통 춤이라고 하였다.

21 요즘에는 럭비선수들이 *haka* 춤을 춘다고 하였다.

22 (A)는 부사적 용법 중 '목적'으로 쓰인 to부정사이다. ①, ②, ③ 명사적 용법 ④ 부사적 용법 중 목적 ⑤ 형용사적 용법

23 부채춤을 가리키는 말이다.

24 부채춤은 한국에서 매우 인기가 있어서 많은 전통 축제에서 볼 수 있다고 하였다.

25 원급 비교이므로 형용사의 원래 형태를 쓴다.

26 아일랜드 사람들이 왜 스텝 댄스를 추는지는 위 글에 나와 있지 않다.

01 People dance to express feelings, give happiness to others, or enjoy themselves.

02 We can think that they are playing good characters.

03 dance, India, fight, good and evil

04 They tell stories through their body movements.

05 The body movements are so powerful that the dancers need to train for many years.

06 They perform a haka with scary faces.

07 to the enemy, their strength to the other team

08 a single person → a group of people

09 are painted

10 It is a traditional Korean fan dance.

11 It's because they want to show different kinds of beauty.

12 They danced the *tarantella* for sick people.

13 We can see people dance the *tarantella*.

14 It is performed before a fight.

01 사람들은 감정을 표현하거나, 다른 사람들에게 행복감을 주거나, 스스로 즐기기 위해 춤을 춘다고 하였다.

02 선한 역할을 맡은 사람은 얼굴을 녹색으로 칠한다.

03 사람들은 많은 이유로 춤을 춘다. 예를 들어서, 인도 춤 카타칼리에서는 사람들이 선과 악 사이의 싸움을 표현하기 위해 춤꾼들이 춤을 춘다.

04 카타칼리 춤꾼들은 몸동작을 통하여 이야기한다고 하였다.

05 동작이 매우 힘이 넘쳐서 춤꾼들은 수년 동안 연습을 해야 한다고 하였다. 'so ~ that'은 원인과 결과를 나타내는 어구이므로 춤동작이 매우 힘이 넘치는 것을 원인으로 하여 문장을 만들 수

있다.

06 하카 춤꾼들은 무서운 얼굴을 하고 이 춤을 춘다고 하였다.

07 마오리족은 적에게 자신들의 힘을 보여 주고자 하카를 추었고, 지금은 럭비 선수들이 상대 팀에게 자신들의 힘을 보여 주기 위하여 하카를 춘다고 하였다.

08 적이나 상대에게 강함을 보여주기 위하여 추는 하카 춤은 전쟁 전에 부족 사람들에 의해서, 혹은 경기 전에 선수들에 의해서 행해지므로 여러 사람이 추는 춤임을 알 수 있다.

09 fans는 색칠되는 대상이므로 수동태를 쓴다.

10 부채춤은 한국 전통 부채춤이라고 하였다.

11 다양한 종류의 미를 보여 주기 위해서 부채를 우아하게 움직인다고 하였다.

12 과거에 사람들이 타란텔라를 춘 이유는 아픈 사람들을 위해서라고 하였다.

13 요즘에는 결혼식과 같은 행복한 날에 추는 춤이라고 하였으므로 사람들이 타란텔라를 추는 것을 보는 것이 가능하다.

14 아두무 춤은 전투하기 전에 춘다고 하였다.

01 uncomfortable   02 ④   03 ④

04 ④

05 (1) wild   (2) hide   (3) bright   (4) popular   (5) scared

06 ③

07 (1) They wanted to show their strength to the enemy.

   (2) Other dancers cheer him up with loud noises.

   (3) Sujin is as brave as a lion.

08 (C) → (A) → (B)   09 ③   10 ④

11 ③   12 (D) → (A) → (C) → (E) → (B)

13 where to find food   14 I agree with you.

15 ⑤   16 ④   17 ②

18 She is as wise as an owl.   19 ②, ⑤

20 ④   21 ③

22 No other basketball player, is as[so] tall as

23 ②   24 ③

25 I was so happy that I sang all day.

26 is as brave as a lion

27 He is so talkative that he can't listen to others.

28 ②   29 ②   30 ⑤

31 *Kathakali* tries to tell a story about a fight between good and evil.

32 The body movements look very powerful.

33 ③   34 ④

35 Because it is so popular.

01 주어진 관계는 반의어 관계이다. comfortable: 편안한, uncomfortable: 불편한

02 give up on ~을 포기하다, on time 정시에

03 '당신이 손을 움직여 공기를 더 시원하게 만드는 평평한 물체'를 가리키는 말은 fan(부채)이다.

04 gracefully: 우아하게

05 bright: 밝은, scared: 겁먹은, wild: 야생의, hide: 숨다, 숨기다 popular: 인기 있는, tame: 길들이다

06 주어진 문장과 나머지 문장에서 express는 모두 '표현하다'를 나타내지만 ③번은 '급행'을 나타낸다.

07 strength: 힘, cheer: 응원하다, brave: 용감한

08 (C) 그림에 대한 의견 묻기 → (A) 의견 말하기 → (B) 동의 및 추가 설명

09 주어진 문장은 좀 더 가까이 볼 것을 권유하는 문장으로 (C)가 적절하다.

10 nervous: 긴장한, disappointed: 실망한, lonely: 외로운, surprised: 놀란, terrible: 무서운

11 한 명의 무용수 뒤에 많은 팔들을 볼 수 있다.

12 (D) 결정의 필요성 언급 → (A) 제안 및 의견 설명 → (C) 반응 및 질문 → (E) 질문에 대한 대답 → (B) 반응 및 확신 표현

15 위 대화를 통해 몇몇 동물들이 춤을 추며 어떻게 의사소통을 하는지는 알 수 없다.

16 원인과 결과를 나타내는 문장이므로 'so ~ that' 구문을 쓰는 것이 적절하다.

17 'No other 단수 명사+동사+ as 원급 as'로 최상급을 나타낼 수 있다.

18 as wise as owl: 매우 현명한

19 '너무 ~해서 …할 수 없는'이란 의미의 'so ~ that 주어 can't 동사원형'은 'too ~ to V'과 같다.

20 'too ~ to V' 혹은 'so ~ that 주어 can't 동사원형'을 쓰는 것이 적절하다.

21 원인과 결과를 이끄는 문장이므로 'so ~ that' 구문을 쓰는 것이 적절하다.

22 원급으로 최상급의 의미를 나타내려면 'no other+단수 명사+동사+as[so] ~ as ...'로 쓰는 것이 적절하다.

23 이어지는 말로 보아 물이 너무 차서 마실 수 없었다는 말이 들어가는 것이 적절하다.

24 가장 긴 밧줄은 D이다.

25 행복한 것이 원인이고 노래를 부른 것이 결과이므로 'so ~ that' 구문을 쓴다.

26 원급 비교를 이용하여 사자처럼 용감하다는 말을 쓸 수 있다.

27 해석: 그는 너무 말이 많아서 다른 사람의 말을 들을 수 없다.

28 give는 4형식 동사이다. 3형식으로 전환할 때 간접목적어에 to 를 부여한다..

29 밑줄 친 (B)는 '종류'라는 의미의 명사이다. 따라서 ②번이 적절하다. 나머지는 모두 형용사로 '친절한, 다정한'이란 의미이다.

30 카타칼리 춤동작은 매우 힘이 넘쳐서 춤꾼들은 몇 년 동안 연습을 해야 한다고 하였다.

31 카타칼리를 추는 춤꾼들은 선과 악의 싸움에 관한 이야기를 한다.

32 춤동작은 매우 힘이 넘쳐 보인다고 하였다.

33 꽃과 날아가는 새는 부채춤의 우아함을 빗댄 표현이다.

34 다양한 종류의 미를 보여 주기 위해 부채를 우아하게 움직이는 것이라고 하였다.

35 부채춤을 한국 전통 축제 장소에서 볼 수 있는 이유는 매우 인기 있어서이다.

단원별 예상문제 p.98~101

01 ④

02 what do you think about that painting?

03 In my opinion[view]

04 They show their love to female birds.

05 They show where to find food.

06 ③

07 (A) there were other dancers
(B) there were more than 10 dancers

08 ⓐ → be held

09 ②   10 ⑤

11 He is funny enough to be a comedian.

12 ⑤   13 as red as   14 ③

15 The dancer is so beautiful that I can't take my eyes off her.

16 ②   17 ④   18 ③   19 ②

20 ④

21 They wanted to show their strength to the enemy.

22 ⑤   23 ⑤

24 They look like flowers or flying birds.

25 colorful *hanbok*, large fans painted in

01 나머지는 모두 상대방의 의견에 동의를 나타내지만 ④번은 이의를 나타낸다.

04 수컷 새들은 암컷 새들에게 그들의 사랑을 보여준다.

05 일부 벌들은 춤을 추며 먹이를 찾을 수 있는 곳을 보여준다.

06 (A) amazed: 깜짝 놀란, amazing: 굉장한, (B) know의 목적절을 이끄는 접속사 that, (C) there is+단수 명사, there are+복수 명사

07 처음 무용수를 보았을 때, 나는 오직 한 명의 무용수만 있다고 생각했다. 그러나 다시 좀 더 자세히 보며, 나는 그녀 뒤에 다른 무용수들이 있다는 것을 알았다. 많은 팔들 때문에 나는 10명 이상의 무용수가 있었다는 것을 추측할 수 있었다.

08 학교 춤 대회가 곧 열릴 것이라는 수동태가 되어야 하므로 be held가 적절하다.

17

09 (A)는 도움을 요청하는 표현으로 ②번과 바꾸어 쓸 수 있다.

10 부채춤은 배우기가 쉽고 아름답다.

11 'so ~ that 주어 can 동사원형'은 '~ enough to V'와 같다.

12 모두 원인과 결과를 나타내는 문장이지만 ⑤번은 그렇지 않다.

13 토마토만큼 머리 색깔이 붉다는 의미이다.

14 각각 ① to move ② so sad ④ as light as ⑤ to swim이라고 쓰는 것이 옳다.

15 take one's eyes off: ~에서 눈을 떼다

16 원인과 결과를 나타내는 말로 가장 적절한 것은 ②번이다.

17 원급으로 최상급의 의미를 나타내기 위해서는 'no other 단수 명사'로 쓰는 것이 적절하다.

18 nowadays는 '요즘에'라는 의미이다. 따라서 these days가 가장 적절하다.

19 적들에게 그들의 힘을 보여 주기 위해서 추는 춤이므로 '겁에 질린(scared)' 표정은 어색하다. scary가 적절하다.

20 요즘에는 뉴질랜드 럭비 선수들이 시합 전에 주로 하카를 춘다고 하였다.

21 하카 춤을 춤으로써 마오리 부족들은 적에게 자신의 힘을 보여 주기를 원했다.

22 특정한 날짜 앞에는 전치사 on이 쓰인다.

23 아두무를 추기 위해서 무엇이 필요한지는 위 글에 나와 있지 않다.

24 춤꾼들의 움직임은 꽃이나 날아다니는 새들처럼 아름다워 보인다고 하였다.

25 부채춤을 추기 위해서는 다채로운 한복과 밝게 색칠된 큰 부채가 필요하다.

서술형 실전문제
p.102~103

01 Jimin's class is going to perform a taekwondo dance.

02 She is good at traditional dances.

03 She thinks that it is easy to learn and it's also beautiful.

04 (1) I am too shy to dance in front of many people.
   (2) I am so shy that I can't dance in front of many people.

05 works so well that

06 The diamond ring is as expensive as the car.

07 She is as slow as a turtle.

08 The party was so enjoyable that nobody wanted to leave.

09 green / wearing black make-up / evil character

10 India, stories, good and evil, men, powerful

11 the dancers look as cute as dolls

12 so fast that

---

01 지민이네 반은 태권도 춤을 공연할 것이다.

02 미나는 전통 춤을 잘 춘다.

03 미나는 부채춤이 배우기 쉽고 또한 아름답다고 생각한다.

04 '너무 ~해서 …할 수 없는'은 'too ~ to V' 혹은 'so ~ that 주어 can't 동사원형'으로 나타낼 수 있다.

05 Brian이 자전거를 또 사지 않으려는 이유는 지금 자전거가 작동이 너무 잘 되서이다.

06 자동차와 다이아몬드 반지의 가격이 동일하므로 원급 비교를 사용하여 나타낼 수 있다.

07 거북이와 동등 비교를 하고 있으므로 'as 원급 as'를 사용하여 문장을 만든다.

08 enjoyable: 즐거운

09 카타할리에서 얼굴을 초록색으로 칠한 춤꾼들은 선한 역할을 맡은 것이고, 악한 역할을 맡은 춤꾼은 검은색 화장을 한다고 하였다.

10 카타할리는 인도 전통 춤이고 이야기가 있는 춤이다. 이야기들은 선과 악의 싸움에 관한 것이며 춤 동작이 매우 힘이 넘친다고 하였다.

11 춤꾼들은 인형과 같이 귀엽게 보인다고 하였으므로 '춤꾼들은 인형만큼 귀여워 보인다.'고 말할 수 있다.

12 발을 너무 빨리 움직여서 그들의 발을 보기 힘들다는 말이 적절하다.

창의사고력 서술형 문제
p.104

|모범답안|

01 (A) a great dancer   (B) a dancer
   (C) try my best to be a great dancer like her

02 (1) |모범답안| The wind was so strong that it blew my hat off my head.
   (2) |모범답안| The soup was so hot that I couldn't eat it.
   (3) |모범답안| She is so friendly that she will throw a party for us.

03 Ireland / wear colorful costumes / as cute as dolls / move their feet so fast / like they're flying

---

01 오늘 나는 Michaela DePrince에 관한 이야기를 읽었다. 이 책을 고른 이유는 나는 그녀처럼 훌륭한 무용수가 되고 싶기 때문이다. 이야기는 매우 인상 깊어서 나는 Tom과 그것을 나누었다. 나는 Tom에게 그녀의 어려움과 무용수가 되기 위한 그녀의 많은 노력들을 포함하여 Michaela의 이야기를 설명하였다. 그녀의 이야기를 읽은 후 나는 그녀처럼 훌륭한 무용수가 되기 위해 최선을 다할 것을 다짐하였다. Tom 또한 나를 많이 격려하여서 나는 그가 매우 고마웠다.

01 ②
02 (1) have fun   (2) take a look
    (3) good and evil   (4) is good at   (5) give up on
03 I'm sure we'll have a lot of fun.
04 ⑤   05 ③   06 ①   07 ⑤
08 ③   09 (B) → (D) → (A) → (E) → (C)
10 She uses her voice to make music.
11 She moves her body to express her feelings.
12 ⑤   13 ③   14 ④
15 She is as busy as a bee.
16 The movie was so moving that I cried a lot.
17 ③   18 ④   19 ②   20 ③
21 (A) The Maori   (B) rugby players
22 They perform a haka to show their strength to the other team.
23 They performed a *haka* before a fight.   24 ③

01 '경찰, 군인 등과 같이 집단 또는 조직의 모든 구성원들이 입는 옷의 특별한 종류'를 가리키는 말은 uniform(제복)이다.

02 have fun 즐거운 시간을 보내다, take a look 살펴보다, good and evil 선과 악, be good at ~을 잘하다, give up on ~을 포기하다

04 위 대화를 통해 왜 지민이네 반이 태권도 춤을 선택했는지 알 수 없다.

05 주어진 문장은 Michaela에 대해 이야기해 달라는 Tom의 부탁에 대한 대답으로 적절하므로 (C)가 적절하다.

06 try one's best = do one's best = 최선을 다하다

07 위 대화를 통해 Michaela DePrince가 무용수로 계속 좋은 일들을 하고 있는지는 알 수 없다.

08 (A) impress: 감명을 주다, express: 표현하다, (B) certain: 확실한, unsure: 불확실한, (C) 의미상 '당신이 이것을 들을 때'가 적절하므로 접속사 when이 적절하다.

09 (B) 춤을 추는 이유 설명 → (D) 춤을 추는 다른 동물들이 있는지 질문 → (A) 대답 및 설명 → (E) 춤에 대한 의견 표현하기 → (C) 동의 표현

10 민지는 음악을 만들기 위해 그녀의 목소리를 사용한다.

11 지민은 그녀의 감정을 표현하기 위해 몸을 움직인다.

12 twice as long as mine이라고 쓰는 것이 적절하다.

13 '~만큼 …할 수 없는'은 동등비교의 부정으로 표현할 수 있다.

14 폭우가 원인이 되어 학교 현장 학습을 취소한 것이 결과이므로 ④번이 적절하다.

15 '벌만큼 바쁜'이라는 동등 비교 표현으로 나타낼 수 있다.

16 원인과 결과를 나타내고 있으므로 'so ~ that' 구문을 활용하여 답할 수 있다.

17 세계의 여러 가지 춤을 살펴보자고 하였으므로 ③번이 가장 적절하다.

18 to부정사에 병렬로 연결되어 있으므로 enjoy라고 쓰는 것이 적절하다.

19 비교 대상으로 미루어 보아 '아름다운'이 적절하다.

20 위 글은 한국 전통 춤인 부채춤에 관하여 정보를 제공하는 글이므로 ③번이 가장 적절하다.

21 각각 마오리 부족과 오늘날의 럭비 선수들을 가리키는 말이다.

22 뉴질랜드 럭비 선수들은 그들의 힘을 보여주기 위해 시합 전에 주로 하카를 춘다고 하였다.

23 마오리족은 싸움 전에 하카를 추었다.

24 strength는 '힘'이라는 의미이므로 the state of being strong 이라고 풀이하는 것이 적절하다.

Magic or Science?

Conversation

시험대비 실력평가　　　　　　　　　　p.112

01 disappear　　　02 ①　　　03 ④
04 ②　　　05 ①　　　06 (1) trick (2) material (3)
prepares (4) necessary (5) pressure (6) expand

01 주어진 관계는 반의어 관계를 나타낸다. disappear: 사라지다
02 '크기, 범위, 또는 양에서 증가하다'를 가리키는 말은 expand(팽창하다)이다.
03 confuse: 혼동하다
04 necessary: 필요한
05 주어진 문장에서 rose는 rise(오르다, 올라가다)의 과거형으로 이와 같은 의미를 가진 것은 ①번이다. 나머지는 모두 '장미'를 뜻한다.
06 trick: 마술, 속임수, material: 재료, 물질, prepare: 준비하다, necessary: 필요한, pressure: 압력, expand: 팽창하다, 확장하다

서술형 시험대비　　　　　　　　　　p.113

01 float
02 (1) see through (2) turn, into (3) burned out
　　(4) cooled down (5) stick to
03 (1) instead (2) float (3) magic (4) pushed
04 (1) It is not good to pick out vegetables that you don't like.
　　(2) I'll give it a try.
　　(3) If you are sleepy, drink a glass of cold water.
　　(4) I signed up for the badminton class.
05 (1) sunburn (2) Hold (3) expands
　　(4) coin (5) escape (6) contract

01 주어진 관계는 반의어 관계를 나타낸다. sink: 가라앉다, float: 뜨다
02 tick to: ~을 고수하다, cool down: 차가워지다, see through: 속을 들여다보다, turn A into B: A를 B로 바꾸다, burn out: 타 버리다
03 instead of: ~ 대신에, float: 뜨다, magic: 마술의, push: 밀다
04 pick out 골라내다, give it a try 시도해 보다, a glass of 한 잔의, sign up for ~을 신청하다
05 hold: 잡다, coin: 동전, sunburn: 볕에 탐, expand: 팽창하다, escape: 탈출하다, 새다 contract: 수축하다

핵심 Check　　　　　　　　　　p.114~115

1 (1) Which country (2) Which sport
　(3) Which one is stronger
2 (1) can't wait (2) looking forward to meeting
　(3) can't wait to see you again

교과서 대화문 익히기

Check(√) True or False　　　　　　　　p.116

1 T　2 F　3 T　4 T

교과서 확인학습　　　　　　　　p.118~119

Listen & Speak 1 A
Which flavor, First, half a cup, Next, mix, freezer, try making

Listen & Speak 1 B
put / picking out / Which, which / that sink in water, float / interesting, float / inside, like, balloon

Listen & Speak 2 A
a glass of, weigh / test / instead of / weigh, put / compare / can't wait to

Listen & Speak 2 B
hasn't rained / lasting, worried / should / clock / seasons, to prepare for, dry season / like / give it a try / can't wait to see your clock

Real Life Communication A
join / signed up for, fall / wait to, tricks / cool, Have you learned / practice / some day

Let's Check
magic, science / interesting / introduces, use science / half / cool, some / balloon / wait to

---

시험대비 기본평가　　　　　　　　p.120

01 ⓔ → see　　02 ⑤
03 Which class did you sign up for?　　04 ①

01 I can't wait to 동사원형: 나는 ~이 무척 기다려져.

04 Mina는 새로운 마술 묘기를 배우게 돼서 신이 나 있다.

06 딸기를 작게 자른 다음 모든 것을 섞어서 냉동실에 넣어야 한다.

시험대비 실력평가 p.121~122

01 isn't it?	02 Sugar	03 ⑤	04 ③
05 물 위에 뜨는 달걀		06 ③	07 ④
08 ⑤	09 ②	10 ⑤	

01 부가의문문으로 앞의 문장의 주어가 it이며 긍정문이므로 'isn't it?'이 적절하다.

02 설탕은 반 컵이 필요하다.

03 집에서 아이스크림을 만들어 볼 것을 제안한다.

04 (A)는 둘 중에서 선택하는 것이므로 which, (B)는 주어가 Eggs이므로 동사는 are, (C)는 주어와 동사가 있는 절이 이어지므로 because가 적절하다.

06 상한 달걀 속에 가스가 찬다.

07 주어진 문장은 시계가 어떻게 도움이 되는지에 대한 대답이므로 (D)가 적절하다.

08 세종대왕이 걷기를 끝내기 위해 무엇을 하는지 알 수 없다.

09 마술 수업에 등록한 상대방에게 '멋지다'라고 호응해 주는 표현이 적절하다.

10 얼마나 오랫동안 미나가 마술 묘기를 연습해 왔었는지는 알 수 없다.

서술형 시험대비 p.123

01 I can't wait to see the difference.

02 She will use a finger.

03 a glass of water weighs more when there's a fish in it

04 (D) → (B) → (E) → (C) → (A)

05 We need to prepare two cups of milk, two cups of heavy cream, half a cup of sugar, and five strawberries.

06 We should mix everything together and put it in the freezer.

02 정 선생님은 물고기 대신 손가락을 사용할 것이다.

03 정 선생님은 재민이와 실험을 통해 물 한 잔이 물속에 물고기가 있을 때 무게가 더 나가는지 아닌지 확인하고 싶어 한다.

04 (D) 시계를 만들 것을 제안 → (B) 어떻게 도움이 될지 질문 → (E) 도움이 되는 이유 설명 → (C) 관심 표현 및 질문 → (A) 대답 및 이유 설명

05 Jane에 따르면 딸기 아이스크림을 만들기 위해 두 컵의 우유, 두 컵의 헤비 크림, 반 컵의 설탕, 그리고 5개의 딸기를 준비해야 한다.

교과서

Grammar

핵심 Check p.124~125

1 (1) to take care (2) to meet (3) for us to stay

2 (1) How come (2) Why (3) How come (4) How come

시험대비 기본평가 p.126

01 (1) stop → to stop

   (2) of you → for you

   (3) did you meet → you meet

   (4) came → come

02 (1) he drinks (2) do you exercise

   (3) she looks (4) did you run

03 (1) It is very important to exercise regularly.

   (2) It is exciting to go to the amusement park.

   (3) It is important to be honest with your friends.

   (4) It is my job to explain it.

01 (1) 진주어로 쓰이는 것은 to부정사이다. (2) 상황에 대한 의견을 나타내는 형용사가 나오므로 의미상 주어로 'for+목적격'을 쓴다. (3) How come을 Why로 바꾸어도 좋다. (4) '도대체 왜 …?'라고 쓰이는 것은 'How come'이다.

02 'How come+주어+동사 …?'로 쓰여 '도대체 왜 …?'라는 의미이고, 'Why+동사+주어 …?' 어순임에 유의한다.

03 가주어 it을 대신하여 진주어 to부정사를 사용하여 문장을 쓸 수 있다.

시험대비 실력평가 p.127~129

01 ② 02 ③ 03 ④ 04 It is fun to learn a foreign language. 05 ② 06 ④

07 ⑤ 08 to read books 09 ④

10 ③ 11 ③ 12 ③ 13 How come she bought the jacket? 14 ⑤

15 ④ 16 It is important not to use your phone while walking. 17 she left 18 ③

19 ③, ④ 20 ③ 21 It is dangerous to tell a stranger where you live. 22 ③ 23 ⑤

24 How come you called me?

21

01 진주어이므로 to부정사를 쓰는 것이 적절하다.

02 'How come+주어+동사' 어순에 유의한다.

03 easy는 사람의 성질을 나타내는 형용사가 아니므로 의미상의 주어로 'for+목적격'을 쓴다. 나머지는 모두 of를 사용한다.

04 '외국어를 배우는 것'이 주어이므로 to learn a foreign language라고 쓴다.

05 주어진 문장의 밑줄 친 부분은 진주어로 쓰인 to부정사이다. ①, ④ 부사적 용법 중 목적 ② 진주어 ③ 형용사적 용법 ⑤ 명사적 용법(목적격 보어)

06 진주어로 쓰일 수 있는 것은 to부정사이며, 의문문에서 '주어+동사' 어순을 이끄는 것은 How come이다.

07 '주어+동사'의 어순을 이끄는 것은 'How come'이고, '동사+주어'의 어순을 이끄는 것은 'Why'이다.

08 진주어로 to부정사를 쓰는 것이 적절하다.

09 It is nice to know how to say hello.

10 모두 가주어 It이지만, ③번의 It은 날짜, 날씨, 거리, 명암 등을 나타내는 비인칭 주어이다.

11 진주어로 쓰일 수 있는 것은 It이다.

12 careless는 '부주의한'이란 의미로 사람의 성격을 나타내는 형용사이므로 의미상의 주어로 'of+목적격'을 써야 한다.

13 'How come+주어+동사' 어순에 유의한다.

14 impossible은 사람의 성격과 관련된 형용사가 아니므로 의미상의 주어로 'for+목적격'을 쓴다.

15 '주어+동사' 어순의 의문문이므로 How come이 적절하다.

16 휴대 전화기를 사용하지 않는 것이라고 하였으므로 to부정사의 부정으로 'not to V'를 쓰는 것에 유의한다.

17 How come이 이끄는 문장의 어순은 '주어+동사'임에 유의한다.

18 wise는 사람의 성격을 나타내는 형용사이므로 의미상의 주어로 'of+목적격'을 쓴다. 절이 이어지고 있으므로 두 번째 빈칸에는 진주어절을 이끄는 that을 쓴다.

19 '부주의하게 운전하는 것'이 주어이므로 주어를 to drive carelessly라고 쓰는 것이 적절하다.

20 모두 가주어 it에 진주어 to부정사가 쓰이지만, ③번에는 전치사 at의 목적어로 동명사 building이 쓰인다.

21 가주어 it을 이용하여 진주어 구문을 문장 맨 뒤로 보내어 같은 의미의 문장을 쓸 수 있다.

22 어순으로 보아 How come이 적절하며, impossible은 사람의 성격을 나타내는 형용사가 아니므로 의미상의 주어 로 'for+목적격'을 쓰는 것이 적절하다.

23 ① hear → to hear ② did you lose → you lost ③ for you → of you ④ you weren't → weren't you

24 How come은 'How come+주어+동사 ~?' 어순임에 유의한다.

01 It is dangerous not to wear your helmet.

02 (1) she is looking (2) did you invite

   (3) the teacher gives (4) we are going

   (5) are you wearing

03 (1) is exciting to travel abroad

   (2) is not easy to read this novel

   (3) know how to use this machine is useful

04 It was stupid of you to say so.

05 How come you put your wallet on the table?

06 for me to climb

07 How come you are going to meet her today?

08 that

09 How come / Why

10 to form good habits

11 A: How come she doesn't say sorry to me?

   B: I think (that) it is not easy for her to say sorry to you.

12 of

13 How come you forgot to bring the book?

14 It was generous of him to lend you his clothes.

15 How come you booked the restaurant?

16 To watch the movie

17 How come / Why didn't you

18 A: How come you study hard?

   B: It makes me happy to study hard.

01 '헬멧을 쓰지 않는 것'이 주어이므로 to부정사 진주어 앞에 부정어 not을 쓰는 것에 유의한다.

02 의문사 why와 how come은 의미는 비슷하지만 어순상의 차이를 보인다. 'How come+주어+동사 …?'로 쓰여 '도대체 왜 …?'라는 의미이지만, 'Why+동사+주어 …?' 어순으로 쓰인다.

03 to부정사구가 주어로 올 경우 주어가 길어지므로 가주어 it을 쓰고 to부정사구는 진주어로 만들어 문장 뒤로 보낸다.

04 '그렇게 말한 것'의 주체가 '너'이며, 사람의 성격을 나타내는 형용사가 쓰이고 있으므로 의미상의 주어로 'of you'를 쓰는 것이 적절하다.

05 'How come+주어+동사' 어순에 유의하여 답을 쓴다.

06 '산을 오르는 것'이 진주어이고 주체는 '나'이므로 for me to climb이라고 쓰는 것이 적절하다.

07 이어지는 답변에서 내가 그녀를 오늘 만나려는 이유를 설명하고 있으므로 '왜 오늘 그녀를 만나려고 하는 거야?'라고 질문했음을 알 수 있다.

08 절을 이끌고 있으므로 진주어 절을 이끄는 that이 오는 것이 적절하다.

09 비슷한 의미를 가졌지만 How come은 '주어+동사' 어순을 이끌고 Why는 '동사+주어' 어순을 이끈다.

10 이어지는 답변으로 보아 '좋은 습관을 형성하는 것은 쉬운가요?'라고 질문했음을 알 수 있다.

11 '너에게 미안하다고 말하는 것'의 주체가 '그녀'이며 easy는 사람의 성격을 나타내는 형용사가 아니므로 의미상의 주어 로 'for her'를 쓰는 것에 유의한다.

12 사람의 성격과 관련된 형용사가 나와 있으므로 의미상의 주어로 'of+목적격'을 쓴다.

13 'How come+주어+동사' 어순임에 유의한다.

14 generous는 사람의 성격을 나타내는 형용사이므로 의미상의 주어로 'of+목적격'을 쓰는 것에 유의한다.

15 How come은 '주어+동사' 어순을 이끈다.

16 '그 영화를 보는 것'이라는 주어를 쓰는 것이 적절하다.

17 'How come+주어+동사'로 쓰이고 'Why+동사+ 주어' 어순임에 유의한다.

18 A: 'How come+주어+동사' 어순이며, '공부를 열심히 하는 것'이 주어이므로 to study hard를 진주어로, it을 가주어로 써서 문장을 완성할 수 있다.

교과서 Reading

확인문제　　　　　　　　　　　　　p.132

1 T　2 F　3 F　4 F　5 T

확인문제　　　　　　　　　　　　　p.133

1 T　2 T　3 T　4 F　5 T　6 T

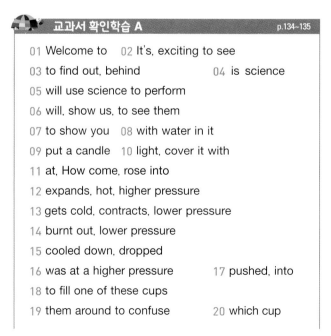

교과서 확인학습 A　　　　　　　p.134~135

01 Welcome to　02 It's, exciting to see
03 to find out, behind　04 is science
05 will use science to perform
06 will, show us, to see them
07 to show you　08 with water in it
09 put a candle　10 light, cover it with
11 at, How come, rose into
12 expands, hot, higher pressure
13 gets cold, contracts, lower pressure
14 burnt out, lower pressure
15 cooled down, dropped
16 was at a higher pressure　17 pushed, into
18 to fill one of these cups
19 them around to confuse　20 which cup

21 It's, one　　22 let's check
23 me the other cups　　24 no water
25 How come, disappeared
26 Before, put, into, the cups
27 absorbed, turned it into
28 stuck to the bottom
29 necessary to us, that
30 for, performance, amazing

교과서 확인학습 B　　　　　　　p.136~137

1 Jina: Welcome to the Super Science Magic Show!
2 It's always exciting to see magic tricks.
3 And it's more exciting to find out the secrets behind them.
4 Some people think the secret of magic is science.
5 Today, Ken, a member of the School Magic Club, will use science to perform his tricks.
6 Which tricks will he show us? I can't wait to see them.
7 Ken: Hello, everyone. Today, I'm going to show you something amazing.
8 Here's a dish with water in it.
9 Now, I'll put a candle in the middle of the dish.
10 Next, I'll light the candle and cover it with a glass. "Abracadabra!"
11 Jina: Look at the water! How come it rose into the glass?
12 Ken: Air expands when it gets hot and creates higher pressure.
13 When it gets cold, air contracts and creates lower pressure.
14 When the flame burnt out, the air inside the glass cooled down.
15 As the air cooled down, the air pressure dropped.
16 So the air outside the glass was at a higher pressure.
17 It pushed the water into the glass.
18 Ken: Now, I'm going to fill one of these cups with water.
19 I will move them around to confuse you.
20 Jina, which cup has the water in it?
21 Jina: That's easy! It's the middle one.
22 Ken: Okay, let's check. See? No water.
23 Jina: Show me the other cups.
24 Ken: See? There's no water.
25 Jina: Wow! How come the water disappeared?

26 Ken: Before the trick, I put a special material into one of the cups.

27 The material absorbed the water and turned it into jelly.

28 Then the jelly stuck to the bottom.

29 If you want to try this trick, it's necessary to use cups that you can't see through.

30 Jina: Thank you for your great performance. It was really amazing!

시험대비 실력평가
p.138~141

01 ②　　02 ③　　03 Ken is a member of the School Magic Club.　　04 ③　　05 ②
06 ④　　07 The water outside the glass rose into the glass.　　08 ②　　09 change
10 ④　　11 ③　　12 absorb　　13 He moved them around.　　14 It is necessary for us to use cups that we can't see through.　　15 ④
16 ③　　17 magic tricks　　18 ④
19 ⑤　　20 ④　　21 The air inside the glass is at a higher pressure. 22 ①　　23 The Amazing Rising Water　　24 How come the water disappeared? 25 ③　　26 ⑤　　27 He moved them around to confuse us.　　28 ④
29 ice and wind

01 Welcome to ~.: ~에 오신 것을 환영합니다.

02 과학을 이용한 마술에 관한 이야기를 하려고 한다.

03 Kevin은 학교 마술 동아리 회원이라고 하였다.

04 공기가 뜨거워질 때 팽창한다면, 반대로 공기가 차가워질 경우 수축하면서 더 낮은 압력을 만드는 것을 유추할 수 있다.

05 불꽃이 다 타버리면 컵 속의 공기는 식어버리므로 'cooled down'이 적절하다.

06 Ken은 물이 든 접시 위의 초를 유리컵으로 덮었다고 하였다. 따라서 ④번은 찾아볼 수 없다.

07 Ken이 유리컵으로 초를 덮었을 때, 유리컵 밖에 있던 물이 유리컵 속으로 올라갔다.

08 Ken은 놀라운 어떤 것을 보여주기를 원하였고, 이는 과학을 적용한 마술이다.

09 글의 내용으로 보아 유리컵의 내부와 외부의 압력 변화로 인하여 물이 움직이게 되는 것을 알 수 있다. difference라고 써도 좋다.

10 이어지는 대화 내용으로 보아 나머지 모든 컵을 보여 달라고 했음을 유추할 수 있다.

11 the jelly는 물을 흡수한 특별한 물질이 변화하여 만들어진 것이다. 따라서 ③번이 가장 적절하다.

12 자연스럽거나 점진적인 방식으로 무언가를 받아들이는 것은 '흡수하다(absorb)'이다.

13 Ken은 컵들 중 하나에 물을 채운 후 컵들을 섞었다.

14 마술을 해 보고자 한다면, 속을 들여다볼 수 없는 컵을 사용해야 한다고 하였다.

15 Ken의 마술은 과학을 이용한 것이며 투명한 유리컵이 아니라 불투명한 컵을 이용해야 한다.

16 밑줄 친 (A)는 가주어 It이다. ①, ④ 비인칭 주어 ②, ⑤ 인칭 대명사 ③ 가주어

17 마술을 가리키는 대명사이다.

18 마술 동아리 회원인 Ken은 마술을 수행하기 위해 과학을 사용할 것이라고 하며 그를 소개하고 있으므로 ④번이 가장 적절하다.

19 이어지는 Ken의 설명으로 보아 왜 물이 유리컵 속으로 올라간 것인지를 묻는 말이 적절하다.

20 (C)에서 물이 담긴 접시가 처음으로 등장하고 (B) 그 접시 한가운데에 초를 놓고 (A) 그 초를 켜는 순서가 적절하다.

21 초가 타는 동안은 뜨거운 공기의 팽창으로 인하여 높은 압력이 만들어지므로 유리컵 내부의 공기가 더 높은 압력을 가진다.

22 '-thing, -body, -one'으로 끝나는 부정대명사는 형용사의 수식을 뒤에서 받는다. 따라서 something amazing 이라고 쓰는 것이 적절하다.

23 '신비한 솟아오르는 물'이 적절하다.

24 How come은 '주어+동사' 어순을 이끄는 것에 유의한다.

25 물을 흡수하면 그것을 젤리로 변하게 한다고 하였다.

26 (C)는 관계대명사 that으로 불완전한 문장을 이끈다. 모두 완전한 문장을 이끄는 명사절 접속사이지만 ⑤번은 관계대명사이다.

27 헷갈리게 하기 위해서 컵을 이리저리 섞는 것이라고 하였다.

28 on one's own: 혼자서, 혼자 힘으로

29 과학자들의 연구에 따르면 얼음과 바람이 바위가 혼자 움직이는 것처럼 보이게 만든다.

서술형 시험대비
p.142~143

01 It is more exciting to find out the secrets behind magic tricks.

02 He will perform his magic tricks.

03 to see magic tricks

04 How come

05 He put the candle in the middle of the dish.

06 It expands.

07 lower pressure

08 Rising, burnt out, cooled, dropped, higher, outside, pushed

09 which has the water in it

10 It sticks to the bottom of the cup.

11 it is necessary to use cups that you can't see through

12 your performance

13 We need to prepare a coin and a bottle.

14 it is important to cool the bottle

15 on the bottom → on the mouth /
spin → move up and down

27 ⓓ–ⓒ–ⓐ–ⓑ

28 the air outside the glass 29 ⑤ 30 expand

31 ② 32 ⑤

01 마술 뒤에 숨겨진 비밀에 관하여 알아내는 것이 더 신나는 일이라고 하였다.

02 Ken은 자신의 마술을 보여줄 것이라고 하였다.

03 가주어 It이므로 진주어를 의미하는 것이다.

04 이어지는 말에서 물이 솟아오르는 원리를 설명하고 있다.

05 Ken은 접시 한가운데에 초를 놓았다.

06 공기가 뜨거워지면 팽창한다고 하였다.

07 공기가 차가워지면 수축하면서 낮은 압력을 만들어 낸다고 하였다.

08 솟아오르는 물 마술이다. 불꽃이 다 타 버렸을 때 유리컵 안의 공기는 차가워지고 압력은 떨어졌다. 유리컵 밖의 높은 압력이 물을 유리컵 안으로 밀어 올렸다.

09 지나는 물이 있는 컵이 가운데 컵이라고 생각하였다.

10 젤리로 변한 물은 컵 바닥에 달라붙는다고 하였다.

11 가주어 it을 활용하여 같은 의미의 문장을 쓸 수 있다.

12 Ken이 한 공연을 가리키는 말이다.

13 마술을 하기 위해서는 동전과 병이 필요하다고 하였다.

14 가주어 it을 활용하여 문장을 쓸 수 있다. '병을 차갑게 하는 것'이 주어이므로 to cool the bottle을 주어로 문장을 만든다.

15 동전을 병 입구에 올려놓는 것이고, 손으로 잠시 병을 쥐고 있으면 동전이 위아래로 움직인다고 하였다. spin: 돌다

영역별 핵심문제
p.145~149

01 ② 02 ⑤

03 (1) turn into (2) cooled down
   (3) see through (4) turned, into

04 ② 05 ②

06 (1) Which flame will burn out first?
   (2) My daughter blew out the candles on her cake.
   (3) Water expands and contracts with changes in temperature.

07 ③ 08 ⓓ → sounds 09 ②

10 ⑤ 11 sink 12 ⑤

13 (A) flavor (B) strawberry (C) mix
   (D) cut (E) put (F) try

14 ④ 15 ② 16 ④ 17 ③

18 It is not easy for her to move the boxes.

19 ③ 20 ④ 21 ⑤ 22 ③

23 How come she made an appointment?

24 for him 25 ⑤ 26 ④

01 '불가능한 일들이 일어나게 만드는 힘을 가진' 것을 가리키는 것은 magic(마법의, 마술의)이다.

02 sink: 가라앉다

03 turn A into B A를 B로 바꾸다, cool down 차가워지다, see through 속을 들여다 보다

04 주어진 문장에서 sink(싱크대)를 가리킨다. ②번의 sink는 '가라앉다'를 가리킨다.

05 mix: 섞다; 혼합물, flour: 밀가루

06 flame: 불꽃, candle: 양초, expand: 팽창하다, contract: 수축하다

07 어느 계란들이 신선한지 묻는 질문에 차이를 구별하고 싶다는 대답은 어색하다.

08 주어가 3인칭 That이므로 단수 동사 sounds가 적절하다.

09 세종대왕은 비가 오랫동안 내리지 않아 걱정했지만 장영실이 시계를 만들어 건기를 대비하기 위해 사용할 수 있도록 한다는 이야기를 듣고 기뻐함을 알 수 있다.

10 '물의 표면 아래로 내려가다'를 가리키는 말은 sink(가라앉다)이다.

11 유진이가 풍선을 갖고 무엇을 하려고 하는지는 알 수 없다.

13 strawberry: 딸기, put A in B: A를 B에 놓다, mix: 섞다, cut: 자르다, flavor: 맛

14 '우리를 위해 나서 준 것'이 주어이며 이것의 주체가 '너'이고 사람의 성격을 나타내는 brave가 있으므로 의미상의 주어로 of you를 쓰는 것이 적절하다.

15 wise는 사람의 성격을 나타내는 형용사이므로 의미상의 주어로 'of+목적격'을 쓰는 것이 적절하다.

16 possible은 사람의 성격을 나타내는 형용사가 아니므로 의미상의 주어로 'for+목적격'을 쓴다.

17 모두 주어로 쓰인 to부정사이지만, ③번은 부사적 용법 중 '목적'으로 쓰여 '~하기 위해서'라고 해석된다. lay: (알을) 낳다

18 '그 상자들을 옮기는 것'이 주어이며 행위의 주체는 '그녀'이므로 'for her to move the boxes'라고 쓴다.

19 절을 이끌고 있으므로 두 번째 빈칸에는 that이 들어가야 하며, 첫 번째 빈칸에는 가주어 It이 적절하다.

20 모두 '주어+동사' 어순이므로 How come이 사용되지만 ④번은 '동사+주어' 어순이므로 Why가 쓰인다.

21 '주어+동사' 어순이므로 How come을 쓴다.

22 ① That → It ② for her → of her ④ play → to play ⑤ did he drink → he drank

23 How come은 '주어+동사' 어순을 이끄는 것에 유의한다.

24 strange는 의미상의 주어로 'for+목적격'을 쓴다.

25 (A)는 '불을 붙이다'는 의미로 쓰인 light이다. ① 빛 ② 전등,

25

(전깃)불 ③ (색깔이) 연한, 엷은 ④ 가벼운 ⑤ 불을 붙이다

26 Jina가 왜 물이 유리컵 속으로 올라간 것인지를 묻고 있으므로 이에 대한 답변이 이어진다고 보는 것이 적절하다.

27 ⓓ 초가 다 탔을 때 유리컵 내부의 공기가 식었음 ⓒ 공기가 식으면서 공기 압력이 떨어짐 ⓐ 그래서 유리컵 밖의 공기 압력이 더 높아짐 ⓑ 압력이 높아진 바깥 공기가 물을 밀어서 유리컵 안으로 들어가게 함

28 유리컵 밖의 공기를 가리키는 말이다.

29 유리컵 밖의 공기 압력이 더 높아지면서 높아진 압력의 공기가 물을 밀어서 유리컵 안으로 들어가는 것이 적절하다. 따라서 pushed라고 써야 한다. pull: 당기다

30 크기, 범위, 혹은 양에 있어서의 증가는 '팽창하다 (expand)'이다.

31 이어지는 대화 내용으로 보아 컵에 물을 채운 것임을 알 수 있다.

32 사라지는 물의 비밀이 가장 적절하다.

단원별 예상문제 p.150~153

01 Which flavor do you want to make? 02 mix
03 ③ 04 sink, float, gas, air 05 ⓒ → use 06 ⑤ 07 She signed up for a magic class. 08 She is looking forward to learning new magic tricks. 09 ⑤ 10 I'm looking forward to seeing the differences. 11 ③
12 ④ 13 It was wise of you to 14 ⑤
15 ④ 16 It is surprising that he won the competition. 17 How come you are home so early?
18 ② 19 ③ 20 **특별한 물질을 숨기기 위해서** 21 ③ 22 ⓐ How do you do it? ⓑ What happens? ⓒ How come the coin moves?
23 expanding 24 ③ 25 trying to escape from the bottle

---

02 '두 개 이상의 물질을 결합하여 하나의 물질이 되게 하다'는 mix(섞다)이다.

03 주어진 문장은 어느 달걀들이 신선한지, 신선하지 않은지에 대한 대답이므로 (C)가 적절하다.

04 달걀이 물에 가라앉을 때, 그것들은 신선하다. 반면에 물에 뜨는 달걀은 신선하지 않다. 상한 달걀은 속에 가스가 찬다. 그것은 풍선 속의 공기처럼 활동한다.

05 that의 선행사는 100 magic tricks이므로 동사는 use가 적절하다.

06 얼마나 오랫동안 지원이가 풍선 마술을 연습했는지는 알 수 없다.

07 미나는 이번 겨울에 마술 수업에 등록했다.

08 미나는 새로운 마술 묘기를 배우는 것을 기대하고 있다.

09 주어진 문장은 How will that work?에 대한 대답으로 적절하므로 (E)에 들어가는 것이 적절하다.

11 I can't wait to ~ = I'm looking forward to -ing: 나는 ~이 무척 기다려져

11 How come은 '주어+동사' 어순임에 유의한다.

12 모두 의미상의 주어로 'for+목적격'을 쓰는 형용사이지만, careful은 사람의 성격에 관련된 형용사이므로 의미상의 주어로 'of+목적격'을 쓴다.

13 wise는 사람의 성격에 관련된 형용사이므로 의미상의 주어로 'of+목적격'을 써서 문장을 완성한다.

14 ① to finding → to find ② is she → she is ③ to not follow → not to follow ④ he is → is he

15 (A) 가주어는 It이 쓰인다. (B) 절을 이끌고 있으므로 that을 쓴다. (C) '주어+동사' 어순이므로 How come을 쓴다.

16 '그가 그 대회에서 우승했다'는 것을 진주어절로 만들어 문장을 완성한다.

17 'How come+주어+동사' 어순에 유의한다.

18 (A)는 '~하기 위해서'라고 해석되는 to부정사의 부사적 용법이다. ① 명사적 용법 중 목적격 보어 ② 부사적 용법 중 목적 ③ 형용사적 용법 ④ 진주어 ⑤ 명사적 용법 중 목적어

19 Ken은 Jina가 혼란을 느끼도록 하기 위하여 컵들을 섞었다.

20 Ken은 마술의 비밀이 특별한 물질 때문이라고 밝혔다. 이를 숨기기 위해서는 속을 들여다볼 수 없는 컵을 사용해야 한다.

21 Ken은 마술 전에 특별한 물질을 컵 하나에 넣었다고 하였으므로 ③번이 가장 적절하다.

22 ⓐ 이어지는 문장이 방법을 설명하고 있으므로 어떻게 하는 것인지 묻는 말이 적절하며, ⓑ 동전이 위아래로 움직인다고 말하고 있으므로 무슨 일이 발생하는지 묻는 말이 들어가는 것이 적절하며, ⓒ 그 원리를 설명하고 있으므로 왜 움직이는지 묻는 말이 자연스럽다.

23 손이 병 안의 찬 공기를 데우면 공기가 따뜻해져서 팽창한다. 팽창하는 공기가 병에서 나가려고 하는 것이므로 'expanding'을 쓴다.

24 병을 차갑게 하는 것이 중요하다고 하였다.

25 병을 탈출하려는 공기 때문에 병 입구에 놓인 동전이 위아래로 움직이는 것이다.

서술형 실전문제 p.154~155

01 It hasn't rained for a long time.
02 He suggests making a special clock.
03 It's because the clock will show the time and the seasons, so they can use it to prepare for the dry season.
04 It is rude of him to take pictures of her without her permission.
05 for him to
06 How come you couldn't catch the bus?
07 It is important to keep
08 How come they are tired?

---

01 오랫동안 비가 내리지 않았다.

02 장영실은 특별한 시계를 만들 것을 제안한다.

03 시계는 시간과 계절을 알려줘 건기를 준비하기 위해 사용할 수 있기 때문에 장영실은 시계가 농부들을 도와줄 것이라고 생각한다.

04 of와 to를 추가한다. rude는 사람의 성격을 나타내는 형용사이므로 의미상의 주어로 'of+목적격'을 쓴다.

05 that절에서 운동하는 주체가 'he'이므로 to부정사 구문으로 바꿀 때 의미상의 주어를 'for him'으로 쓸 수 있다.

06 답변에서 버스를 타지 못한 이유를 설명하고 있으므로 '왜 버스를 타지 못했니?'라는 질문을 쓰는 것이 적절하다.

07 진주어로 to부정사를, 가주어로 It을 써서 나타낼 수 있다.

08 'How come+주어+동사' 어순임에 유의한다.

09 Ken은 컵들 중 하나에 특별한 물질을 넣었다고 하였다.

10 컵 안에 있는 물이 젤리로 변한 이유는, Ken이 넣어둔 특별한 물질이 물을 흡수하여 그것을 젤리로 변하게 만들었기 때문이다.

11 'How come+주어+동사' 어순이고, 'Why+동사+주어' 어순임에 유의한다.

12 차가운 병 속의 공기를 따뜻하게 하기 위해서 손으로 병을 쥐는 것이고, 병 속의 공기가 따뜻해지면서 공기가 팽창한다. 이 팽창하는 공기가 병에서 나가려고 하는 것이다.

13 ⓑ 병을 차갑게 하고 ⓓ 병 입구에 동전 하나를 올려둔 후 ⓐ 병을 두 손으로 잡고 ⓒ 얼마간의 시간이 지나면 동전이 움직일 것이다.

01 세종대왕은 건기가 너무 오래 지속되고 있었기 때문에 농부들을 걱정했다. 그가 농부들을 도울 방법을 찾을 때 장영실은 특별한 시계를 만들 것을 제안하였다. 세종대왕은 어떻게 그 시계가 농부들을 도와줄 수 있을지 궁금했다. 장영실은 시계가 시간과 계

절을 보여주므로 건기를 준비하는데 사용될 수 있다고 설명했다. 다행히도, 장영실은 시간과 계절에 대해 많이 알고 있어서 그는 이것을 발명하기 위해 노력했다.

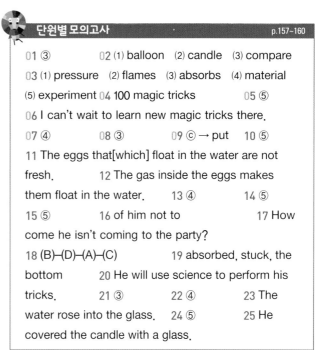

01 '음식을 얼리거나 언채로 유지되도록 하기 위한 장치 또는 공간'을 가리키는 것은 freezer(냉동고)이다.

02 balloon: 풍선, candle: 양초, compare: 비교하다

03 flame: 불꽃, material: 재료, 물질, absorb: 흡수하다, pressure: 압력, experiment: 실험, bleed: 피흘리다

07 미나는 전에 마술 묘기를 배운 적이 있다.

07 I can't wait to ~: 나는 ~이 무척 기다려져. = I'm looking forward to ~ing

09 mix와 병렬구조를 이루는 동사로 put이 적절하다.

10 Jane은 섞은 것을 얼마나 오래 냉동실에 두어야 하는지 알 수 없다.

11 물에 뜨는 달걀들은 신선하지 않다.

12 달걀 안에 있는 가스가 그 달걀들을 물 위에 뜨게 만든다.

13 '주어+동사' 어순이므로 How come, clever는 사람의 성격을 나타내는 형용사이므로 to부정사의 의미상 주어로 'of+목적격'을 쓴다.

14 possible은 사람의 성격을 나타내는 형용사가 아니므로 의미상의 주어로 for him을 쓰는 것이 적절하다.

15 모두 가주어 It으로 쓰였지만 ⑤번은 명암을 나타내는 비인칭 용법이다.

16 to부정사의 부정은 'not to V' 형태이며, mean은 사람의 성격을 나타내는 형용사이므로 'of him'을 쓰는 것에 유의한다.

17 'How come+주어+동사' 어순임에 유의한다.

18 (B) 마술 전에 미리 특별한 물질을 넣어 둠 - (D) 이 물질이 물을 흡수하고 물을 젤리로 만듦 - (A) 그 젤리는 컵 바닥에 들러

27

붙음 - (C) 그러므로 이 마술을 하기 위해서는 반드시 속이 들여다 보이지 않는 컵을 써야 함.

19 컵 안에 있는 특별한 물질이 물을 흡수하고 그것을 젤리로 변하게 했다. 그리고 그 젤리는 바닥에 달라붙었다.

20 Ken은 자신의 마술을 위해 과학을 이용할 것이라고 하였다.

21 'I can't wait to ~'는 '나는 ~이 무척 기다려진다.'라는 뜻으로 'I'm looking forward to -ing'로 바꾸어 쓸 수 있다.

22 'How come+주어+동사' 어순이므로 How come을 쓰는 것이 적절하다. 'Why+동사+주어' 어순임에 유의하자.

23 물은 유리컵 안으로 솟아올랐다.

24 초가 얼마나 탔는지는 위 글을 읽고 답할 수 없다.

25 Ken은 초에 불을 붙인 후 유리컵으로 초를 덮었다.

교과서 파헤치기

Lesson
5

1 enter, 입장하다   2 suspect, 용의자   3 bean, 콩

4 bottom, 맨 아래 (부분)   5 thief, 도둑   6 half, 반, 절반

7 clue, 단서, 실마리   8 cross, 건너다   9 delete, 삭제하다

10 bat, 방망이, 배트   11 accident, 사고

12 detective, 탐정   13 riddle, 수수께끼

14 escape, 탈출하다   15 hide, 숨기다   16 stamp, 우표

단어 TEST Step 1   p.02

01 구역, 블록	02 반, 절반	03 삭제하다
04 사고	05 던지다	06 어딘가에
07 용	08 맨 아래 (부분)	09 용의자
10 거짓말하다	11 탈출하다	
12 ～ 밖에, 밖으로, 밖에		13 단서, 실마리
14 숨기다, 숨다	15 탐정, 형사	16 다행히
17 콩	18 두 번, 두 배	19 공간
20 ～의 안에, ～의 내부에		21 축하
22 장면	23 이상한	24 도둑
25 상	26 안전하게	27 설명하다
28 똑바로, 일직선으로		29 마침내
30 사라지다	31 접다	32 하나도 ～ 않다
33 해결하다	34 수수께끼	35 단추
36 마음껏 드세요	37 ～을 적다	38 ～을 뒤집다
39 도둑을 잡다	40 A를 B로 채우다	41 공짜로
42 ～이 일어나던 때에		
43 ～에 이르는데 성공하다		

단어 TEST Step 2   p.03

01 button	02 scene	03 clue
04 throw	05 bottom	06 strange
07 explain	08 fold	09 cross
10 half	11 somewhere	12 delete
13 twice	14 finally	15 hide
16 lie	17 straight	18 accident
19 solve	20 disappear	21 bean
22 suspect	23 escape	24 luckily
25 congratulation	26 space	27 outside
28 prize	29 riddle	30 safely
31 detective	32 candle	33 thief
34 stamp	35 dragon	36 fill A with B
37 turn over	38 make it to ~	39 for free
40 at the time of	41 write down	42 catch a thief
43 help yourself		

Listen & Speak 1 - A

want to play, that, bought / what, it / like, dragons, seahorses, need to use, to play / sounds fun, Can you explain how to use

Listen & Speak 1 - B

riddle, twice in a week, once, never in a day / I have no idea / get it, Can you explain why / year, no, day / get it

Listen & Speak 2 - A

look at / How did you make it / First, in half, make a triangle, Second, fold the top, bottom line, Third, both ends, to make ears, Then, turn, over / sounds easy

Listen & Talk 2 - B

detective / didn't see, this week, about / all of, disappeared / did, do / First, looked around, Then, suspects, Finally, found, thief / don't tell, watch, later

Real Life Communication

solve / First, a bag of beans, needs to cross a river / can only hold, one more / Are you saying, take, at a time / Can you explain how to move everything across, safely

Let's Check

smells, good / going to, for dinner, Help yourself / Can you explain how to make / First, fill, with, Then, add, on the top / delicious / Would, like / thanks

---

Listen & Speak 1 - A

Jimin: Do you want to play the new game that I bought?

Brian: Sure, what is it, Jimin?

Jimin: It's like a soccer game but the players are dragons and seahorses. You need to use these buttons to play.

Brian: That sounds fun. Can you explain how to use the buttons?

Jimin: Sure.

Jack: Kelly, here's a riddle. You can see this twice in a week, once in a year, but never in a day. What is this?

Kelly: I have no idea.

Jack: It's the letter "E."

Kelly: I don't get it. Can you explain why?

Jack: Well, there are two "E"s in the word "week," one "E" in the word "year" but no "E"s in the word "day."

Kelly: Aha! Now I get it.

Tom: Yujin, look at my paper fox.

Yujin: That's cute. How did you make it?

Tom: First, fold a paper in half to make a triangle. Second, fold the top of the triangle to the bottom line. Third, fold both ends of the bottom line to the top to make ears. Then, turn it over and draw a face.

Yujin: That sounds easy.

Jane: Minsu, do you know the TV show about the student detective?

Minsu: Yes. I love that show, but I didn't see it this week. What was it about?

Jane: Well, all of the bikes at school disappeared.

Minsu: So, what did he do?

Jane: First, he looked around the school. Then, he met some suspects and asked questions. Finally, he found the thief. The thief was ....

Minsu: No, don't tell me! I'll watch it later.

Emily: Junsu, do you want to solve a riddle?

Junsu: Sure, what is it?

Emily: There is a farmer. First, the farmer buys a fox, a duck, and a bag of beans. Then, the farmer needs to cross a river.

Junsu: What's the problem?

Emily: The boat can only hold the farmer and one more thing.

Junsu: Are you saying that the farmer can take only one thing at a time?

Emily: Yes. Also, the fox will eat the duck or the duck will eat the beans if the farmer isn't there. Can you explain how to move everything across the river safely?

Junsu: Hmm ....

Minjun: Wow! Something smells really good, Mom. What is it?

Mom: We're going to have tacos for dinner. Help yourself.

Minjun: Can you explain how to make a taco?

Mom: First, fill your tortilla with vegetables and meat. Then, add some sauce on the top.

Minjun: Sounds delicious!

Mom: Would you like some cheese?

Minjun: No, thanks.

01 Welcome to, Escape
02 enter, first our
03 solve, riddles, escape
04 be found, inside
05 are, ready, think
06 hit by, on
07 Luckily, badly hurt, see
08 suspects, questioned by
09 reading, time, accident
10 said, was walking
11 was making breakfast
12 Who hit, explain
13 have, Write, down
14 move to, next
15 accident happened in
16 made it to
17 much harder, escape
18 gets, from, clothing
19 reads, won, event
20 surprised, quickly opens
21 won our, event
22 have won, prize
23 During, choose, item, free
24 to, on
25 can't wait to
26 Truly yours
27 However, real, deletes
28 Can, explain why
29 There, usually, days
30 have, answer
31 Write, down, free

01 Welcome to
02 enter the first room
03 need to solve some riddles
04 be found, inside
05 are, ready to think like
06 was hit by, on
07 Luckily, wasn't badly hurt, didn't see
08 were questioned by

09 reading a book at the time of the accident

10 said, was walking

11 was making breakfast

12 Who hit, explain why

13 Write it down 14 can move to

15 accident happened in   16 made it to

17 However, much harder to escape than

18 gets, from, clothing store   19 reads, won

20 surprised, quickly opens

21 won our   22 Congratulations, have won, prize

23 During, choose, from, for free

24 Come to, on   25 can't wait to see

26 Truly yours

27 However, thinks that, isn't real, deletes

28 Can, explain why

29 There are usually, days

30 have the answer

31 Write it down, are free to go

24 11월 31일에 우리 가게로 오세요.

25 우리는 몹시 당신을 보기를 기대합니다.

26 안녕히 계십시오, Kay Brown

27 그러나 Jay는 그 행사가 사실이 아니라고 생각하고 이메일을 삭제합니다.

28 왜 그런지 설명할 수 있나요?

29 단서: 한 달은 주로 30일 또는 31일이 있습니다.

30 답을 가지고 계신가요?

31 그것을 적으면, 당신은 자유롭게 가실 수 있습니다!

---

1 '탈출 탑'에 오신 것을 환영합니다.

2 당신은 저희 탑의 첫 번째 방에 들어갈 것입니다.

3 당신은 탈출하기 위하여 몇 개의 수수께끼를 풀어야 합니다.

4 단서들은 방 어딘가에서 발견될 수 있습니다.

5 그러면 당신은 셜록 홈스처럼 생각할 준비가 되었나요?

6 Doodle씨는 일요일 오후에 차에 치였습니다.

7 다행히 그는 심하게 다치지 않았으나 그는 운전자를 보지 못했습니다.

8 세 명의 용의자들이 경찰에게 심문을 받았습니다.

9 A씨는 사고가 일어난 시간에 책을 읽고 있었다고 말했습니다.

10 B씨는 그의 개를 산책시키고 있었다고 말했습니다.

11 C씨는 아침을 만들고 있었다고 말했습니다.

12 누가 Doodle씨를 치었을까요? 왜 그런지 설명할 수 있나요?

13 답을 가지고 있나요? 적어 보세요.

14 그런 다음, 당신은 다음 방으로 갈 수 있습니다.

15 단서: 사건은 오후에 일어났습니다.

16 축하합니다! 당신은 두 번째 방에 오는 데 성공하셨습니다.

17 그러나 두 번째 방은 첫 번째 방보다 탈출하기 훨씬 더 어렵습니다. 행운을 빕니다!

18 Jay는 그가 가장 좋아하는 옷 가게로부터 이메일을 받습니다.

19 제목은 "당신은 '행운의 날' 행사에 당첨되었습니다!"라고 적혀 있습니다.

20 Jay는 놀랍니다. 그는 재빨리 그것을 엽니다.

21 당신은 우리의 '행운의 날' 행사에 당첨되었습니다!

22 축하합니다! 당신은 특별한 상품을 받게 되었습니다.

23 '행운의 날' 행사 동안, 당신은 우리 가게에서 일곱 가지 상품을 아무거나 공짜로 선택할 수 있습니다!

---

1 Welcome to the Escape Tower.

2 You will enter the first room in our tower.

3 You need to solve some riddles to escape.

4 Clues can be found somewhere inside the room.

5 So, are you ready to think like Sherlock Holmes?

6 Mr. Doodle was hit by a car on Sunday afternoon.

7 Luckily, he wasn't badly hurt, but he didn't see the driver.

8 Three suspects were questioned by a police officer.

9 Ms. A said she was reading a book at the time of the accident.

10 Mr. B said he was walking his dog.

11 Ms. C said she was making breakfast.

12 Who hit Mr. Doodle? Can you explain why?

13 Do you have the answer? Write it down.

14 Then you can move to the next room.

15 Clue The accident happened in the afternoon.

16 Congratulations! You made it to the second room.

17 However, the second room is much harder to escape than the first one. Good luck!

18 Jay gets an email from his favorite clothing store.

19 The title reads "You won our Lucky Day event!"

20 Jay is surprised. He quickly opens it.

21 You won our 'Lucky Day' event!

22 Congratulations! You have won a special prize.

23 During our Lucky Day event, you can choose any seven items from our store for free!

24 Come to our store on November 31.

25 We can't wait to see you.

26 Truly yours, Kay Brown

27 However, Jay thinks that the event isn't real and deletes the email.

28 Can you explain why?

29 Clue There are usually 30 or 31 days in a month.

30 Do you have the answer?

31 Write it down and then you are free to go!

구석구석지문 TEST Step 1

Listen and Speak 1-C

1. Try to solve

3. are under, gets wet, explain why

4. because, a sunny day

Let's Write

1. It, last

2. at home

3. Suddenly, heard a sound

4. went into, was broken

5. looked outside, was holding, was throwing

6. broke

7. can, explained

Culture & Life

1. famous riddle

2. needs to solve, go into

3. that, asks him

4. Which, walks on four legs

구석구석지문 TEST Step 2
p.20

Listen and Speak 1-C

1. A: Try to solve this riddle.

2. B: Sure.

3. A: Four people are under one umbrella, but nobody gets wet. Can you explain why?

4. B: Yes! It's because it's a sunny day!

Let's Write

1. It was last Sunday.

2. Dohun was at home.

3. Suddenly , he heard a sound in the next room.

4. When he went into the room, the window was broken.

5. When he looked outside, Sujin was holding a baseball bat and Ted was throwing a ball to his dog.

6. Who broke the window?

7. How can it be explained?

Culture & Life

1. This is the famous riddle of the Sphinx.

2. Oedipus needs to solve it to go into Thebes.

3. This is the question that the Sphinx asks him.

4. Which creature walks on four legs in the morning, two legs in the afternoon, and three legs in the evening?

단어 TEST Step 1   p.21

01 ~ 사이에	02 등장인물	03 힘
04 용감한	05 ~을 통해	06 (색상이) 밝은
07 강한, 힘 있는	08 적	09 표현하다
10 싸움, 다툼	11 부채	12 숨다
13 응원하다	14 겁먹은, 무서워하는	
15 의사소통하다	16 ~ 뒤에	17 무서운
18 열다, 개최하다	19 인기 있는	20 의상, 복장
21 흥미 있게도	22 암컷의, 여성의	23 바람이 많이 부는
24 전통적인	25 오늘날에는	26 의견
27 원래, 본래	28 수컷의, 남성의	29 공연하다
30 편안한	31 완전히	32 야생의
33 두 사람, 남녀	34 우아하게	35 내 의견으로는
36 ~이 허용되다	37 살펴보다	38 ~을 포기하다
39 정시에	40 최선을 다하다	41 ~처럼 보이다
42 소리를 내다	42 계속 열심히 하다	

단어 TEST Step 2   p.22

01 character	02 female	03 popular
04 brave	05 communicate	06 bright
07 enemy	08 express	09 fan
10 sure	11 wild	12 couple
13 traditional	14 between	15 windy
16 gracefully	17 costume	18 behind
19 interestingly	20 through	21 male
22 totally	23 nowadays	24 scary
25 opinion	26 hide	27 originally
28 movement	29 perform	30 fight
31 powerful	32 cheer	33 comfortable
34 strength	35 take a look	36 try one's best
37 in my opinion	38 give up on	39 on time
40 make a sound	41 sound like	42 be good at
43 be allowed to		

단어 TEST Step 3   p.23

1 popular, 인기 있는   2 behind, 뒤에

3 movement, 움직임   4 drop, 떨어뜨리다   5 wild, 야생의

6 strength, 힘   7 brave, 용감한   8 fan, 부채

9 originally, 원래, 본래   10 hide, 숨다

11 express, 표현하다   12 field, 들판

13 perform, 공연하다   14 uniform, 제복

---

15 cheer, 응원하다   16 comfortable, 편안한

대화문 TEST Step 1   p.24~25

Listen & Speak 1 A-1

what, think about, painting / look like, having fun / In my opinion, enjoys dancing

Listen & Speak 1 A-2

what, about this painting / interesting, smiled when, first saw / Me, too, look happy

Listen & Speak 1 B

some male birds dance / Why, dance / to show, love, female birds / any other animals / bees, where to find food / way to communicate / totally agree with you

Listen & Speak 2 A-1

my voice, Listen to, soft, cool, sure / my body to express, movements, Why don't, like, sure, feel great / make sounds, dance

Listen & Speak 2 B

What, reading / story about / tell, more / lost, when, After that, difficulties, gave up on / worked, hard to be, to be, right / try my best / Keep up, work, sure, make it

Real Life Communication

what, will be held / perform / decide what to do / How about, opinion, easy to learn, beautiful / sounds like / is good at / I'm sure / give it a try

Let's Check

dancing girls, amazing / only see / Look more closely, behind / didn't know, other dancers behind her / right, I'm sure, more than

대화문 TEST Step 2   p.26~27

Listen & Speak 1 A-1

Jane: Minsu, what do you think about that painting?

Minsu: Umm ... The people look like they're having fun.

Jane: I agree. In my opinion, the dancing boy really enjoys dancing.

Listen & Speak 1 A-2

Brian: Jimin, what do you think about this painting?

Jimin: In my opinion, it's interesting. I smiled when I first saw it.

Brian: Me, too. The dancers in the painting look happy.

Listen & Speak 1 B

Emily: Hojun, did you know that some male birds dance?

Hojun: No. Why do they dance?

Emily: They dance to show their love to female birds.

Hojun: That's interesting. Do you know any other animals that can dance?

Emily: Yes, some bees dance to show where to find food.

Hojun: That's cool! In my opinion, dancing is a great way to communicate.

Emily: I totally agree with you.

Listen & Speak 2 A-1

Minji: I use my voice to make music. Listen to my music. My voice is soft and cool. I'm sure you will like it.

Jimin: I move my body to express my feelings. Look at my movements. Why don't you jump like me? I'm sure you'll feel great.

Sujin: I use my hands to make sounds. Come and listen to my music. I'm sure you'll want to dance when you listen to it.

Listen & Speak 2 B

Tom: What are you reading, Kelly?

Kelly: I'm reading a story about Michaela DePrince.

Tom: Michaela DePrince? Can you tell me more about her?

Kelly: Sure. Michaela lost her parents when she was three. After that, she had a lot of difficulties. But she never gave up on her dream of becoming a dancer.

Tom: Wow, she worked very hard to be a good dancer. Kelly, you also have a dream to be a dancer, right?

Kelly: Yes. I will try my best to be a great dancer like her.

Tom: Keep up the good work. I'm sure you can make it.

Real Life Communication

Junsu: You know what? The school dance contest will be held soon.

Emily: That's right. I heard Jimin's class is going to perform a taekwondo dance and Tim's class is going to do a K-pop dance.

Brian: We should also decide what to do.

Mina How about a Buchaechum? In my opinion, it is easy to learn, and it's also beautiful.

Emily: That sounds like a good idea. But who will teach us?

Brian: Mina is good at traditional dances. Can you help us, Mina?

Mina: Of course, I will. I'm sure we'll have a lot of fun.

Junsu: Great. Let's give it a try.

Let's Check

Jenny: Look at the dancing girls, Dongjun. Aren't they amazing?

Dongjun: Girls? I can only see one dancer.

Jenny: Look more closely. Do you see many arms behind her?

Dongjun: Wow. I didn't know that there were other dancers behind her.

Jenny: That's right. I'm sure there are more than 10 dancers.

본문 TEST Step 1 p.28~29

01 Why, dance

02 express, happiness, enjoy themselves

03 take, different kinds, around

04 tells, story

05 stories through, body movements

06 fight, good, evil

07 playing, characters, green

08 eveil, wear, make-up

09 Interestingly, allowed to

10 movements, powerful, train

11 When, visit, may meet

12 perform, traditional, scary

13 originally performed, fight

14 show, strength, enemy

15 looked, scary as, before

16 Nowadays, perform, show, other

17 traditional, fan dance

18 wear colorful   19 with, painted, bright

20 move, gracefully, different, beauty

21 movements, as beautiful, flying

22 so popular that, traditional

본문 TEST Step 2 p.30~31

01 Why, dance

02 to express feelings, to others, enjoy themselves

03 Let's take, different kinds of dance

04 tells, story

05 stories through, body movements

06 a fight between good and evil

07 who are playing good characters, green

08 who are playing, wear black make-up

09 Interestingly, are allowed to dance

10 so powerful that, need to, for

11 may meet, *haka* dancers

12 perform, traditional, with scary faces

13 originally performed by, fight

14 to show their strength, enemy

15 looked as scary as, before fighting

16 Nowadays, usually perform, to show, to the other team

17 traditional Korean fan dance

18 wear colorful *hanbok*

19 with, that are painted

20 move, gracefully, different kinds of beauty

21 look as beautiful as, flying birds

22 so popular that, can see it

1 사람들은 왜 춤을 추는 걸까요?

2 사람들은 감정을 표현하고, 다른 사람들에게 행복감을 주거나 스스로 즐기기 위해 춤을 춥니다.

3 세계의 여러 가지 춤을 살펴봅시다.

4 Kathakali에는 이야기가 있습니다.

5 춤꾼들은 몸동작을 통해 이야기합니다.

6 이러한 이야기들은 대개 선과 악의 싸움에 관한 것입니다.

7 선한 역할을 맡은 춤꾼들은 자신의 얼굴을 초록색으로 칠합니다.

8 악한 역할을 맡은 춤꾼들은 검은색 화장을 합니다.

9 재미있는 것은 Kathakali 춤에서 남자들만 춤추는 것이 허락된다는 사실입니다.

10 몸동작이 매우 힘이 넘쳐서 춤꾼들은 수년 동안 연습을 해야 합니다.

11 사람들이 뉴질랜드를 방문할 때, 그들은 haka 춤꾼들의 무리를 만날지도 모릅니다.

12 그 춤꾼들은 무서운 얼굴로 이 전통 춤을 춥니다.

13 이 춤은 원래 마오리족에 의해 싸움 전에 행해졌습니다.

14 그들은 적에게 그들의 힘을 보여 주고 싶었습니다.

15 그 춤꾼들은 싸움하기 전의 야생 동물들만큼 무섭게 보였습니다.

16 요즈음, 뉴질랜드에서는 럭비 선수들이 다른 팀에게 그들의 힘을 보여 주기 위해 게임 전에 주로 haka 를 보여 줍니다.

17 부채춤은 한국 전통 부채춤입니다.

18 춤꾼들은 다채로운 한복을 입습니다.

19 그들은 밝은 색으로 칠해진 커다란 부채를 가지고 춤을 춥니다.

20 그 춤꾼들은 다양한 종류의 미를 보여 주기 위해 부채를 우아하게 움직입니다.

21 그들의 움직임은 꽃 또는 날아다니는 새들처럼 우아하게 보입니다.

22 한국에서, 부채춤은 너무 인기가 있어서 사람들은 많은 전통 축제에서 그것을 볼 수 있습니다.

1 Why do people dance?

2 They dance to express feelings, give happiness to others, or enjoy themselves.

3 Let's take a look at different kinds of dance around the world.

4 *Kathakali* tells a story.

5 The dancers tell stories through their body movements.

6 These stories are usually about a fight between good and evil.

7 Dancers who are playing good characters paint their faces green.

8 Those who are playing evil characters wear black make-up.

9 Interestingly, in *Kathakali*, only men are allowed to dance.

10 The body movements are so powerful that the dancers need to train for many years.

11 When people visit New Zealand, they may meet a group of *haka* dancers.

12 The dancers perform this traditional dance with scary faces.

13 This dance was originally performed by the Maori before a fight.

14 They wanted to show their strength to the enemy.

15 The dancers looked as scary as wild animals before fighting.

16 Nowadays, in New Zealand, rugby players usually perform a *haka* before a game to show their strength to the other team.

17 *Buchaechum* is a traditional Korean fan dance.

18 The dancers wear colorful *hanbok*.

19 They dance with large fans that are painted in bright colors.

20 The dancers move the fans gracefully to show different kinds of beauty.

21 Their movements look as beautiful as flowers or flying birds.

22 In Korea, *Buchaechum* is so popular that people can see it in many traditional festivals.

Listen and Speak 2 - C

1. going to, culture event, want to join
2. Sounds
3. enjoy dancing, sure, a lot of fun

Culture & Life

1. Italy
2. In the past, sick people
3. Nowadays, couple's dance
4. on, such as weddings

Culture & Life

1. Kenya
2. is performed, fight
3. is also called
4. jump high
5. When, cheer, on, loud noises

Lesson 7

구석구석지문 TEST Step 2 p.39

Listen and Speak 2 - C

1. A: I'm going to a culture event in our town next week. Do you want to join me?
2. B: Sounds interesting.
3. A: We can enjoy dancing from many countries. I'm sure we'll have a lot of fun.

Culture & Life

1. *Tarantella*, Italy
2. In the past, people danced the *tarantella* for sick people.
3. Nowadays, it is a couple's dance.
4. People dance the *tarantella* on happy days such as weddings.

Culture & Life

1. *Adumu*, Kenya
2. This dance is performed before a fight.
3. It is also called a jumping dance.
4. Dancers jump high in the air.
5. When a dancer jumps, other dancers cheer him on with loud noises.

단어 TEST Step 1 p.40

01 맛	02 안전한	03 차이, 차이점
04 탈출하다, (액체, 가스가) 새다		05 채우다
06 냉동고	07 대신에	08 가라앉다
09 뜨다	10 번개	11 압력
12 비밀	13 ~ 뒤에	14 준비하다
15 볕에 탐	16 팽창하다	17 마술, 속임수
18 재료, 물질	19 비교하다	20 흡수하다
21 불꽃	22 수축하다	23 사라지다
24 실험	25 마른, 비가 오지 않는	
26 혼동하게 하다	27 오르다, 올라가다	28 무게를 재다
29 마술, 마법	30 자외선 차단제	31 잡다, 쥐다
32 양초	33 연습	34 필요한
35 오랫동안	36 차가워지다	37 ~을 신청하다
38 시도해 보다	39 ~을 (바꾸지 않고) 고수하다	
40 타 버리다	41 골라내다	42 속을 들여다 보다
43 A가 B로 변하다		

단어 TEST Step 2 p.41

01 coin	02 fill	03 practice
04 magic	05 disappear	06 dry
07 expand	08 candle	09 sunburn
10 flavor	11 sink	12 absorb
13 secret	14 instead	15 lightning
16 material	17 sunscreen	18 difference
19 contract	20 mix	21 experiment
22 necessary	23 safe	24 trick
25 flame	26 prepare	27 confuse
28 float	29 escape	30 compare
31 pressure	32 weigh	33 rise
34 freezer	35 pick out	36 burn out
37 stick to	38 for a long time	39 cool down
40 turn A into B	41 sign up for	42 give it a try
43 see through		

단어 TEST Step 3 p.42

1 disappear, 사라지다 2 contract, 수축하다
3 mix, 섞다 4 sink, 가라앉다 5 expand, 팽창하다
6 float, 뜨다 7 confuse, 혼동하게 하다
8 material, 물질, 재료 9 trick, 속임수, 마술
10 freezer, 냉동고 11 weigh, 무게를 재다

12 absorb, 흡수하다 13 magic, 마술의
14 experiment, 실험 15 secret, 비밀
16 practice, 연습

Listen & Speak 1 A

Which flavor, How about, First, half a cup, Next, cut, into, mix, freezer, easy to make, isn't, Why don't, try making

Listen & Speak 1 B

why, put / picking out / Which eggs, which / that sink in water, float, shouldn't eat / interesting, float / Because, inside, acts like, balloon

Listen & Speak 2 A

a glass of, weigh / can test / fish / can use, instead of / How, work / weigh, put / weigh, compare / can't wait to, difference

Listen & Speak 2 B

hasn't rained for / dry season, lasting, worried / should, to help / special clock / How, help / seasons, to prepare for, dry season / sounds like, going to / give it a try, a lot / can't wait to see your clock

Real Life Communication A

join / sounds interesting, signed up for, fall / Which class / magic class, can't wait to, tricks / cool, Have you learned / more practice / some day

Let's Check

are, reading / magic, science / sounds, interesting / introduces, use science, learned about half / cool, some / balloon trick / can't wait to see

Listen & Speak 1 A

W: Today we'll make ice cream. Which flavor do you want to make? How about strawberry? First, mix two cups of milk, two cups of heavy cream, and half a cup of sugar. Next, cut five strawberries into small pieces. Then, mix everything together and put it in the freezer. That's it. It's easy to make, isn't it? Why don't you try making it at home?

Listen & Speak 1 B

B: Yujin, why did you put the eggs in water?
G: I'm picking out the bad eggs.
B: Which eggs are fresh, and which ones are not?

G: Eggs that sink in water are fresh. When eggs float in water, they're not fresh. You shouldn't eat them.
B: That's interesting. Why do the bad eggs float?
G: Because they have gas inside. The gas acts like the air in a balloon.
B: Oh, I see.

Listen & Speak 2 A

B: Ms. Jeong, does a glass of water weigh more when there's a fish in it?
W: Yes, it does. We can test it now.
B: But how? We don't have a fish.
W: We can use a finger instead of a fish.
B: How will that work?
W: I'll weigh a glass of water first. Then I will put my finger in the water and weigh it to compare.
B: Oh, I can't wait to see the difference.

Listen & Speak 2 B

King Sejong: It hasn't rained for a long time.
Jang Yeongsil: Yes. The dry season is lasting too long. The farmers are very worried.
King Sejong: We should do something to help them.
Jang Yeongsil: How about making a special clock?
King Sejong: A clock? How will that help?
Jang Yeongsil: The clock will show the time and the seasons. We can use it to prepare for the dry season.
King Sejong: That sounds like a good idea. But who's going to make it?
Jang Yeongsil: I'll give it a try. I know a lot about time and the seasons.
King Sejong: Okay, I can't wait to see your clock.

Real Life Communication A

Brian: Mina, will you join our tennis club?
Mina: It sounds interesting, but I signed up for a special class this fall.
Brian: Which class did you sign up for?
Mina: I signed up for a magic class. I can't wait to learn new magic tricks there.
Brian: That sounds cool ! Have you learned magic tricks before?
Mina: Yes, I learned some before, but I need more practice.
Brian: I hope I can see your magic tricks some day.

Let's Check

B: What are you reading, Jiwon?
G: I'm reading a book about magic and science.
B: That sounds interesting.
G: Yes. This book introduces 100 magic tricks that

use science. I've learned about half of them.

B: That's cool. Can you show me some of the tricks?

G: Sure. I can show you a balloon trick now.

B: Great! I can't wait to see it.

본문 TEST Step 1

p.47~48

01 Welcome to, Super, Magic

02 It's, exciting, see, tricks

03 more, find out, behind

04 secret, magic, science

05 member, science, perform, tricks

06 show, can't wait

07 show, something amazing

08 dish with water

09 put, middle, dish

10 light, cover, with

11 How come, rose into

12 expands, hot, higher pressure

13 gets, contracts, lower pressure

14 burnt out, lower pressure

15 cooled, pressure dropped

16 outside, higher pressure

17 pushed, water, glass

18 fill one, with water

19 move, around, confuse

20 which cup, water

21 easy, middle one   22 let's check

23 me the other cups

24 There's no water

25 How come, disappeared

26 Before, put, into, cups

27 absorbed, turned, into

28 stuck to, bottom

29 try, necessary, use, through

30 for, performance, amazing

본문 TEST Step 2

p.49~50

01 Welcome to, Science Magic

02 It's, exciting to see

03 to find out, behind

04 secret, is science

05 will use science to perform, tricks

06 will, show us, wait to see them

07 to show you something amazing

08 with water in it

09 put a candle, middle

10 light, cover it with

11 Look at, How come, rose into

12 expands, gets hot, creates higher pressure

13 gets cold, contracts, creates lower pressure

14 burnt out, lower pressure

15 cooled down, dropped

16 outside, was at a higher pressure

17 pushed, into

18 going to fill one of these cups with

19 them around to confuse

20 which cup   21 It's, middle one

22 let's check   23 me the other cups

24 no water   25 How come, disappeared

26 Before, put, into one of the cups

27 absorbed, turned it into

28 stuck to the bottom

29 want to try, necessary to use, that, see through

30 for, performance, amazing

본문 TEST Step 3

p.51~52

1 지나: 특별 과학 마술 쇼에 오신 것을 환영합니다!

2 마술을 보는 것은 항상 신나는 일입니다.

3 그리고 마술 뒤에 숨겨진 비밀을 알아내는 것은 더 신나는 일입니다.

4 어떤 사람들은 마술의 비밀이 과학이라고 생각합니다.

5 오늘 학교 마술 동아리 회원인 Ken은 마술을 수행하기 위해 과학을 사용할 것입니다.

6 그는 우리에게 어떤 마술을 보여 줄까요? 무척 기다려지는군요.

7 Ken: 안녕하세요, 여러분. 오늘, 저는 여러분에게 놀라운 무언가를 보여 주려고 합니다.

8 여기에 물이 담긴 접시가 있습니다.

9 이제, 저는 접시 한가운데에 초를 놓을 것입니다.

10 그다음에 초를 켜고 유리컵으로 초를 덮어 보겠습니다. "아브라카다브라!"

11 지나: 물을 보세요! 어째서 물이 유리컵 속으로 올라간 거지요?

12 Ken: 공기가 뜨거워지면 팽창해서, 더 높은 압력을 만듭니다.

13 공기가 차가워지면 수축해서, 더 낮은 압력을 만듭니다.

14 불꽃이 다 타 버렸을 때, 유리컵 속의 공기는 식어 버렸습니다.

15 공기가 식었으므로, 기압이 낮아졌습니다.

16 그래서 유리컵 밖의 공기 압력이 더 높아졌습니다.

17 높아진 압력의 공기가 물을 밀어서 유리컵으로 들어가게 된 것입니다.

18 Ken: 이제, 이 컵들 중 하나를 물로 채워 보겠습니다.

19 여러분을 헷갈리게 하려고 이 컵들을 섞어 보겠습니다.

20 지나, 어떤 컵에 물이 있을까요?

21 지나: 쉽네요! 가운데 컵이에요.

22 Ken: 좋습니다, 확인해 봅시다. 보셨죠? 물이 없군요.

23 지나: 다른 컵들도 보여 주세요.

24 Ken: 보셨죠? 물이 없네요.

25 지나: 왜! 어째서 물이 사라진 거죠?

26 Ken: 마술 전에, 저는 특별한 물질을 컵 하나에 넣어 두었습니다.

27 그 물질은 물을 흡수하고, 그것을 젤리로 변하게 했습니다.

28 그러고 나서 젤리는 컵 바닥에 달라붙었습니다.

29 여러분이 이 마술을 해 보고자 한다면, 속을 들여다볼 수 없는 컵을 사용해야 합니다.

30 지나: 멋진 공연 고맙습니다. 정말 놀라웠어요!

본문 TEST Step 4~Step 5　　p.53~56

1 Jina: Welcome to the Super Science Magic Show!

2 It's always exciting to see magic tricks.

3 And it's more exciting to find out the secrets behind them.

4 Some people think the secret of magic is science.

5 Today, Ken, a member of the School Magic Club, will use science to perform his tricks.

6 Which tricks will he show us? I can't wait to see them.

7 Ken: Hello, everyone. Today, I'm going to show you something amazing.

8 Here's a dish with water in it.

9 Now, I'll put a candle in the middle of the dish.

10 Next, I'll light the candle and cover it with a glass. "Abracadabra!"

11 Jina: Look at the water! How come it rose into the glass?

12 Ken: Air expands when it gets hot and creates higher pressure.

13 When it gets cold, air contracts and creates lower pressure.

14 When the flame burnt out, the air inside the glass cooled down.

15 As the air cooled down, the air pressure dropped.

16 So the air outside the glass was at a higher pressure.

17 It pushed the water into the glass.

18 Ken: Now, I'm going to fill one of these cups with water.

19 I will move them around to confuse you.

20 Jina, which cup has the water in it?

21 Jina: That's easy! It's the middle one.

22 Ken: Okay, let's check. See? No water.

23 Jina: Show me the other cups.

24 Ken: See? There's no water.

25 Jina: Wow! How come the water disappeared?

26 Ken: Before the trick, I put a special material into one of the cups.

27 The material absorbed the water and turned it into jelly.

28 Then the jelly stuck to the bottom.

29 If you want to try this trick, it's necessary to use cups that you can't see through.

30 Jina: Thank you for your great performance. It was really amazing!

구석구석지문 TEST Step 1　　p.57

Real Life Communication B

1. Which class, sign up for

2. take, class, like playing, about

3. take the computer class, can't wait to

4. sounds

Culture & Life

1. Atlantic Ocean, Triangle

2. A number of, have disappeared

3. come

4. still

Culture & Life

1. Egypt

2. that were used to build, weigh about

3. it possible to move

4. still a mystery

구석구석지문 TEST Step 2　　p.58

Real Life Communication B

1. A: Which class do you want to sign up for ?

2. B: I want to take the badminton class. I like playing badminton. How about you?

3. A: I want to take the computer class. I can't wait to make a computer program there.

4. B: That sounds cool!

Culture & Life

1. North Atlantic Ocean – The Bermuda Triangle

2. A number of airplanes and ships have disappeared in the Bermuda Triangle.

3. How come?

4. It's still a mystery.

Culture & Life

1. Egypt – The pyramids

2. Some of the rocks that were used to build the pyramids weigh about 70 tons.

3. How was it possible to move such heavy rocks back then?

4. It's still a mystery.

1. Egypt – The pyramids